ERIN'S BLOOD ROYAL

ALSO BY PETER BERRESFORD ELLIS

The Ancient World of the Celts, 1999

The Chronicles of the Celts, 1999

Celt and Roman: The Celts in Italy, 1998

Celt and Greek: Celts in the Hellenic World, 1997

Celtic Women: Women in Celtic Society and Literature, 1995

The Druids, 1994

The Celtic Dawn, 1993

Celt and Saxon: The Struggle for Britain AD 410–937, 1993

A Dictionary of Celtic Mythology, 1992

The Celtic Empire, 1991

A Dictionary of Irish Mythology, 1987

The Rising of the Moon, 1987

Celtic Inheritance, 1985

The Celtic Revolution, 1985

The Boyne Water: The Battle of the Boyne, 1976

Hell or Connaught:
The Cromwellian Colonisation of Ireland 1652–1660, 1975

History of the Irish Working Class, 1972

ERIN'S BLOOD ROYAL

The Gaelic Noble Dynasties of Ireland

PETER BERRESFORD ELLIS

palgrave

First published 2002 by PALGRAVE™
175 Fifth Avenue
New York, N.Y. 10010
Companies and representatives throughout the world.

PALGRAVE is the new global publishing imprint of St. Martin's Press
LLC Scholarly and Reference Division and Palgrave Publishers Ltd.
(formerly Macmillan Press Ltd.).

ISBN 0–312–23049–4

Library of Congress Cataloging-in-Publication Data.
Ellis, Peter Berresford.
Erin's blood royal : the Gaelic noble dynasties of Ireland / written by
Peter Berresford Ellis.—Rev. ed.
      p.   cm.
   Includes bibliographical references (p.) and index.
   ISBN 0–312–23049–4 (cloth)
   1. Ireland—Kings and rulers—Biography.   2. Ulster (Northern
Ireland and Ireland)—Kings and rulers—Biography.   3. Leinster
(Ireland)—Kings and rulers—Biography.   4. Connacht (Ireland)—
Kings and rulers—Biography.   5. Munster (Ireland)—Kings and
rulers—Biography.   6. Celts—Ireland—Kings and rulers—Biography.
7. Aristocracy (Social class)—Ireland—History.   I. Title

DA916.1.E45   2001
941.5'0099—dc21   00–064029

Design by Letra Libre, Inc.

First PALGRAVE edition: March 2002
10   9   8   7   6   5   4   3   2   1

Printed in the United States of America.

I am a ghost upon your path,
An ethereal wisp.
But you must know one word of Truth
Can give a phantom breath.

—Donal IX MacCarthy Mór (d. 1596),
last regnant King of Desmond,
Aisling—thruagh do mhear meisi
(A sorrowful vision has deceived me)

CONTENTS

PART THREE

RANK AND MERIT

Sixteen pages of illustrations appear between pages 226 and 227.

THE MAN WHO WOULD BE PRINCE

WHEN THE FIRST EDITION OF THIS BOOK WAS PUBLISHED in London in the late summer of 1999, it carried a foreword by The MacCarthy Mór, Prince of Desmond. It also included a section on his family and their claims of descent from the royal Eóghanacht house of the MacCarthys, kings of Munster and Desmond.

Terence McCarthy had his pedigree registered at the Irish Genealogical Office in 1980; his arms had already been confirmed in 1979, and he was given "courtesy recognition" by the Chief Herald of Ireland in 1992 as The Mac-Carthy Mór, Chief of His Name. Being thereby recognized by the Irish state, Dick Spring, then Tánaiste (Deputy Prime Minister) and Minister for Foreign Affairs, wrote to McCarthy on April 11, 1995, approving his request that the title could be entered in his Irish passport. His pedigree and titles were subsequently recognized by the Castile and Leon King of Arms of Spain and registered with other foreign heraldic jurisdictions. In February and June 1998 an Italian Arbitration Court, at Casale Monferrato, gave two judgments in his favor when he took legal proceedings to authenticate his titles and rights against claims of his being bogus.

The MacCarthy Mór had become one of the most active, outspoken and widely publicized representatives of the old Gaelic nobility of Ireland. He was the author of several published works on Irish history and the Gaelic aristocracy. He had become patron of the MacCarthy clan societies, patron of the Royal Eóghanacht Society and of his reconstituted dynastic Military

Order of the Golden Chain (Niadh Nask) as well as patron of a Royal Eóghanacht Gallowglass Guard, which featured prominently in the 1999 St. Patrick's Day ceremonials in New York City. The Gallowglass Guard's officers were received and blessed by Cardinal O'Connor, Archbishop of New York, and invited to a breakfast reception by Mayor Rudolf Giuliani at Gracie Mansion, the mayor's official residence. The MacCarthy Mór, as well as being honorary president of the Cashel Heritage and Development Trust, was patron of the Cashel Arts and Heritage Society and the Cashel Writers' Circle.

After his recognition by the Irish state, he received numerous foreign knighthoods, awards and honors, including an honorary doctorate for his work on Irish history. He had been given civic receptions by the Irish President, Mary Robinson; the Lord Mayor of Cork; the mayors of Waterford and Clonmel; and other civic leaders and dignitaries in Ireland. In the United States he was honored by state governors and made colonel of the South Carolina State Guard and given an honorary colonelcy in Alabama.

As a convert to the Eastern Orthodox Church, he was bestowed, in March 1998, with the style *Orthodoxissimus Princeps*, or Most Orthodox Prince by Evloghios I, Metropolitan of the Autonomous Metropolitanate of Western Europe of the Ukrainian Orthodox Church.

His entry in *Debrett's People of Today* was already substantial by the 1995 edition.

It seemed, in early 1999, that MacCarthy Mór was an obvious choice to be invited to contribute a polemic foreword to this study on the surviving heads of the old Gaelic nobility of Ireland. The first edition of this work duly carried that foreword.

The volume was already in print when, in late July 1999, one of the great impostures of recent times was revealed. A public announcement by the Chief Herald of Ireland on July 21, 1999, maintained that Terence McCarthy's pedigree was "without genealogical integrity." Therefore the confirmation of arms by the Genealogical Office was declared invalid and the "courtesy recognition" of Terence McCarthy as The MacCarthy Mór was null and void.

The ramifications of the affair ran so deep that on September 29, 1999, the Minister for Arts, Heritage and Gaeltacht, Síle de Valéra, was forced to admit in the Dáil, the Irish Parliament, answering a question on Terence McCarthy, that the procedure by which "courtesy recognition" had been given to Gaelic titles during the 1980s and 1990s was flawed. The Minister announced that a comprehensive review of the procedures involved would be undertaken by the Irish Government. In the meantime, no further recognitions of claimants to old Gaelic titles would be made until that review has been carried out. As time passed and no further action followed, she announced that she had reversed her decision to set up a review group and that the matter would now rest in the hands of the Chief Herald and the Genealogical Office.

Meanwhile, a private genealogist, Seán Murphy, was gaining much publicity in attacks on the Chief Herald and Genealogical Office concerning the recognitions given to Irish Chiefs, labelling several other Chiefs as bogus and berating the Genealogical Office for not moving immediately to remove their recognitions. By mid-2000 the Chief Herald had decided to review the pedigrees of The Maguire, The O'Long, The O'Dochartaigh, The O'Carroll, The O'Ruairc and The MacDonnell of the Glens. The Genealogical Office was quick to point out that this did not mean that the situation of these Chiefs was similar to that of Terence McCarthy, only that the Genealogical Office needed to be reassured of the flawlessness of the pedigrees previously approved.

However, by July 2001, these reviews had been stalled while the Genealogical Office sought legal advice from the Attorney General's Office concerning certain legal issues raised by The Maguire. In view of the continued campaign by Seán Murphy against the Chiefs and the Genealogical Office, the Chief Herald emphasized: "Mr. Murphy is acting independently in these matters and the Office has neither rejected nor approved of his findings; he has copied some of his reports to us and these would have to be taken into account in due course, in conjunction with all other relevant materials, in the event that reviews go ahead."

The publicity surrounding the imposture of Terence McCarthy has brought those genuine survivors of the old Gaelic Irish aristocracy into an invidious position whereby they have been collectively depicted as figures of fun; Disneyland characters in a pretend world. Terence McCarthy's high profile has, in fact, turned out to be highly damaging.

I am thankful, therefore, to my publishers for allowing me the opportunity to remedy the misinformation contained in the first edition, correcting and presenting some new material that I had previously considered irrelevant. I am indebted to them for also allowing me the opportunity to tell, in brief form, the strange story of Terence MacCarthy, in chapter 12 entitled "The MacCarthy Mór Affair."

When the complete history of Terence McCarthy is written, I think he will be recorded as one of the great impostors of our day. His name will be included with such historical impostors as Olive Wilmot, daughter of a house painter, who claimed to be Princess Olive, daughter of His Royal Highness, the Duke of Cumberland; Stefan Mali, the Montenegran, who claimed to be Tsar Peter

III of Russia; Anna Anderson, who claimed to be the Grand Duchess Anastasia, daughter of Tsar Nicholas II; and a Devon servant girl, Mary Baker, who was able to pass herself off as Princess Caraboo of Javasu among the rich and famous in Victorian London. Terence McCarthy's story is, perhaps, as fascinating as any of the historical figures who he claimed were his ancestors.

Peter Berresford Ellis
August 2001

INTRODUCTION

THIS IS ESSENTIALLY THE STORY OF the surviving families of the old Gaelic Irish aristocracy whose ancestors were kings, princes and nobles in Ireland until the English Tudor Conquests of the sixteenth century. The heads of these families still maintain their Gaelic titles, and the majority of them are given "courtesy recognition" by the modern Irish state as "Chiefs." The families with which this book are concerned are the ancient Milesian Gaelic families, not those families who arrived in Ireland with the Normans and adopted the Irish language and social system, such as the Joyces, the Burkes, or the Barrys. Neither is it concerned with those families who are members of the Irish Peerage, holding such titles as the Knight of Glin, the Marquess of Waterford or the Duke of Leinster.

The Irish Gaelic aristocracy is the oldest traceable nobility in Europe; written genealogies survive from the seventh century A.D. and were transcribed from oral traditions handed down for a thousand years before Christianity reached Ireland. The history of these families, therefore, can be said to encompass three thousand years of Irish experience and folklore. These families have survived today as a last link with an ancient civilization that has been pushed to the verge of extinction. Indeed, the "utter extinction" of that culture was the declared colonial policy of England from 1541 onward. The history of the practical application of that policy is one that makes uncomfortable reading.

Surprisingly, the history of the native Gaelic monarchy of Ireland and its destruction is one that is barely acknowledged in modern Ireland, where the popular perception of history generally begins with the 1798 uprising and the republican struggle for independence. The concept of Gaelic kingship is barely understood. Many years ago, at a lecture on Irish kingship in Dublin, a student, apparently wishing to demonstrate his support for the policy of egalitarianism, interrupted the professor by declaiming the popular Irish saying: "But we are *all* king's sons!" The lecturer responded irritably: "That may be; but we can't all prove it!"

In Ireland, any history of kings and princes, albeit native ones, is generally an unfamiliar territory. Modern Irish historiography, apart from a few notable exceptions, seems geared to the intention of either proving its impeccable republican credentials or trying to demonstrate that republican ideology was not a popular Irish philosophy and that Ireland would have been content with domestic self-government remaining within a United Kingdom framework. That latter school of historiography, popularly called Revisionist during the last decade, has not become part of the mainstream historical doctrine. The history of Ireland is either seen from the anti-imperialist pro-Irish standpoint or from the pro-British Unionist stand. In both approaches, however, monarchy in Ireland has become synonymous only with English monarchy.

Sometimes, in what appears to be almost a conscious attempt to keep to a republican "purity," the Irish state bureaucracy expunges references to native monarchy in the most unlikely places. It is taken to the point of ignoring the provenance of many of the great art treasures of Ireland. Some years ago a catalogue describing the twelfth-century "Shrine of the Book of Dimma" made a passing mention that an inscription on it "refers to Thaddeus O'Carroll, who died in 1152." The catalogue failed to explain that the inscription was actually an acknowledgment that the shrine was made on the instructions of King Tadhg Ó Cearbhaill (Thaddeus O'Carroll) of Ely.

The catalogue, describing the now - world famous "Processional Cross of Cong" from the twelfth century, detailed everything about it except that it bore the name of King Tairrdelbach Ua Conchobhair (O'Conor) of Connacht, also High King (d. 1156), who commissioned the great artwork. In referring to the fifteenth-century Cross of Lislaughtin, the catalogue mentions that "the O'Conor family built a Franciscan monastery at Lislaughtin" where the cross was made. Yet it fails to mention that the family was the royal dynasty of Connacht who endowed the monastery and financed the construction of the cross. Such examples would, of themselves, fill a book.

There is a popular perception, which has its origins in the propagandists of Tudor England, that the kings and princes of Ireland were quaint, barbaric chiefs of small warring tribes, mainly famous for being cattle rustlers. Even Charles J. O'Donnell of Carndonagh, himself the descendant of the princely house of Tirconnell, who endowed the prestigious O'Donnell lectures at Oxford and other universities, suggested that the idea of referring to kings in Ireland was "an ignorant practice."

It has become almost a cliché to state that without a knowledge of the past, we cannot understand the present nor create a sound springboard to the future. Cliché or not, it is still a truism.

The story that follows is of a much-neglected area of Irish history. No assessment of the history of Ireland can ever be complete without a consideration of the story of those dynasties that ruled the country for at least two thousand years prior to the English Tudor Conquests. It is a story of a struggle against a foreign empire; a survival against incredible odds—endurance against confiscations, the destruction of books and records, genocidal warfare, artificial famines and an enforced dispersal of the princes and their people throughout the world in a manner as incredibly poignant as the Jewish diaspora.

It is a story made vivid by the personalities of the individual members of these aristocratic families. Some inevitably sold out under the pressure; some went down fighting; some merely vanished "underground," continuing to live in Ireland surrounded by loyal countrymen who did not betray them to the new authorities. Others were forced to flee into exile where their progeny gave of their remarkable talents to other nations. They became presidents of France, Chile, Argentina, Mexico, the United States. A descendant of the princes of Tirconnell became a prime minister of Spain. Three were High Chamberlains of Austria, the equivalent of first minister under the emperor. Numerous others rose to be generals and admirals not only in the armies and navies of Europe but in many other quarters of the world. Others became diplomats, ambassadors and viceroys. The last Spanish viceroy to Mexico was Juan O'Donoju (O'Donoghue), who devised the plan that made Mexico independent in 1821. Coincidentally, in 1834 the elected president of Mexico was Miguel Barragan, son of a Berrigan who was an officer in Spain's Irish Brigade. Some exiles married into other European royal dynasties. Even Elizabeth II of England can, perhaps ironically, boast the O'Brien kings of Thomond in her ancestry. Many were compensated in their exile with foreign honors, awards and titles.

The stories of these families are the sum total of the Irish experience, not only prior to invasion but in the aftermath of conquest. They are representative of how the Irish, in differing ways, came to terms with the conquest of their country.

These families, however, claim titles that were "abolished forever" under English law, a law system that also abolished the native Irish law system, and it is English law that the modern Irish state has now inherited. In trying to genuflect to the Gaelic Ireland that existed prior to the Tudor Conquests, the modern Irish republic had become entangled in a legal problem. By what legal authority can the modern state recognize titles of nobility that existed in a predecessor state, prior to the acts of abolition by the conquerors between 1541 and 1613, under a law system that no longer prevails? The Irish civil service solution, accepted by the newly created Genealogical Office in 1944, has merely created complications that have led to the problems facing the Irish government today.

However, what delineates these surviving Gaelic aristocratic dynasties, with their continued allegiance to their legally extinct titles, is the preservation of a fidelity to an ancient and highly civilized culture that went down in a holocaust of blood, flame and famine under the ruthless colonial policy of an unsympathetic alien power.

A Note on Names

READERS MAY WONDER AT FINDING variant spellings for what appear essentially the same name. This is not merely the result of sixteenth- and seventeenth-century English administrators straining to render Irish names into English phonetics. The attempts to render Irish sounds into English certainly causes confusion. The name Ó Dochartaigh has been rendered, with or without the "O," as Doughtery, Doherty, Dockerty, Daughtery, Dorrity, Dogherty and so on. Ó Domhnaill may be rendered not only as O'Donel, but with almost as many *n*s and *l*s as you like, as O'Donnell or O'Donell. However, there is also the problem of grammatical cases in Irish. If the name was heard in the vocative form, it might be regarded as a different name. The easiest example of this is the name Séamas, which becomes Shéamais, phonetically "*hamish,*" and which is accepted now as a separate proper name by its rendition into English phonetics. Additionally if Éildhe had a grandson, he would become known as Ó hÉildhe, Anglicized as Hely. Conchobar may equally be found as Conchobhair and Conchúir (pronounced *kru-húr*) and rendered into Anglicized form as Conor or Connor. I have tried to maintain some standardization wherever possible.

PART ONE

The Extinction and Survival of Gaelic Aristocracy

CHAPTER ONE

THE GAELIC ARISTOCRACY

THE INDIGENOUS GAELIC ARISTOCRACY OF IRELAND is, without doubt, the most ancient in Europe. Most of the families have pedigrees that stretch back more than fifteen hundred years; and, if we accept the validity of the ancient genealogical records, some can date their ancestry back three thousand years. The Irish royal houses have genealogies, contained within these early records, tracing their descent, generation by generation, from the sons of Golamh, otherwise known as Milesius or Míle Easpain (soldier of Spain), who, according to tradition, invaded Ireland at the end of the second millennium B.C. He is regarded as the progenitor of the Gaels.

Many scholars are unhappy at placing complete faith in these early genealogies based on oral transmission to the early Christian period. Professor Thomas O'Rahilly even rejected placing any reliance at all on the oral traditions, saying, "The fact is that no trust can be placed in the pedigrees of pre-Christian times."[1] Some of his contemporaries disagreed. Professor Eoin MacNeill was more cautious and believed that they "are probably fairly authentic in the main as far back as 200 B.C."[2] In recent years, scholars have come to a better understanding and acceptance of the accuracy of oral traditions. We must also remember that these family pedigrees were being maintained in written form at least from the seventh century A.D.

Whether we accept pre-Christian oral traditions or not, the fact remains that the antiquity of the Irish Royal Houses rivals only that of the royal Bagration family of Georgia, who traced their descent from the Armenian (Bagratuni) nobles of the third century A.D. and are considered "the most ancient family of the old Christian East." According to the *International Edition of The Royalty Peerage and Nobility of Europe* (1997), commenting on the modern bearers of Gaelic titles: " . . . despite these facts, their existence is largely unknown to all except academic historians and genealogists."

The bulk of the early Irish collections of genealogies is impressive. The earliest material comes from the seventh century A.D., when, having adopted the Latin alphabet, the Irish were committing their extensive knowledge to written form. Among the oldest fragments of Irish poetry collected by Kuno Meyer were four genealogical poems, one of them giving a genealogy of the Munster King Cathal II Cú-cen-máthair (d. A.D. 641) and the others of Leinster kings.[3] These poems, known as *forsundud*, or praise poems, were to princes of Irish dynasties extolling their ancestry. Professor Myles Dillon has pointed that the *forsundud* is the oldest surviving form of Irish poetry and compares to other ancient Indo-European poetic forms, such as the Sanskrit Vedic *narasamsyah* songs in praise of princes and their ancestry. Dillon writes: "I would now suggest that these oldest Irish quatrains are true *nayasamsyah*, that is to say stanzas composed by the bard to be recited on the occasion of a king's inauguration. . . ."[4]

The *forsundud* were handed down orally for a thousand or more years, being added to with each generation, before finally being committed to writing. It was a poetic form still being used when the chief bard of Ó Ceallaigh of Hy-Maine (A.D. 1375) wrote such a genealogical poem about the Eóghanacht dynasty of Munster. The word *forsundud* implies illumination, casting light upon a matter. The same root is found in *fursaintid*, the order of the third degree of wisdom of the study to become an *ollamh*, the highest qualification of learning and now the modern Irish word for "professor."

The earliest surviving complete genealogical manuscripts date from the early twelfth century. References show that many genealogical books have been lost or destroyed. Even so, that which remains is considerable. There has been an attempt to print these remarkable manuscripts. The first volume in the projected series was edited by M. A. O'Brien as *Corpus Genealogiarum Hiberniae*, appearing in 1962.

At the time of the Anglo-Norman invasion of Ireland in the late twelfth century, the island was divided into a number of provincial kingdoms. Giraldus Cambrensis, in his *Expugnatio Hibernica*, reported that Ireland was a pentarchy of Munster, Ulster, Leinster and Connacht together with Meath, as the seat of the "High Kings."

Prior to the late tenth century, the principal Irish kingdoms consisted of Munster (Royal House of MacCarthy); Ulster (Royal House of O'Neill); Leinster (Royal House of MacMorrough); and Connacht (Royal House of

O'Conor). Within these kingdoms were many petty "kingdoms" whose rulers were akin to princes, dukes, counts and barons, but all giving allegiance, though sometimes unwillingly, to the king. There was also a theoretical "High King" elected by and from the ranks of the provincial dynasties, enjoying what the heraldic expert Gerard Crotty has described as a "precedence of honor" rather than an executive position.[5] The position of the "High King" was a symbolic acknowledgment of the common origin and unity of the Irish peoples. Until the onset of the Christian period, this High Kingship alternated between the Uí Néill (O'Neill) and their kindred clans and the Eóghanachta (MacCarthys) and their kindred clans. After the start of the Christian period, the Uí Néill dominated the High Kingship, making it a struggle between northern and southern branches. Some O'Neill propagandists claim that the concept and office of High Kingship was only an Uí Néill prerogative, but the records are clear.

The High Kingship was centered in the "middle kingdom," Midhe, from which the Anglicized Meath gets its name, and consisted of Meath, Westmeath and parts of adjoining counties. In the twelfth century it had been reduced to no more than a petty kingdom. Its position will be discussed in chapter 2.

This High Kingship, together with the Irish legal system, a fairly standard written language and a common mythology and religion, marked a sense of unity that was not present in many other lands that contained such a multiplicity of kingdoms, such as the Iberian and Italian peninsulas, the territory now known as France, or even England itself prior to its tenth-century unification under Athelstan (A.D. 925–939), who melded the Anglo-Saxon and Danish kingdoms into one by conquest.

The Uí Néill and the Eóghanachta, in being acknowledged as the only original legitimate claimants to the High Kingship at this time, claimed their descent from the two sons of Milesius, Eremon and Eber Fionn, who were the progenitors of the Gaels in Ireland and who divided Ireland between them—Eremon ruling in the north and Eber Fionn in the south.

However, in the tenth century, another dynastic family was able to seize the High Kingship. The rulers of a rebellious clan in northern Munster (Tuaidh Mhumhain = Thomond), called the Dál gCáis (descendants of Cas, later to become known as the O'Briens), managed take possession first of the throne of Munster and then of the High Kingship itself by means of force. The most famous member of the Dál gCáis dynasty was Brían Bóroimhe (Anglicized as Brian Boru, d. 1014) and hence the name of O'Briens or descendants of Brían. Under his rule the High Kingship became, for the first time, a centralized, executive power over the kingdoms. It would be wrong to say that the seizure of kingship by force was meekly accepted by the other dynasties. The Eóghanachta in Munster refuted Dál gCáis claims in arms, not just with opposition to the High Kingship but to the claim to the Munster throne itself. The Eóghanachta were pushed back on the territory of Desmond (Deis Mumhan—south Munster), which was to remain their kingdom until the Elizabethan conquests.

Later in the twelfth century, another powerful dynasty seized the High Kingship by similar military means. This dynasty was the Uí Briúin, or O'Conors of Connacht. To further secure their power base, by the Treaty of Glanmire in A.D. 1118, the O'Conors forced the Dál gCáis and Eóghanachta to accept the partition of the Kingdom of Munster into the kingdoms of Thomond (north Munster—O'Brien) and Desmond (south Munster—MacCarthy). Thus, at a stroke, the O'Conor High Kings weakened the power of these rival dynasties. But before the O'Conors could further assert a strong centralist power over the other kingdoms, King Dermot MacMorrough of Leinster went abroad to seek help from the Angevin emperor, Henry II, in order to secure his kingdom against the High King, Ruaidri Ua Conchobhair (Rory O'Conor).

In the twelfth century, the kingdoms of Ireland, with their new centralizing High Kingship, were already under threat from the rapidly expanding Norman empire, which we retrospectively call the Angevin Empire.

What sort of places were the kingdoms ruled over by the Gaelic kings at this time? If an equitable social order, if literacy and advancement in the arts and known sciences are yardsticks by which to judge civilization, then Ireland had produced one of Europe's outstanding cultures. The kingdoms had become Christianized during the fifth century. From this time the Irish intellectual class turned from a centuries-old orally transmitted culture to committing their vast wealth of knowledge, poetry and legends to written form. Seizing the impetus of the new faith with enthusiasm, the Irish religious of both sexes took their learning and literacy to many other peoples. Singly and in groups, they brought Christianity to the pagan Anglo-Saxons and taught them the art of writing. They spread their foundations further, as far east as Kiev in the Ukraine, north to Iceland and the Faroes, and through France, Germany, Spain and Italy. And the peoples of Europe were welcomed to the great centers of learning in Ireland itself. Durrow, in the seventh century, boasted students from eighteen different nations.

Even the Viking raids, beginning in A.D. 795, did not upset the Gaelic order. The Vikings settled down in seaports and set up their own petty kings to rule their settlements. Dublin was formed in 841 under King Olaf. The Irish managed to contain the warlike ambitions of these Vikings. The Munster king,

Ceallacháin I (ca. 944–952), whose campaigns are recorded in the twelfth century romance *Caithreim Cheallacháin Chaisil*, broke Viking power in his kingdom and made them acknowledge his rule. More famous is the final breaking of Viking territorial ambitions in Ireland by the High King Brían Bóroimhe, who defeated the combined Viking army at Clontarf in 1014. The Viking city colonies had already begun to merge before this into an Irish cultural ethos, with their petty rulers acknowledging the Gaelic kings.

The Irish kingdoms were rich in agriculture, pastoral farming, mining—even gold was mined and worked in several parts. There was a rich trade and regular contact with Europe, especially in intellectual exchanges. Imports and exports flourished. The fortresses and the castles, and architecture in general, were more than merely functional and, for the climate, well constructed, as can be seen by what has survived the ravages of time. For example, standing in the Gallarus oratory, on the Dingle Peninsula, two and a half miles east of Ballyferriter, one cannot help being impressed by its construction. One of the best examples of corbel pattern building, its construction is of dry stone masonry arranged to slope slightly downward and outward to throw off the rain. Considering that this is probably over twelve hundred years old and that, in spite of being constructed without any mortar, not a drop of rain has entered the building in that time, we must acknowledge the Irish builders of that period. The Irish round towers, built as defensive structures against Viking raids, with conical caps, such as the one at Ardmore, County Waterford, are further examples of advanced building techniques. King Cormac's Chapel at the old Munster capital of Cashel built in the period 1127 to 1134 remains another fascinating demonstration of how architecture was developing under the patronage of the kings.

The Irish kings ruled rich courts and patronized both artists and artisans. The illuminated gospel books and other such works; the amazing book shrines, such as that for the Book of Dimma and the Domnach Airgid; the processional Cross of Cong and the processional Cross of Lislaughtin, County Kerry; the Shrine of St. Patrick's Bell; the Ardagh Chalice; the Derrynaflan Chalice; and other masterpieces of Irish metalwork leave one gasping in amazement at artistic and technical brilliance that remained unsurpassed in succeeding centuries. Many of these pieces were commissioned by the Irish kings and nobility. The spectacular Cross of Cong is inscribed as being commissioned by the King of Connacht, Tairrdelbach (Turlough) O'Conor in 1125. The fascinating Shrine of St. Lachtin's Arm carries an inscription asking for prayer for Cormac III MacCarthy, King of Munster; the Shrine of the Book of Dimma is inscribed as commissioned in the twelfth century by the O'Carroll of Ely; the fifteenth-century Ballymacasey Cross is inscribed as commissioned by The O'Connor

Kerry; and the Derrynaflan hoard includes a stag device badge, which is the symbol of the Eóghanachta dynasty, which had connections with Derrynaflan. The royal courts were havens of patronage and hospitality for the Irish artists. The popular notion that their work was solely the product of support by the Irish ecclesiastical centers is incorrect. Kings did, in fact, endow ecclesiastical centers but also encouraged secular colleges and personal patronage.

The royal courts were replete with lawyers; theologians and philosophers; medical men, for medical practice was also highly advanced as well as the laws governing it; historians or chroniclers; poets; musicians; and astronomers. Musical notation manuscripts also survive from the twelfth century. Cashel Diocesan Library still contains a treatise on music written by a musical scholar at Cashel during the reign of Dermod I (1144–1185) and dated 1168.

With regard to astronomy, Dr. Dan MacCarthy of Trinity College has recently examined twelve of the Irish annals and chronicles. He collated and examined, for the first time, all observations made of astronomical phenomena between 442 and 1133. What emerged was a body of record of eclipses, comets, aurorae and even a supernova, all carefully and accurately set down; some ninety-two astronomical observations. Dr. MacCarthy checked these records using a computer and found that between 627 and 1133 some thirty-one observations were found only in these Irish records. No other European textural evidence has been found. But the references corresponded to non-European (mainly Chinese and Japanese) sightings, and, when calibrated with the Irish records, the Irish observations were in precise accord.

In 1054 the Italians recorded what appeared to be a supernova in the Crab Nebula, dating it to April 19, 1054. This is significant because it is the date of the death of Pope Leo IX. But Irish astronomers had placed it nearly eight weeks later. Who was right? A comparison with Chinese and Japanese records proved that the Irish astronomers were accurate. The Italians had altered the observation to make it concur with the death of the pope.

Left to themselves, the Irish kingdoms could perhaps have continued developing as the great intellectual centers of Europe. But the one thing the Irish had not developed was a ruthless military capability. The Irish, like their fellow Celts, took an attitude to warfare that had not altered in a thousand years. Combat was still a matter of personal honor, and often an entire battle could depend on a single combat between two champions. Warriors were individuals, not merely part of some mindless killing machine. True, as we shall examine later, there were warrior groups, but these were generally royal bodyguards. There were no standing armies in Ireland such as had developed in Rome, nor was warfare held in the same cultural esteem in which the Germanic peoples held it. Therefore, the Irish had no centralized, trained force to withstand an assault by a more ruthless foe. And in the twelfth century they were faced with just such an enemy.

Viking Norsemen had settled in the area that was to be named after them—Normandy—and in 991 Charles III, King of the Franks, had ceded control of the territory to the Norse chief, Rollo, whom he recognized as first Duke of Normandy. These Normans quickly merged their lifestyle into that of the Franks, another people of Germanic origin. Both were thirsty for the conquest of new lands. By the twelfth century the Norman empire had grown considerably and consisted of Normandy, Brittany, Maine, Anjou (from which the term "Angevin empire" derives), Touraine, Aquitaine, Gascony, England, Cornwall and a tenuous overlordship of parts of Wales and Scotland. It was obvious, at some stage, that Ireland would be the next step for the Norman expansion.

In 1066 William of Normandy conquered England. Although he claimed the title "King of England," his dominions were primarily in the south. Indeed, after his conquest, he remained in England barely three months, leaving it to his half brother Odo to attempt to secure Norman domination in the country. He returned for a military campaign a year later and spent a few years in the country. England, therefore, was merely one province of the empire centered in Anjou, the main residence of the Norman kings. This was the position in 1169 when the first Norman lords invaded Ireland. It was not, as some misrepresent it, an English invasion.

When King Dermot arrived at Henry's court in Aquitaine, Henry was not particularly keen to gather an army to invade Ireland. However, he did not put any obstacle in the way of any of his Norman liegemen who might like an adventure. So King Dermot found an ally in Richard FitzGilbert, Earl of Pembroke, and a member of the de Clare family, descended from the Dukes of Normandy. He has taken his place in Irish history as "Strongbow." Dermot promised Richard his daughter's hand in marriage; as Dermot had no sons, Richard thought this meant he would inherit the Kingdom of Leinster. He was in for a rude awakening, for primogeniture had no status in Irish law. Richard sent troops with Dermot to Ireland in August 1167, a force defeated by the High King and his ally O'Ruairc of Breifne; another band of Normans and Flemings landed in Wexford on May 1, 1169. Then on August 23, 1170, "Strongbow" himself arrived. The initial victories, plus the death of King Dermot on May 1, 1171 and "Strongbow's" claim to be king (a position the Irish could not accept under their laws of succession, as discussed in chapter 2), caused Henry II to reconsider his position. He doubtless feared that

"Strongbow" might make himself King of Ireland and become a threat to him. So, on October 17, 1171, Henry II landed near Waterford with his army as much to keep the original adventurers in obedience to his feudal authority as to conquer Ireland. The result of this military campaign was that the High King, Ruaidri Ua Conchobhair, having abdicated his position under law and acting only as King of Connacht, signed the Treaty of Windsor on October 6, 1175. By this treaty, Ruaidri recognized Henry II as his paramount lord, but Henry II went further and declared himself paramount Lord of (all) Ireland. It is true that Henry had received several submissions from the Irish kings and nobles during his months in the country. Among the major rulers who submitted were King Dermot MacCarthy of Desmond, King Donal O'Brien of Thomond and the O'Ruairc of Breifne.

One of the great debating points of history is that Pope Adrian IV (1154–59) granted a Bull Laudabiliter, which gave Henry II, of the Angevin Empire, full permission and support to "enter the island of Ireland in order to subject its people to law and to root out from them the weeds of vice." In return for this papal approval, Henry II agreed to pay an annual tribute to Rome of one penny for every household in Ireland. The bull is thought to have been issued about 1155, many years before the invasion. In Norman terms, the Bull Laudabiliter was seen as the "legal" basis for the invasion of Ireland.

It became almost fashionable for many nineteenth-century Irish Catholic nationalists to claim that the Bull Laudabilter was forged or to emphasize that Pope Adrian IV was one Nicholas Breakspear, an "Englishman." He was, indeed, the only Anglo-Saxon to become Bishop of Rome. However, why should the fact that Adrian was an Anglo-Saxon, whose people had recently been conquered by the Normans, be of any significance? After all, Henry II was born in Le Mans, in Maine, died in Anjou, was buried at Fontevrault Abbey and was the French-speaking ruler of a predominantly French-speaking empire. Had the prelate been Irish, he would not have been more removed from Henry II. The Anglo-Saxons were still not assimilated into that empire, and conflict was still erupting between Norman overlords and their Anglo-Saxon vassals throughout England. Any conclusion that Adrian's cultural background had per se some "national" bearing on the issuing of the bull is illogical.

The eighteenth-century *Généalogie de la Royale et Sérnissime Maison de Mac-Carthy*[6] reported the tradition that, when Donnchadh O'Brien was deposed from the throne of Munster, he went on a pilgrimage to Rome, and "made a present of his crown of massive gold and other regalia to the pope" before he died there in 1064. It has been speculated that this action was interpreted by the popes, in their role as feudal princes, as being an act of submission, giving them the right to dispose of Ireland. Was Donnchadh's crown the same crown sent by a later pope to Henry II in 1186 to confirm his fiefdom in Ireland?

In fact, many nineteenth-century Irish Catholics found it hard to accept that the Church of Rome, as a temporal and feudal institution, was not a friend to the Irish nation. It was forgotten that the church in Ireland at this time had been in conflict with Rome for many centuries. The Irish church disagreed on several fundamental matters of theology with Rome, but, most important, it stood in opposition to the feudal social system espoused by Rome. In this fact, more than theology, lay the reason for Rome's enthusiastic advocacy of an invasion and conquest of Ireland.

Historians Mary Hayden and George Moonan explain: "Each clan had its own bishop, and its own priests. . . . The clan allotted to its clergy, for their support, certain lands . . . looked after by an officer who was generally a layman. The clergy of a clan mostly lived in communities under their bishop, so that the church was both tribal and monastic."[7]

In other words, the Irish church, while it was building up its own ecclesiastical laws, called the *Penetentials*, which were generally inspired by Roman custom, still found itself constrained by the Irish native law, popularly called Brehon law, from the word *breitheamh*, which means "judge," and the social system it generated. Irish law was ancient. It is regarded by scholars as the oldest surviving codified law system in Europe. In chapter 2 we will examine its ancient Indo-European origins and its parallels with the Hindu Laws of Manu, and also compare the Irish law texts to the Sanskrit of the Hindu texts, both being of common Indo-European root. The Irish had an amazing respect for and obedience to the law compared with other ancient peoples, and their ancient literature is full of the high regard that they gave their *brehon* (judge) and *ollamhain* (professors). An *ollamh* could even speak before a king, and kings and princes had to obey the judgment of the *brehons*.

Under this social system, there was no such concept as primogeniture inheritance. Kingship was electoral although within the same families. There also was no such concept as absolute ownership of land nor right of alienation of the land. Kings were not law makers but only officers of the established law and could be deposed by being forced to abdicate if they became either negligent or despotic. Women's rights were protected under the law, and offenses against women, even sexual harassment, are listed in native Irish law. Women could aspire to office in all the professions and, in certain exceptional circumstances, might become head of a clan and a leader in battle. There was even a highly advanced "medical health service" whereby sick maintenance (including curative treatment, attendance, and nourishing food) had to be made available to all who needed it, no matter their station in life. The exceptional working of the Irish system was undoubtedly due in large part to the clan system.

Dr. William E. Montgomery feels that the clash between the Irish system and the crushing slavery of feudalism then emerging out of Europe was inevitable. He points out that the original system was undergoing change, first by the change to Christianity and second by contact with the Danes, who had formed several city-states on the coast of Ireland. There is no denying that from the start of the eleventh century a system of territorial lords was arising particularly in Munster. Some fifty or so territorial lords (such lordships were held by someone with a Gaelic title) were clearly feudal in essence and were at the bestowal of the king. In 1588 Sir Warham St. Leger compiled a report for Elizabeth's Privy Council in which he enumerated the major territorial lordships subject to Donal IX MacCarthy Mór as King of Desmond. There is little evidence of this territorial lordship practice, the equivalent of an English "Lord of the Manor," outside of Munster, although Dr. Katharine Simms, in her article "The O'Hanlon, O'Neill and Anglo-Normans in 13th Century Armagh," pointed out that The O'Hanlon was granted a feudal lordship in 1300 by an O'Neill king.[8]

What was happening has been described by Montgomery as "the steady march of time," which "advanced the feudalization of the land, which in Aryan races seems always to have gone hand in hand with increase of population."[9]

Laurence Ginnell, in his book *The Brehon Laws*, has commented:

The idea of private property in land was developing and gathering strength, and land was generally becoming settled under it. The title of every holder, once temporary, was hardening into ownership, and the old ownership of the clan was vanishing, becoming in ordinary cases little more than a superior jurisdiction the exercise of which was rarely invoked.[10]

However, by the time of the Norman invasion, the change was only beginning in Munster. Even in Munster it was a new concept that one could have a feudal relation with the king. Doubtless, left to themselves, the Irish might have developed slowly over the centuries their own feudal ideas. As Montgomery says: "the growth of the power of the Chief, the idea of landlord and tenant was still strange to the Irish mind and its compulsory imposition on an unwilling people [by the Norman invasion] was probably a fatal mistake." The persistence of the native equitable communal laws against the complete feudal, private property of the Anglo-Norman system is without parallel. The reason for this was imposition by force rather than the continuance of natural development. This natural development, starting probably a century before the Norman invasion, was certainly not fast enough for the temporal princes of the Roman church. Montgomery comments:

> The Church lands were in the first place probably granted by the tribe from the common stock, and the Brehon Law recognizes to a very remarkable extent the claim of "the tribe of the Saint" to support. The most important influence exerted by the Church on the system of land holding is that it undoubtedly did much, from more or less selfish ends, to aid free alienation of land. The *Corus Brescna* shows that, in the cause of acquisitions, the Church had made great inroads on the restrictions imposed on alienation by the tribal system; and that even in allotments a succession attack had been made on the original inviolability of tribal possession as far as regards alienation to the Church.

He further observes: " . . . at the end of the 10th or beginning of the 11th Century the Irish people were in a state of transition from common property to several ownership, the Brehon writers themselves favouring the theory of private property."[11] However, attempts to change the Irish social system were generally unsuccessful before the Norman invasion.

Rome had long been dismayed at the lack of a centralized Irish political state ruled by a strong autocrat. This was why the emergence of the O'Brien and O'Conor dynasties was encouraged by the agents of Rome. Rome, as a feudal power, sought to extend that feudal power to Ireland, where feudalism was still generally an alien concept. The Irish church's most zealous reformer was Maelmaedoc Ó Morgair (St. Malachy), born in Armagh in 1095. He paid two visits to Rome in the early and mid-twelfth century. One can argue that St. Malachy was the real architect of the invasion by convincing Rome that its feudal policies could be brought about only by a strong outside force. Even Malachy's friend, St. Bernard of Clairvaux, with whom he stayed, seemed surprised at the invective with which Malachy denounced his fellow Irishmen, calling them "beasts, not men." "In all the barbarism which he had yet encountered, he had never met such a people so profligate in their morals, so uncouth in their ceremonies, so impious in faith, so barbarous in laws, so rebellious in discipline, so filthy in life . . ."[12] Was it with irony that St. Bernard wondered how "so saintly and lovable man could come of such a race"?

It must be remembered that the bishops of Rome of this period regarded themselves as temporal princes, with more feudal power than most emperors, and that they often led their own armies into battle to assert that power and reap tribute from those they subjugated.

When Henry II finally took his armies to Ireland and began to force the Irish kings to submit to him, Pope Adrian's successor, Pope Alexander III, wrote to him. Three of his letters are extant, confirming that he recognized Henry II as "Lord of Ireland."[13] The excuse of nationality could not be leveled against Alexander III. He was one Rolando Bandinelli from Sienna, and his concern for Ireland was simply to exercise his feudal rights and claim the financial tribute from Henry II.

Many of the Irish clergy followed the leadership of St. Malachy. The Irish bishops and abbots "concluded that the defects and backward state of their Church and nation were justification for subjecting their native land to a foreign king as one destined by Heaven and the Vicar of Christ to reform otherwise hopeless abuses."[14] During the winter of 1171/72 a council of Irish bishops convened in Cashel, the Munster capital, passing several decrees that were submitted to Henry II for confirmation. As well as purely ecclesiastical affairs, some of the decrees attacked the Irish social system and sought to bring it in line with feudalism, freeing all church property from the jurisdiction of the clan assemblies and placing all clergy, for the first time, above the law, excusing them from paying fines if found guilty of transgressing the law, even if they committed homicide. The Cashel Synod decided "the divine offices shall be celebrated according to the forms of the Church of England" (i.e., still the Roman church at this date). Professor Edmund Curtis comments: "The bishops indeed went the whole way to oblige Henry and, if we are to believe reputable chroniclers of the next century, each of them gave him a letter with his seal attached, confirming to Henry and his heirs the kingdom of Ireland."[15]

The Irish church now came in line with Rome. All the Irish were ordered to pay feudal tithes to the parish priest (each clan territory now becoming a parish) in whose parish they lived. Henry II wrote acknowledging the Pope's feudal superiority in a letter to Alexander III in 1173, which is found recorded in Thomas Rhymer's *Foedera*. The annual payment for Ireland, as a vassal state, was duly paid by Henry II to the Pope.

John of Salisbury, in his *Metalogicus*, recorded that the Pope, in return, sent Henry a golden ring adorned with an emerald to be worn to symbolize his authority, on Rome's behalf, over Ireland. So it is quite clear that when Ireland became the newest province of the Norman Angevin Empire, with several of its kings having submitted to Henry II as *Dominus Hibernia* (Lord of Ireland), Ireland had, constitutionally, become a papal fiefdom with the Angevin Emperors merely as middlemen. The bishops of Rome, as temporal feudal princes, had conspired in the conquest of Ireland, asserting themselves as feudal lords of all the lands of Europe and even beyond, taking their feudal authority from

God, whom they represented on earth. In this position they were able arbitrarily to give Ireland into the charge of Henry II in return for payment.

Henry II, in a passing fit of generosity, thought to bestow the "Kingship of
Ireland" on his nineteen-year-old son John, in 1186. He had already crowned
his eldest son, Henry, as "King of England" in June 1170, demonstrating that
England was regarded only as one of the provinces of the empire. But "young
Henry" died in Turenne on June 11, 1183. Enthusiastically, Henry II even
sought permission and papal sanction from Urban III (Uberto Crivelli of
Milan) for the use the title "king" instead of "lord." Urban III, naturally, demanded more money for the proposed change of title and sent three papal
legates to Henry II bearing a crown of peacocks' feathers set in gold for the inauguration ceremony.

But 1186 turned out to be a bad year for Henry. His son Geoffrey, now
heir to the throne, was killed in an accident in a tournament in Paris in August
and there was a growing dispute between his sons Richard and John over their
claims to the empire. Henry changed his mind, deciding that John might become too big for his boots. Three years later Henry II was dead.

Henry II's son Richard I (Coeur-du-Lion, the Lionheart) spent even less
time in England than his father. Few of his subjects even noticed when Richard I
died, contrary to the romantic tales centered around the myths of Robin Hood.
Although "King of England" for ten years, he spent only six months there. Apart
from his crusading period, he preferred to spent his time in the duchy of
Aquitaine. As historian Mike Ashley remarks, in *British Monarchy* (Robinson,
1998): "The English, in their usual way of preferring the legend to the facts, have
long cherished the memory of a man who, in fact, had no interest in England
other than as a source of revenue, and who was a ruthless fighting machine who
made enemies of most of the royalty of Europe."[16]

Henry II's next surviving son, John, became the new Angevin emperor on
June 2, 1199. John tried to secure his power as king by murdering Arthur, his
nephew and son of his older brother Geoffrey, who had a superior claim for the
throne under the primogeniture system. John proceeded to lose most of the
empire in what is now France. In fact, in 1204, the heartland of Normandy was
captured by the Franks. He fell back on England. It is only then, although
dominated by its Norman ruling class, that England begins to emerge as a central kingdom and not just a Norman province.

John was excommunicated by Pope Innocent III (Lotario dei Conti di
Segni), but then, as now, money talked. John formally submitted himself to In-
nocent III. On May 15, 1213, at the House of the Templars at Ewell, near
Dover, John assigned the "kingdom of England" and the "lordship of Ireland"

to Pope Innocent III. The Pope then regranted the kingship of England and lordship of Ireland to John on condition that John acknowledge, for himself and his heirs and successors, Rome's temporal feudal authority under bonds of fealty and homage as vassals of the Bishop of Rome in his capacity as a temporal feudal prince. John and his heirs agreed to pay the Bishop of Rome an annual tribute of 700 marks for England and 300 marks for Ireland.

This act was solemnly ratified in St. Paul's Cathedral, London, on October 3, 1213, in the presence of Nicholas, Cardinal Bishop of Tusculum, and sealed with a golden bull on behalf of Innocent. The confirmation of this act is recorded in the Charter Rolls and in Thomas Rhymer's *Foedera*. Ireland, therefore, continued to be a papal fiefdom at the whim and gift of the bishops of Rome but with the Norman kings of England, emerging from the chaos of Henry II's Angevin Empire, as middlemen. John had tried to regain his lost Angevin territories, retaining some, but was generally unsuccessful. And, under the new papal deal, the Irish kings and princes were instructed, on pain of excommunication, to obey the authority of the English kings as their paramount lords.

The Irish kings not only resented this, they appealed as to the injustice of it directly to the Bishop of Rome. The kings of England now were trying to destroy the Irish legal system. In 1246 Henry III decreed that "all the laws and customs which are observed in the realm of England should be observed in Ireland." Edward I (1272–1307) asked his justiciar in Ireland, Robert D'Ufford, to report in 1277 as to the possibility of extending English law to Ireland. Edward II (1307–27) issued a royal order to admit the Irish to "the protection of English law" in 1321.

In the face of this, "The Remonstrance of the Irish Princes to Pope John XXII" was sent in 1317:

> Let no one wonder that we are striving to save our lives and defending as we can the right of our law and liberty against cruel tyrants and usurpers, especially since the said King, who calls himself Lord of Ireland, and also the said Kings, his predecessors, have wholly failed in this respect to do and exhibit orderly government to us and several of us.[17]

The Statutes of Kilkenny of 1366, declared by the English administration in Ireland, tried to abolish native Irish law and encroach on the authority of the Gaelic Kings and princes. However, the statutes actually had the effect of recognizing that they were still a strong power and stipulated that those "who continue to live under their own chiefs by Brehon law, are regarded as outside the protection of English law and liberty."

The fact was that English law was used only in a few isolated areas in Ireland where the colonists had established themselves. Irish law continued in the majority territory governed by the Irish kings. Indeed, most of the colonists, from 1169 onward, had found Irish law more equitable and had adopted the Irish language, law, customs and dress. Families like the Barry family, Blake, Brown (Le Brun), Burke, Butler, Cusack, Dillon, Fitzgerald, Joyce, Nugent, Plunkett, Roche, Taafe and Walsh all became indistinguishable from the Gaelic Irish.

It was mainly towards these "degenerate English," as these Gaelicized families were called, that colonial legislation, especially the Kilkenny Statutes, for spreading English law was aimed. Under these statutes intermarriage was forbidden; the adoption of Irish forms of names, the use of the language, the method of holding land, even the toleration of Brehon law, still more submitting to its judgments, was considered high treason by the English administration.

Perhaps the most fascinating thing about the Statutes of Kilkenny was their effect in not only recognizing the continued existence of the Gaelic kingdoms but the existence of a "middle nation," the Anglo-Irish who had merged themselves into Irish culture. What is more to the point, it demonstrated that the English administration had little control over the colonists.

Even the Kingdom of Leinster, which had been the first area entered by the Normans and settled, was by no means conquered. When Richard II landed with his army in Waterford on June 1, 1399, accompanied by the dukes of Exeter and of Albemarle and the Earl of Gloucester, he was faced with a formidable foe in Art Mór Mac Airt (MacMorrough Kavanagh), King of Leinster (1375–1416). Art Mór had already defeated the army of the Viceroy, Roger Mortimer, and de facto heir to the English throne, at Kelliston near Carlow. Mortimer was slain in the battle. King Art Mór was an exceptional commander who would not be drawn into a battle until conditions favored him. Similarly he did not respond to offers of negotiation on unfavorable terms, showing that he also had astute political acumen.

When a frustrated Richard II demanded his surrender, Art Mór replied, according to the *Annals of Loch Cé*: "I am rightful King of Ireland [*sic*], and it is unjust to deprive me of what is my land by conquest." Before Richard could do anything further, there came news of opposition to his own kingship in England. He had to hurry back to England where Henry, Duke of Lancaster (Bolingbroke), had invaded the country with ten ships and three hundred men and seized the throne as Henry IV. The result of the English regnal power struggle was that Ireland, for a century afterward, continued to be ruled by its own Gaelic kings and princes, secure in their kingdoms, with the Gaelicized Anglo-Norman lords protected in their earldoms and estates and baronies. Indeed, the Ó Raghaillighs of Lough Oughter, County Cavan, were so unassailable that they were issuing their own coinage through the fourteenth century. Under the settled condition of the Irish kingdoms there was a new flowering of Irish learning, much influenced by the new Arabic ideas in medicine permeating the European universities. The Irish language contains the largest corpus of medical literature written in any one language prior to 1800. There was a new outpouring of literary endeavors and a new school of courtly poetry. It was "the beginning of a Gaelic literary renascence."[18] Many manuscript books were composed and recopied from older books during this period before the coming of printing technology. Even new studies on the law system were produced, and the *Senchus Mór* was rewritten with careful glosses. In addition, Irish scholars were translating avidly from Greek, Latin, Hebrew, Arabic, French and English. During the fifteenth century Arthurian tales became popular, and many versions of these were produced in Irish.

The position of the Irish kings and the aristocracy continued unchanged until the reign of the Tudor King Henry VIII, who was crowned in 1509, at the age of eighteen. In many ways, until this time the situation in Ireland with the English crown's relationship to the native kings and princes paralleled that of India under the British raj. Until Indian independence in 1947, the English crown had made treaties with many of the native kings and princes of the Indian subcontinent. One has to remember the vastness of India and that it was never a homogeneous unit. Some fourteen major languages and fifteen hundred dialects are spoken there.

Under British rule, native kings and princes still ruled a major part of the subcontinent under British suzerainty. These native kings and princes ruled half the landmass and one-quarter of the entire population. There were some six hundred of them, ranging from the powerful Nizam of Hyderabad, whose principality was the size of Italy with a population of 14 million, down to the Siem of Nongliwai in Assam, whose authority extended over a few hundred people in an area of a few hundred acres. While these princes had absolute authority over international affairs in their states, British Residents "advised" them, acting on behalf of the Viceroy in the name of the "King-Emperor of India," the English Crown.

During the 1920s, as India began approaching independence, there was an attempt to set up a "Council of Princes." One policy favored by the English Crown was to created a union of the nations of the subcontinent by means of a federation of the princely states. However, Congress, then the Indian independence movement, and especially Mohandas Gandhi, believed that the Indian princes, in accepting British suzerainty, had merely become India's "badges of slavery." Although the English Crown had solemnly signed treaties with these princes guaranteeing their autonomy, political "expediency," the standard morality, caused the Crown unilaterally to discard the treaties. The princes were told that they must take their states either into the new state of India or into that of Pakistan.

The Nizam of Hyderabad, a Muslim with a large number of Hindu subjects, tried to keep his state independent. The Hindus rose up and wanted to join India. Troops marched in, and his ancient capital Hyderabad is now in Pakistan while southern areas of the kingdom went to India. The Maharajah of Kashmir, a state the size of Ireland, decided to join India. His people were mixed, Moslem and Hindu. A state of conflict still exists in a partitioned Kashmir. The Republic of India eventually abolished the power of the Indian princes but "courtesy recognition" is still given to their titles and most still own their personal palaces and estates.

Between 1175, with the Treaty of Windsor and the accession of Henry VIII, the Irish kings and princes stood in almost the same position as those Indian princes, still ruling their ancient kingdoms and principalities and theoretically deferring to the suzerain authority of the English crown as a paramount lordship.

In 1533 Henry VIII began his break with the Church of Rome and declared himself head of a separate Church of England. The most important aspect of this separation was that Henry VIII was not simply breaking with Rome on the religious matters but on the feudal level, and that meant a loss of revenue to the papal coffers.

As early as 1515, and again in 1533, Henry VIII had ordered accounts of the "State of Ireland, and Plan for Its Reformation" to be compiled. The 1533 assessment reported that there were

> more than 60 countries, called territories (*regionis*) in Ireland, inhabited with the King's Irish enemies . . . where reigneth more than 60 chief captains, whereof some calleth themselves Kings, some Kings' peers, in their language, some princes, some dukes, some archdukes . . . and obeyeth to no other temporal person . . . [19]

The report gives a lists of the names of these holders of Gaelic titles. The same report says that there are "more than 30 great captains of the English noblefolk that followeth the same Irish order." It goes on to show that the Gaelic kings and Anglo-Irish nobles ruled most of Ireland still, two-thirds under the native kings and one-third under the Gaelicized Anglo-Irish. Only in a few tiny pockets, cities and walled towns, particularly on the coast, did the native Irish law hold no sway at all. It was pointed out to Henry VIII that "all the English folk of the said countries be of Irish habit, of Irish language, and of Irish conditions, except the cities and walled towns." And even most of the municipal governments of these cities and walled towns paid tribute to the Gaelic kings. The inhabitants of Cork city, for example, paid The MacCarthy Mór £40 per annum.

The King's Council in Ireland was asked to send some recommendations to John Alen, Master of the Rolls, on how the English ambition of making Ireland as indistinguishable from England in language, law, and social order might be accomplished. The recommendations were simple.[20] It was pointed out that in reality, England controlled only the Pale, which was not above twenty miles in diameter around Dublin. The term "Pale," from which the colloquial English phrase "beyond the pale" comes, is from the Norman-French *pal*, a stake used to make a fence as a limit or boundary. Calais was called the English Pale until 1558, when the English Crown finally lost this last piece of the former Angevin territory. It was then feared that, at any time, the Dublin Pale could also follow the Calais example and revert to the Irish.

The recommendations submitted to Henry argued that the temporal lords of Ireland had long been opposed to the rule of the kings of England. "Item, another hurt is, the committing the governance of this land to the lords, natives of the same. . . ." John Alen considered the matter for some time and in 1537 wrote a letter advising Henry VIII's commissioners in Ireland that it would be better for Henry to be recognized as "King of Ireland" and "then induce the Irish Captains [Gaelic Kings and nobles] as well by their oaths as writings, to recognize the same which things shall be, in continuance, a great motive to bring them to due obedience. . . ."[21]

In 1541 Henry VIII ceased to use the title *Dominus Hiberniae* (Lord of Ireland) and became the first English king to style himself *Rex Hiberniae* (King of Ireland). Therefore, Ireland's constitutional position changed from being a papal fiefdom, in which the kings of England, as lords of Ireland, once accepted the bishops of Rome as paramount lords and ruled Ireland exercising "but a governance under the obedience of the same."[22]

From the Irish viewpoint, it could be argued that Henry VIII, in ceasing to acknowledge the feudal dues of the Bishop of Rome, had freed the Irish kings and princes from their feudal dues to Henry, for their ultimate feudal authority was the Bishop of Rome. They therefore had no further obligation to acknowledge any English king's jurisdiction in Ireland by a claim to European feudal law. The point was certainly recognized at once by the papal administration of

Pope Paul III (1534–50), who realized that Henry VIII of England was "stealing" the papal fiefdom not only of the "Kingdom of England" but of the "Lordship of Ireland." Pope Paul III wrote to the King of Ulster, Conn Bacach O'Néill, in 1538, addressing his letter "To Our Most Dear Son in Christ, Conn Ó Neale, the Greater, Our Noble King of Our Realme of Ireland."[23] In this letter Pope Paul III revoked the grant made by Adrian IV's Bull Laudabiliter and confirmed by letters of Alexander III and Innocent III, and formally released all the Irish princes from the feudal duty of obedience to the English king as "Lord of Ireland."

A report, dated April 17, 1539, from the O'Conor King of Connacht claimed that Conn Bacach O'Néill had plans to march an army to Tara and there have himself proclaimed King of Ireland, with the support of the Fitzgerald, Earl of Desmond.[24] O'Néill and Aodh Dubh Ó Domhnaill did join with FitzGerald, Earl of Desmond, but before any formal inauguration was made, the Irish army was defeated by the English forces of the Lord Deputy at Belahoe, recorded in the *Annals of Connacht* for 1539.

The new policy of the Bishop of Rome was to reestablish a dynasty in Ireland that would recognize him as feudal prince of the country. On April 24, 1541, Pope Paul III wrote to Conn Bacach O'Néill that he had "heard with grief how that Island is by the present King reduced to such impiety and devastated with such cruelty." He "exhorts the whole Irish people to persevere in the Faith they received from their fathers." He goes on to say that he "holds that Ireland specially dear, as these Nuncios, John [Codurious] and Alphonsus [Salmeron] and Raymond will report."

A mission of these three papal nuncios had been sent to the King of Ulster. What was the purpose of that mission? What did they communicate to the Irish kings? Was their purpose to ensure that the kings rejected Henry VIII's new claim to the Kingship of Ireland and the abandonment of Ireland's status as a papal fiefdom? Indeed, Pope Clement VIII (1592–1605) later endorsed the struggle to maintain the papal fiefdom of Ireland against the authority of Protestant England. He did so in response to an appeal by The O'Neill, Florence MacCarthy Mór, MacDonagh MacCarthy of Duhallow and James, the Earl of Desmond. On April 18, 1600, Clement VIII issued a Bull of Indulgence to "archbishops, bishops, prelates, chiefs, earls, barons and people of Ireland." Clement acknowledged that the Irish "have long struggled to recover and preserve your liberty . . . to throw off the yoke of slavery imposed on you by the English . . . we grant to all of you . . . plenary pardon and remission of all sins, as usually granted to those setting out to the war against the Turks for the recovering of the Holy Land."[25]

However, Pope Paul's intercession with King Conn Bacach O'Néill proved fruitless. The Ulster king became one of the first to offer his submission to Henry VIII in 1541, surrendering his Gaelic title and taking from Henry the English title Earl of Tyrone.

From 1541 Ireland was to constitute a separate realm called the Kingdom of Ireland, but with the English kings as heads of state. This position remained until January 1, 1801, when the Kingdom of Ireland became part of the United Kingdom of Great Britain and Ireland.

On June 26, 1541, the Lord Deputy, Sir Anthony St. Leger, wrote to Henry VIII telling him that a parliament had been summoned in Dublin at which Henry's decree to be King of Ireland was endorsed.[26] There were attending, says St. Leger, two earls, three viscounts, sixteen barons, two archbishops, twelve bishops, as well as Donough O'Brien, the King of Thomond, a doctor named O'Nolan and a bishop and deputies assigned by O'Brien to represent him in parliament. The Ó Raghailligh Mór and many other Irish nobles had attended. In fact, the tenth Earl of Ormond, James Butler, had to volunteer his services to translate the words of Henry VIII's emissary to the parliament from English into Irish, not so much, it has been pointed out, for the Gaelic lords attending but for the Anglo-Irish lords who did not speak any English.

In the wake of Henry VIII's assumption of the kingship of Ireland came the announcement of the policy to "utterly abolish" all Gaelic titles, the native law system, the social system and methods of land holding in Ireland. As a Master of the Court of Wards, Sir William Parsons (ca. 1570–1650), was to state: "We must change their course of government, apparel, manner of holding land, language, and habit of life. It will otherwise be impossible to set up in them obedience to the laws and to the English Empire."[27]

The first step on that road to bring the Irish nation into obedience to England was that all holders of Gaelic titles were to be asked, with threat of force, implied or real, to surrender their titles and clan lands to the English Crown. If they took an oath of allegiance to the same Crown, they would be granted English titles and returned such portions of their former estates as deemed fit, to hold by feudal tenure from the English Crown. Any such surrenders, of course, meant an acknowledgment of the new religious order in which the English king was now head of the church and not the Bishop of Rome.

CHAPTER TWO

GAELIC DYNASTIC LAWS
OF SUCCESSION

WHAT MADE IT DIFFICULT FOR THE NORMANS and subsequently the English to establish control over Ireland? Had the kingship laws and the social order, with the system of land tenure, been close to the English feudal law system, or had Ireland shared the concept of the divine right of kings, in which the king and the law were inseparable, then the nature of the conflict might have been different. However, the Irish law system and government of kings was so different from the Anglo-Norman system that struggle and eventual dominance of one system over the other was inevitable. As soon as Henry VIII made himself king and demanded the surrender of the Irish kings on a feudal basis, unaware of the intricacies of the laws that governed them, war became unavoidable.

According to the ancient chroniclers, it was an eighth-century B.C. High King, Ollamh Fódhla, who ordered the laws of Ireland to be gathered. They were called the Laws of the Fénechus, or Féini (the tillers of the land). He is also said to have founded the great Féis Temhrach (Festival of Tara), held every three years, at which the laws were discussed and revised. The laws are now popularly called the Brehon laws.

The laws were the result of many centuries of transmission by oral tradition before being codified in the early Christian era. They show fascinating parallels with the Vedic Laws of Manu in India and are echoed in the Welsh law system, the Laws of Hywel Dda, named after King Hywel ap Cadell, who ruled Wales between A.D. 910 and 950. He decreed that the laws of Wales be gathered and examined by an assembly presided over by Blegwywrd, Archdeacon of Llandaff, and set down in a single law book.

The first known codification of the Irish law system was in A.D. 438, when High King Laoghaire established a nine-man commission to examine the laws, revise them and set them down in writing. Three leading *brehons* (judges) of the day, Dubhtach maccu Lugir, Rossa and Fergus, sat on the commission. Dubhtach is referred to in other sources as King Laoghaire's Chief Brehon and Druid. Laoghaire sat on the committee with Dara, King of Ulster, and Corc, King of Munster, indicating the importance of these two kings above the other kings of Ireland. In deference to the new faith, three Christian advisors sat on the committee, Patrick, Benignus and Cáirnech.

The committee eventually codified the laws into the *Senchus Mór*. This was the civil law and divided into the Cáin Law, which applied to all Ireland, and the Urradus Law, the local law under which certain laws applied to particular provinces. The criminal law was set down in the *Book of Acaill*. Even in the fifth century the "law language," called the *Bérla Féini*, was already archaic and demonstrated how old the Brehon system was at that time; for the laws were remembered in the form handed down for many centuries. The codification of A.D. 438 is said to have produced no *new* laws but was a setting down of those already in use with some addition of Scriptural or canon law. The introduction to the *Senchus Mór* states: "What did not clash with the word of God in the written Law and in the New Testament, and with the conscience of the believers, was confirmed in the laws of the Brehons by Patrick and by the ecclesiastics and the Kings of Erin; and this is the *Senchas Mór*."

The earliest surviving record of the laws in their most complete form is found in the *Leabhar na hUidre* (Book of the Dun Cow) dating from the eleventh and twelfth centuries.

The Brehon system is unique. What makes it one of the most fascinating ancient law codes in world jurisprudence is that the basis of the system of criminal liability was compensation for the victim or victim's family and rehabilitation for the perpetrator; not merely a system of vengeance. Compensation was more important, and the provision of compensation by the transgressor was paramount. The culprit or his family had to contribute to the individuals and to the society who had been wronged.

The laws and their archaic language are comparative with Vedic Laws of Manu. The similarity between Old Irish and Sanskrit is demonstrable proof of the common Indo-European origin. Professor Calvert Watkins pointed out that

Old Irish represent[s] an extraordinarily archaic and conservative tradition within the Indo-European tradition. . . . The classical Old Irish nominal and verbal system of the eighth century of the Christian era is a far truer reflection of the state of affairs in Indo-European than is the Latin system of more than a thousand years before . . . the structure of the archaic Old Irish sentence can be compared only with that of the sentence in Vedic Sanskrit or the Hittite of the Old Kingdom.[1]

Professor D. A. Binchy, examining the oldest records of the Irish law tracts, in particular the *Bretha Nemed*, says it indicates, in language and law, a system harking back to Indo-European times.[2] Much has now been written on the Vedic - Old Irish similarity, especially by Myles Dillon.[3] In terms of kingship, even the terminology is related—the Irish *Rí(gh)* compared to the Gaelish Celtic *Rix*, the Latin *Rex* and the Sanskrit *Rajan* (Hindi = *raj*). Certainly the English king from the Gothic *kunnings* has no relationship, but a surprising harking back to the concept appears in the English words "rich" and "reach." The ancient Indo-European concept was that a king *reached* forth his hand to protect his people. Also in Old Irish, for example, *rige* was not only the concept for kingship but also the word for the act of reaching. Therefore, in many Indo-European cultures, from India to Ireland, we have the concept of a deity with a "long hand" who reached it out to encompass his people— Lugh Lamhfada (Lugh of the Long Hand) has his Vedic equivalent in Dyaus. Oenghus Olmuchada of the Long Hand is said to have ruled Ireland in 800 B.C. The Uí Néill's ancient symbol of the Red Hand doubtless stems from this concept. It is the hand of a just ruler.

The Irish word *aire* for noble has its comparison in the Sanskrit *ayra*, from which the word Aryan comes from, now much perverted by Nazi philosophy. Similarly *nemed*, rendered as a name and word for privilege in Irish, is cognate with the Sanskrit *namas*, meaning a sacred person. The Indians also had a form of election of their kings (*parisad sam iti*), as did the Irish, and both cultures shared the condition that a king had to be without physical blemish. Another fascinating point in the cultural tradition of both peoples was the idea of the division of five kingdoms (the Irish word for a province still is *cúige* from the Old Irish *cóiced* (a fifth), in which a central kingdom exerted a theoretical obligation over the others. This kingdom was designated Midhe (the origin of Meath in Ireland, still sometimes referred to in memory of the kingship as Royal Meath), meaning "middle." In Sanskrit the Hindu kingdom was designated Madhya, having exactly the same meaning.

Central to the clash between the Irish and their invaders were these laws reflecting an entirely different social concept and philosophy of life. More significant was the different successional laws and the constraints put upon an Irish ruler. While an Irish king had to be of the "blood royal," he also had to be elected to office by his family. His succession relied on his *derbhfine* who formed the kinship electoral college.

Irish society, being kin-based, was categorized in law in the following manner: the *innfine* were the male great-great-grandchildren of the original head of the family. That five generations could be alive at one time was so unusual as to be discounted, although their rights are listed in law. There was an expressive aphorism *cúig glúine ó rígh fo rámhainn*—[there are] five generations from king to spade (i.e., to having a grave dug). The *iarfine* were the male great-grandchildren but the law indicates that their rights to be part of the electoral college as heirs to any property, real or ideal, were negligible.

The *derbhfine* were the male grandchildren who were the usual basis of the electoral college. The *geilfine* were the male children of an existing ruler. The *Book of Acaill* frequently mentions the *derbhfine* as seventeen in number. Probably the idea of seventeen male grandchildren existing at any one time and capable of taking part in an electoral college was not beyond the realm of possibility. This number is mentioned in the tract "On Succession."[4]

So the head of a family, a Chief of whatever degree, and the king himself, was elected by an electoral college consisting of his family, which was generally called the *derbhfine*, or true family, consisting of the sons, grandsons, and even great-grandsons of a common ancestor. According to the law, a king was appointed *do thaobh a ghlun ngeineamha*—by virtue of his ancestry. A king of whatever rank was also a member of his *derbhfine*, and on his death his title became inheritable property within the limits of his *derbhfine*. In our modern law concepts we might call this title an "ideal property" of the *derbhfine*.

Eoin MacNeill points out in *Early Irish Laws* that this succession was a combination of the elective with the hereditary principle and was a logical application of the Irish laws of inheritance.[5] But the decisive criterion for election to kingship was *febas*, or personal ability and standing. Part of that standing could be the *febas* of a candidate's father and grandfather, so if they both had held the kingship, his claim would be strengthened. Professor T. M. Charles-Edwards points out: "Seniority is a rejected principle unless other considerations should be equal."[6]

Election often narrowed to one of the three generations of the *derbhfine*, but this was not an unbreakable rule. Donnchadh Ó Corráin made a survey of Uí Cheinnsealach dynasty within a given period and found that their succession could be expressed in these percentage figures:

54% were sons of kings, though not necessary the eldest son, and of these only a small number [he lists six] succeeded directly after their father. With the majority, other relatives intervened in the kingship.

16% were grandsons of kings.

3% were great-grandsons of kings.

20% were great-great-grandsons and further removes

7% were of unknown lineage.[7]

In the kingdom of the northern Uí Néill, especially between A.D. 879 and 1260, the figures were: 66 percent the sons of kings, 15 percent the grandsons, and 3 percent great-grandsons.

However, it was not unusual to find candidates elevated to kingship even outside of the confines of the *derbhfine* and outside of the five generations of the *innfine*. Among the Eóghanacht, for example, the famous Cormac II mac Cuilennáin (d. 908) was eleven generations removed from his last regnant ancestor while Dub-dá-Bairenn mac Domhnaill (d. 959) was sixteen generations from his. However, at least half the kings elected were the sons of previous kings, and this election was usually made by the three generations of the family.

It was a principle of Irish law that all the *derbhfine* of a king or Chief were of suitable age. The male *aimsir togú*, or age of choice, was seventeen years. No one under that age could succeed to a title or, indeed, inherit property. For a female, the *aimsir togú* was fourteen years. To be elected to office, kings had to possess the necessary accomplishments; they had to be of sound mind and body. Stress was put on their intellectual powers, although military prowess was also important. As potential heirs to a title, particularly to a kingship, they were styled *Rígdamnae (Materies Regis)*, kingship material. This title, therefore, implied their eligibility to the kingship by being within the requisite degree of kindred. Dr. James Hogan has pointed out: "In short a Rígdomna was a prince whose father, grandfather, or great-grandfather had been a king."[8]

The electoral college of the *derbhfine* did not, of course, have to wait until the title had become vacant to meet and vote for the successor among themselves. Certainly from the twelfth century the practice was to appoint an heir-apparent, or *tánaise*, Anglicized as tanist, during the life of the king. The king or Chief could make the nomination himself from any member of his *derbhfine*. Any debate among the *derbhfine* could then take place during the lifetime of the king or chief so that his successor was able to assume his title without challenge.

Indeed, in the law tract *Críth Gabhlach* the term for the royal heir apparent, *tánaise ríg*, is explained by the sentence "because the whole clan looks forward to his kingship without opposition to him." David Greene has shown that the word actually derives from the past participle of *to-ad-ni-sed* and translates as "the awaited one." Only as it developed later did it come to mean "second in respect of dignity and function."[9]

To sum up the important point of difference between Irish kingship succession and that of the Anglo-Normans, we may quote Lawrence Ginnell:

> An eldest son did not succeed merely because his father had been king, if there was an uncle, nephew, brother, cousin or other member of the *Damhnae Ríg* better fit for the position; and the Tanist was usually such a relative, and not a son. The same rules applied to the election of sub-kings. . . .[10]

However, the law did not expressly forbid the succession of the eldest son, providing he was qualified and had the support of the electoral college. Because of this, some scholars have mistakenly argued that the law of kingship succession was naturally evolving away from the original method in favor of primogeniture.

In *Gaelic and Gaelicised Ireland in the Middle Ages*, Kenneth Nicholls, K. Lydon and M. MacCurtain pointed out:

> In practice it often happened if a Chief was long lived and survived all his younger brothers, his son would qualify [for the succession] thus introducing a form of pseudo-primogeniture which has led some writers to the mistaken conclusion as to the existence of true primogeniture among such families as, for example, The MacCarthy Mór, where son followed father for six generations between 1359 and 1508. Simply because no MacCarthy Mór during the period was outlived by a younger brother or at least one strong or able enough to take the lordship.[11]

Some years later, however, delivering his May 1976 O'Donnell lecture at University College, Cork, entitled "Land, Law and Society in Sixteenth Century Ireland," Nicholls broke ranks with his academic comrades by stating:

> While admitting that conclusions in this field are open to controvertion, my impression is that the difference in forms of land holding between the lordships of purely Gaelic origin and those of the Gaelicised Anglo-Normans had, by the sixteenth century, become of little significance, at least so far as Connacht and the west midlands were concerned. In Munster a residue of feudal practice still survived along with the rule of primogeniture succession. . . .
>
> In Gaelic Thomond, too, we find a recognition of primogeniture in the rule which gave children of a deceased elderly brother preference in partitions over their senior but cadet uncles.

This highly controversial suggestion was immediately dismissed by his colleagues. Hogan and Ó Corráin have dismissed the argument that senior son inheritance, which scholars have identified as "pseudo-primogeniture," became part of O'Neill dynastic law.[12]

We may admit that there were cross influences between the Irish and English law systems by the sixteenth century. Even in vocabulary we find departures from ancient law terms and borrowings, such as (a)*turnae* = attorney; *seicdedúir* = executor; *réléas* = release; and hybrid terms such as *oighridhe agus sighinoighridhe* for "heirs and assignees."[13] However, can we accept the thesis that the Brehon law of succession had altered to one of primogeniture? I share the view of James Hogan, an expert on Brehon kingship and successional law, expressed in his study "The Irish Law of Kingship with special reference of Ailech and Cenél Eoghan."[14] He had already pointed out that it had been noticed that for certain periods the eldest male heir succeeded to the throne of an Irish kingdom—sons succeeding their fathers. He also pointed out that this was not forbidden under Brehon law. The eldest son could succeed his father, being a member of the *derbhfine*, providing he was not challenged by that *derbhfine*.

This pattern of succession was noticed among the Uí Néill kings after the death of Domhnall Ua Néill (d. A.D. 1325). Hogan stressed: "The Uí Néill kings failed to substitute a lineal, that is, hereditary kingship, for the traditional succession of collaterals by election." Father-to-son inheritance was not contrary to Brehon law, merely, as is pointed out in "Geinealaighe Fearmanagh," highly unusual.[15] It is certainly not, as Nicholls argues, a change of successional law.

This custom of "nonopposition" or "opposition" to the heir-apparent became very significant in the period after the abolition of Gaelic titles. It can be argued that Gaelic titles had survived during the three hundred years after their abolition by two means that are found in Brehon successional law. The first means is a succession by a passive tanistry (*tánaise cen fresabra*), and the second is succession by an active tanistry (*tánaistecht gnímarthach*).

In both active and passive tanistry, the eldest son could certainly succeed to the title, and often did so when Brehon law continued to hold sway. But this inheritance was not simply based on the fact that the candidate was the eldest male heir. If the title did pass down to the eldest male heirs after the English conquest, it could be argued that it did so on the basis that the eldest male heir gained the title because he was not challenged by any member of the *derbhfine* and that no challenger (*agóideoir*) presented an opposition (*an fresabracht*), or that such a challenger did not receive the approval of the *derbhfine*. So the eldest male heir inheritance is within the keeping of the Brehon law when the family's *derbhfine* gives tacit approval to the title holder. It could be argued that such families took the position of a *derbhfine tostanach* to the *tánaiste*—that is, a passive or silent *derbhfine*—which allowed the eldest male heir to assume the title *cen fresabra* without opposition.

The most important point is that no holder of a Gaelic title could at any point declare Brehon law to be invalid in the successional rules of his title. The law stood above the title holders as expressed in the *seanfhocal* (proverb) *Is treise dli ná tiarna* (The law is stronger than a lord). The Irish kings, unlike the kings (and queens) of England, were not lawmakers nor were they the embodiment of the law. This difference was central to the mistakes of the Tudor politicians in their dealings with Ireland.

English kings were the embodiment of the English law. That they are still seen so symbolically is indicated by the fact that all prosecutions in the United Kingdom are carried out as "the Crown versus the defendant." In republics it is usually the state or the people in whose name prosecutions are made. But in the United Kingdom the crown prosecutes by virtue of its unique place above the law of the land. The Irish kings, however, were hemmed in and constricted by Irish law to the point where they could only promote the common wealth of their people for they, too, could be brought to account by law. A king was merely an officer of the law *established*. The law texts demonstrate quite clearly that the king was subject to the law in the same manner as the lowliest member of his *tuath* (people or tribe). In the *Críth Gabhlach* comes an admonition: *Is treise tuatha ná tiarna* (A people are stronger than a king or lord). It goes on to ask why this is so and states very clearly that it is because the people ordain the king, the king does not ordain the people.

Kings sat as judges in the courts but always with a *juris peritus* or *Brehon* and a scribe. While the judgment of the king's court might be given in the name of that king, it is clear from the extensive and technical corpus of law that the king consulted with his *Brehon* before reaching any verdict. Indeed, it was an essential part of the king's household to support the lawyers (*Brehons*) and professors of learning, especially in matters of genealogy and history (*ollamhain*), and musicians, poets and storytellers. So revered were the learned classes that the leading scholars were treated as on the same noble level as the kings.[16]

It becomes clear from the law that if the king, or any Chief, attempted to surrender his title on behalf of his kingdom on behalf of his heirs and successors, he simply could not do so. He could surrender his body; he could make a treaty, within certain parameters; and he could abdicate office for himself, as many Irish kings did. But there are plenty of examples to demonstrate that no king could abrogate the law or any part of it, especially the successional system.

In debating the appointment of a tanist, should the *derbhfine* ever become deadlocked regarding the succession of a candidate, an appeal could be made to the overlord of the clan. For example, in Tudor times, The O'Donel was recognized as overlord of northern Connacht at a time when the Chieftainship of the Burkes was in question. Aodh O'Donel, while in Mayo, was asked to arbitrate in the matter. In Munster during the Tudor period, MacCarthy Mór was acknowledged as overlord of O'Sullivan Mór and the O'Sullivan Beare and had the sole right to present them with the white rod of office. So each major king was responsible for any deadlocked successional within his territory.

Before leaving the subject of successional law, it will inevitably be asked whether a woman could inherit a title. It is certainly true that women feature prominently in Old and Middle Irish literature, and we have the famous example of Queen Medb. Her traditions may well be interlinked with those of a sovereignty goddess, but in the "Ulster Cycle" as well as in the histories and genealogies she appears as a real person. She is given as the daughter of a High King, Eochaidh Feidhlioch. She is said to have had several husbands and lovers. Her most famous husband was Ailill Mac Máta, who was the handsome commander of her royal bodyguard. Medb rules Connacht in her own right and not as the consort. She appears as a flesh-and-blood ruler.

The only woman, however, to appear on the "High King Lists" is Macha Mong Ruadh, listed as the seventy-sixth monarch of Ireland, daughter of Aodh Ruadh, who is said to have reigned from 377 B.C. for seven years. She is an Ulster queen, of the line of Ir son of Míle, so not of the usual Uí Neill lineage from Eremon, son of Míle. Macha is said to have founded Emain Macha (Navan, County Armagh) and, indeed, Armagh itself (Ard Macha—Macha's Height). She succeeded on the death of her father, who had ruled jointly with his brothers or cousins, Dithorba and Cimbaeth. It is more likely that they were cousins, as Macha is reported to have married Cimbaeth. She is frequently confused with other Machas. The ancient texts cite at least five, one of whom was undoubtedly a war goddess, while another is also clearly a legendary figure, being the wife of the mythical invader Nemed.

We have many examples in Celtic society, although mostly outside of Ireland, of female rulers. Onomaris, Cartimandua and Boudicca are famous examples of queens in their own right. Even within Irish society we have several examples of women leaders commanding their clans in battle. We have fleeting examples of Étain ní Fínghin Már Mac Carthaigh leading a wing of the army of the Desmond king at the victory of Callan in the thirteenth century. We have Éabha Ruadh ní Murchú leading her clan into battle in the same period. She wound iron bars into her hair and refused to take any English prisoners. And we have a reference to Máire ní Ciaragáion, ruler of a clan in Fermanagh. There is also the example of Fionghuala (Inghean Dubh—the "dark daughter," b. A.D. 1555), who married the Prince of Tyrconnell and acted as his chief political advisor in the wars against the English, taking the field herself to command a victorious army at the Battle of Doire Leathan, in Donegal, in 1590.

The twelfth-century collection of genealogical lore about women, called *The Banshenchas* (History of Women), would suggest that women were entitled to achieve positions of power under Brehon law. The explanation might lie in the *Cáin Lánamna* that if there is no male heir, a woman may be called the *banchomarbae* (female heir) and, like any male, have the right to make formal legal entry into her rightful inheritances. If she marries a landless man or someone from another *tuath* (tribe), she makes the decisions and pays his fines and debts indeed, as Medb was clearly doing for Ailill. But, after her death, the rights and properties of a *banchomarbae* normally reverted to her own kin, her father's *derbhfine*, and did not pass to her husband or to any sons that she may have had by him. References in the *Bretha Crólige* mention women in a military leadership capacity.

The obvious objection, in a system of law such as the clan system, to female succession is that it naturally leads to the alienation of the title and lands of the *tuath* by intermarriage with people from outside the *tuath*. Thus we also see in the *Cáin Lánamna* the provision that after the female's life her inheritance rights revert to her father's family. "The female heir is here referred to who has had the father's and grandfather's land, and though she should desire to give it to her sons, she shall not give it unconditionally."[17]

We are told that this right was confirmed by the female judge Brígh Briugaid in the legal tract *Uraicecht Bec*, which arose when the Brehon Sencha Mac Ailella gave a wrongful judgment on female rights.

The rights are clarified by Thurneysen, who says: "if there is no male heir a daughter or daughters inherit all chattels, and may inherit all other property as well."[17] This has been confirmed in other analyses of the law: "If there is no male heir, all the movable property is given to the female heir, and the immovable property without obligation to provide military service."[18] As titles are deemed "ideal property," that is, "movable property," I would argue that this seems a clear indication of female succession in particular circumstances.

Technically, the woman does not pass into the *fine*, or family, of her husband for the purposes of inheritance but remains in the *fine* of her father. But her children do pass into the *fine* of her husband. The only property in land she can transmit to her heirs is property acquired for services rendered (*orba cruib ocuss sliastal*) or by gift (*ar dúthracht*). If she did become a Chief, she could not appoint one of her own children as tanist, and the title would remain with her father's *derbhfine*, presuming, at the time of her death, a suitable candidate had emerged from that *derbhfine*. The period of her chiefship was considered only a lifetime "stop-gap." The law is precise: "When there are no sons . . . the whole estate goes to the daughters for life; and they are restrained from alienating it wrongfully and it is restored to the *fine* after them."

So a woman cannot acquire more than a life interest as *banchomarba*.

Because the circumstances in which a female heir was necessary arose so infrequently, few female rulers are recorded in ancient Ireland.

Women's rights in all other aspects of Brehon law were far superior to those of their English sisters. The Irish laws gave more rights and protection to women than any other western law code at that time or until recent times. Women could and did aspire to all professions as the coequals of men. They could be political leaders, command their people in battle as warriors, be physicians, local magistrates, poets, artisans, lawyers and judges. Women were protected by laws against sexual harassment, discrimination and rape. They had the right of divorce on equal terms from their husbands with equitable separation laws and could demand part of their husband's property as a divorce settlement; they also had the right of inheritance of personal property and the right of sickness benefits.

This was the system that Henry VIII and his administrators in Ireland now faced, a social order that they set out to methodically destroy. They knew that unless it was eliminated it would be hopeless to attempt to bring Ireland into the growing empire of England. Without an understanding of the Irish social order and law system, it is impossible to fully understand the turmoil into which Ireland was about to be plunged.

CHAPTER THREE

THE "UTTER ABOLITION"
OF GAELIC TITLES

THE FIRST GAELIC NOBLE TO SURRENDER HIMSELF under Henry VIII's new "surrender and regrant" policy was Turlough Ó Tuathail.[1] Ó Tuathail surrendered his title and clan lands because he was threatened by aggressive military policy from the English Pale on which his lands bordered. His clan was domiciled in northern Wicklow, adjacent to Dublin. Henry, writing to his Lord Deputy and Council in Dublin, was aware of the military situation:

> The lands of O'Reilly, O'Connor and Kavanagh etc. we take to lie so upon the danger of our power, as you may easily bring them to any reasonable conditions, that may be well desired of them. The other sort, as O'Donnell, MacWilliam, O'Brien etc, we think to lie so far from our strength there, as, without a greater force, it will be difficult to expel them out of their country, and to keep and inhabit the same with such as we would thereunto appoint; albeit we may easily correct and punish any of them as the case shall require . . . we think that you may easily bind all them which lie upon our strength, to all the conditions whereunto Turlough O'Toole is bound.[2]

Henry VIII had an astute eye for strategy. Those Gaelic kings and nobles whom his armies could dominate by military strength were to be approached first. Turlough Ó Tuathail had agreed to surrender his chiefship and his lands and, in return, the lands were, in part, regranted to him as King Henry pleased, to use under English law and habits, and he promised to bring his children up to speak English. He would no longer use the title "The Ó Tuathail." However, a descendant, using title The Ó Tuathail, was still leading his clan one hundred years later during the 1641 uprising. His successor to the title was forced to flee to France and joined the Irish Brigade of the French Army, in which eight of his sons served. In 1944 Charles Joseph Antoine Thomy O'Toole, Comte O'Toole de Leinster, living in the Avenue des Champs Elysées, Paris, claimed to have succeeded his father in 1889 as The O'Toole of Fer Tire, and his pedigree was accepted by the Irish Genealogical Office. The title is now in abeyance so far as the Genealogical Office's records show.

Within a short time, the new English policy had succeeded in netting some important members of the Irish nobility, including Conn Bacach O'Neill, King of Ulster, Murrough O'Brien, King of Thomond and an Anglo-Irish "Chief" Ulick na gCeann Bourke, The MacWilliam Uachtar. Conn Bacach Ó Néill surrendered his title at Henry's palace at Greenwich on October 1, 1542. We will return to him shortly.

The next most important "catch" was Murrough O'Brien, fifty-seventh King of Thomond, who surrendered to Henry VIII at Greenwich on Sunday, July 1, 1543. He was rewarded with the title Earl of Thomond. Now we find an interesting sleight-of-hand acceptance of the Brehon law of succession by Henry VIII. Under tanistry, Murrough's nephew, Donough O'Brien, was his heir-apparent. Yet Murrough had a son who, by English rules, should have succeed Murrough as Earl of Thomond. Donough, however, was created Baron Ibrickan. It was agreed that he would succeed his uncle as second Earl of Thomond and that the title would thereafter descend through first born male heirs. To square their consciences under primogeniture, Murrough's son would take the title Baron Inchiquin.

Sir Thomas Cusack, acting as Lord Justice, wrote gleefully to the Duke of Northumberland on May 8, 1553, that the policy of forcing the Irish kings to surrender to Henry VIII was working out very well. "The making of O'Brien an Earl made all that country obedient. . . . Irishmen were never so weak, and the English subjects never so strong as now."[3]

The next "catch" was the powerful Gaelicized Anglo-Norman Lord Ulick na gCeann, The MacWilliam Uachtar (Upper) of Galway, who surrendered his chiefship to become Earl of Clanricade on the same day as O'Brien. Although an Anglo-Norman lord, MacWilliam Uachtar, and his cousin MacWilliam Iochtar (Lower) of Mayo governed their families and those dependent on them as Irish clans, spoke Irish and obeyed Irish law. Now MacWilliam Uachter took the English title and promised to obey English law and speak English.

The surviving documentation setting out the terms and conditions for the submissions of the Gaelic kings and aristocracy show precisely what was intended by Tudor policy. The Gaelic titles, and the laws of tanistry under which they were passed down, were to be totally abolished. The essential condition of surrender was the acceptance of the English common law and the primogeniture system. The Articles of Submission for the King of Ulster, Conn Bacach O'Neill, was: "He utterly forsake the name of O'Neill." The abolition of this title was confirmed by a speech Sir John Davies when he was appointed Speaker of the Commons in the Dublin Parliament of 1613. Sir John said: "What was the principal cause that Sir Henry Sidney held a Parliament in the eleventh year of Queen Elizabeth but to extinguish the name of O'Neill and entitle the Crown to the great part of Ulster?"[4] In both instances, of course, it is not a surname that is being discussed, but the Gaelic title *The* O'Neill. If there had been any confusion in examining Tudor policy, the text of the Elizabethan Act of Attainder of Shane O'Neill makes clear that it is the title The O'Neill that "shall henceforth cease, end, determined, and be utterly abolished and extinct forever."[5] Dr. Constantia Maxwell points out that Elizabeth I, by this Act, declared the title of The O'Neill abolished and her Crown entitled to the whole of Ulster.[6]

A cultural point needs clarification. In referring to a Chief, in this case, O'Neill, an Irish speaker, would have simply said O'Neill. *"Mise O'Neill"* (I am O'Neill), Eoghan Ruadh is famously said to have introduced himself. In the English language there arose a tendency to put the capitalized word "The" before the name to emphasize that this was the head of the clan. Others would have their forenames appended.

The Act of Elizabeth makes clear that

> what person soever he be that shall hereafter challenge, execute, or take upon him that name of O'Neill, or any superiority, dignity, preeminence and jurisdiction, authority, rule, tributes, or expenses, used, claimed, usurped, or taken heretofore by any O'Neill, of the lords, captains, or people of Ulster, the same shall be deemed, adjudged and taken high treason against your Majesty, your crown and dignity. . . .[7]

When King Murrough, The O'Brien, of Thomond, surrendered his title, the first item of the submission was: "1, Utterly to forsake and refuse the name of O'Breene [*sic*], and all claims that he might pretend to by the name; and to use such name as it should please the King to give unto him."[8]

In Leinster, King Caothaoir Mac Airt, MacMorrough Kavanagh King, who had succeeded in 1547, was persuaded to surrender his title and on February 8, 1554, he was created Baron Ballyanne. One wonders why he was not given the greater carrot of an earldom like O'Brien and O'Neill and later MacCarthy Mór. We know that the colonial administration "persuaded him" by taking two of his sons as hostages to ensure his surrender. Yet he was removed by his *derbhfine* within a year of surrendering and died four years later. Caothaoir was succeeded to the kingship not by his sons but by a cousin, Murchadh Mac Muiris. This cleaving to Brehon law obviously presented the English administration with problems, but it persuaded the new MacMorrough Kavanagh, Murchadh, to surrender also and replace his title with that of Baron of Coolnaleen. The last to claim the title of King of Leinster was Domhnall Spáinneach mac Donnchadha in 1595. He chose to abdicate after the general Irish surrender in 1603 rather than surrender the kingdom, and he died in 1632.

In Connacht, the way was made easier by the split in the O'Conor royal dynasty into three separate houses—The O'Conor Roe, O'Conor Don, and O'Conor Sligo. O'Conor Sligo surrendered his title in 1567 at Hampton Court and, it is said, was offered an earldom, which he declined. No evidence of this appears in the State Papers. But the kingship of Connacht was contested between O'Conor Roe and O'Conor Don, and Connacht had been partitioned between the two branches. It had been reunited in the fourteenth century under O'Conor Roe but soon split again. By the mid-sixteenth century it was again a single kingdom ruled by Dermot, the O'Conor Don. In 1568 Tadhg Buidhe O'Conor Roe had surrendered his title for a knighthood. However, King Dermot O'Conor Don proved the more difficult "catch." Finally, the English "President of Connacht," Sir Edward Fytton, invited King Dermot to his castle for "talks" in 1571. For the Irish and, indeed, all the Celts, the laws of hospitality were sacred. Fytton did not respect such niceties and made King Dermot his prisoner.

In the following year, King Dermot's tanist, or heir-apparent, Aodh (Hugh) O'Conor, together with the son of O'Conor Roe, led a rescue party to Fytton's castle and succeeded in releasing King Dermot. War erupted in Connacht. But by 1576 the English forces were achieving the upper hand. The forces of Aodh O'Conor, who appeared as commander of King Dermot's army, managed to hold out until 1581 before surrendering to Lord Deputy Sir John Perrot. King Dermot died in 1585. In that year "The Composition of Connacht" was agreed, in which the titles of O'Conor Don, O'Conor Roe and O'Conor Sligo were "abolished and made extinct forever." The O'Conor titles were to be exchanged only for English knighthoods, presumably in retaliation for King Dermot's refusal to submit immediately.

Another major problem, so far as the English administration was concerned, was the kingdom of Desmond. The King of Desmond, Donal VIII

(1516—ca. 1558) had actually toyed with the new proposals and in 1552 he obtained a grant of "English liberty" for himself, his younger son and tanist Donal and daughter as a means of ensuring the inheritance of either his son or daughter to the ownership of his estates and personal property. This was in violation to Brehon law. However, Donal VIII died sometime between 1552 and 1558 and Donal IX The MacCarthy Mór came to the throne. Donal IX was an astute leader and was concerned with protecting his kingdom by diplomacy first and by force if there was no other choice. He was an Irish poet of considerable merit. Several of his poems survive, such as *Aisling-thruadh do mhear meisi* (A sorrowful vision has deceived me) and *Och an och! a Mhuire bu de* (Alas! Alas! O benign Mary). He was married to Honora FitzGerald, daughter of the thirteenth Earl of Desmond.

Although the Kingdom of Desmond had been compressed back by this time in Counties Cork and Kerry by the encroachments of the Palatine earldoms of Desmond (FitzGerald) and of Ormond (Butler), Donal still ruled a sizable kingdom. Sir Warham St. Leger reported that he controlled at least fourteen "countries," ruled by petty chiefs and several lordships, that paid him rents and services. Although pressed to surrender his title as king, Donal seemed expert at avoiding the issue. There is no reference to any such surrender during the reigns of Henry VIII, Edward VI, Mary or in the first years of the reign of Elizabeth I.

Perhaps a demonstration of how frustrated the Tudor administration became with Donal lies in the fact that in 1565 David Roche, Lord Fermoy, organized the kidnapping of the king. He was taken as a prisoner to London where, under duress, he was forced to accept the title Earl of Clancare. But Donal IX MacCarthy Mór was, as previously said, an astute politician. When in 1760 Sir Isaac Heard, then Norroy King of Arms (later Garter King), and Ralph Bigland, then Clarenceux King of Arms, compiled a history of the Royal House of MacCarthy for the Muskerry MacCarthys entitled *Généalogie de la Royale et Sérénissime Maison de MacCarthy*, they had this to say about the incident:

> Donal MacCarthy Mór, King of Desmond, being taken prisoner by David, Lord Roche of Fermoy, Sir Henry Sydney, then Lord Lieutenant of Ireland, mistrusting the rebellious intentions of Gerald, the last Earl of Desmond, sent Donal MacCarthy Mór to England, to the intent that by Her Majesty Queen Elizabeth's good usage to him, he might be made an instrument against the said Desmond. Her Majesty did so effectually prevail on him by Royal gifts and fair promises that she engaged him to surrender into her hands his Kingdom of Desmond and to take it back from the Crown by English tenure. She paid the

expenses of his journey, conferred many ample privileges on him, *left him in full possession of all his royalties*, and power of appointing Sheriffs at will in his territory, at the same time she created him Earl of Clancarré and Baron of Valentia by letters patent bearing date the 7th year of her reign, anno 1565. Donal on his return to home was so much despised by his vassals and followers for his new titles that he rejected them immediately, and after the example of O'Néill in Ulster, took to arms in the South, assumed the title of King of Munster and sent ambassadors to the Pope and King of Spain for assistance. . . . [9]

The English heralds compiling this account admit that Elizabeth left him in "full possession of all his royalties." Donal had actually managed to get the compiler of the letters patent to refer to him by the royal title MacCarthy Mór so that he was both Earl of Clancare and, simultaneously, MacCarthy Mór. In the Gaelic context, MacCarthy Mór embodies the royal status as head of the Eóghanachta, just as in the time of the Roman Empire the surname Caesar was adopted by the emperors as the title of imperial dignity. The same meaning applies to the names of the other royal dynasties.

Once safely back in his kingdom, Donal IX proclaimed that he was still King of Desmond. The mayor of Waterford, in 1569, complained to Sir William Cecil about "MacCarthy Mór, who refuses the new titles of Earl, and is offended with any one that calleth him Earl of Clancar."[10] The war between King Donal and the English lasted until 1569, when he was again forced to surrender and make submission to Elizabeth. This time his only son, Tadhg, had been taken to Dublin Castle to be held as a hostage in return for Donal's good behavior. Donal still remained Earl of Clancare in English eyes, but documents showed that he never used the title and simply stuck to the Gaelic form as MacCarthy Mór, thus still implying his continued royal status supported by his letters patent. When he died in 1596 he went into history as the last regnant King of Desmond; his son Tadhg, Lord of Valentia, had escaped from Dublin Castle and died in France before his father. There was no clearly appointed tanist, and the title was disputed in the chaos that followed the devastating conquest of Munster, then being subjected to plantation by a new wave of English colonists.

In the wake of initial surrenders in 1541 to 1543, there came the surrender of members of the lesser aristocracy. The Mac Giollaphádraig (MacGilpatrick) of Ossory, then chief of an area in Upper Ossory, surrendered. MacGilpatricks had been petty kings of Ossory, a subkingdom of Leinster at the time of the Anglo-Norman invasion. It had stretched from Waterford in the south to the Slieve Bloom mountains in the north, along the west bank of River Nore (An

Fheoir). It was a kingdom that Richard, Earl of Pembroke ("Strongbow"), seized by conquest. Donal MacGiollaphádraig (d. 1185) was the last king of all Ossory. The territory had then shrunk to the Upper Ossory ruled by The MacGilpatrick of Tudor times. He submitted on the terms laid down:

> First, the said MacGilpatric doth utterly forsake and refuse the name of MacGilpatric, and all claim which he might pretend by the same; and promiseth to name himself, for ever hereafter, by such name as it shall please the King's Majesty to give him.[11]

There was a further essential item.

> . . . the said MacGilpatric, his heirs and assignees and every other the inhabiters of such lands as it shall please the King's Majesty to give unto him, shall use the English habits and manner, and, to their knowledge, the English language, and they, and every of them, shall to their power, bring up their children after the English manner, and the use of the English tongue.

There followed the surrender of The O'Grady of Clan Donghaile, The MacNamara of Clancullen and The O'Shaughnessy, each of whom received English knighthoods, although it had initially been recommended that they could "swap" their Gaelic titles for the title of Baron. The O'Kennedy of Ormond, The O'Carroll of Ely, The O'Meagher of Ikerrin, The MacMahon of Cocobaskin, The O'Conor of Corcoro, The O'Loughlin of Burren, The O'Brien-Arra, The O'Brien of Oghonagh, The O'Dwyer of Kylenemana and "The O'Mulrion de When" are all listed as coming forward to surrender their names and titles. "William O'Carroll" of Ely later surrendered personally all his estates into Chancery on August 2, 1578, and was granted a small portion of these lands back to hold as an estate for "a knight's fee."

The surrender of the King of Ulster, Conn Bacach O'Neill, was a major step forward in the process. However, Hogan does not agree.

> The submission of Conn Bacach in 1542, in common with most of the native princes, is an event the significance of which has been somewhat overrated. It is certain that the Irish kings did not regard their submission as involving the abandonment of the old order. It did not enter their heads that their own immemorial social and political scheme of life was suddenly to disappear because they recognised the English King as overlord. But even the partial introduction of English land tenures was bound to antagonise a people so closely wedded to custom and tradition, and it was this feeling of antipathy that enabled Seán (*an Díomais*) to come forward as the champion of the native order against

the feudalising and Anglicizing programme for which, at the time, his own father Conn (Bacach) seemed to stand; and, again, towards the close of the century a similar racial resurgence carried Aodh Ua Néill away from his English
ideas and leanings, and moved him to seek for himself the traditional inauguration accorded to the Kings of his line at Tulach Og.[12]

It is hard to imagine that the Irish kings were as naive as Hogan suggests.
Whatever their expectations, the conditions of their surrender seem unequivo-
cal. The 1570 Act, referred to by Sir John Davies (1569–1626), James I's Attorney General for Ireland and Speaker of the Dublin Parliament, in his *A
Discovery of the True Causes Why Ireland was Never Entirely Subdued* (1612), declared that the clan system and all chiefships were to be totally abolished. And
as to whether the Irish aristocrats knew the results of their surrenders, most of
the intellectuals of Ireland were perfectly aware of what was going on and
would have advised the kings.

Aonghus mac Daighre Ó Dálaigh (ca.1540–ca.1600) was poet to The
O'Byrne of Wicklow. In a poem called *Dia Libh a Laochradh Ghaoidheal* (God
be with the Irish host) he states:

Torment it is to me that, in the very tribal gathering, foreigners proscribe
them that are Ireland's royal Chiefs, in whose own ancestral territory is given
to them no designation but that of a lowly outlaw's name.

For "outlaw" he used the term that translates as "wood-kerne" but that the
English used as a general name for all Irish outlaws. The poem became well
known and is first recorded in the *Leabhar Branach* (Book of the O'Byrnes). It
has been translated many times; one of the most popular translations is by
Pádraic Pearse. That these bards and *ollamhain* were effective in such matters is
attested by a letter from Lord Justice FitzWilliam, writing to William Cecil
(Lord Burghley), complaining that the plan of Anglicization was being frustrated by poets. He speaks of "the discountenance of heraldry and the preva-
lence of rhymers who set forth the beastliest and most odious of men's doings."

We may be sure that one of the main pressures on the Irish kings and
princes for their initial surrender was the fear of the use of greater force against
their peoples and territories. A few years before the first surrenders, in 1536,
Lord Leonard Gray (afterwards Viscount Graney), then Lord Deputy, had
marched an army throughout Ireland. It was then that Donal Mór, The Ó
Morchoe, described as a "Chief Captain of Ireland," being of the cadet line of
the Kings of Leinster, surrendered to Lord Grey and agreed on May 10, 1536,
to hold his country and "lordship" from the English Crown.

Sir John Davies pointed out that the result of the Lord Deputy's display of force was that "the principal septs of the Irishry, being all terrified, and most of them broken in this journey, many of their chief lords, upon this Deputy's return, came to Dublin and made their submissions to the Crown of England, namely, the O'Neills and O'Reillys of Ulster, MacMorrough, O'Byrne and O'Carroll of Leinster and the Bourkes of Connacht."[13]

Several of the lesser nobility were persuaded to surrender for expectation of bettering their own positions. Sir John Davies says:

> Hereupon the Irish captains of lesser territories, which had even been oppressed by the greater and mightier—some with risings outs, other with bonaght, and others with cuttings and spendings at pleasure—did appeal for justice to the Lord Deputy, who upon hearing their complaints, did always order that they should all immediately depend upon the [English] King, and that the weaker should have no dependency upon the stronger.[14]

A bonaght, from the Irish *buannacht*, was the tax levied on a district for the wages and provisions of soldiers who were protecting it. By extension, it eventually became a word for a mercenary soldier.

English diplomacy used the argument that if these lesser Chiefs and Chieftains surrendered to the English king, he would then "protect them" and give them greater independence than if they continued their allegiance to their native princes. Greed thereby entered into the argument, for the English documentation shows that the administrators emphasized the "iniquities" and "injustice" of the native Irish taxation system to these petty chiefs. It was, of course, no more unjust than any other taxation system whereby public monies had to be raised for the welfare and defense of the people. How many of these petty chiefs were fooled into thinking they would escape payment of taxation, not realizing that they were going to be infinitely worse off under Tudor taxes, is not known. It is impossible to believe that they would have been more than a handful.

Some of the petty chiefs did initially manage to inveigle the system to their advantage, according to Davies. In stating that James I had to clear up some of the ambiguities of the previous Tudor administration, he admits that in Elizabeth I's reign

> ... there were many Irish lords who did not surrender, yet obtained Letters Patents as the captainships of their countries, and of all the lands and duties belonging to those captainships; for the Statute which doth condemn and abolish these captainries usurped by the Irish doth give power to the Lord Deputy to grant the same by Letters Patent.

Therefore, some Letters Patent actually acknowledged certain nobles as "captains of the nation." James I had sent two special commissions to Ireland to clear up any anomalies in case the Letters Patent could be construed as confirming the Gaelic titles.

Davies was referring mainly to the Letters Patent issued on the direction of Lord Deputy Sir Henry Sidney. In fact, there was little ambiguity in them. On February 11, 1570, Sidney had signed an agreement with Faghne O'Farrell, The O'Farrell of Annaly, County Longford, who was Chief of the Clan tSédin, one of the two branches of the O'Farrells. The O'Farrell surrendered to Sir Henry and agreed that "the captainship of that portion of the said county . . . shall from henceforth be utterly abolished . . . and that the said Faghne O'Farrell shall receive and take, by Letters Patent from the Queen's Majesty . . . the names and styles of seneschal." Therefore it is clear that The O'Farrell had given up his Gaelic titles and agreed to adopt the English designation.

Davies speaks of Sir Henry Sidney's policy in this manner:

> For, the first to diminish the greatness of the Irish lords, and to take from them the dependency of the common people, in the Parliament which he held eleventh of Elizabeth, he did abolish their pretended and usurped captainships and all exactions and extortions incident thereunto. Next to settle their seignories and possessions in a course of inheritance according to the course of the Common law, he caused an Act to pass whereby the Lord Deputy was authorised to accept their surrenders and to regrant estate unto them, to hold of the Crown by English tenures and services.[15]

It depended on the degree of one's Gaelic title as to what English title was offered in its place. These ranged from an earldom for most provincial kingships to a barony for the Maquire of Fermanagh to a knighthood for The Ó Raghailligh of Cavan. Some of the Gaelic aristocrats were considered of less significance and were given titles ranging between the now-defunct seneschal to major domo, serjeant, and esquire—these latter then meant titles of dignity and authority below a knight.

Dr. John O'Donovan, writing to Morgan William O'Donovan on October 25, 1841, comments: "I am satisfied that none of the name of O'Donovan ever had a title; never! not even that of knight! . . . It does not appear that any of that family ever got a title under the Crown of England except Sir Owen, who fought at Kinsale 1601–2."[16] It may be that Dr. O'Donovan was not considering that seneschal, serjeant or esquire were, in those days, titles of lesser gentry.

Donal na gCroiceann (of the Hides) had been inaugurated as The O'Donovan by The MacCarthy Reagh, Prince of Carbery, in 1560. He died in 1584. It is not clear who was The O'Donovan for the next seven years. However, in 1591, the son of Donal na gCroiceann received the white wand of office from MacCarthy Reagh. In spite of his acknowledged fealty to his rightful prince, the following year, on February 12, 1592, the English Lord Chancellor, Adam Loftus, received his surrender. In 1608 Donal O'Donovan surrendered the lands of Clan Cathail against native law. Dr. O'Donovan, in a subsequent letter to Morgan William O'Donovan, wrote that he believed that Donal was then unsuccessfully challenged under Brehon law by his second son, Teige, for the chiefship.[17] Donal received a regrant of his real estate in 1613 and seems to have accepted a mere "esquire" in place of his Gaelic title.

Many of the lesser chieftains, such as The O'Molloy, The MacMahon and The O'Hanlon, were given grants of land to hold on a "knight's service" or as "serjeant." Certainly it was made clear in a letter of December 1, 1587, granting some land to "Ogie" O'Hanlon that the grant was made "provided that no person shall have any title claiming as O'Hanlon or tanist, which titles are abolished."[18] A grant issued in February, 1571 clearly states that any local authority and fees that were formerly paid to a Chief and his tanist were now to be paid to the persons holding the English titles: "these customs not to be called by Irish names but to be known as the fees of the Chief Serjeant and Under Serjeant"[19]

Gradually, the Tudor "Kingdom of Ireland" was emerging with feudal titles of manorial and baronial jurisdiction, reaching their height in the palatine earldoms of Desmond and Ormond. There was now a system of chartered boroughs, with the capital at Dublin deemed a royal borough, and with lords' towns, such as Waterford, having "Breteuil rights." Ireland was ruled, in the absence of the king, by his viceroy, who had been Lord Deputy during the "Lordship of Ireland," but even under the new "kingdom" the viceroy was usually styled as Lord Deputy. The system now allowed for no holder of a Gaelic title to exist. These titles were not only abolished under Statute Law but by the *jus commune*, the unwritten law of English administered in the king's courts, based on a universal usage and embodied in commentaries and reported cases—common law. Only feudal titles granted by the English Crown had any legal existence in the new "Kingdom of Ireland."

The surrenders and the switch from one system to another were not peaceful processes. Many of the Irish nobility did not submit as meekly as the English administration hoped for. The fierce opposition that was encountered caused the Tudors to abandon the original plan to simply Anglicize the population.

Under Queen Mary, they started an experiment in Leinster, clearing the land of the natives and settling it with English colonists—a policy of "ethnic cleansing." This "transplantation" policy, as it became known, was tried in Munster and in Ulster, but it was to have its most marked effect on the Irish psyche during the Cromwellian administration of the mid-seventeenth century, when the Irish population was ordered into a "reserve" west of the River Shannon, in County Clare and the province of Connacht.

CHAPTER FOUR

THE STRUGGLE FOR SURVIVAL

THE STRUGGLE OF THE IRISH AGAINST THE TUDOR Conquests lay in the attachment of the aristocracy and the people to the Irish law, language and culture. This fierce adherence to their social system against the alien system that Henry VIII was trying to impose on the country lasted for well over a century. The result of it was a brutal conquest by a foreign power that had the effect of changing the law, the social system and the status of the language. The changes were forced on the population of Ireland under duress by the use of force majeure. As pointed out by Antony Carty, the Evershed Professor of International Law, England's only right to govern Ireland was "a legal title by right of conquest."[1]

From the perspective of Irish law, to what extent could the surrender of the Irish kings and aristocracy to the English Crown be considered a legal action? It has already been pointed out that, under Brehon law existing at the time of the conquest, an Irish king, and even a lesser chief, was not a creator of law, nor was a king above the law. Irish kings and chiefs were subject to the law and could not afford to ignore it.

The *Críth Gablach*, the best known of the law texts, has clear instruction that begins:

> These are the qualifications of a just ruler with respect to his people that he does not violate them by falsehood, nor force, nor superior strength; let him be a just, sound mediator between weak and strong. There are moreover three other things they demand from the King; let him be a man of full righteousness

on every side, let him be a man who inquires after knowledge; let him be an abode of patience.

As has been explained, the kings and chiefs sat as judges in the law courts, but always sat with a Brehon and other learned people.[2] The writer of one of the law texts on kings says: "There are four rights which the King pledges his people to observe. The rights of *Fénechus* law first; it is the people that acclaim it." The obedience of the king to the law was not meant as a slight to the king, explains the text, "for the law, like the king, was ordained by the people."

Any attempt to surrender his title on behalf of the kingdom and on behalf of his heirs and successors, and, further, to surrender the rights of his people, was simply incompatible with Brehon law. A king could surrender his body, he could make a treaty within limitations, or, indeed, he could abdicate office for himself, and many Irish kings did abdicate when they felt they could no longer contribute to the welfare of their people by holding office. Ruaidri Ua Conhobhair. who abdicated his kingship in 1184 to enter the Monastery of Cong, is one of the best examples of such an abdication. But no king or chief could abrogate the entire law and successional system. Any king or chief attempting to do so could be dismissed from his office and his tanist, or heir apparent, could be appointed—or, should the tanist support him, a new successor.

This is precisely what began to happen the moment the Irish kings began their surrender to Henry VIII. It led to the bloody Tudor Wars of Conquest and the even more brutal conquests and devastations of the seventeenth century.

It is clear from Irish written sources from the start of the Tudor surrender and regrant policy that those members of the Gaelic aristocracy became the object of scorn and derision among the intellectual classes. One anonymous Irish text says:

> Pride they [the Gaelic nobility] have bartered for a lowly mind, and bright perceptions for gloominess; this flaccid disposition of the erstwhile gallant host may in all earnest stand us in lieu of a sermon. They, the flowers of the freeborn clans of Tara's armies, have run out the term of their prosperity; envy has brought down her elbow on them, so that an eclipsing deluge has overwhelmed them. Their wonted good luck they have all forgotten, their battleground and their athletic feats; their ire, their turbulence, their aggressiveness; prowess of clean handed loyal warriors. No stripling now is seen to challenge combat, nor soldier's gear to hang by his pallet, nor sword to suck the hand's palm, while frost congeals the ringlet of the hair. No more the target is seen slung on the broad back, nor hilt girt to the side at coming of the moon, nor smooth soft skin coming into contact with chainmail; all this must once upon a

time have been a dream. Their cheerfulness of spirit, their appetite for diversion and their propensity to give away, they have relinquished; likewise their charge in the fight, their industry in depredations so that they being thus are not living men at all.[3]

The same view was shared by the poet of The O'Carroll of Ely, who says not one of the Irish Chiefs has life in him. His ten bitter verses name the leading Irish princes:

Fúbún fúibh, a shluagh Gaoidheal,
ní mhaireann aoinneach agaibh:
Goill ag comhroinn bhur gcríche
re sluagh síthe bhur samhail

Shame on you, oh men of the Gael,
not one of you has life in him;
The foreigner is sharing out your country among themselves
and you are like a phantom host

The O'Neills of Aileach and Navan
the King of Tara and Tailltean
in foolish submission
they have surrendered their Kingdom
for the earldom of Ulster.

O Nobles of the Island of ancient (King) Art
evil is your change of dignity.
O ill-guided cowardly host
henceforth say nothing but "shame!"[4]

Soon incredulity at what certain of the kings and their nobles were doing turned to action. The action began in Ulster.

The King of Ulster, Conn Bacach O'Neill, had surrendered to Henry VIII at Greenwich on October 1, 1542, and accepted the English title Earl of Tyrone. His son Ferdorcha, now called "Matthew" by the English, was told that he would inherit the earldom by the law of English primogeniture and until that time would be styled Baron of Dungannon.

Shortly after returning to Ulster, Conn Bacach's *derbhfine* met and refused to regard Ferdorcha, Baron of Dungannon, as a legal successor and heir to Conn; nor, of course, could they support the surrender by Conn of his kingship. They simply disowned him. On January 31, 1543, three months later,

Conn Bacach wrote an anguished letter to Henry VIII pleading for help.[5] Conn Bacach was driven out and sought refuge among the English of the Pale. He died in exile there in 1559.

The *derbhfine*, having rejected Ferdorcha because of his acceptance of an English title, elected as new King of Ulster Conn Bacach's youngest son, Seán an Díomais, known to the English as Shane the Proud. He was duly installed as king at the ancient inauguration site of Tulach Og. His cousin Turlough was named as tanist. Seán an Díomais was so secure in his position that in 1562 he actually paid a "state visit" to Elizabeth I's court, where he took the opportunity to explain to her about the Brehon law of succession.[6] According to the Holinshed *Chronicles:*

> He pretended to be King of Ulster, even as he said his ancestors were, and affecting the manner of the "Great Turk," was continually guarded with 600 armed men, as it were his Janissaries, about him, and had in readiness to bring into the field, 1,000 horsemen and 4,000 footmen.[7]

The same rejection of the surrender of the title and abrogation of the law occurred even among the Gaelicized Norman-Irish Bourkes. MacWilliam Uachtar returned from England in 1543 with his title Earl of Clanricade. Suspiciously, within months, in 1544, the new Earl of Clanricade was dead. When his eldest son, Richard, attempted to proclaim himself head of the clan with the title of second Earl he was rejected by his *derbhfine*, who elected a cousin, named Ulick. A dynastic struggle commenced and it was not until 1550/51, with the help of English troops, that Richard was placed in control of the MacWilliam Bourkes.

Even O'Brien was rejected in Thomond. That O'Brien knew well the consequences of his surrender is demonstrated in an interesting incident recorded beforehand. When the Lord Deputy Andrew St. Leger went to Limerick in February 1541 to meet with Murrough O'Brien, the fifty-seventh King of Thomond, who had come to the throne in 1539, the purpose was to open negotiations about the surrender of his title. St. Leger reported that the king asked for time to consult his *derbhfine* on the proposition. The English interpretation of this was given in a report stating that Murrough O'Brien demanded time to consult with his kinsfolk "forasmuch as he was but one man, although he were captain of his nation."[8]

Did Murrough O'Brien understand, and if he did, was he able to explain fully to his *derbhfine* what was actually being asked? Did he really surrender his title of king to Henry VIII at Greenwich and become Earl of Thomond with the foreknowledge and approval of his *derbfhine?* It seems unlikely that they realized all the consequences and were happy to accept Murrough O'Brien returning to Thomond with an English title. They could have been led to believe that this title was in addition to his own for, during the rest of Murrough's life, there is no report of any disturbance.

When Murrough died in 1551 and was succeeded, as we saw in chapter 3, by his nephew Donough, Baron of Ibrickan, there seemed to be no problem. The problem arose when Donough set about ensuring that his title as second Earl of Thomond, and his role as head of the O'Briens, would pass to his eldest son under the new English method of primogeniture. The *derbhfine* now saw the break with Irish law and elected Donal O'Brien of Dough, the brother of Murrough, as The O'Brien, King of Thomond. They rejected Donough, the second Earl of Thomond. Donal was then inaugurated in 1553, according to custom, at Magh Adhair, where there stood a sacred tree under which The O'Brien had been invested for many centuries. Donal was also supported by his half-brother Turlough. Faced with a general insurrection of the people of Thomond, the second Earl took refuge in Clonroad Castle and sent messages to the English Lord Deputy for military help. Within five weeks Donough was dead, probably of a wound sustained in the attack on Clonroad Castle by his own people.

Donough's son Conor who, under the English law, now became the third Earl of Thomond, also sent appeals to the English for military aid. But this was not a good time for the English administration. Edward VI, who had succeeded his father in 1547, died on July 6, 1553, in the middle of these events. There was the attempt to establish Jane Grey, daughter of the Duke of Suffolk, as English queen to continue the Protestant Reformation in England. However, by July 19, 1553, Mary had become queen and started to return the country to Catholicism. The problems of the English Crown, and the fact that a condition of surrender of the Irish nobility was that they accept the reformed Anglican faith, caused the authorities in Ireland some confusion. The Earls of Thomond had recognized Henry as head of the church for himself and his heirs and successors. Should the English administration send an army to support the third Earl as a Protestant against Donal, calling himself King of Thomond, as a Catholic? Mary was asked for her express orders. She vacillated, and it was not until March 1558, five years later, that she decided that English domination in Ireland was more important than religious questions. Her new Lord Deputy, Sir Thomas Radcliffe, Earl of Sussex, arrived with a powerful army at Limerick. Mary was dead by November 1558, and Elizabeth I was Queen and resumed Protestantism as the national religion.

Donal, King of Thomond, was no match for the armies of Lord Sussex. Eventually he was forced to retreat and seek refuge with the King of Ulster. Conor O'Brien, third Earl of Thomond, with the help of Lord Sussex, was placed in control of Thomond on the feudal terms agreed by his grandfather. According to Ivar O'Brien: "He followed his father's example by forswearing the traditional title of 'The O'Brien' and promising to be loyal to the English Crown." This ceremony took place in Limerick Cathedral on July 10, 1558 and "was sworn upon the sacraments and on the relics of the Church with bell, book and candle . . ."[9]

Yet this was not the end of the O'Brien dynastic struggle. After Lord Sussex's victorious English army had withdrawn from Thomond, Donal returned from Ulster and for some years a civil war continued in the kingdom. But with the third Earl able to call on English troops, it was a losing struggle. Eventually an exhausted Donal concluded a peace with Conor. In return for dropping his claims to the Gaelic title, Conor interestingly agreed to compensate Donal for his "loss of rights." Donal, of course, had no rights under English law but he certainly had rights under Brehon Law. Was this a recognition of those rights by the third Earl? Donal, in return, agreed to move into Ennistymon Castle and accept the third Earl's position.

It was still not the end of the dynastic conflict. Harassed by criticism and attacks from the O'Brien *derbfhine*, Conor finally rose up against the English but was defeated and fled to France in 1571. He sought pardon and died in 1581, having formally surrendered his estate as an act of contrition. His son Donough became the fourth Earl. But still the dynastic problems continued. That Donough was still regarded as a royal prince in the people's eyes is seen from one of the poems of Tadhg Mac Dairé Mac Bruaideadha (1570–1652), chief *ollamh* and poet to Donough. He wrote, addressing Donough, with what seems to be a warning to him not to betray the people of Thomond.

Teirce, daoirse, dith ana,
Plágha, cogtha, conghala,
Díombuaidh catha, gairbh-shíon, goid,
Tre ain-bhfír flathafásaoid.

Death, servitude, want of provisions,
Plagues, wars, conflicts,
Defeat in battle, rough weather, rapine,
They arise through the falsity of a prince.

Tadhg was known for his biting verses. At the age of eighty-two, he was hurled over the cliffs to his death by English soldiers.

On August 17, 1585, the then Lord Deputy, Sir John Perrott, signed an agreement with Donough, the fourth Earl of Thomond, and Murrough, third Baron Inchiquin, which agreed to divide the lands of Thomond on an English feudal model. Seventeen lesser Chiefs of Thomond, four merchants with ostensibly English names, the Bishop and Dean of Killala and the Bishop Elect, Dean and Archdeacon of Kilfernora signed their assent to this agreement. The principal clause was: "They agree to abolish all captainships, tanistships and all elections and customary divisions of the land."[10]

In an effort to get everyone to agree, some Chiefs were persuaded by being allowed to keep their Gaelic title for the term of their lives. For example, Seán MacNamara, otherwise The MacNamara Fionn, was allowed to use his title for the rest of his life, but the English stipulated that "after the death of the said 'Shane' all duties and customs as belonging to the name M'Nemarra Fynn, being but extorted, shall be extinguished." The same condition was made for Donel Reagh MacNamara, for "after the death of the said Donnell the customs claimed as belonging to the name M'Nemarrae Reigh shall cease." Similar conditions were down laid for "Tege" Mahowne, Owny O'Loghlyn and Mahown O'Byrne.

The Letters Patent of 1587 are full of the names of Chiefs whose titles had been abolished. A grant to William Bourke of Loughmask, County Mayo, says no one can make a claim as "MacWilliam Uachtar or tanist, which names are abolished." This was the usual formula. A grant to Ross MacMahon, on May 1, 1587, states that the grant "shall not prejudice the rights of any of the Queen's subjects except any arising from the title of M'Mahowne or tanist which names are abolished." On April 11, 1587, that Conal O'Molloy of King's County, formerly "Chief and Captain of his Nation," was given an estate to hold as a knight but could make no claims "arising from the name O'Molloy and tanist which *titles* are abolished."[11]

The O'Dochertaigh of Inis Eoghain, Seán, surrendered on June 28, 1587, and was knighted and allowed to hold certain lands but could no longer claim to be The O'Dochertaigh. "The titles O'Dockertie and tanist are abolished," say the Letters Patent. Some Chiefs were allowed to receive fees from former clansmen, but these were now called tenants. However, "these customs [are] not to be called by Irish names but to be known as the fees of the Chief Serjeant and Under Serjeant." When Lucas Dillon was given the office of Seneschal of the barony of Kilkenny West, County Westmeath, on March 13, 1577/8, it was expressly stated "The Irish customs taken under Irish names by the former captains (chiefs) [are] abolished."

Even so, it was clear that many still rejected the English abolition of the titles and laws and that dynastic wars were breaking out where the *derbhfine* refused to acknowledge the authority of their Chiefs and tanists to surrender.

On March 20, 1570/1, "Conley M'Goghegane" (The MacGeoghegan) "reputed Chief of the Name, had refused to surrender his name (title) of Magogegane or captain of that name . . . and the Queen desiring to change the name of captain to seneschal, a degree or name more usual in places of civil government" ordered that "Conley" be removed. The title of "seneschal of Kenalagh in Co Meath" was then offered to the former Chief's son, Ross MacGeoghegane. We can hazard a guess as to the manner in which Elizabeth's administration "removed" The MacGeoghegan.[12]

On November 3, 1570, "Conwicke," The O'Farrell Buidhe of Clonconnogher, refused to surrender his title. The Lord Deputy merely ordered his "removal" as Chief.

> The Deputy, considering that the country is now shire ground, and no longer under Irish law, has resolved that the office of captain should be extinguished and that Her Majesty's laws, and the currency of her writs, shall take place as is convenient, but believes the services of some such office necessary, till the authority of a sheriff be better known.

The Lord Deputy then ordered that Tadhg Buidhe M'Hubbert O'Farrell should take the office of "Chief Serjeant of Clonconnogher."[13]

We can only speculate as to what happened to these "displaced" Chiefs after their arrest by the English authorities.

Charles Blount, Lord Mountjoy (1555–1629), who became Lord Deputy in 1601, appeared to be somewhat bemused by the vehemence with which the Irish princely families rejected those relatives who surrendered their titles and clung to Brehon law and by the complexity of the dynastic struggles that followed. He wrote to William Cecil, Lord Burghley, in 1603: "Believe me out of my experience, the titles of our honours do rather weaken than strengthen them in this country."

Quoting this letter, Constantia Maxwell sums up the situation thus:

> The weakness of Henry's policy lay in the fact that by negotiating with the chieftains only, he neglected the mass of the clansmen. By tanistry, the Irish law of succession, a chieftain's authority descended not necessarily to his son, but to the strong man elected by the clan. Henry assumed that he was himself the absolute owner of all Irish lands, and acted accordingly, but the tribesmen naturally resented being deprived of their share of the tribe lands, and losing

their power of election with regard to their Chiefs. The English king, governed by feudal principles, confused the office of chieftain with the ownership of land, and made his bargain with individuals who were really subordinate to a system and could not bind their successors. There had always been domestic intrigues within the clans; these were now increased ten-fold by English policy. The Chiefs could not stand out against the public opinion of the clansmen, and as time went on they were literally unable to keep their agreements with the Crown. This blunder led to the breakdown of Henry VIII's policy under Elizabeth.[14]

Indeed, within a few years, if not months in some cases, of submitting to the English administration, "the Chiefs . . . soon began to repent of their bargain."[15] Unrest and opposition were increasing. Edmund Tremayne, clerk of the Privy Council, was sent to Ireland to make an assessment of the situation for Elizabeth I. In 1573 he reported that "[English] Law can take no place without the assistance of the sword."[16] Tremayne's report, entitled "Discourse whether it be better to govern Ireland after the Irish manner or reduce it to the English government," was, of course, an argument for direct rule from England. He says the role that the chiefs were now playing was intolerable and *fons et origo malorum.*

St. Leger interpreted the view of the Irish aristocracy to English law in this way: "It is the death to all the lords and chieftains of both factions to have English government come among them, for they know that if the English government be established here, their Irish exactions is laid aground; the which to forego, they had as lief die."[17]

The English Chief Justice of Connacht, Rokeby, writing to William Cecil in 1570, said: "So beastly are this people, that it is not lenity that will win them . . . it must be by fire and sword, the rod of God's vengeance. . . ." Maxwell sums up: "Gradually it was realised, however, that it was hopeless to graft feudal conceptions upon the clan system, and Elizabethan statesmen decided that war was the only satisfactory method by which peace might be obtained."[18]

An interesting example of how the Irish kings and nobility began to oppose the "surrender and regrant" policy took place during the reign of Edward VI in 1548. The O'Moore of Leix and O'Connor of Offaly had not submitted. Brían, The O'Moore, had been driven to declare that he would hear "no more name of the King of England in Ireland than of the King of Spain."[19] The O'Moore and O'Connor presented a considerable threat to the colonists in the Pale, being adjacent to their now-expanding territory, to the southwest. On a pretext of inviting the two Chiefs to some festival, and relying on the Irish respect for the laws of hospitality to allay their fears, the newly appointed Lord Deputy,

Edward Bellingham, seized them and dispatched them as prisoners to the Tower of London. Their clan lands were then declared confiscated.

From an English viewpoint, this would have been good strategy had the Chiefs operated under the same feudal laws as the English. However, the tanists of both Chiefs pointed out that according to Brehon law, the land did not belong to the Chiefs but to the inhabitants; therefore, the Chiefs could not forfeit it. In the absence of the Chiefs, the tanists controlled matters. Bellingham marched English troops into these territories and the people resisted. The war resulted in the near extermination of the clans and the residual population was driven from the land so that it could be settled by colonists.[20]

Yet the counties of Leix and Offaly were still not crushed. Ten years later, on June 13, 1558, a special commission was given to Sir Henry Radcliffe, the lieutenant of the newly named "King and Queen's counties," to "punish with fire and sword the Irish of the said counties otherwise called Leix and Offaly, Irre, Glinnahirry and Slemarge, Magowghegans, O'Moloyes, Ossories etc." The clans that were to be particularly crushed were "the O'Duns, O'Carrolls, Sinnots (alias the Foxes), O'Mollaghelins, MacOwghlans, O'Maddens, O'Kellies, O'Kennedies and O'Maughers (O'Moores)."[21]

Even then we find the remnants of the O'Moore clan led by Ruaidri Óg (Young Rory) and his son Eoghan (Owny) fighting in alliance with Fiach MacHugh of the O'Byrnes in 1572. Both Ruaidri Óg and Eoghan were killed at that time. Eoghan had instructed that if he were killed in battle, his head should be cut off and buried in a certain spot so that it should not fall into the hands of the English. Here we have an echo of the ancient Celtic belief that the soul dwelt in the head, which is why the ancient Celts venerated the head. They collected the heads of those they had admired and respected, those who had fallen in battle, even those of their enemies, and took them to sacred spots, to sanctuaries, or consigned them as votive offerings in sacred rivers.

After the defeat at Kinsale and the arrival of James VI of Scotland on the throne of England as James I, it was reported that in the area there "was not a Moore or a Connor to be heard of" and "the Byrnes, the O'Tooles, the Kavanaghs, and all the rest continued good subjects."[22]

Perhaps one of the most heartrending stories of the conquest and the loyalty of the people to their Chief came from the kingdom of Desmond. One of the Eóghanacht nobles, Ó Súileabháin Beare, head of a cadet branch of Ó Súileabháin Mór of Kenmare, had fought at Kinsale. He was Donal Cam, known to the English as The O'Sullivan Beare (1560–1618). In the wake of the defeat, Donal Cam heard that Sir George Carew, appointed Lord President of Munster (later created Earl of Totnes), was about to attack the O'Sullivan heartland on the Beara Peninsula. Donal Cam had several castles there but one, in particular, was Dunboy Castle. After Kinsale, he gathered many survivors of the battle and set out for home. He was joined by Donal MacCarthy, illegitimate son of King Donal IX, recently dead, and therefore a claimant to the title Mac-Carthy Mór. Another Chief who joined Donal Cam was The Connor Kerry.

O'Sullivan Beare and several of his men left Dunboy and went to Ardea Castle, on the other side of the peninsula, to met a Spanish ship that was landing arms. Richard MacGeoghegan was appointed Constable of the Dunboy in the Chief's absence.

The Earl of Thomond, now fighting for the English, was asked to reconnoiter the Beara Peninsula. He did so, ravaging and burning O'Sullivan Beare territory. On June 1, 1602, Thomond invested Dunboy and called on Mac-Geoghegan to surrender. He refused. A few days later Carew arrived and took command. He had brought up artillery and began to bombard the castle with its few hundred defenders. Watching the collapse of Dunboy's defenses was Thomas Stafford, who wrote *Pacata Hibernia*. He described the massacre that took place. Once a breach had been made, Captain Doddington and Lieutenant Kirton led their men into the castle. Their orders appeared to be "no quarter" and neither did they give any. Forty Irishmen, realizing resistance useless and unable to surrender, managed to break away from the fighting and threw themselves into the sea, hoping to swim to safety. Carew commanded his boats to row after them, and each one of them was killed, clubbed, stabbed or shot while in the water. At the end of the fighting there were only seventy-five survivors crowded into a cellar of the castle, who offered to surrender. This was refused and, as dusk was falling, a guard was placed to prevent their escape. In the morning twenty-six men were allowed out. At first Carew ordered his cannons to fire into the cellar to bury the survivors under fallen masonry. Then he changed his mind and allowed the surrender. MacGeoghegan, mortally wounded, was stabbed to death. The survivors were then handed to the Earl of Thomond who, perhaps as a means of demonstrating his loyalty to the still-suspicious English overlords, hanged fifty-eight of them in pairs in the English camp.

The massacre of Dunboy put cold determination into O'Sullivan Beare. He organized his forces into a "flying column," not unlike Tom Barry's Cork No. 3 Brigade, which was to fight almost in the same area during the War of Independence in 1919 to 1921. O'Sullivan Beare held out for six months on the Beara. It was no mean feat. Munster was already a near desert. In 1583, after the earlier campaigns, the English had confiscated 574,628 acres, driven off the Irish and placed English settlers on the land. Ten further years of warfare had not improved the situation. O'Sullivan's people were suffering. The

villages were burned, the people were butchered. There were no supplies either in foodstuff nor in armaments. Time was not on O'Sullivan Beare's side.
News came that a considerable English force commanded by Sir Charles
Wilmot (later Viscount Wilmot of Athlone) was marching against his territory. O'Sullivan Beare sent his young son to safety in Spain and with him went
a twelve-year-old cousin, Philip O'Sullivan, who was to grow to manhood as a
soldier and sailor and turn into a foremost Irish historian. His work *Historia
Catholicae Iverniae Compendium*, published in Lisbon in 1621, was a detailed
history of the Elizabeth conquest told from an Irish viewpoint. He died in
Spain around 1660.

It was then that the O'Sullivan Beare called upon the surviving members
of his household and told them of the approach of the English army. They
would be shown little mercy. Their only hope, he told them, was to march
north, to seek refuge and protection with Brian Ó Ruairc, the Prince of
Breifne, who was still holding out. It was a distance of two hundred miles
through now hostile territory and at the height of winter. On December 31,
1602 O'Sullivan Beare gathered a thousand of his people at Glengarriff on the
north side of Bantry Bay. They were mostly old men, women and children,
protected by four hundred soldiers of which thirteen had horses. Other
groups, under other commanders, were to leave later. O'Sullivan Beare and
his followers set out from Glengarriff through the winter mountains carrying
all the food they had—enough for one day's rations each. The atrocious winter weather, the hardship of the march and attacks from English skirmishers
resulted in a terrible rate of attrition.

On January 14, 1603, the survivors arrived at the Leitrim Castle of Ó Ruairc, Prince of Breifne. There were only thirty-five survivors; of which sixteen
were soldiers. The others were the surviving civilians, including Dermot O'Sullivan and his wife, the parents of young Philip who was then in safety in Spain.
The O'Connor Kerry and other leaders bringing three hundred more survivors
arrived later. The O'Ruairc gave them what hospitality he could until a ship
could be found to take the noncombatants as refugees to Spain. O'Sullivan
Beare was anxious for revenge and decided to stay, joining Prince Brian Maguire
of Femanagh in fighting during what proved to be the final days of the war.

Donal Cam, The O'Sullivan Beare, was to die in exile in Spain in 1618. The
Spanish king bestowed the title Conde de Berehaven on him; in actuality, it was
a Spanish translation of his Irish title as *Tiarna na Beara*. He, like many other
Irish nobles who had to flee into exile, was warmly welcomed in Spain. As late as
1792 the Spanish Council of State acknowledged that "by the mere fact of settling in Spain, the Irish are accounted Spaniards and enjoy the same rights."[23]

Even after the defeat at Kinsale and the submission and eventual flight of the leading nobility, such as O'Neill, O'Donel, Maguire and others, there was still a stubborn refusal by the Irish people to abandon Irish law. Sir John Davies, writing to the Earl of Salisbury from Dublin on November 8, 1610, reported that he had accompanied the Lord Deputy and commissioners to County Cavan to start the Plantation of Ulster. A total of 3,785,057 acres were about to be confiscated and made ready to receive the new colonists. First the natives had to be removed. The leading Irish, who had survived the wars, were summoned to hear the proclamation that was to order them off their lands. Sir John Davies says:

> When the proclamation was published touching their removal (which was done in the public session-house, the Lord Deputy and Commissioners being present), a lawyer of the Pale retained by them did endeavour to maintain that they had estates of inheritances in their possession which their Chiefs Lords could not forfeit. . . . [24]

Davies says that it had to be made clear "whether the case be ruled by our law of England which is in force, or by their own Brehon Law, which is abolished and adjudged no law, but a lewd custom."

> those lands in the county of Cavan, which as O'Reilly's country, are all holden of the King; and because the captainship or chiefry of O'Reilly is abolished by Act of Parliament by Statute second of Elizabeth, and also because two of the chief lords elected by the country have been lately slain in rebellion, which is an attainder in law, these lands are holden immediately of His Majesty."[25]

"This estate of the chieftain or tanist hath been lately adjudged no estate in law . . . ," he emphasizes and goes on, showing his lack of understanding of Brehon law, to argue that even under the law, James I had supreme rights over the people and the clan lands.

> For he that was O'Reilly or chieftain of the country, had power to cut upon all the inhabitants, high or low, as pleased him; which argues they held their lands of the chief lord in the villeinage, and therefore they are properly called natives; for *nativus* in our old register of writs doth signify a villein. . . . Thus, then, it appears that, as well by the Irish custom as the law of England, His Majesty may, at his pleasure, seize these lands and dispose thereof.[26]

The term "cutting" is only an English form of the Norman *tallage*—probably deriving from *tal*—a yielding of cows—which was a tax on tenants towards public expenses. Sir John might have known his common law, but his knowledge of the Brehon system of land tenure was abysmal.

Hogan, who is honest in his admittance that he is no admirer of Brehon law, sums up the situation:

> This [Brehon] law of sovereignty, distinct from anything known to Roman or Feudal Europe, remained a living reality down to the end of the native order. As we have already remarked, the sixteenth century witnesses a revival of traditional sentiment and ideas in Ulster, and in general, under the pressure of Tudor England, Gaelic Ireland revealed itself to be traditionalists to the core. The Gaelic intellectuals, poets, historians, and jurists, equally with the ruling aristocracy, continued to live in the past, and to insist on development along lines entirely congenial to the native genius.[27]

CHAPTER FIVE

"EXTINCT FOR EVER"?

BY THE BEGINNING OF THE REIGN OF JAMES I of England, according to the conquerors of Ireland and the law system they had imposed, all Gaelic titles had, in the words of the Act of 1587, been deemed to "henceforth cease, end, determined and be utterly abolished and extinct for ever."[1] As a corollary to this, all Brehon law was abolished in the wake of the English victory over the Irish at Kinsale. But the enforcement of the new English system did not happen all at once, and many parts of Ireland clung to its own law system during the succeeding century. The difficulties of enforcing English law may be seen from the number of times that the English administration had to repeat their claim that Brehon law was abolished.

The King's Bench issued a decision in 1608, endorsing a judgment given earlier announcing the abolition of Brehon law and enforcement of English common law.[2] John Davies mentions this judgment was followed by "A Royal Proclamation," to similar effect, in 1605 reiterating that Gaelic titles and estates were to be surrendered and would be met by regrants of the estates under English law with, where warranted, the bestowal of English titles. There is evidence that many Irish aristocrats now came forward expecting to receive incontestable titles, but a grant of a title was made conditional on their giving up the clan relationship and chiefdom in favor of them being mere landlords in English feudal terms and many of their former clansmen becoming their tenants.[3]

The proclamation in question had been issued in Ireland on behalf of James I by the Lord Deputy, Sir Arthur Chichester, on March 11, 1605.[4] One of the main aims of the proclamation was apparently to isolate the remaining chiefs from their people by prohibiting the people from obeying them. It declared that

> tenants or inhabitants . . . are not to be reputed or called the natives or natural
> followers of any other lord or chieftain whatsoever, and that they and every of
> them ought to depend wholly and immediately upon His Majesty, who is both
> able and willing to protect them, and not upon any other inferior lord or
> lords. . . .

By way of further reinforcing the policy, the first "Irish" Parliament to meet in twenty-seven years assembled in 1613, and a bill was passed whereby the Irish were put at the jurisdiction of English law. Those members of the Irish aristocracy, specifically the Chiefs who had not formally surrendered or acknowledged the ending of the chiefdoms and clan systems, were to be forcibly removed. In that single year, seven clans from Leix were forcibly removed to County Kerry and dispersed together with twenty-five petty chiefs, mostly from the O'Farrells of County Longford and the O'Byrnes of Wicklow. Their lands were then confiscated and given to colonists.[5]

John P. Prendergast, an eminent lawyer and historian, sums up James I's continuation of the Tudor policies against the Irish aristocracy:

> The Irish gentlemen who did not forfeit their estates received proportions (intended to be three-fourths of their former lands, but often only one-half or one-third, as the English "were their own carvers"), as immediate tenants of the king. Their lands were liable to forfeiture if the Chief took from any of his former clansmen any of his ancient customary exactions or victuals; if he went coshering on them as of old; if he used gavelkind, *or took the name of the great O, whether O'Neill, or O'Donnell, O'Carroll or O'Connor.*[6]

"Coshering," which is an Anglicized word deriving from the Irish *cos* (a foot) meant an act of wandering. In this instance it referred to a Chief who made a tour of his territory. Under Brehon law, those with whom he stayed had to offer him hospitality. However, there seemed a change in what a cosherer was, probably due to the unsettled times, when many members of the Gaelic aristocracy were "on the run." An Act for the Suppressing of Cosherers and idle wanderers' describes cosherers in this way:

> Many young gentlemen of this kingdom that have little or nothing to live on
> of their own, and will not apply themselves to labour or other honest industri-
> ous courses to support themselves, but do live idly and inordinately, coshering

upon the country and pressing themselves, their followers, their horses, and their grey-hounds upon the poor inhabitants sometimes exacting money. . . . [7]

The term "gavelkind" comes from the Irish *gabáil cenél* meaning "maintaining the tribe."

Prendergast continues:

> On his death, his youthful heir was made ward to a Protestant, to be brought up in Trinity College, Dublin, from his twelfth to his eighteenth year in English habits and religion—often after his enforced conformity, all the more embittered, like Sir Phelim O'Neill, against English religion. The wandering *creaghts* were not to become his tenants at fixed money rents. He covenanted that they should build and dwell in villages and live on allotted portions of land "to keep them as grievous as to be made bond slaves." Unable to keep their cattle on the small portions of land assigned to them, instead of ranging at large, they sold away both corn and cattle. Unused to money rents, though of victuals they formerly made small account because of their plenty, they were unable to pay rents; and their lords finding it impossible to exact them fled to Spain. Similar Plantations followed in Leitrim, Longford, King's County and Wexford, except that in some (as in Leitrim) one-half of the lands of the Irish were seized.[8]

The term *creaght* is another Anglicization of the Irish *caoraidheacht*, meaning an act of wandering and later a foray or raiding party in search of cattle and also a cattleherd and herdsman, like the cattle drovers of the American West in the nineteenth century, who herded their cattle in search of good pasture, living and sleeping as itinerants.

Prendergast attributes his information that any Gaelic landowner who called himself The O'Something or The MacWhoever would be deprived of his land and rights to a letter of Sir Arthur Chichester to King James I dated October 30, 1610.[9]

A penal code against the Catholic Irish had been emerging since the reign of Elizabeth I. Sons of Gaelic aristocrats and gentlemen were taken as "wards of court" and sent to be educated in England, in English language, attitudes and law as well as in the Protestant religion. The purpose was, of course, to completely eradicate Irish culture and the Catholic religion. However, in 1625 it was decreed that landowners of sizable estates could take an oath of civil allegiance as opposed to the oath of supremacy, which had previous recognized the English Crown as head of the church. At the same time the English Crown set up a commission to examine what were called "defective titles" to estates.

Landowners were allowed to hold land only if they could prove it had been held in their family by primogeniture for over sixty years, that is from the time of the original "Surrender and Regrant" of 1541. This, of course, led to many confiscations of estates, for such proof was almost an impossible demand.

In 1634 a Statute of Wills and Uses confirmed that the crown could intervene in the education of any Irish gentleman's heir-apparent and that those should be forcibly sent to be educated in the Protestant faith, English law and custom. Lord Deputy Thomas Wentworth, as early as 1635, was drawing up a new scheme to drive all Chiefs still clinging to the clan system out of Connacht and resettle the clan lands with new English colonists. That can only be interpreted to mean that some Connacht Chiefs had survived the initial attempt to eradicate them and were cleaving to the native system.

In 1641 the Irish uprising began in the north and spread quickly throughout Ireland. One of the pertinent aspects of this uprising was that the main Irish forces were coming from the clan structures, and these clans were still led by their Chiefs. For example, on October 12, 1641, the Chiefs of the O'Rourkes in Leitrim, the O'Farralls in Longford, the O'Byrnes and O'Tooles of Wicklow and Kavanaghs of Wexford, whom one would have thought had disappeared before this time, were leading their peoples as their forefathers had done. The major leader of the uprising was Sir Phelim O'Neill, later to be joined and superseded by his kinsman Eoghan Ruadh O'Neill (1590–1649), the nephew of Aodh, The O'Neill (1550–1616). Eoghan Ruadh, a general in Spanish service, was regarded by many Irish as a candidate to the throne not only of Ulster but as one who could reinstate the High Kingship. His initial victories ended with his premature death at Cloughoughter Castle, County Cavan.

A poignant illustration of the survival of the Brehon law of succession is found during the reign of Charles II. There were two rivals for the lands given to the head of the O'Rourke family, which in O'Rourke eyes meant that there were two rivals for the title Ó Ruairc of Breifne. Eoghan Óg, son of Eoghan Mór, of Dromahair was one claimant, and the other was Aodh of Kilnagen. Charles II had actually given the lands to Father Patrick Maginn, chaplain to his queen. Aodh of Kilnagen was the tenant on these lands but claiming ownership. Eoghan Óg petitioned King Charles II in 1662, who sent an emissary Captain Owen Lloyd to Jamestown, County Leitrim, to inquire into Eoghan Óg's claim—not, of course, to the chiefship, as it did not exist in English eyes. When Father Patrick Maginn heard this, his "honour of conscience urged him" to write to the *ollamhain* of Connacht to ask who was the rightful chief of the O'Rourkes and, thereby, who should have the land in question. The reply was signed by the *ollamhain* of Connacht—the Uí Mhaoil Chonaire, the Uí

Dhuibhgeanain and the Uí Chuirnín. They were unanimous that Eoghan Óg, son of Eoghan Mór, was without question The Ó Ruairc of Breifne. Father Patrick cleared his conscience by authorizing Eoghan Óg to collect a substantial sum of rent from Aodh as his tenant.[10]

Indeed, many of the Irish nobles in exile still maintained their *Brehons*. As a postulant for admission to the Royal Spanish Order of Calatrava, Arthur O'Neill, in 1662, submitted a pedigree drawn up by Tulio Conreo (O'Mulconry) who claimed to be "Coronista General" of the Irish nobility.[11]

Through the seventeenth century, some Gaelic titles survived as well as the Brehon laws under which they were governed. Some of the holders of titles did surrender when faced with no other choice; others like Aodh (Hugh) O'Neill, "Earl of Tyrone," resumed the style "The O'Neill, Prince of Ulster" as soon as he sought political refuge abroad. He was buried under that title in Rome in 1616, where his tomb may still be seen in San Pietro in Montorio, in the Via Garibaldi. As a legal point, it could be argued that O'Neill never accepted that the surrender of his title while under duress was binding. When he did surrender on April 3, 1603, the first item of the document states that he "vows he will continue a loyal subject to the King's person, crown, prerogative and laws, *utterly renouncing and abjuring the name and title of O'Neill.*"[12]

There were two major and decisive blows given to the remnants of the Gaelic aristocracy following the end of the 1641 uprising and Oliver Cromwell's military campaigns in Ireland of 1649/50. By 1652 it was estimated that one-third of the total Irish population had perished by war and attendant diseases arising from the devastations during this conquest. Following this, the English administration began to enact policies that were designed to eradicate the Irish peoples by ordering them, first into a "reservation," that is, the territory west of the River Shannon, in the province of Connacht and County Clare. The towns and rich lands in those areas were to be used as English military garrison lands. Any Irish person found on the east bank of the River Shannon after May 1, 1654, could be, and was, executed on the spot. Many were. Some 7,708,238 statute acres were confiscated. An estimated 100,000 Irish men, women and children were seized from their villages between 1654 and 1660 and shipped off to the New World colonies, mainly Barbados, to serve as "indentured laborers" who, because they were provided to the plantation owners free by the government, usually were treated in worse fashion than the African slaves, whom they had to buy. A further 40,000, mostly the former members of the Irish Army and many of the Gaelic aristocrats, fled to Europe where they were welcomed at the courts, and into the armies, of France, Spain and Austria.

The restoration of Charles II alleviated the situation somewhat, although his administration's land settlement of 1662, with the court of claims of 1663, did little to put the Irish back in control of all the property they had held before the Cromwellian Conquest. It was still, of course, against the law to use Gaelic titles, although many members of the Gaelic aristocracy did reemerge in this period and several sat in James II's Dublin parliament of 1689.

The Williamite Conquest continued to crush the old system even further, if further it could be crushed. James II had been no friend to Ireland and was committed to maintaining English imperial rule. One of the essential planks of that rule was the land settlement, confiscations of rich farming land from the native Irish and its redistribution to the colonists. However, as James began to fight for his own power base and was driven out of England, he had begun to concede certain rights to his "Kingdom of Ireland." His colonial Irish Parliament repealed Poynings Law, making the Irish Parliament subservient to the English Parliament, and declared it independent from England. This Parliament was predominantly an Anglo-Irish one with only a small section of the wealthier natives who could speak English being allowed to sit in it. Acts were passed that made all religions equal under the law, with the order that each sect should support their own priests or ministers. But the primary desire of the Parliament was to repeal the Cromwellian land settlement. When this matter came up, James threatened to dissolve the Parliament. But with his son-in-law, William, Prince of Orange, about to land in Ireland with an army, James reluctantly assented to the bill that stated that the landowners of 1641 and their heirs could recover their confiscated property and declared that the Cromwellian and later Acts of Settlement were invalid.

The Irish gave their full support to James II, who was in alliance with Louis XIV of France, who was using James in his greater European plan. To counteract Louis's ambitions in Europe, a Grand Alliance had been set up at Augsburg in which William of Orange was a principal member. So also was Pope Innocent XI. It has become one of the later ironies of Irish history that the army of William of Orange, in their conquest of Ireland, was supported by Pope Innocent. There were Catholics in William's army just as there were Protestants in James II's army. Since the nineteenth century, Ulster Unionists have been fed the myth that William "overthrew the Pope and Popery" at the Battle of the Boyne in 1690.

The Boyne, in military terms, was not even a decisive battle. It was a year later, on July 12, 1691, that the defeat at Aughrim sealed the future of Ireland. Some seven thousand Irish and their allies were killed with four hundred officers, most of them the scions of the old Gaelic nobility and the Gaelicized old

Anglo-Irish families. Colonel Charles O'Kelly, himself of an old chiefly family, observed that on that day the Irish lost "the flower of their army and nation."[13]

The Irish fell back on Limerick and eventually negotiations opened. By October 3 a treaty was signed. A principle point of this treaty was that religious toleration was guaranteed. Those Irish who wanted to return home could do so unmolested, and not all the Irish who had supported James II would have their estates confiscated. Those Irish soldiers who did not want to remain under the new regime would be allowed to leave for Europe. Some twelve thousand immediately did so and formed the famous Irish Brigade of the French Army, created by Justin MacCarthy, Viscount Mountcashel. Another Irish Brigade was formed in Spain in 1709 and smaller brigades in various countries where the refugees were welcomed.

Once the remnants of the Irish army were safely out of Ireland, the Williamite administration failed to ratify the Treaty of Limerick. Some 1.5 million statute acres were confiscated for a new colonization scheme. Just after the surrender of Limerick, only 14 percent of Irish land was in native hands. By 1778 this had decreased to only 5 percent. The Acts of James II's Dublin Parliament, XIII and XV, which declared all religions should be equal under the law and that each priest and minister would be supported by his congregation only, acts that the Treaty had guaranteed, were abolished. There would be no religious toleration and only the Established Church of England was recognized. A series of Penal Laws against Catholics and all dissenting Protestant sects began to be enacted. Intermarriage between people of different religions was forbidden. Presbyterian ministers were liable to three months in jail for delivering a sermon, a fine of £100 for celebrating the Lord's Supper and so forth. If a couple was found to have been married by a Presbyterian minister, they were dragged into an Anglican church and denounced as guilty of the sin of fornication.

All Irish Catholics were immediately banned from being able to own property above a few pounds sterling in value. They could not own guns or any other weapons. They could not own a horse above the value of £5. They were forbidden from practicing in any profession—they could not become doctors or lawyers or hold office in the army, navy, customs and excise or municipal employment. Presbyterian and other dissenting Protestants were also excluded in the same manner. An Act of 1704 excluded all Presbyterians from holding office in these professions. In 1715 a further act made it an offense for Presbyterian ministers even to teach children, and this was punishable by three months' imprisonment. The "religious liberty" won by William of Orange, which the Ulster Orange Order celebrates by their marches today, actually caused 250,000 Protestant Ulstermen to emigrate to the colonies of America between 1717 and 1776 alone in order to find religious freedom. There they became prominent in the American War of Independence and adherents of re-publicanism, which they transmitted to Ireland. In the republican uprising of 1798, in County Antrim alone, some thirty-six Presbyterian ministers were named as local leaders of the United Irishmen movement. Of that number, five were executed by hanging, five were transported for life, ten received terms of imprisonment, nine were forcibly exiled, four escaped into voluntary exile and three were acquitted on guarantees of their future good behavior. The change of perception to history came after 1834 when Ulster Presbyterians were al-lowed to join the elite Anglican Orange Order and soon took it over.

The betrayal by the Williamite administration of the provisions of the Treaty of Limerick, especially the breaking of the guarantee of religious free-dom for all denominations, was a further scar on the Irish psyche. In 1745, when the Irish Brigade of the French Army played the key role in the defeat of the English at Fontenoy, they charged the English lines with the battle cry: "*Cuimnighidh ar Luimneach agus ar fhéile na Sasanaigh!*"—Remember Limerick and the English treachery!—meaning the breaking of their word in the treaty.

So, in the eighteenth century, Ireland had sunk into the darkness of the Penal Laws in which some 85 percent of the people of Ireland simply did not exist so far as civil rights were concerned. Only Anglicans were allowed full rights and able to own land and pursue the professions.

Of the sixty kings and aristocrats listed by the English administration in 1534, a mere handful had survived the turmoil of continuing conquests and dev-astations. A few of these chiefly families went "underground" in Ireland, while others, the most notable members of royal dynasties, had been forced into exile. With the start of the Penal Law period we can say that the conquests had finally brought about the general destruction of the Brehon law and Irish social system. The Irish language had been reduced to the language of the peasantry and working classes. A poignant example of the language shift is demonstrated in the *Reminiscences* of Michael Kelly, the Dublin-born singer and composer (1764–1826). Kelly, who became a friend of Mozart, sang the parts of Don Curzio and Don Basilio in the first performance of "The Marriage of Figaro." He sang before the Holy Roman Emperor, Franz I (later Franz I of Austria), and, after the performance, he was introduced to the emperor. The emperor, learning that he was Irish, told him that there were a number of his compatriots at the court. He turned and introduced several titled Irishmen. He does not identify them all but among them might have been Austria's Finance Minister, Count Joseph O'Donnell and his son Field Marshal Maurice O'Donnell, married to Princess Christine of Belgium. They addressed Michael Kelly in Irish. Kelly did not speak Irish. The emperor remarked upon this fact with curiosity. Kelly, unthinkingly, told the emperor "only Irish peasants" spoke the language. The titled Irish exiles pretended not to hear him. In his *Reminiscences*, Kelly had the grace to reflect: "I could have bitten out my tongue."[14]

Those chiefly families in Europe, usually recognized by the monarchs of those countries in which they settled and bestowed with titles of those countries, often found it easier to maintain their genealogies and rights to Gaelic titles than those left behind in Ireland.

A *Pacte de Famille* happened in 1901 in Paris where the heads of some of the O'Neill branches met and confirmed the Jorge O'Neill, a peer of Portugal, as The O'Neill, Prince of Clanaboy. They also believed him to be entitled to use the title of Comte de Tyrone. However, this acknowledgment to the headship of Cenél Eoghain and the title is not without dispute. O'Neill then dropped his Portuguese title but was formally addressed as Most Serene Highness by Popes Leo XIII and Pious X and was so enrolled on the Register of Portuguese Nobility.

In Ireland it became the practice of many families, in order to keep some house or small estate within the family, to designate one of their number to "convert" to the Anglican faith, for only an Anglican could own land. Through this means could a family keep security of tenure. Of course, not all families were so united, and often a son, brother, uncle or cousin would convert and then denounce their family to maintain total possession of the property.

Some chiefly houses had, of course, converted wholeheartedly—the O'Briens, the O'Donovans and the O'Morchoes among them. Many merely followed the nomination scheme. Others existed as "nonpersons" under the penal laws, their identity known only to the local population. Now and again they might emerge into record, as when the English traveler Arthur Young made his tour of Ireland and discovered two nobles families.

> At Clonells [Clonalis], near Castlerea, lives O'Connor, the direct descent of Roderick O'Connor, who was King of Connaught six or seven hundred years ago. The common people pay him the greatest respect and send him presents of cattle etc., upon various occasions. They consider him as the prince of a people involved in one common ruin.[15]

The MacSweeneys of Doe walked the roads of Donegal rather than become tenants of their conquerors and were sheltered by those members of their extended family who had accepted the conquest. Confirmation that many holders of Gaelic titles led double lives even in eighteenth-century Ireland is confirmed by Daniel Corkery, when commenting on the observations of Arthur Young:

> When the O'Connells were writing business letters, or indeed putting their hands to any official documents whatever, they signed themselves Connell, omitting the distinctively Gaelic O. But when anyone of them succeeded in making his way on the Continent and found himself at last of some importance in the world, little by little he came to sign himself O'Connell again: that, he resumed the Gael. Of the Connells, Young could have made some report; of the O'Connells none.[16]

After the relaxation of the Penal Laws, perhaps in the mistaken belief that it was only those Penal Laws that proscribed the use of Gaelic titles, The O'Conor Don began to use his title publicly, and several O'Conor Dons stood successfully for Parliament during the nineteenth century.

Arthur Young noted the survival of another Gaelic prince: "Another great family in Connaught is MacDermot, who calls himself Prince of Coolavin. He lives at Coolavin in Sligo, and though he has not above one hundred pounds a year, will not admit his children to sit down in his presence."

The titles, therefore, were passed down in a surreptitious manner within the family during the Penal period so that the state could not interfere. But, of course, these families were known and paid tacit deference by the local people who had been their former clansmen. So an "underground aristocracy" was managing to survive in Ireland in addition to those exiled in Europe. Outwardly, such people were known simply as Connor or MacDermot, but, it seems, the old Chiefs were still acknowledged when it was safe to do so.

The O'Connells, once hereditary Constables of Ballycarbery Castle, then a principal residence of the MacCarthy Mór, Kings of Desmond, and afterward petty chieftains, settled at Derrynane. Daniel Corkery has pointed out that they omitted the "O" from their name unless travelling in Europe. They were still able to assert a chiefly authority in the area. Dr. Denis Gwynn points out an interesting example of this.[17] The family kept a crooked knife, said to be an old pruning knife, which was of no value, except that it had been handed down from one chieftain to another as a symbol of their authority. When Captain Whitwell Butler, a revenue collector of West Kerry, went to Derrynane to see Muiris-an-Cipín (Maurice "Hunting Cap" O'Connell, 1727–1825) on business, he needed safe conduct to get out of the area. Captain Butler was hated for his exactions from the local people. Maurice was, in fact, an uncle of Daniel O'Connell, "The Liberator," and the incident happened in 1782.

Muiris handed the knife to his nephew, an O'Sullivan of Couliagh, and told him to escort Captain Butler and his men out of the area. "Angry faces met them as they walked out through the little village of Caherdaniel at the back of Derrynane, but young O'Sullivan let them see the crooked knife, and the crowd melted away." As Daniel Corkery confirms:

> So long as any of the O'Connells, the chief's nephew, or his most abject menial, bearing the crooked knife, accompanied the Captain there was no fear of his being molested; and, as a matter of history, he was not set upon and beaten until he had himself persuaded the knife-bearer to leave him and return home.[18]

By the beginning of the eighteenth century, the aristocratic and intellectual classes of Ireland had been smashed, destroyed or driven into exile. The seventeenth century had seen the completion of what had been described so vividly by Fearflatha Ó Gnímh (ca. 1540–1640), bard to The O'Neills of Clanaboy. He begins with a caution:

> *Níl eigeann eagla an ghallsmmaicht*
> *damh a hanstaid do do nochtadh:*
> *atá an chríoch réidhse rí Néill*
> *do chrú fíréin dá folcadh.*

> [Fear of the foreign law does not permit me to tell (of Ireland's) sore plight; this smooth land of royal Niall is being washed with innocent blood.]

O Gnímh goes on, however, to describe the chaos and loss.

> Ireland's learned are dead,
> Stuff of wise man and free poet,
> Successor to them isn't left
> Nor the stuff of an *ollamh*'s soul.

> At an end, all at one time,
> Ulster's schools, Leinster's learned,
> Of Munster poets not a tenth alive—
> That slaughter left no remnant.

The secular and ecclesiastical colleges of Ireland had been smashed, and if any Catholic Irishman wanted to acquire an education, he had to go to Europe. It had already been enacted that no Irish Catholics could be tutors or teachers,

and in 1695 even going abroad to seek an education became a punishable of-
fence. The other alternative was attendance at the illegal "hedge schools."
These schools were held in isolated spots where lookouts could be posted to
alert the scholars of the approach of English soldiers. An itinerant schoolmas-
ter, usually a man of sound and serious scholarship, would try to keep alive the
fragments of an education in children—an education banned by the Penal
Laws. In the shelter of hedges, in caves and other remote locations, Irish poetry, Greek, Latin, advanced mathematics were taught. These schools continued until Catholic Emancipation in the nineteenth century.

Through the seventeenth and eighteenth centuries, books in the Irish language—grammar books, dictionaries, tracts on history and philosophy—were
printed in such places as Louvain, Antwerp, Paris, Rome and Lisbon, and attempts were made to smuggle them back into the country. As a seventeenth-
century poet, Aindrias Mac Marcais wrote:

Gan gaire fa ghniomhradh leinbh

There is no laughter at children's doings,
Music is prohibited, the Irish language is in
chains.

Much knowledge was lost in this suppression, including a general knowledge of Brehon law. Without brehons to advise them, it is no wonder that
many of the "underground" chiefly families began to forget the exact requirements of the old laws of succession. Not even Brehon law books were generally
available to guide them. W. K. O'Sullivan explained:

> During the first part of the eighteenth century the possession of an Irish book
> made the owner a suspect person, and was often the cause of his ruin. In some
> parts of the country the tradition of the danger incurred by having Irish man-
> uscripts lived down to within my own memory; and I have seen Irish manu-
> scripts which had been buried until the writing had almost faded, and the
> margins rotted away, to avoid the danger their discovery would entail at the
> visit of the local yeomanry.[19]

But many Irish books and manuscripts did survive in spite of systematic
burnings, burials and "drownings." Ironically, many law books lay forgotten in
private collections owned by the Anglo-Irish families. Charles Graves
(1812–1899), the grandfather of the famous poet Robert Graves, began a study
of the Irish law system. He was a Dubliner, a graduate of Trinity College,

Dublin, and a professor of mathematics who became Anglican Bishop of Limerick, Ardfert and Aghadoe. He was also an expert on Ogam, the early Irish form of writing, and became president of the Royal Irish Academy in 1860. It was in February 1852 that Dr Graves petitioned the English government to establish a commission to collect, edit and translate the surviving Brehon law manuscripts in the cause of academic knowledge. He was supported by James Henthorn Todd (1805–69), founder of the Irish Archaeological Society and Regius professor of Hebrew at Trinity. Surprisingly, but in a spirit of conciliation with the rising tide of the Irish movement for self-government, a royal commission was appointed on November 11, 1852, to direct, superintend and carry into effect the transcription, translation and publication of the law system as the *Ancient Laws and Institutes of Ireland.* Six volumes were published between 1865 and 1901.

However, until then, many Chiefs in Ireland worked from only a faint memory of the law, which became tradition. Others merely accepted English primogeniture.

As Ireland was allowed to pass into a more liberal age, with the Catholic Emancipation Act of 1829 and other reform acts, and with a newly enfranchised electorate moving toward demands for self-government, those possessing the old Gaelic titles began to reassert them in public. The O'Donoghue of the Glens (1831–91) became member of Parliament for Tipperary (1857–65) and Tralee (1865–85) and used his title in public. He was referred to by his title even in the English newspapers and the *Hansard Parliamentary Report.* The O'Donovan and The O'Conor Don also began to use their titles publicly.

Another O'Connor was using a Gaelic title even before that. This was the rather colorful Roger O'Connor, from Connorville, County Cork (1762–1834), who claimed to be The O'Connor Kerry. There has not been a detailed examination of his genealogy, but the claim might well have been genuine. He was educated as an Anglican at Trinity College, Dublin, and called to the English Bar in 1784. He joined the republican United Irishmen and was arrested in 1797 but acquitted of sedition. Rearrested in 1798, the year of the uprising, he was sent to Fort George in Scotland in March 1799. In 1801 he was escorted to London but in 1803 was allowed to return to Ireland. He rented Dangan Castle, Trim, which burned down soon after he had insured it for £5,000. He eloped with a married lady and, finally, in 1817, he was arrested for highway robbery, holding up the Galway coach. His defense was that he had not wanted money but meant simply to retrieve the love letters of his friend, Sir Francis Burdett. To the astonishment of the judge, he was acquitted. He published a curious work entitled *The Chronicles of Eri: being the history of the Gaal Sciot Iber: or, The Irish People;*

translated from the original manuscripts in the Phoenician dialect of the Scythian language. Printed in London, in 1822, it was mostly his own fictional account of Ireland's early history.

Even more curiously, his son, who likewise maintained his descent from the ancient kings of Ireland, Feargus Edward O'Connor (1794–1855), became the famous Chartist leader. Born at Connorville, graduate of Trinity College, Dublin, called to the Irish Bar, he became a Member of Parliament for County Cork (1832) seeking repeal of the Union. He turned to radical agitation and settled in England, founded the weekly *The Northern Star*, helped to organize the People's Charter of the Working Men's Association and became one of the best-known radical leaders of the nineteenth century, being elected as Member of Parliament for Nottingham (1847–52).

Charles James Patrick Mahon (1800–91) claimed to be The O'Gorman Mahon. He was a barrister from County Clare and represented Ennis in Westminster from 1847 to 1852. A traveler and adventurer, an officer in the tsar of Russia's bodyguard, a general in Uruguay and commander of a Chilean naval fleet against Spain and a colonel in the Brazilian army, his adventures became legend. He also fought in the Union army during the American Civil War and finally joined Napoleon III's chasseurs. A friend of Bismarck, he took up residence in Berlin. He was a noted duelist and survived thirteen encounters. He returned to Ireland in 1873 and won the Clare seat for the Westminster Parliament in 1880, losing it in 1885. He then represented Carlow from 1887 to 1891.

But the emergence of those claiming Gaelic titles threw up several curious anomalies. In 1821 we are told that George IV, visiting Ireland, was approached by a Colonel O'Hanlon who claimed to be The O'Hanlon and demanded the right to the office of hereditary royal standard bearer north of the Boyne.[20] It would be bizarre had George IV given any credence to this individual whose claim was based on the right of a Gaelic ancestor, whose title had been abolished by English law, to carry an O'Neill royal banner. The title, The O'Hanlon, actually had been made extinct on December 1, 1587, when a grant of land to "Oghie O'Hanlon" "provided that no person shall have any titles claiming as O'Hanlon or Tanist, which titles are abolished."

Similarly, and no more curious, was the appearance of The O'Conor Don bearing a flag dubbed the "standard of Ireland" at the coronation of Edward VII at Westminster Abbey in 1902[21] and claiming to hold the right to carry it by his Gaelic title that had been abolished by English law on July 15, 1585. This was the Right Honorable Charles Owen O'Conor (1838–1906), who maintained he was a direct descendant of the "last High King," Ruaidri Ua Conchobhair, and therefore "senior chief of Ireland," claims that were total nonsense. Indeed, the carrying of this hastily devised "standard," even though a fabrication, by O'Conor Don was seen as another sop to the rising tide of Irish political nationalism.

There also began to emerge a bizarre way of arbitrarily adopting Gaelic titles. The method was simply to adopt the title as a name by Deed Poll. The Reverend William Hanlon, the rector of Inishshannon, County Cork, claimed to be The O'Hanlon, and so adopted it as a name by Deed Poll on February 14, 1907. The Reverend Hanlon died on April 26, 1916, and his grave in Innishannon Old Cemetery bears the legend "Commonly called 'The O'Hanlon.'"

This example was followed by Pierce Charles Mahony (1850–1930) who adopted the name of "The O'Mahony" of Kerry by Deed Poll in 1912. Samuel Trant McCarthy, the High Sheriff and Deputy Lieutenant of County Kerry, a former judge of the British India Imperial Civil Service who had retired to Kerry, adopted the title MacCarthy Mór as his name by Deed Poll on July 1, 1921. His legal name therefore became "Samuel Trant McCarthy MacCarthy Mór." Just how many of these curious Deed Poll claims were made might make an interesting area of further research.

There was, however, a growing small band of those maintaining Gaelic titles who were asking for some form of recognition from the English Crown. Among them was the Reverend Thomas Arthur MacMorrough Murphy (1865–1921), rector of Kilkernan, County Dublin, and a graduate of Trinity College, Dublin. He had resumed the surname O'Morchoe by Deed Poll on September 3, 1895, and asserted his claim to be The O'Morchoe. In 1904 he published a booklet entitled *The Succession of the Chiefs of Ireland.*

The O'Morchoe, on a questionable basis, argued that Brehon law was merely eldest male heir inheritance. He says:

> Within the last two generations the representatives of the former Chiefs have reassumed the style and title of their ancestors, and courtesy recognition is accorded them, both officially and by the public. They are received at the Royal and Vice-Regal Courts by their titles, and are so described in official documents.

The O'Morchoe seems confused, for at one point he says that the Gaelic titles are "officially recognised" and that "a certified copy of a pedigree in Ulster's Office has been issued which describes the pedigree as 'establishing the right of—to be Chief of his Sept.'" On the other he correctly states that the English Crown does not determine the right to use the title.

> It would seem but justice that the Crown [of England] as the Fountain of Honour, and in accordance with the precedents to be now quoted, would grant a

similar form of recognition in the case of the Irish Chiefs to that which is afforded to the native nobility of other countries that have come under the British Crown. To admit the titles at Court and not to determine the right to use them is unsatisfactory.

Of course, the issuing of a pedigree, certified or otherwise, by Ulster's Office—then the heraldic office for all Ireland—expressing the establishment of a *right* to claim the Chiefship was not a recognition of the title. There is a subtlety of language here.

The O'Morchoe gave some rather weak precedents on the use of foreign titles recognized by the English Crown. He misinterprets the law by thinking that the Act 11 of Elizabeth I merely "reserved the rights of the Chiefs and recognised them by patents" (i.e., Letters Patent) whereas the act made such titles "utterly extinct."

The O'Morchoe's claim, disregarding the Irish law that no holder of a Gaelic title could surrender his titles on behalf of heirs and successors, believed that Henry VIII's Act had been one which the Irish kings and aristocracy had willingly accepted. "The Act of His Majesty Henry VIII, previously referred to, merged all such independence, whether actual or implied, in such a title, in the Crown. All Ireland became a feud of the King, and then Chiefs held as feudal lords from the Crown." That was the English intention but not, as we have demonstrated, the Irish reality.

The O'Morchoe's claim was:

> The evidence in support of a claim to represent a former recognized Chief must be a pedigree registered in Ulster's Office. Once the right to the use of the titles shall have been determined by the official act of the Crown, it becomes only a question of the proof of the claimant's pedigree that he is the lineal male representative of the last recognised Chief. To determine the right to the use of the titles rests with the Crown as the Fountain of Honour; and although the titles have been recognised by courtesy at the Royal and Viceregal Courts, yet the absence of any official act either to determine the right to their use or to accord them a definite precedence, as in the case of the Maltese Nobles, leaves the matter in an unsatisfactory state, which only the Crown can settle.

The English Crown was, in fact, irrelevant to the continued existence of Gaelic titles. As the early years of the twentieth century progressed, the English Crown was to become even more irrelevant in the political wishes of the Irish people in their reassertion of an independent state.

Perhaps one of the most famous characters in modern Irish history was a descendant of the Ó Rathaille chiefly line of County Kerry. This was of the same clan as the poet Aodhagán Ó Rathaille, who wrote that his family had served the Eóghanacht kings before the Christian period. The O'Rahilly's family is sometimes mistaken as being of the Breifne O'Reillys. The family had ceased to use the "O" during the years of suppression, and the family lived as plain "Reilly." The "O" was revived by Michael Joseph O'Rahilly (1875–1916). He was not consistent about its use until 1911, when he then adopted The O'Rahilly[22] as a nom de plume for his writings. It appears that, both at that time and subsequently, it was assumed that he had adopted it as a title but he never actually did so.

The O'Rahilly had joined Sinn Féin and was closely involved with the production of the journal *Sinn Fein*. From May 6, 1910 through 1911 he was the anonymous author of a series called "The Arms of the Clans," each article dealing with two clan names. That the author did not fully understand the nature of the subject is demonstrated by his ascribing the personal arms, crest and motto of the Chief as belonging to the clan itself and to any person bearing the name. This mistaken conception is something that occurs even today.

The O'Rahilly, while disagreeing with the timing of the 1916 uprising in Ireland, nevertheless fought in the insurrection and was killed at the General Post Office in Dublin, the insurgent headquarters during the fighting. There is still an O'Rahilly, Michael, although he is not inclined to use the title nor is he recognised by the Chief Herald of Ireland. His mother was Elgin Barry, a sister of Kevin Barry, executed by the British in 1920. Madam O'Rahilly had attempted to rescue her brother from Mountjoy Jail just before his execution but was unsuccessful. She married Richard ("Mac") The O'Rahilly in 1935. The O'Rahilly was a barrister and he joined Nobel laureate Seán MacBride (a former chief of staff of the Irish Republican Army and son of the executed 1916 leader Major John MacBride and actress Maud Gonne) in forming Clann na Poblachta in 1946. The party joined a coalition Irish government in which MacBride was foreign minister from 1948 to 1951. The O'Rahilly became treasurer of the party. He later joined MacBride in forming the Irish section of Amnesty International. Madam O'Rahilly died in December 1997.

It is interesting that Arthur Griffith, founder of Sinn Féin, approved the idea of the resumption of Gaelic titles "as part of the counter-movement aimed at de-Anglicization." A *Sinn Fein* editorial, doubtless written by Griffith, said: "We thoroughly approve of the representatives of the old Irish aristocracy reassuming their titles."[23] It should be pointed out that Griffith was never at any time a republican. He had formed Sinn Féin in 1904 as a dual-monarchist party using the model of the Austro-Hungarian Empire for a his ideal of a Anglo-Irish Empire. It was mistakenly believed by the English government that Sinn Féin was the driving force behind the 1916 uprising. Sinn Féin, therefore, became a rallying symbol of the republic in popular perception among the Irish. Republicans joined it and changed the dual-monarchy concept to the republican ideal by adopting a new constitution in 1917. Griffith's subsequent role in the Treaty negotiations, accepting a partitioned Ireland with the Free State within the British Commonwealth, begins to make more sense in light of his ideas of dual monarchism with England.

Marcus Burke, The O'Rahilly's biographer, believed that in the 1840s prominent nationalists like The O'Gorman Mahon and The O'Donoghue had adopted Irish titles in this "anti-British context."[24] This was certainly not so of O'Donoghue of The Glens nor of others who merely publicly reassumed the titles they believed they had inherited and did not "adopt" them.

In December 1918 a general election was to change the face of Ireland. At the dissolution of the Westminster Parliament the Irish Party, pledged to achieve "Home Rule," held 68 seats; there were 10 held by Independent Nationalists and 7 seats held by Sinn Féin; the Unionists held only 18 seats. In the new General Election Sinn Féin, pledged to making a unilateral declaration of independence and asserting an Irish republic, won 73 seats out of the total 105. The Irish Party was reduced to 6 seats and the Unionists increased their seats to 26, many of the extra seats being held on the split vote between Sinn Féin and the Irish Party. In accordance with their manifesto, the Sinn Féin Members of Parliament withdrew from Westminster and established an Irish Parliament in Dublin, called the Dáil. They invited all Irish elected representatives to take seats in the new assembly and they issued a Declaration of Independence on January 21, 1919.

The London government's reaction was to declare the Dáil an illegal assembly and commence to arrest these democratically elected representatives. This led to the War of Independence. In spite of the continuance of this war and attempts by the English administration to destroy Sinn Féin's credibility with the electorate the January 1920 municipal elections gave Sinn Féin control of 72 town and city councils. Coalitions of Sinn Féin and the Irish Party took joint control of a further 26 town and city councils. Thus 98 out of 127 town and city councils recognized the Dáil as the legitimate government in Ireland.

Again in June 1920 elections for county and rural district councils and boards of guardians saw Sinn Féin win control of 28 out of the 32 county councils (giving republican control of five out of the nine Ulster counties); they also won 186 out of 206 rural district councils and 138 out of 154 boards of guardians.

Arbitrarily, the English government pushed through a Government of Ireland Act (1920) setting up "Home Rule" parliaments in Dublin and Belfast, with the idea of partitioning Ulster. The problem in Ulster was that five out of the nine counties had voted overwhelmingly for the republic and only four counties were for the maintenance of union. Once more, arbitrarily, London declared a General Election in May 1921 for the two parliaments, bringing in proportional representation in the hope of decreasing the support given to Sinn Féin. Even so, the state of the parties in an all-Ireland context was that Sinn Féin held 130 seats, the Irish Party won 6 seats, and the Unionists had 44 seats. Partition was foisted on Ireland at gunpoint.

On July 11, 1921, in the wake of these elections, negotiations with "the Irish representatives" and the London government began. On December 6, 1921, under threat of the renewal of "an immediate and terrible war," the Irish plenipotentiaries, without authority from the Dáil, signed the "Articles of Agreement for a Treaty between Great Britain and Ireland." It was placed before the Dáil as a fait accompli giving Ireland a Free State within the British Commonwealth but, under Clause 11, allowing the representatives of the Unionist Belfast parliament, already set up, one month from the passing of the ratification of the Treaty to withdraw, if they so wished, from the Free State and rejoin the United Kingdom.

On January 7, 1922, the Treaty was approved by the Dáil by 64 votes to 57. Some republican representatives, such as Laurence Ginnell, had been out of the country and thus not able to cast a vote. Of the Irish Army commands, twelve were against the Treaty and only seven were supportive of it. The result was a slide into civil war, which ended in 1923 after a bloody and bitter conflict.

In June 1922 a general election was held to decide support for the Treaty. Although the Treaty spoke initially of a thirty-two county Free State, the territory under the control of the Belfast parliament did not take part, so only 128 seats in the 26 counties were actually contested. Pro-Treaty candidates won 58; Republicans won 36; and Labour, Farmers and Independents held 34.

On December 6, 1922, the Free State came into being. On December 7, only twenty hours later, the Belfast Unionist Parliament petitioned King George V, under Article 11 of the Treaty, to be allowed to withdraw from the Free State and rejoin the United Kingdom.

The Free State came into being inheriting the (English) statute and common law under which Ireland had been governed for three hundred years. Some voices had been raised earlier regarding attempts to revive the spirit of

Brehon law, not the actuality of it, as a means to create an intrinsically Irish law system. The barrister Laurence Ginnell, an Irish Party member of Parliament and later a Sinn Féin deputy in the Dáil of 1919 to 1921, the distinguished author of a book on Brehon law, was one who was interested in this concept. In practical terms, this meant the reconsideration of the philosophical principles of the Brehon system.

Another legal mind who supported the idea at the time was barrister and King's Counsel James Creed Meredith, who had been entrusted by the Irish Government of 1919–1921 with drafting the Constitution and rules for the republic's law courts. Creed Meredith became President of the Irish Supreme Court. In one instance, while hearing a case, he actually pointed out that he considered English common law retrograde in a matter of women's rights and applied Brehon law to give judgment in favor of the appeal of an unmarried mother for medical expenses. According to historian Dorothy Macardle: "This created an interesting link with old Irish principles of justice and preserved continuity between the old Brehon Law of Ireland and the Republican courts."[25]

However, when the Free State emerged, the inherited English law system was accepted and no further consideration was given to the matter. As the Free State moved, with the 1937 constitution, into being a "dictionary republic" and from thence to a sovereign republic, by referendum, on April 18, 1949, the laws of the state remained unaltered. Under that law system all Gaelic titles were still "utterly extinct." This being so, a curious dissonance emerged between those holding Gaelic titles and the state bureaucracy.

CHAPTER SIX

"COURTESY RECOGNITION": A CONFLICT OF PERCEPTIONS

FOLLOWING THE CHANGE OF STATUS OF IRELAND to Henry VIII's new kingdom, in 1552 the English administration established a heraldic officer called the Ulster King of Arms. The first to hold this office was Bartholomew Butler, who had served as Hampnes Pursuivant in 1529, Rouge Croix in 1535 and York Herald in 1538. On February 2, 1552, Edward VI invested Butler as Ulster King of Arms—the heraldic officer for all of Ireland. His son, Philip, became Athlone Pursuivant of Arms, his assistant. The task of the office was concerned with the recording of the titles granted or recognized by the English Crown in the new Kingdom of Ireland. While it could, and did, eventually draw up genealogies for Gaelic aristocratic families, especially during the more liberal nineteenth century, it did not, nor could it in law, take cognizance of any Gaelic titles. Much depended on the individual character of the Ulster Herald and how he interpreted his office. Sir Arthur Vicars, for example, was supposed to have accepted, on the genealogical certificate of O'Morchoe, that he had a *right* to claim a Gaelic title.

After the Free State came into being, Ulster's Office continued to operate from the Bedford Tower in Dublin Castle, fulfilling the same functions it had discharged since 1552. The Free State was, of course, part of the British Commonwealth, and the head of state was still the English Crown in its capacity as head of that Commonwealth. Therefore there was no inconsistency with the continued jurisdiction of the Crown's herald over the whole of Ireland.

In 1940 Sir Neville Wilkinson, the Ulster King of Arms, died. Thomas Sadlier, the Deputy Ulster, continued to administer the office. Eamon de Valéra's new constitution of 1937 had, however, removed the Crown as head of state with its personal representative, the Governor General, since 1922 no longer a viceroy. Under Articles 12/1 he had instituted the office of President of Ireland (*Uachtarán na hÉireann*) "who shall take precedence over all other persons in the State." So far as the authority of the Ulster King of Arms was concerned, a gray area existed. On December 11, 1936, de Valéra's External Relations Act was introduced, which delimited the functions of the Crown in the field of external relations of the Free State but maintained the link with the British Commonwealth. This remained the position until the 1949 Declaration of the Republic and the repeal of the External Relations Act. At this point the Irish state was deemed to have left the Commonwealth. Did, technically, the Ulster King of Arms continue to have heraldic jurisdiction over all of Ireland between 1937 and 1949 by virtue of the English Crown's position as head of the Commonwealth? It is a debatable point. Certainly some heraldic experts have pointed out that as King George VI of England was Crowned King of Ireland on May 12, 1937, and the 1937 Constitution was not enacted until July 1, 1939, coming into force from December 29 of that year the act could not retrospectively alter the legal authority of his herald.

Whatever the ambiguities were, in 1943 the continuance of the office of the Ulster King of Arms in Dublin Castle came to the attention of Dr. Richard Hayes, Director of the National Library of Ireland, and Dr. Edgeworth Anthony Lysaght (1887–1986), who had adopted Edward MacLysaght as the form of his name in 1920. In 1943 he had joined the staff of the National Library. MacLysaght was to create the new Genealogical Office. He later admitted that he was "an amateur in genealogy and an ignoramus in heraldry."[1] However, he was to be Chief Genealogical Officer and Keeper of Manuscripts from 1943 to 1955 as well as chairman of the Irish Manuscripts Commission.

Son of the Cork novelist Sidney Royce Lysaght (1860–1941), MacLysaght had been a republican in politics since his youth. When in 1917 David Lloyd George made an attempt to hustle Irish leaders into an agreement by summoning a gathering of representative Irishmen to find a basis for a settlement between Nationalists and Unionists, called the Irish Convention, MacLysaght was one of the 104 delegates who sat for the 8 months. Coincidentally, Walter MacMorrough Kavanagh, The MacMorrough, was another. MacLysaght was then a young farmer and amateur publisher. He sat on the commission with the approval of the Sinn Féin leadership and reported to them daily on discussion. At one point the Archbishop of Dublin, Dr. John Henry Bernard, a scholar who had been a divinity professor and Fellow of Trinity College, Dublin, had to rebuke MacLysaght for "threatening" the Convention on Sinn Féin's behalf.[2] MacLysaght was imprisoned during the War of Independence (1919–21) by the British authorities. He served as an Irish senator from 1922 to 1925 and later joined Fianna Fáil when it broke away from Sinn Féin under Eamon de Valéra in 1926. This gave him ready access to leading members of the Fianna Fáil government party, and de Valéra was now Prime Minister. It is important to appreciate MacLysaght's background because it helps to partially understand his attitude, which led to subsequent events. His personal contact with Prime Minister de Valéra resulted in the Irish Government sanctioning the expropriation of the Heraldic Museum and offices of the Ulster Kings of Arms on March 31, 1943, and the confiscation of all manuscripts and properties connected with the office. Dr. Edward MacLysaght was then appointed Chief Genealogical Officer with the remit of setting up a new office as a subsection of the National Library of Ireland.

That this move was viewed with some concern by the English Crown's heraldic offices may be seen by the initial reluctance of the Garter King of Arms, Sir Algar Howard, to accept the validity of the new Irish office. Indeed, the office of the Ulster King of Arms was, in fact, removed to the College of Arms in London, without its original records and properties, and a new Ulster King of Arms appointed. The office later combined into the Norroy and Ulster King of Arms and still exists. It continues to exercise its authority over Northern Ireland, as part of the United Kingdom territory.

There grew up a general but unsustainable myth that the Genealogical Office was but a continuance of Ulster's office and that its Chief Genealogical Officer, who seemed to take the title Chief Herald after the Irish Free State became a republic in 1949, was but the continuance of the Ulster King of Arms. The Dublin office was, however, a new creation by the Irish State and not the inheritance of the historic heraldic office established in 1552, which was now in London.

Such myths and discrepancies are, perhaps, understandable within the confusion caused by the creation of any new state and we must remember that a new state of Ireland was in the process of being created. The problem arises only where the Genealogical Office itself claims its authority from 1552. For example, on August 25, 1990, the Chief Herald, Donal Begley, was introduced as the twenty-third "Chief Herald," and it was stated that his office had been created in Tudor times. Neither the Chief Herald nor Denis Lyons TD, the Minister of State for Culture, the Chief Herald's superior, who attended these proceedings, felt obliged to correct this misstatement.

For those maintaining or seeking recognition for Gaelic titles, this background meant a problem was looming.

De Valéra had been aware of the survival of many of the Gaelic princely families. In preparing the 1937 Constitution, he had even considered the idea of creating a "Prince President" based on the model of Prince Louis Napoleon of France (later Napoleon III), who had become President of the Second Republic.

Emissaries had sounded out Lord Inchiquin (The O'Brien) as the direct descendant of the High King Brían Bóroimhe.[3] Sources close to de Valéra at this time said that not only The O'Brien, but also several Anglo-Irish peers, were considered. Three were specifically mentioned. One was the eighth Viscount Powerscourt (1880–1947), who had been a senator in the Free State. Another name mentioned was the eighth Earl of Granard (1874–1948), a former Deputy Speaker of the United Kingdom House of Lords, who became a Free State senator from 1922 to 1934. The third name was Eduard Carl Richard, eighth Count von Taafe of the Holy Roman Empire (1898–1967), who had returned to Ireland to live in Dublin and pursue the profession of a gemologist. The naming of these non-Gaelic peers in the matter of the presidency would indicate that de Valéra was not particularly concerned with securing a link to Gaelic Ireland. He merely was considering a representative from any distinguished Irish family.

In 1944 Edward MacLysaght, as Chief Genealogical Officer, started to give some consideration to the idea of giving "recognition" to those claiming Gaelic titles. The problem, he felt, was how these titles could be recognized by the state. That something had to be done by the new Genealogical Office was obvious. Several chiefs had been asserting their titles, listing themselves in *Thom's Directories* and in *Whitaker's*.

MacLysaght, admitting that he knew nothing of nobility law, was, however, aware that the new 1937 Constitution (Article 40.2) stated:

1. Titles of nobility shall not be conferred by the State.
2. No titles of nobility or honor may be accepted by any citizen except without the prior approval of the Government.

He apparently did not realize that if the Irish state wished to give "courtesy recognition" to the Gaelic titles, it could simply do so under the international usages then current. It was the "Gaelic" aspect that appeared to confuse him. There was no problem giving courtesy recognition to those holding titles issued during the Kingdom of Ireland period of 1541 to 1801, nor to those bestowed by the successor state of the United Kingdom of Great Britain and

Ireland (1801–1922). Courtesy was also paid to foreign titles, even titles of states that had ceased to exist, such as the Holy Roman Empire, which Napoleon abolished in 1806. Similarly, the state did not question the right of Count George Noble Plunkett (1851–1948), a Papal Count, to use his title. Why, then, was there such a problem with the Gaelic titles inherited from the old kingdoms of Ireland prior to the Tudor Conquest of the country?

There can be only one answer, and one that appears to be confirmed by MacLysaght's reported conversation on the matter with de Valéra. Knowledge of the subject of the native nobility had reached such an abysmally low level that these titles were not even considered to be titles of nobility. Three hundred years of historical propaganda had demeaned the role of the Gaelic aristocracy to the point where Charles O'Donnell, a Member of Parliament between 1906 and 1910, himself descended from the Princes of Tirconnell, could, twenty years before this time, say it was "an ignorant practice" to talk of kings in Ireland.[4] This attitude was all-pervasive in the modern Irish psyche. MacLysaght consulted de Valéra and the resultant decision, made without any reference to academic authorities, either historical or legal, has remained the basis of the Genealogical Office's policy on the subject of Gaelic titles.

MacLysaght recalled:

> When in 1943 the question of the recognition of Chiefs came up for consideration I—being then Chief Herald—consulted the Taoiseach, Mr. de Valéra, and he agreed that the chieftainries were designations rather than titles and that consequently we [the Genealogical Office] should go ahead and, after thorough investigation, formally register any person claiming to be the Chief of his Name when the evidence was found acceptable.[5]

I am not alone in finding this passage incredible. Heraldic expert Gerard Crotty also found it extraordinary, leaving aside the point that MacLysaght was not appointed as Chief Herald in 1943 but was then only the Genealogical Officer.[6] Crotty agrees that the piece of semantics worked out by de Valéra and MacLysaght appeared to be an attempt to avoid confronting the reality that a Gaelic title was, in fact, a title of nobility. The attempt to find a word that would avoid this fact, and the choice of "designation," seems less than worthy of de Valéra's reputed pedantry. Amusingly, it is merely a dictionary synonym for a title. A designation is "a distinctive name; personal appellation, hereditary or not, denoting or implying office or nobility or distinction or merit."

The sleight-of-hand that Gaelic titles were not titles but merely "designations" pointed to the implication that MacLysaght must have thought that the Genealogical Office was empowered to create a designation and that this was not the same thing as creating a title. Yet we see the immediate contradiction in the very first list of Chiefs whose designations were recognized by MacLysaght. This was published in the official government publication *Éire Iris Oifigiúil* (December 22, 1944). Among them is MacDermot, *Prince of Coolavin*. In recognizing that MacDermot was a *prince* of an Irish territory, even such a small one, the Genealogical Office, with Government approval, was clearly recognizing a *title* and not a "designation" in its meaning of the word. Matters get even more complicated when, as we shall see, MacDermot was, in reality, Prince of Moylurg, and "Prince of Coolavin" was an unhistoric title bestowed by the local people of the Coolavin estate. It is also fascinating to note that, in the first official announcement in Irish by the Government of the recognition of these "designations," the phrase *úsáide na gairme*—"use of the *title*"—crept in. *Gairm rí* is a title of a king, and *gairm uaisleachta* is a title of nobility.

It is hard to accept the theory that de Valéra and MacLysaght were acting in the belief that they were not recognizing titles that already had a historical existence. Nor that they believed they could, somehow, have the authority to bestow such historic titles as modern designations guided by rules devised within the Genealogical Office. The attitude of some subsequent Chief Heralds is to hotly deny that they are making a creation of any sort. Yet one Chief Herald, Donal Begley, at a public inauguration ceremony for The O'Long of Garranelong in 1990, was quite clear what he was doing. He said: "Accept this parchment *designating you* as O'Long of Garranelongy and Chief of the Name *by my office under the authority of the Government of Ireland*." He was not thereby merely "recognizing" an already existing O'Long but creating one on the authority of the Irish government. As previously mentioned, the appropriate Minister of State was in attendance and did not correct the fact that Mr. Begley was claiming to be "granting the title of Chief to *Mister* Denis Long."

The action of the Chief Herald's Office was not to acknowledge existing titles used in a previous Irish state but to arbitrate and designate who held the title on the basis of a primogeniture descent system derived from the very laws that abolished the titles and made them "utterly extinct." This caused immediate merriment in academic and legal circles. Edward MacLysaght admitted:

> Our action at the Genealogical Office in recognizing Chiefs encountered some opposition from a few historians and Celtic scholars on the ground that to determine chieftainry by primogeniture was a departure from the principles of the Gaelic Irish system. We argued . . . that to reject primogeniture would result in taking no action at all in the matter.[7]

This was a curious justification for what was clearly a legally questionable and even unconstitutional decision. It also demonstrated MacLysaght's lack of knowledge of the situation concerning the legal framework of giving courtesy recognition to titles of former states. Why the office felt that it did not need to consult experts in the field remains a mystery. These courtesy recognitions began as an internal civil service office procedure. There was no Act of the Irish Parliament or ministerial approved written guidelines instructing the office on the methods of "recognition." What was happening, therefore, was that an office of the Irish government was taking upon itself to arbitrate over the recognition of titles bestowed in a former state by the act of retrospective alteration of the dynastic laws by which those titles were governed.

In 1998 an Italian court ruling concerning Gaelic titles, while dealing with the case of a bogus title holder, made the following relevant observation on international law concerning such matters:

> Although it is true that the Chief Herald of Ireland has recognized several Gaelic titles . . . the actual legality of such an act must in itself be highly questionable and has never been determined in any Irish Court. A Civil Servant, irrespective of whatever titular office he may hold, is bound by the laws of his own State. As English Common law has abolished Gaelic Chiefly titles, their very recognition by the Chief Herald of Ireland, even as a courtesy, must logically be questionable if not actually illegal under existing Irish Law. Nor, as this Court has previously ruled, could the mere fact that the Chief Herald grants such courtesy recognition to the bearers of Gaelic titles gives him any lawful authority over them, whether to alter their original forms or nature, annul their laws of succession, or in anyway to negate their hereditary rights vested therein.[8]

This view was known to many people in the area of nobiliary studies at the time.

By 1944 Edward MacLysaght had decided to draw up what came to be known as *Clár na dTaoiseach*—the Register of Chiefs and Chieftains. The first announcement of the courtesy recognition of Chiefs was made in the Government Gazette *Éire Iris Oifigiúil* of December 22, 1944:

> For centuries and until immediately after the disbandment of the Gaelic system, the *derbhfine*, who could trace their ancestors for four generations, elected the successor of the Chief.
>
> Later, the Chief was chosen from one of such a family according to seniority.

The Gaelic genealogists always accepted this latter tradition in addition to the practice of election.

With respect to the following, the Genealogical Office examined their pedigrees in accordance with primogeniture, from the last Chief to be inaugurated or who had that particular distinction *de facto*, confirming his progeny.

Their names are listed in this office as Chiefs as well as by their family names, and their positions are acknowledged by "courtesy recognition."

In addition to the list, the names of two Chiefs are given who have a legal right to claim the title but the office has not made a confirmation of the lineage.

In certain cases, not mentioned here, even though a claim of a Chief is made from ancient Chiefs we have no knowledge of it.

In other cases even though we have knowledge of a Chief, we have no claims or usage of the title at the Genealogy Office.

If the list is added to from time to time, the Chiefs names will be announced in the *Iris Oifigiúil*.

The chiefs given "courtesy recognition" were:

MacDiarmada (MacDermot, Prince of Coolavin)
MacGiolla Chuda (MacGillycuddy of the Reeks)
Ó Ceallacháin (O'Callaghan)
Ó Conchobhair Donn (O'Conor Don)
Ó Donnchadha an Ghleanna (O'Donoghue of the Glens)
Ó Donnabháin (O'Donovan)
Ó Murchadha (Mac Murrough)
Ó Néill Clann Aodha Bhuidhe (O'Neill of Clanaboy)
Ó Sionnaigh (The Fox)
Ó Tuathal Fear Tíre (O'Toole).

It was stated that The Ó Gráda (O'Grady) and Ó Ceallaghin (O'Kelly) "while not representative of Chieftainries in the strict sense, having long been styled under [these designations] and, their pedigrees duly authenticate, are on record at the Genealogical Office."

A slightly different English version of the announcement was given in *Thom's Directory* for 1945, and the name of O'Brien of Thomond, O'Donel of Tirconnell and O'Morchoe was then added. It was also announced that the title of MacDermot Roe was dormant. *Thom's* acknowledged that the titles had originated from and been passed down by Brehon law succession but went on:

The descent of the following, by primogeniture from the last inaugurated or *de facto* chieftain, has been examined by the Genealogical Office, Dublin Castle. Subject to the possible survival in some cases of senior lines at present unidentified, they are recorded at the Genealogical Office as Chiefs of the Name and are recognized by courtesy. Certain Chiefs whose pedigree have not been finally proved are included in this list on account of their prescriptive standing.

This was a reference to The O'Grady and O'Kelly, whose names are referred to in the same manner as in the *Iris Oifigiúil*.

Immediately, another problem arose. If the Genealogical Office was merely recognizing an *existing title*, the reference to "designation" that kept slipping into the more correct term "title" departed from its objective by placing new additions on the chiefly titles. When The O'Grady was finally fully recognized, he was designated "The O'Grady *of Kilballyowen*," the territorial designation being an entirely new addition that no O'Grady had used in the past. The title had simply been "The O'Grady." Gerard Crotty observes: "A number of other chiefs seem also to have acquired additional designations of this kind, through the courtesy of the Office."[9] MacLysaght does confess that he had reservations about the nature of the title The O'Grady, for, as Crotty points out, "in creating a new designation, which after all is a title, he came perilously close to infringing [on] Article 40 of the Constitution," which says that the Irish State cannot confer titles.

The Genealogical Office apparently decided that the Gaelic titles should be based on the Tudor English attempts to translate the Gaelic forms. "Chief of the Name" was added. This also presented anomalies with the Office recognizing both The MacDermot, Prince of Coolavin, and The MacDermot Roe as "Chiefs of the Name." As Gerard Crotty pointed out in bemusement:

> Both of these belonged to the Moylurg house. Logic must surely demand that both cannot have been simultaneously Chief of the Name. While both may be described as chieftains, depending on how we understand that term, only the Prince of Coolavin could have been chief of the whole sept: MacDermot Roe represented a minor though yet considerable branch and may best be referred to as a chieftain.[10]

Another problem later arose for some people in the matter of heraldic territorial authority. It was argued that, having signed the Treaty of Rome, which forbade member states from making territorial claims over other states in either legislating or attempting to have judicial authority, the Irish Republic's territorial claim over Northern Ireland appeared to breach this agreement. The Prime Minister, Bertie Ahern, was to explain that Articles 2 and 3 of the

Constitution, which made such claims, were merely "expression[s] of an aspiration." In 1998 the matter was resolved when those articles were amended in accordance with an expression of the aspiration of a majority of Irish people for reunification rather than stating a territorial claim. Yet the point that worried heraldic experts was that the Chief Herald's Office, as a civil service department of the Irish State, was making territorial claims by exercising heraldic jurisdiction within Northern Ireland, which encroached on the judicial role of the Norroy and Ulster King of Arms. Did the Genealogical Office have legal authority to arbitrate on the pedigrees of those within the Norroy and Ulster King of Arms territory? Similar concerns have been raised as to whether the Office also could arbitrate in the matter of titles held by citizens of other countries, such as Spain and Portugal and the United States, which refuses to allow its citizens to bear any title of nobility.

Between 1944 and 1989 the Genealogical Office's list remained substantially unaltered, although the second Chief Herald to hold office, Gerard Slevin (1919–98), gave courtesy recognition to a new MacMorrough Kavanagh. On January 2, 1959, after the Borris line had ended without male heirs in primogeniture terms, the Genealogical Office registered a pedigree and a grant of arms to William Butler Kavanagh of the Ballyhale line and recognized him as The Mac Murrough Kavanagh, Chief of His Name. It is further accepted that Gerard Slevin appears to have placed a slip of paper to the *Clár na dTaoiseach*, the Register of Chiefs, with the name of William Butler Kavanagh and his son written on it. Curiously, the Genealogical Office seemed to encourage, or at least made no attempts to deny, the belief that the line was considered dormant. Standard reference works such as *Debrett's*, *Burke's Irish Family Records* (1976) and several other studies, including Ida Grehan's *Irish Family Histories*, repeated this claim. In *Burke's Introduction to Irish Ancestry* (1976), and printed opposite an article on the Irish Genealogical Office by Gerard Slevin, Edward MacLysaght was able to claim the title had been dormant since 1958. This allowed two lobbies to emerge—one supporting the son of the daughter of the penultimate MacMorrough Kavanagh, who had died in 1953, and the other supporting an elected "chief" of a Kavanagh clan society. The Genealogical Office stated that records for that period have failed to turn up copies of relevant supporting documents or correspondence and requested William Butler Kavanagh to send copies of the relevant correspondence. The Chief Herald stated:

> I am not prepared to make any further entries in *Clár na dTaoiseach* except on
> the basis of a fresh, rigorous and independent examination of the available ev-

idence and records and, in particular, that I am not prepared to make such an entry on the basis of arms granted or pedigrees registered by one or other of my predecessors, unless the documents and evidence on which those decisions were based is available to me for review.[11]

MacMorrough Kavanagh complied with the Genealogical Office's request. On May 22, 2000, the Chief Herald wrote to the tanist of MacMorrough Kavanagh that the file containing correspondence concerning his family had come "to light." The file contained the evidence that the family knew existed. Brendan O'Donoghue added: "I am sorry that the failure until now to turn up the old file here has led to unnecessary correspondence as to the events of 1958–1962. Now, however, there can no longer be any doubt but that Mr. Slevin recognized your grandfather and, in turn, your father as The MacMorrough Kavanagh." Indeed, Gerard Slevin had written to Madam MacMorrough Kavanagh on June 26, 1962 that with the death of William Butler Kavanagh in that year his eldest son "automatically becomes Chief of the Name according to our records."

In 1969, Robert McDonnell was given courtesy recognition by Chief Herald Slevin as MacDonnell of The Glens, descendants of the Kings of Dál Riada. This was reported in the *Irish Times* of September 10, 1969.

In 1989 other courtesy recognitions began to be made. One of the most astonishing recognitions of a Gaelic title by the then Chief Herald, Donal Begley, was that of The Joyce of Joyce's Country. The name Joyce is from the Norman personal name Jois. They arrived in Connacht in the thirteenth century. They became Gaelicized, intermarried and proliferated, but they were considered "degenerate English" and one of the "Twelve Tribes of Galway." Joyce's Country was to be found in the barony of Ross (County Galway). By no stretch of the imagination could a Joyce be regarded as possessor of an ancient Gaelic chiefly title.

However, there is some confusion as to the reasoning why Joyce appears on the Chief Herald's list of Gaelic Chiefs. Gerard Crotty, in his capacity as Heraldic Adviser to the Standing Council of Irish Chiefs and Chieftains, and writing on behalf of Mr. Joyce in a note to the author of June 22, 2000, felt that there was never any intention of implying that the Joyces were Gaelic. The inclusion of this title in the list stemmed from the strongly Gaelicized character of the Joyces, who had apparently had Chiefs "after the Irish fashion." The style used by the Genealogical Office in referring to Mr. John Edward Joyce was "Joyce of Joyce's Country" without the prefixed "The."

The current Chief Herald, Brendan O'Donoghue, appeared to confirm this, writing to both the author and to the Standing Council of Irish Chiefs and Chieftains. "While John Joyce is accepted as head of the Joyce family, he has never been officially recognized as a Gaelic Chief of the Name."[12]

Although John Joyce was introduced to the Irish President, among the Gaelic Chiefs, Gerard Crotty argued that he was introduced as an Irish Chief not a Gaelic Chief. Crotty stated: "Mr. Begley, when Chief Herald, once told me that the number of non-Gaelic families whose heads could be considered eligible for recognition as Irish Chiefs was very limited. I presume that the criterion for this has to be whether such families had been so Gaelicized as to have had 'chiefs after the Irish fashion.'"[13]

Nevertheless, the perception among many was that Mr. Joyce had, indeed, been given recognition as a Gaelic Chief. At a lecture given by Gerard Crotty to the Irish Congress of Genealogy, in Trinity College, Dublin, during September, 1994, with Chief Herald Donald Begley in the chair, a questioner from the audience demanded to know how Mr. Joyce, as head of a Norman family, could be recognized as a Gaelic Chief. Crotty recalls that he passed the question to the Chief Herald, who said it was his right to accept or reject any application which came before him and that Mr. Joyce's [great?] grandfather was described on his tombstone as "Chief of his Name."

The question remained as to the nature of Gaelic Chiefs. Were the Gaelic titles that were being recognized belonging to the descendants of the original kings and princes of Milesian origin, or were they to include some of the Gaelicized family heads, such as the Joyce family? If the latter were so, similar recognitions might have to be made for such families as the Fitzgeralds, Barrys, Blakes, Burkes, Lacys and Powers, arriving in the twelfth or thirteenth centuries and merging into the Irish social system.

All these matters were leading to discord between the Genealogical Office and the Chiefs. The core of the problem appeared to be that the Irish Government had not appointed properly qualified heralds to take charge of the Office from the time it had been established. Usually the person appointed Chief Herald was the Director of the National Library, a civil service administrator not qualified in heraldry, genealogy or international nobiliary law—let alone Brehon law of dynastic succession. The problems became more marked as the holders of the Gaelic titles banded together and found a collective voice.

In June 1991 Terence Maguire, recently recognized by the Chief Herald as The Maguire, Prince of Fermanagh, was visiting the Heraldic Museum in Dublin and saw the banners of those Gaelic title holders who had been given courtesy recognition hanging there. He later wrote that he asked himself

"Would it not be beneficial to our country if these Gaelic princes were to come together and form a Council?" He wrote to each Chief on the *Clár na dTaoiseach*, proposing a meeting to discuss the formation of a Council.[14]

Conor O'Brien, Prince of Thomond, replied: "I strongly believe that we should have some say in the future of Ireland, not political but certainly cultural and economic, as we are, whether we like it or not, the representatives of the old Gaelic Order and represent a very large number of people world wide."[15]

President Mary Robinson was also enthusiastic about the idea and invited the Chiefs to a reception at *Aras an Uachtaráin*, the presidential residence, on the day of the inaugural meeting. The Maguire asked the Chief Herald, Donal Begley, to attend. Bord Fáilte (the Irish Tourist Board), being informed, announced that it would sponsor an official lunch. Jury's Hotel in Dublin offered the use of its services for the proposed council meetings.

On October 5, 1991, for the first time in centuries, representatives of the Gaelic aristocracy of Ireland met together. Thirteen of those holding recognized Gaelic titles attended, with Admiral Pascual O'Dogherty representing The Ó Dochertaigh and his tanist together with Messrs. John and Patrick Joyce. Also invited to attend was Gerard Crotty, a graduate of University College, Cork, a Trustee of the State Heraldic Museum and published expert on heraldic matters as well as a founder of The Heraldry Society of Ireland. He was elected Honorary Secretary to the Council, a position he held until 1995, when he became Heraldic Adviser to the council.

The first chairman was The Maguire, Prince of Fermanagh. Letters from Irish Prime Minister Charles Haughey and Chief Herald Donal Begley greeted the establishment of the *Buanchomhairle Thaoisigh Éireann* (Standing Council of Irish Chiefs and Chieftains), as it was named. Letters of advice were offered by the Lord Lyon King of Arms, Sir Malcolm Innes, explaining the method of how the Standing Council of Scottish Chiefs had been established.

During the debate on the draft constitution, the problem that has continued to bedevil the Irish Gaelic title holders emerged. Terence McCarthy, the *soi-disant* MacCarthy Mór, was accepted as the most academically qualified in this field, having studied heraldry, genealogy and Irish history. Terence, for reasons we will discuss in chapter 12, had become a firm adherent of Brehon law succession. He correctly pointed out that there were differences between the Irish and Scottish positions on Chiefship. The Lord Lyon was an officer of the Crown of Scotland, a Crown still in existence; therefore, the Scottish chiefs held their titles under that Crown. Irish Chiefs, contrary to this, derived their titles from a state that had existed prior to 1541, when Henry had created his Kingdom of Ireland. Irish Gaelic titles were not a creation of this "Crown of

Ireland," which, indeed, had abolished all Gaelic titles. Nor were these titles a creation of the modern Irish State of which the Chief Herald was only a civil servant, unlike the Lord Lyon King of Arms. Any legal or judicial authority of the Chief Herald of Ireland did not apply to the Irish Chiefs. Scottish Chiefs were subject to the Lord Lyon King of Arms, representing his monarch. The Chief Herald's recourse to primogeniture ruling on their titles was arbitrary and without authority. It was a retrospective change of dynastic law by a successor state. The arguments were correct if their advocate was bogus.

At the July 25, 1992 meeting, Gerald Crotty reiterated that no one could alter the mode of succession of the Chiefs, "which by their nature emanated from Gaelic titles. In this connection the simple resort to primogeniture by the Office of Arms in 1943 had been most arbitrary."

Eventually a constitution was drawn up making the council have the status of a company limited by guarantees. Its objects were:

a. To consider matters affecting Irish Chiefs, Chieftains and the Clans they represent
b. To submit its views and interests to Government, to Department of State, to local authorities, to Press and Public and to Associations connected with Clan and Family in Ireland and overseas
c. To educate the general public in matters connected with the rights, functions and historical position of Irish Chiefs and Chieftains
d. To take such steps as may seem expedient to protect the titles, armorial bearings and other appurtenances of Chiefs and Chieftains from exploitation or misuse in trade or otherwise
e. To promote and preserve the Gaelic heritage of Ireland
f. Any other objects related to the above objects.

The problem created by the Genealogical Office during 1943/44 could not simply be ignored. During the January 30, 1993 meeting, Terence McCarthy, for what turned out to be his personal agenda, again pointed out that he could never accept that the Chief Herald had any judicial authority over holders of Gaelic titles. The Irish Peers Association, composed of those holding Anglo-Irish titles, did not look to the Chief Herald as an authority on the nature and descent of their titles; neither, he argued, should holders of Gaelic titles. He believed that the council should move toward a position of taking responsibility for the recognition or nonrecognition of those claiming to hold Gaelic titles under the dynastic laws that governed them. A committee to do this was eventually set up by the council.

Unfortunately, the difference between the Office and the Chiefs continued. The Office of the Chief Herald simply refused to move from the procedure it had adopted based on English primogeniture law. When the Chief Herald sent a memo to the Chiefs trying to exert his authority over the Council, the Council drafted and sent back a response that pointed out that "The authority of the Chief Herald of Ireland, acting for and on behalf of the Irish State, is cognitive and not creative. The 'act of recognition' is just that, recognition of an existing and inalienable right! Chiefs and Chieftains are not created by the Chief Herald but *recognized* by him." While the Council expressed its determination "to give the Chief Herald every support in the proper discharge of his duties," several matters were felt to be an improper discharge of that duty.

The relationship continued to deteriorate, exacerbated by the public campaigning of Terence McCarthy, who at the time spoke with the authority of one of the major figures among the Irish Chiefs. Terence McCarthy became the goad that seemed to force the Office into more reaction rather than attempting to deal with the fundamental problem.

The National Cultural Institutions Act of 1997, which brought the Genealogical Office under the Board of the Library, even went so far as to make the remarkable claim that any coat of arms granted or confirmed by the Office should be the copyright of the Board of the Library (Section 13.2). The Act came into being in 1999.

Yet another problem had begun to emerge affecting the public perception of the legitimacy of the antiquity of the Gaelic title holders—the formation of Clans of Ireland Limited, which, significantly for some Chiefs, was established with offices in the Chief Herald's office. However, the current Chief Herald has asserted:

> As regards Clans of Ireland Ltd., I understand that this organisation was provided some years ago with limited office facilities at the premises occupied by the Genealogical Office in Kildare Street. The organisation no longer occupies this office accommodation. There is not, and has never been, any working or other relationship between Clans of Ireland Ltd. and the Genealogical Office.[16]

Clans of Ireland Ltd. was formed as an independent company dedicated to assisting Irish clan societies and families to organize and hold gatherings. Government grants to help fund these clan gatherings were made available. Clans of Ireland Ltd., in fact, wrote to the officers of clan associations telling them that funds from Bord Fáilte, a government body, could be made payable only to those that joined the organization.[17]

The problem was that these clan societies, in electing their officers, were encouraged to elect a "chief" or "honorary chief." This obviously led to a debasing, in the minds of the general public, of those who held a genuine Gaelic title. A chief became merely someone elected at a public meeting of a clan association. The problem was explained to the Clans of Ireland Ltd. by both the Council and individual Chiefs and scholars. However, Clans of Ireland Ltd., controlled by a board of directors, has refused to acknowledge or advise its constituent clan associations that an office holder in a clan society taking on the title of chief or even honorary chief, as some do, was insulting and debasing to genuine Gaelic title holders. Furthermore, the title was the "ideal property," in legal terms, of the genuine chief and his *derbhfine*. Should a clan association of, as an example, the O'Husseys meet and elect as their principal officer someone styling himself "Chief of the O'Husseys" when there existed a genuine chief of that name, then the elected officer could be sued in the courts to protect that "ideal property."

More irony followed in that Pádraig Flynn, Minister for Justice in Albert Reynolds's Fianna Fáil Government in 1992 and, since 1993, a European Commission member with responsibility for Social Affairs, allowed himself to be elected as "The O'Flynn" at one of the clan association rallies. How does this equate with the prohibition on the creation of titles?

As these problems continued and seemed to compound, what started out as scholastic disagreements began to take on "personality" aspects as others joined in. The current writer, whose histories and articles were known for expressing views on the Brehon laws and for being critical of the reinvention of the legal basis of chiefship, was contacted by Terence McCarthy. My reply to him was to question the validity of chiefship without the support of Brehon law.[18] I was subsequently invited to contribute scholastic pieces to his publications and finally decided to write a study on the surviving Gaelic aristocratic families, approaching the chiefs singly and collectively, seeking their cooperation.

Being invited to give a talk on the legal basis of the descent of their titles on July 17, 1998, I naturally approached the matter as an academic subject, not realizing that I was becoming embroiled in "personality clashes," for it was presumed, as I subsequently learned, that several people attending believed that I was merely an acolyte of Terence McCarthy and not an independent scholar.

Terence McCarthy appeared to believe that his position was invulnerable and was presenting himself as the leading advocate of the "Brehon law camp." His style of advocacy was such that several people, who had begun to suspect that his claims were fraudulent, questioned his claims. I had accepted, along with Dr. Katharine Simms and many other authorities, that the recognitions given to McCarthy by the Chief Herald were based on a properly authenticated family pedigree. The debate concerning his claims, I believed, involved only whether his Gaelic title was valid under tanistry or primogeniture. No approach was made to me to indicate that his pedigree might be bogus until after the publication of the first edition of this book.

A Professor Marco Horak had, apparently, publicly repeated several assertions concerning Terence McCarthy's claims to the title and of his rights as MacCarthy Mór. McCarthy was confident enough to take legal action against him. As Professor Horak was a member of the Union of the Nobility of Italy, both plaintiff and defendant agreed to pursue the matter in the Italian courts. Due to the controversy, the court had to be uniquely qualified in the subjects of heraldry, genealogy and nobility law. Defendant and plaintiff agreed to a court of arbitration consisting of experts in the field and that they would accept its verdict as being without appeal.

The arbitration court met at Casale Monferrato, Italy, in 1997 and 1998. The President of the Court was Dr. Roberto Messina, a holder of several nobiliary orders and an expert and author of numerous publications on heraldry, genealogy and nobiliary rights. He was assisted by two judges: the Marchioness Professor Bianca Maria Rusconi, also holder of several honors, an expert in heraldry, genealogy and nobiliary rights, and Professor Riccardo Pinotti, also holder of numerous honors, General Administrative Secretary of the Most Serene Republic of San Marino, Coordinating Consultant of the Republic's Numismatic Office and, further, an expert in genealogy, heraldry and nobiliary rights. All three judges had published in their respective areas.

The judges began to examine the three thousand pages of photocopied documents placed in evidence before them on December 2, 1997. The matters considered by the learned judges resulted in the handing down of two verdicts. The first verdict was registered by the district attorney in Casale Monferrato in the Republic of Italy and dated February 27, 1998. It consisted of seventy-four pages of closely reasoned comments on the evidence that had been presented by both sides. The second verdict was registered on June 22, 1998, and this consisted of a further forty pages of reasoned judgment.

The judgments confirmed The MacCarthy Mór's right in international law to his title. The first judgment declared that he bore the titles The MacCarthy Mór, Prince of Desmond, Lord of Kerslawny, Hereditary Head of the Niadh Nask, and that he legally bore the arms of the Eóghanacht Royal House of Munster and had, as head of a sovereign house, the rights of *jus majestatis* and *jus honorum* that constituted the prerogative of *fons honoroum*, according to the same rights that had been proven to have existed in the person of King Donal IX of Desmond.

The second verdict dealt more specifically with Dr. Horak's claim that The MacCarthy Mór had no legal right to claim the right to be hereditary head of a nobiliary order, the Niadh Nask, whose history we shall deal with in a later chapter (see chapter 13). Dr. Horak argued that MacCarthy Mór had no right to dispense nor bestow the order. This was not a question of whether Terence McCarthy had a right to dispense or bestow a dynastic order but whether the *title* he represented was empowered to do so. The judges found against Dr. Horak and said it had been proven that knighthood had existed as a rank in Gaelic Ireland before the advent of the Anglo-Normans in 1169 and that the Niadh Nask was a dynastic honor of nonchivalric knighthood that was recognized in international law as a nobiliary body corporate and politic, being so recognized by various States and by the International Commission for Orders of Chivalry. The judgment went on:

> It must be accepted that the Chiefship of the Eóghanacht Royal House of Munster, with the title of The MacCarthy Mór, Prince of Desmond, with all the prerogatives therein lawfully vested, including the full possession of *Fons Honorum* with the absolute ownership of The Niadh Nask, or Military Order of the Golden Chain, has always descended, and continues to descend by the Laws of Tanistry as set forth in the Gaelic Law Codes known, collectively, as the *Fénechus* or *Senchus Mór*, because primogeniture was never adopted by the MacCarthy Mór Dynasty. Therefore it follows that the Republic of Ireland, accepting, in full, English Common Law as the basis of its Legal Code, has absolutely no jurisdiction in any matter determined by Brehon law, and, according to the accepted principles of International Law, any pretended right or juridical power asserted by it to resolve any schism arising in the Eóghanacht Royal House of MacCarthy Mór must be considered *Ultra Vires* particularly given the fact that the actual laws of succession are "unknown to the Legal Code" of that State. Such an act of interference would be, from any perspective, unconstitutional, have nothing whatever to do with that State, and of no legal effect in International Law.[19]

The Italian Court had been presented with copies of documents by Terence McCarthy, *not originals*, together with copies of his books on the Eóghanacht kingship. The ruling of the Italian judges was based on the fact that Terence McCarthy came before them with recognitions by the Irish State together with all the subsequent recognitions and honors that he had gathered on the groundwork of those recognitions. The court was not aware of any investigation by the Genealogical Office into Terence McCarthy's background at that time, nor that the basis on which he had been granted recognition was not the same as the arguments he was placing before the Italian court. The court simply accepted that the Irish state had investigated and authenticated Terence McCarthy's claims. In retrospect, the Genealogical Office should have sent a representative to the arbitration, having been given notice that it was to take place. Without challenge, the Arbitration Court simply accepted Terence Mc-Carthy's new claims as being those already authenticated by the Genealogical Office of Ireland.

Terence McCarthy had scored a singular victory in his campaign to maintain the title.

What is lost, by the fact that the Italian judgments relating to Terence Mc-Carthy have now been shown as "unsafe," is the general principle reflected by the Italian ruling, that the dynastic laws of titles held in previous states cannot be retrospectively altered. However, it can now be argued by the primogeniturists that the Italian judgment is "null and void" so that it is not binding in any way on all member states of the European Community, which, from January 1999, under the Treaty of Maastricht, would have been the case.

The legal rulings led to a series of commentaries written by expert international legal opinion in support of the Italian judges' interpretations. Several of these commentaries, among them one written by a United States chief judge, J. Michael Johnson, and doctors of law Mitchell L. Lathrop and David V. Brooks, were collected and, together with the certified legal translations of the Italian judgments, which had been registered in the United States and other international legal jurisdictions, were published as *A New Book of Rights*[20] Once again, unfortunately, the legal reality of the position on dynastic succession is now blurred by the bogus nature of Terence McCarthy's position. The song is condemned with the singer.

The Honorable Chief Judge John Johnson of the United States Federal Court, a practitioner in the Supreme Court, a member of the U.S. Judge Advocate's Office and a specialist in international law, in his comments on the judgments, underlined the most important aspect applying to all Gaelic titles.

> The court took cognizance of the fact that the Constitution of the Republic of Ireland forbids the bestowal of titles by the Government. It carefully distinguishes, however, this proscription from the transmission of existing titles by inheritance. It was specifically observed that the use of inherited titles has never been forbidden to either Irish citizens or visitors to the republic and, in fact, its constitution guarantees and protects the right of property, including that—such as hereditary titles—of an incorporeal nature. The court reasoned that it would be unconstitutional—essentially equivalent to the creation of a title—for the government of the Irish Republic to change the form of inherited titles by

alteration of their historical nature, status, manner of succession, coat of arms, or their inherent quality. This view was recognized to be consistent with principles of International Law which deny any retrospective authority to successor states with regard to sovereign houses whose rule antedated their own.[21]

Judge Johnson reemphasizes this point:

> the court . . . specially commented with regard to the relative recent recognition of "Chiefly Titles" by the Republic of Ireland, through the agency of the Chief Herald. Such "recognition" of existing rights, it noted, confers no additional authority pursuant to International Law upon the Government of the Republic of Ireland. Hence, that Government possesses no legal authority to alter the status or the historic nature of the dynastic rights.

The leading U.S. legal counsel, Dr. David Brooks of North Carolina, also sought to emphasize that essential point.

> Whilst the Republic of Ireland may, as it has chosen to, recognize the existence of . . . Gaelic titles . . . by granting "courtesy recognition" to the Chiefs thereof, it does not thereby acquire any right to alter the form, historical status or laws of descent of those Houses. This is an important point, since the law code of the Irish Republic is based upon English Common Law, which respects the principle of primogeniture, while it is evident that the Chiefship of a Gaelic House can only legally exist under the Brehon Laws and descend by tanistry.

Coincidentally, at the time of the publication of the judgments and commentaries, a not dissimilar case regarding dynastic law of a deposed royal house was being heard by the Bundesgerichtshof (German Supreme Court). The case arose from an action of Prince Frederick William of Prussia, great-grandson of the last German Kaiser. The Prince's late father, then head of the former Sovereign House of Hohenzollern of Prussia, Prince Louis Ferdinand, had disinherited his eldest son after he had contracted a morganatic marriage, in 1981, to a lady Ehrengard von Reden. The Hohenzollern dynastic laws said that the head of the Royal House of Prussia had to marry a daughter of a sovereign house. Miss von Reden did not have that qualification.

Prince Frederick William decided to pursue the matter in the German courts. Whereas two lower courts, basing their judgments on modern German law, found that Prince Frederick had every right to succeed his father like any other German citizen, the Supreme Court ruled on December 2, 1998, that Hohenzollern dynastic laws of inheritance were still applicable to claims made concerning property, of which a title is party. The German courts, representing the state, could not retrospectively alter them.[22]

Prince Frederick William of Prussia had to give way to his nephew Prince George Frederick, aged twenty two, who became the head of his house and pretender to the German throne. The verdict of the German Supreme Court was greeted with satisfaction by Wilfried Rogasch, an expert on dynastic history at the German Historical Museum in Berlin, as well as other international experts.

However, Dr. Rainer Kramer, of Berlin, wrote to the author to emphasize that the German Court could only deal with the subject of property inheritance without mentioning succession to a title. However, titles are interpreted as "ideal property" and the succession was thereby implied rather than stated. The court was technically concerned to see if the "brandenburgisch-preussiche Hausverfassung" (the dynastic law in question) could be valid under the German Constitution which, in 1919, had abolished all titles and ranks of nobility. The decision, he argues, was merely confirmation that if people have special opinions as to how the possessions of their families should be inherited they may follow them as long as they are neither unreasonable nor against German law. Quite rightly, Dr. Kramer agreed that the Supreme Court, representing the state, could not retrospectively alter the former dynastic method of inheritance as such a decision would have been against the German Constitution.

However, the parallel was lost in certain quarters in Ireland.

The matter of the Brehon laws of succession was put to the current Norroy and Ulster King of Arms, Thomas Woodcock, who immediately supported the fact that only the Brehon law of dynastic succession was valid as a means of claiming a Gaelic title. He said: "One should not apply a common law inheritance system to a title which only existed under Irish Brehon Law; if you argue that Irish Brehon Law and the Gaelic titles could not be abolished by conquest, then the inheritance system under that law, i.e., the laws of tanistry, must be applied."[23]

Encouraged by his success, Terence McCarthy then succeeded in obtaining a recognition by the Castile and Leon King of Arms of Spain. McCarthy had a residence within Spanish heraldic jurisdiction. Once again the Spanish Herald was guided by the Irish State recognitions and by the judgment of the Italian courts. And once again the herald was quite clear on the matter of recognizing Gaelic titles as being governed only by the Irish laws of tanistry. The Castile and Leon King of Arms is the Marquis de la Floresta of the Spanish Royal Academy of Heraldry and Genealogy.

The Spanish Herald, of course, had no trouble in recognizing Gaelic titles as *titles of nobility*, which passed down only through the Brehon law of dynastic succession. Furthermore, this recognition had been made by a learned herald who received his appointment from the Crowned Head of Spain, and it was approved under Royal Decree by the Spanish Ministries of Public Administration and Ministry of Justice.

On July 18, 1998, the Standing Council of Chiefs and Chieftains, at their annual meeting, unanimously acknowledged that their titles stemmed from Brehon law. On January 9, 1999, they again reaffirmed that fact, with the corollary that there was no legal power to retrospectively change those laws of succession. They agreed to continue to meet with the Chief Herald of Ireland in the hope of bringing the courtesy recognition of the state into line with international law.

In 1997 Brendan O'Donoghue had been appointed as Director of the National Library and, thereby, as Chief Herald with a brief to revise the working practices of the Genealogical Office. It had been realized that there were some inherent problems in its function. Almost at once, the new Chief Herald was caught up in the challenge to Terence McCarthy's authenticity. When initially asked for a statement on recognizing Gaelic titles, he stated the policy of his office:

> When the practice of recognizing Chiefs of the Name was introduced in 1944, it was made clear that recognition was based on descent by primogeniture from the last inaugurated or *de facto* chieftain. Subject to the possible survival in some cases of senior lines then unidentified, the persons concerned were recorded at the Genealogical Office as Chiefs of the Name. There are no proposals to change the practice of the Genealogical Office in this regard.[24]

However, he has now admitted that "there is no basis for the practice in the Constitution or in statute law" and argues that "the Genealogical Office does not grant titles" in spite of the peculiarities of the situation with regard to the Gaelic chiefly titles. "Titles are not created and do not exist because of recognition: on the contrary recognition has been granted on the basis of evidence submitted by applicants as to their use of an existing courtesy title." While this should be self-evident, one has to judge the statement in context to the problems that have been created.[25]

Disarmingly, however, the Chief Herald has made the statement: "In so far as this Office is concerned, Chiefs of the Name are free to do what they wish in the matter of succession. Their actions are not matters to be either disputed or approved by the Genealogical Office." But this statement is hard to square with the statement that the Genealogical Office will dispute chiefly titles handed down by tanistry. What is that but a disapproval of the dynastic laws of the

Chiefs? It also implies a contradiction that "the Genealogical Office neither claims nor assumes legal authority over Gaelic titles, or any others."

The revelation of Terence McCarthy's fraud caused questions to be raised in the Dáil on September 29, 1999, and the Minister of Arts, Heritage and the Gaeltacht, Síle de Valéra, announced a review of the entire system of recognition of Gaelic titles, indicating that recognitions given in the 1980s and 1990s were flawed. Therefore, no further courtesy recognitions were to be made by the Chief Herald of Ireland until the inquiry was finalized and a procedure was agreed to. In 2001 the minister changed her mind and announced that the matter would be left to the Chief Herald and no government commission would be held.

Brendan O'Donoghue believes that the State is doing no more or less than recognizing that "X" is the most senior descendant in the male line of a person who was the last inaugurated or de facto Gaelic Irish Chief. In granting courtesy recognition, he believes, his office simply accepts that the person may use the style or designation "Chief of the Name" and/or a particular style if used traditionally in his family.[26] If this is, indeed, the reality, then it raises many questions about the current form of recognitions granted by the Genealogical Office.

Anthony Carty, Eversheds professor of international law at the University of Derby, believes that a confusion has arisen in the attempts to restore Irish polity "if not exactly as it had been, at least in a form, adapted to the present, which was, as far as possible, approximate to what had been lost." He considers that the dispute about Gaelic titles "is a product of this confusion in the Irish imagination." While on one hand the civic tradition of Irish nationalism, proclaiming freedom and equality and independence from the British state would insist that titles of nobility could not be conferred by the state, the general rule need not exclude a constitutional amendment to admit the historical exception for the sake of ancient Gaelic titles. "I think the appropriate solution would be to have the Irish Constitution amended to regularize the confirmation of the ancient Gaelic titles in accordance with the principles of the Brehon law. This would be consistent with the attempt to restore other aspects of Gaelic identity."[27]

Professor Carty finds the

> conduct of the Chief Herald . . . very unsatisfactory. I think the issues thereby raised are extremely important because they represent a fundamental confusion of legal identity of the Irish State and can only be deeply impoverishing to Irish culture. This is not an esoteric or somehow archaic matter. The enthusiasm for a common European Union identity in Ireland is not an adequate

compensation, because the latter supposes, for other Europeans, that they still have to sort out the terms of their own national identity.

While the Chief Herald still believes that international law has no bearing on the way the Irish State gives courtesy recognition to the old Gaelic titles, he points out that there is no evidence that those holders of such Gaelic titles who purport to have adopted the tanistry system have made any effort to implement a procedure that would remotely resemble the tanistry system of Brehon law days. Even if such a system was adopted, he feels, it would be simply a recipe for further controversy and dispute and demean the status "Chief of the Name." One hesitates to point out that since the primogeniture rulings in 1944, the controversies and disputes and the demeaning of Gaelic titles could hardly become worse.

Because Terence McCarthy hailed the Brehon system in an attempt to ensure his bogus claim to be The MacCarthy Mór, it is quite evident that the prejudice felt against him personally for his actions now encompasses Brehon law succession. McCarthy has managed to totally obscure what was an essentially scholastic argument on the historical and legal reality. Many people believe that now the Irish government inquiry on the system of recognitions has been dropped, the state will continue to opt for primogeniture descent and thus finally sever any basis with the culture from which the Gaelic aristocracy arose. Some maintain a faint hope that the Irish state might give initial recognition to the primogeniture heirs with the provision that the families could then reinstate tanistry succession for future generations, thus recreating the reality of Gaelic culture. Without this return to Brehon law, however, there is no historical reality in Gaelic chiefship, and such Gaelic titles should be allowed to quietly pass into historical obscurity.

The Gaelic aristocratic families, having survived more than two thousand years in most cases and having endured centuries of sustained assault to make them extinct, will doubtless continue to survive, whatever the bureaucracy of the current state demands. They will take pride in their family pedigrees, but without Brehon law succession, their "titles" will be a mere fantasy without historical substance. Is there an irony in the fact that the founding fathers of the modern Irish state aspired, in the words of Pádraic Pearse, the leader of the 1916 uprising, to an Ireland "not free merely, but Gaelic as well" while the state is now trying to force the survivors of the Gaelic titled families to give up the old Gaelic laws of dynastic succession and follow English primogeniture? Professor Carty seems correct in viewing it as a "confusion in the Irish imagination." As Gerard Crotty has written, the surviving Gaelic aristocratic families form one of the richest threads in the tapestry of Gaelic Ireland.[28] It would be a myopic society, indeed, that would destroy such a profound cultural link with its past, a link stretching back to the primordial roots of the nation, by ignoring or recreating it in a modern "never-never land" setting.

PART TWO

The Families

CHAPTER SEVEN

THE KINGDOM OF
MUNSTER (DESMOND)

MUNSTER IS THE MOST SOUTHERLY AND SOUTHWESTERLY province of Ireland. Geographically, it is the largest of Ireland's four modern provinces, comprising the six counties of Cork, Kerry, Waterford, Tipperary, Limerick and Clare and covering 9,317 square miles. Prior to A.D. 1118 it was, therefore, the largest of the Irish kingdoms. The Irish name is Mumu, of which there is no satisfactory definition. In the popular genitive case, it is Mumhain, to which the Norse added *stadr*, meaning a place; and thus the Anglicized form is Munster. Latin texts refer to it as Momonia or Mumonia.

Munster stands apart from the other provinces of Ireland in that in ancient mythology and legend it is considered the land of primordial beginnings. It appears as a place of origin, the place where most of the mythical invaders of Ireland landed. In Munster the occult powers were supreme, for it was not only the place of origin but a place of ending, an alpha and omega of the Celtic world. Here, off the coast, was Tech Duinn, the gathering place of the dead souls where the god Donn would collect them and transport them to the Otherworld. It is not without significance that the ruling house of Munster was referred to in some texts as The House of Donn. It is in Munster, in Kenmare Bay, that the sons of Míle Easpain landed. Here Míle's son Amairgen, claimed as "the first Druid" in Ireland, cried out his extraordinary incantations, which could have come straight from the Hindu *Bhagavad Gita*. Thus, we are reminded once again of the Indo-European origin of the Irish. Scota, the wife of

Míle Easpain, was killed by the children of Danu, the Tuatha Dé Danaan. She is said to be have been buried in Scota's Glen, three miles from Tralee, County Kerry.

Indeed, it has been argued that it was in Munster that Irish literacy had its beginnings. Ogham, the earliest form of Irish writing, frequently referred to in Irish myth and sagas, is said to have been the gift of Ogma, god of eloquence and literature. The sagas refer to great libraries of Ogham books, written on bark and wands of hazelwood, in the manner of the first Chinese recorded books. The surviving Ogham inscriptions are, however, on stone. There are 369 such inscriptions, some found where Irish missionaries traveled, but the bulk in Ireland. Of these, the highest density is not only in Munster but in the extreme southwest. There are 121 surviving inscriptions in County Kerry alone. Dr. Mairtín Ó Murchú has suggested that Ogham, therefore, originated in this area of Munster.[1]

The religious significance of Munster is seen in the story of its first Gaelic king, Eibhear Fionn (Eber Finn). The sons of Golamh, or Míle Easpain, the progenitor of the Gaels, landed and fought with the Tuatha Dé Danaan for the possession of Ireland. Having achieved victory, the sons agreed to divide the country between them. One son, Eremon, took the northern half of Ireland called Leth Cuinn; he became the progenitor of the Uí Néill. Another son, Eber Fionn, took the southern half of Ireland, which was called Leth Mug Nuadat, and he became progenitor of the Eóghanacht. Later Uí Néill scribes referred to the southern half as "Leth Mug," omitting one important word, so that it could be translated as "the slave's half." This was part of the later propaganda war between northern and southern dynasties which denigrated the right of southern kings to the High Kingship. But the proper name was Leth Mug Nuadat, which means "half of the slave of Nuada." Nuada was a major god of the Celts. The word "slave" in this context merely indicates that the early rulers of Munster thought of themselves as servants of the god in much the same way that the early Christian Irish declaimed themselves as *giolla* (servant or follower) of St. Patrick or St. Brigit or *mael* (servant) of St. Ruan, St. Maedoc, and so forth. It does not imply that they were literally slaves. Interestingly, while the Uí Néill claimed Eremon was the elder and senior of Míle's two sons, the Eóghanacht maintained that Eber was the senior. The arms of MacCarthy Reagh de Toulouse bears the inscription under the family motto: "*Sinnsior Clanna Milead*" (*sinnsear* being senior, eldest, a chief of the family).

The size of ancient Munster and its power, not to mention its Indo-European origins, may be seen in its early composition. The kingdom was divided into five "provinces" ruled by a "High King" from a central kingdom who extended his rule over the four lesser kings.[2] It was the pattern that then emerged as an all-Ireland polity.

The genealogies of the kings of Munster begin with one of the earliest *fursundud* (genealogical poems) attributed to Luccraid moccu Chíara writing in the seventh century. He wrote it in praise of the ancestry of King Cathal Cú-cen-Máthair (d. A.D. 641).[3] Most other genealogies survive from the twelfth century, tracing the descent of the kings from Eber Fionn, who ruled, according to most chroniclers, in Anno Mundi (Year of the World) 2737. In Hebrew tradition, the year of creation corresponds to 3761 B.C., although James Ussher (1581–1656), the Dublin-born Archbishop of Armagh, computed the date of creation as 4004 B.C. However, according to the chronicles, the Milesian, or Gaelic, settlement in Ireland is dated at the end of the second millennium, usually considered to be 1015 B.C.

The early Christian scribes felt the need to trace their kings back to Adam. Míle Easpain, therefore, shared an ancestor whom all the Gaelic nobility claimed as the thirty-sixth generation in descent from Adam. This genealogy, tacked on by Christian scribes to the traditions of oral genealogies, claims that Feinius Farsaidh, son of Baath, son of Magog, at the time of the Tower of Babel, devised the Gaelic language and was progenitor of the people.

As noted, while O'Néill sources maintain that Eremon was the senior son of Míle, Eóghanacht sources also claim Eber as the elder son. Between 691 B.C. and A.D. 146 some twenty-four Munster kings were also listed as High Kings of Ireland. Only the Uí Néill and Eóghanachta lines succeeded to the High Kingship until the Christian era. Duach Donn Dalta Deagha appears in the early Christian period as the last Eóghanacht to hold the office; he did so for ten years.

From Eber Fionn, the Munster genealogies trace father to son down forty-eight generations to Eóghan Mór, from whom the Eóghanachta take their dynastic name. It is particularly significant to our discussion on the name of Eber Fionn's half of the country that Eóghan Mór was also known as Mug Nuadat. A text compiled in the thirteenth century, *Cath Maige Léna* (Battle of the Plain of Léna), gives a full account of the deeds of Eóghan. It claims that Eóghan, as a youth, helped the servant of a Munster fortress builder called Nuadhu Dearg in building a fort and thus earned his nickname, Mug, meaning "servant." It is more likely that the connection of the king is linked with the pagan divinity whose name, Nuadat, appears to mean "cloud maker."

Eóghan Mór is said to have reinforced the ancestral divisions of Ireland into two equal halves, setting the border between Átha Cliath Meadhraighe (Maaree, southeast of Galway) and Baile Átha Cliatha (Dublin). He is recorded as dying in battle at Magh Léna (Moylena, just north of Tullamore, County

Offaly) in A.D. 192. However, conservative scholarship accords Conall Corc, who died after A.D. 438, the role as the first proven historical king of Munster. He served with St. Patrick on the nine-man commission to make the first known codification of the native Irish law system. It was he who established his capital on the Rock of Cashel, County Tipperary.[4]

Forty-nine Eóghanacht kings reigned at Cashel between 438 and 963. This last was the year when, after the death of Donnchadh II mac Cellacháin Chaisil, the Dál gCais of northern Munster seized the throne by force. Mathgamain mac Cennétig, King of Thomond (Thuaidh Mumhan, or north Munster) grabbed the Munster throne. But he was assassinated in 976 by Maelmuad mac Bríain, ruler of the Eóghanacht Rathlind. He assumed the throne until Brían Bóroimhe killed him in 978 and reestablished the Dál gCais dynasty, expanding his power by military means to become High King. From then on the Ua Bríain of Thomond and the Eóghanacht Chaisil fought until the Treaty of Glanmire in 1118 partitioned Munster into two kingdoms, Desmond and Thomond.

The leading branch of the Eóghanacht royal dynasty took the surname MacCarthy from Carrthach, King of the Eóghanacht Chaisil, who died in 1045. His son Muiredach became the first "Mac Carrthach" (d. 1092) and hence MacCarthy in Anglicized form.

THE MACCARTHY MÓR, PRINCE OF DESMOND (MACCARTHAIGH MÓR)

High Kingship politics played a great part when the Treaty of Glanmire in 1118 established the Kingdom of Desmond, dividing Desmond, the major part of Munster, from Thomond of the O'Briens. Tairrdelbach (Turlough) O'Conor of Connacht wished to claim the High Kingship for himself and his successors, and that necessitated weakening the O'Briens, who had by then provided three High Kings in the persons of Brían Bóroimhe (d. 1014), Tairrdelbach (d. 1086) and Muirchertach (d. 1119). When the High King Muirchertach O'Brien summoned Tairrdelbach Ua Conchobhair to help him crush the Eóghanachta in Desmond, Tairrdelbach and his men dutifully marched to join him.

Tadhg MacCarthy, the leading Eóghanacht prince, whose aim was to drive the usurping O'Briens from the Munster throne, had taken up positions with his army at Glanmire in Cork. Muirchertach was confident of victory. *MacCarthaigh's Book*, written under the patronage of The MacCarthy Reagh, reports the event:

Turlough O'Conor, Murchad O'Mael Seachlainn and Aodh son of Donnchadh Ó Ruairc, came into the assembly of Tadhg son of MacCarthaigh, and
made an enduring treaty with him and with Cormac (his brother) against
Muirchertach, son of Toirdhealbach and Sliogh Briain (the Dál gCais). It was
then that Muirchertach O'Briain was parted from the kingship of Munster and
Ireland.[5]

In other words, Muirchertach's allies refused to wage war on the
Eóghanachta and forced the High King to accept a treaty allowing the
Eóghanachta to rule in south Munster (Desmond) while the O'Briens had to be
content with north Munster (Thomond). A year later the Muirchertach was
dead and Tairrdelbach Ua Conchobhair was High King. No O'Brien took the
High Kingship after that. *MacCarthaigh's Book* presents the newly recognized
MacCarthy kingdom of Desmond as a continuing kingdom and its crown con-
tinuing to pass through the Eóghanacht dynasty. However, MacCarthy kings
often claimed to be titular "kings of the two Munsters" (both Desmond and
Thomond).

Tadhg I MacCarthy Mór (1118–23), the grandson of Carrthach, was the
first of the Eóghanacht line of MacCarthy kings to rule the new kingdom of
Desmond following the Treaty of Glanmire, returning the MacCarthy dynasty
to their ancient capital of Cashel for the first time in 150 years. Twenty-five
MacCarthy kings ruled Desmond, down to Donal IX MacCarthy Mór
(1558–96), the last regnant king.

Many of the Eóghanacht kings were "king bishops," a Christian inheritance of the pagan sacral kingship of former times. One of the great literary
kings of the Eóghanacht was Cormac II MacCuileannáin (836–908), who was
King Bishop of Cashel. Born in Cashel, he succeeded to the kingship in 902
and married Gormflaith (ca. 880–947), daughter of Flann Sionna, an Uí Neill
High King of Ireland. Gormflaith was a poetess in her own right and herself
the subject of a romantic cycle of tales and poems. *Triamhuin Ghormflaithe* (the
Tragedy of Gormflaith) was considered one of the great medieval romances.
She is not to be confused with another Gormflaith (ca. 955–1042), who was
queen of both Dublin and Munster.

However, Cormac II was another of the literary kings of the Eóghanacht.
Some of his lyrics appear in the twelfth-century *Leabhar na Nuachonghbhála*
(Book of Leinster). But his literary fame arises from his authorship of *Sanas
Chormaic* (Cormac's Glossary), an early Irish lexicon. Cormac was also respon-
sible for the compilation of the *Saltair* (the Psalter of Cashel) and for his in-
volvement in helping produce the *Lebor na Cert* or *Leabhar na gCeart* (the Book

of Rights), setting out the privileges, tributes and duties of Irish kings and nobles in mnemonic verse. After being revised two centuries later on the orders of Brían Bóroimhe, it was used as a standard for centuries. The work also gives the genealogies of leading families.

The book also contains a very interesting account—*Senchas Fagbála Caisil andso sis agus Beandacht Ríg* (the Story of the Finding of Cashel), an account of how King Conal Corc came to choose Cashel as the seat of the Munster kingdom. This story also mentions how, sixty years after the event, when Nad Froich Mac Cuirc was on the throne, St. Patrick came to Cashel. St. Patrick and a native Munster bishop, Ailbe, who established the Abbey of Emly, converted Nad Froich Mac Cuirc and baptized him at Cashel. St. Ailbe is, of course, the patron saint of Munster, and is regarded by scholars as pre-Patrician, arriving in Ireland before Patrick to preach Christianity.[6]

While Brían Bóroimhe justly receives credit for breaking the power of the Danes at Clontarf in 1014, little notice has been taken of Cellachán Mac Buadacháin (d. 954), who actually broke the Norse attempts to dominate in Munster by a series of victories over the Danes. The Norse were isolated in their port city-states of Cork, Limerick and Waterford and made to pay tribute to the Munster kings. In the twelfth century Cormac III, the best-known, perhaps, of the MacCarthy king bishops at Cashel, commissioned the story of Cellachán to be set down in writing. *Caithreim Cheallacháin Chaisil* (the Battle Saga of Cellachán of Cashel) was written sometime between 1127 and 1138, and the earliest surviving manuscript is in the Royal Irish Academy.[7]

Cormac reigned in two periods. The first was 1123 to 1127. It is implied in both the *Annals of Innisfallen* and in *MacCarthaigh's Book* that Cormac attempted to reunite all Munster under Eóghanacht control. In 1125 he captured the Dál gCais capital of Limerick and thereafter is referred to as King of Munster. However, in 1127 he is reported as being "deposed by the nobles of Munster"; perhaps the *derbhfine* did not want to enter into an all-out war with the Ua Bríain again. Cormac's younger brother Donnchadh II succeeded to the kingship while Cormac retired into a religious life at the Abbey of Lismore.

However, within months Donnchadh had proven himself an unworthy successor. He was sent into exile in Connacht while Cormac was returned to reign until 1138. Now Cormac found that instead of fighting the Ua Bríain, the Kings of Thomond were actually asking for an alliance against the power of the O'Conors of Connacht, who were attempting to annex part of Thomond to their territory.

Cormac has a tenuous link with another great literary work. Christiaus, or more properly Giolla Christa MacCarthy, a first cousin of Cormac, was Abbot of Ratisbon (Regensberg, the old capital of Bavaria). In 1149 an Irish monk from Munster called Marcus wrote in Latin a saga called *The Vision of Tngdal*, which is regarded as one of the great medieval vision tales of the Otherworld. Tnugdal is a knight of Cashel, who, dining with some friends in Cork, falls into a deep sleep. We follow his journey to the Christianized Otherworld. Some 154 manuscript copies in Latin survive as well as 100 manuscripts containing the translation of the text in Irish and a score of other European languages. In an introduction to a new English translation by Dr. Jean-Michel Picard (1989), Yolande de Pontfarcy says "it is also an Irish production and cannot be fully appreciated if not understood in its Celtic context."[8]

But perhaps Cormac is best known for the famous building on the Rock of Cashel, Cormac's Chapel. He ordered it begun in 1127, and it was consecrated in 1134. It appears to be the earliest Romanesque Church in Ireland. Firmicius, the Abbot of Regensberg, is recorded as sending four of his best craftsmen to help with the work. The monastery of St. James at Regensburg (Ratisbon) was founded by Muiredach Mac Robartaigh (Marianus Scotus, d. 1088) and became a Benedictine abbey. It was regarded as an Eóghanacht foundation beyond the seas. The elaborately decorated sarcophagus inside Cormac's Chapel is popularly said to have been that of King Cormac himself. However, scholars believe that it originally was made for King Tadhg (1118–1123). It was only returned to the chapel at the beginning of the nineteenth century. The copper crozier found inside, said to be proof of the interring of a "king bishop," is actually dated to a century after Cormac lived. This crozier, ornamented with Limoges enamel, now in the National Museum, Dublin, is compared to a similar enamel in the Victoria and Albert Museum and must have belonged to another bishop.

Cormac III was assassinated in 1138 by his erstwhile allies, the O'Briens. *The Annals of Innisfallen* state:

> Cormac, son of Muireadach MacCarthaigh, king of the two provinces of Munster [Desmond and Thomond], and defender of all Leth Mug, the most pious and valorous of men, the best for bestowing food and clothes [on the poor], was, after building the church of Cormac at Cashel and twelve churches at Lismore, treacherously killed by Diarmuid Súgach, son of Mathghamhain Ó Conchobhair Ciarraige [O'Connor Kerry] and Ó Tailcín, at the instigation of Toirdhealbhach son of Diarmaid Ó Bríain, in his own court at Magh Tamhnach.

That the royal court of Cashel was a highly civilized and literate one is, perhaps, stating the obvious. Apart from the works just mentioned, one fascinating opus is a treatise on music written at Cashel in 1168. This was kept in the Cashel Diocesan Library. From the early medieval manuscripts it is clear that music played an important role in Irish courtly life. Irish manuscripts of musical notation survive from this period also.[9]

On Cormac's death, his brother, Donnchadh, returned from exile and reigned from 1138 to 1143. He attempted to punish the O'Briens for his brother's death but was himself taken prison by Toirdhealbach and died in captivity.

King Dermod I (1144–1185), the son of Cormac, has been placed second only to Dermod MacMorrough of Leinster in the demonology of Irish traitors. This is due to his submission to Henry II even before his kingdom was threatened. King Dermod had suffered years of continuous attacks on Desmond by the Dál gCais kings. The polity of Desmond was not stable. A strong kingdom was possible only by political means and alliances. *MacCarthaigh's Book* reveals how Dermod I supported the O'Conors and MacMorrough against the O'Briens during this turbulent period.

H. A. Jefferies, in "Desmond: The Early Years and the Career of Cormac MacCarthy," observes: "Dermod MacCarthy created one of the most powerful and united kingdoms of pre-Norman Ireland, and the endurance of Clan Mac-Carthaigh as a major political force in south Munster throughout the later middle ages was due in no small part to the work of this remarkable king."[10]

King Dermod had heard reports of the landing of Norman knights and their men-at-arms during 1169 and 1170. In October, 1171, the Angevin emperor Henry II himself went to Waterford. With the defeat of the High King's army and the submission of other Irish kings and nobles, Dermod realized that the Normans were a foe who needed to be treated with consideration. Dermod certainly did not possess an army that could defend Munster when the High King's army had already been defeated. He went to see the Angevin emperor, then encamped at Waterford. The *Annals of Innisfallen* say "*ina theg an sin*" (he went into Henry's house), which is interpreted to mean that he submitted to Henry as his feudal lord. Hot on his heels came the Thomond king, Domhnall Mór O'Brien, who also submitted.

Dermod saw submission to Henry, acknowledging him as his "overlord," as being no different from submission to Ruaidri Ua Conchbhair as High King. He saw it as another alliance to a powerful king against possible threats to his own kingdom. Now that the High King of Ireland had been rendered impotent by the Normans, he could not guarantee protection against the ambitions of the O'Briens.

The Normans were swift to repudiate the treaty. Dermod was murdered, according to the annals of the Regensburg monastery, on November 6 by the Norman knight named Geoffrey de Cogan. Cogan was immediately slain by

Domhnall Mór na Curra, who succeeded Dermod as Donal I of Desmond. *The Annals of Innisfallen* record Donal's obituary in 1206 thus:

Domhnaill, son of MacCarthaigh, High King of Munster, died in Corr Tige Meuc Urmainn this year on the Kalends of December (first of the month) as regards the day of the solar month, and on Friday, as regards the day of the week. It was he, of all the contemporary Kings of Ireland, who was most feared by the foreigners. During the twenty years he held the kingship, he never submitted to the foreigner; and though an army of foreigners and Gaels often cam against him, he gave them at all times no more than was their due, while at other times, he gave them nothing. And it was he who slew Geoffrey de Cogan, the most hated kerne that ever was in Ireland, and he flayed this Geoffrey. And it was he who inflicted the rout of Bern Meic Imuir, and who successfully attacked the castles of Lios Mór, Dun Cuireda, In Cora and Mag Ua Mairgili, and the castles of Uí Meic Caille. By him nine Justiciars were slain and twenty-one battles fought in Munster, and many other exploits were performed.

In the thirteenth century Norman knights were moving into Desmond and kings were forced to protect themselves. In November 1259 the Norman Lord of Ireland, Henry III, granted all Desmond to John FitzThomas as his fiefdom. John FitzThomas swiftly moved to take over this rich kingdom and invited King Donal II (1247–1252) to Airloch Castle on guarantees of personal safety to discuss matters. Once again the sacred trust of hospitality was flouted. FitzThomas murdered the Desmond king and attempted to assert his authority throughout the kingdom.

Finghín V (1252–1261) of Rinn Róin became King of Desmond and immediately took the field against FitzThomas and his Normans. He destroyed six Norman strongholds, castles that they were building to dominate the kingdom. FitzThomas called on William de Dene, the Norman justiciar, for aid, and a large Norman army marched into Desmond. On July 24, 1261, the army of the King of Desmond met that of King Henry III's personal representative in Ireland, the lord justiciar himself, with his armored knights and men-at-arms. The battle site was at Callann near Kenmare. One wing of the King of Desmond's army was commanded by his daughter, Étain. Never had the Normans suffered such a defeat. John FitzThomas and his son Maurice were killed along with eight Norman barons, twenty-five knights and thousands of men-at-arms. Professor Edmond Curtis comments:

The important result of Callan was the check it gave to what seemed the inevitable triumph of Norman English speech, culture and law in the south west corner, the conquest of which would have extinguished native Desmond. For centuries not a single English settler dare now set foot in the country of the MacCarthys. . . .[11]

Technically, this is not entirely accurate. Milo de Courcy managed to ambush King Finghín near Kinsale in 1262 and kill him. Cormac, Finghín's brother, then became Cormac V (1262) and was joined by the Princess Étain, who seems a formidable military commander but, alas, we know little about her. Together they met the army of the new lord justiciar, Richard de la Rochelle, with his second-in-command, Walter de Burgo, on the slopes of Mangerton, County Kerry. The battle was another victory even though the King of Desmond fell in the thick of the fighting. His cousin Donal Ruadh became Donal III, reigning between 1262 and 1302. His long reign was due to the fact that, as Curtis has pointed out, though for the wrong battle, "for centuries not a single English settler dare now set foot in the country of the MacCarthys."

When Donal III was succeeded by his son, Donal Óg (1302–06), *The Annals of Connacht* record his passing in these terms: "Domhnall Ruadha Mac-Carthaigh, King of Desmond, the most generous and valorous, the most terrible and triumphant of the Gaels of all Ireland in fights and forays, dies after a victory of repentance this year (1302)."

The term "victory of repentance" meant he received the last rites of the church.

By the late fourteenth century, the Norman barons were back in Desmond, carving out palatine estates, self-governing principalities. Among the first Normans settlers were the Fitzgeralds, who were eventually to take the title Earls of Desmond, and the Butlers, who became Earls of Ormond—west Munster. However, this time they sought liaisons and alliances with the Desmond kings. One of the most peaceful reigns in Desmond was that of Donal Óg (Donal V) (1359–90) of which the *Annals of Innisfallen* record:

> there was none of his contemporaries, neither foreigner nor Gael, more
> comely, more humane, or more powerful than he, nor was there in his time one
> of greater generosity, prowess, kindliness o[r] truthfulness. He died in his castle
> of Loch Léin and was buried in the same monastery as his father after a victory
> of penance and devotion. And no other calamity was so notable at that time.

His son Tadhg II na Mainistreach MacCarthy Mór (1390–1428) stands out as important as the children of two of his three sons became the progenitors of important branches of the royal dynasty. His senior surviving son, Domhnall, continued the kingly line until Donal IX (d. 1596); his next son, Cormac, became Tiarna Chois Leamhna (Lord of Kerslawny) and Tanist of Desmond. The *Annals of Loch Cé*, noting his death in 1473, says: "The son of Mac-Carthaigh Mór, Cormac, son of Tadhg, son of Domhnall Óg, Tanist of Des Mumha, died this year." Tadhg's third son, Dermod, died without issue. It is from that second son, Cormac, that the current claimants to the title Mac-Carthy Mór descend.

The last King of Desmond, the end of a line of twenty-four kings from Tadhg I (1118–23), was Donal IX (ante 1558–96), of whom we have given some account in the first part of this work. In terms of territory, the kingdom had shrunk back into Cork and Kerry. Donal ruled from his estate at Killarney. The Norman Earls of Desmond (Fitzgeralds) and of Ormond (Butlers) had deprived him of much of the kingdom, but the ordinary Irish people still looked upon Donal as their king, even though the Norman Earls governed palatine estates. Donal IX was another literary king, and, as has already been mentioned, some of his poems are extant.

He had several illegitimate children and, by his wife Honora, sister and daughter of FitzGerald Earls of Desmond, he had a daughter and a son. We have already examined how Donal IX, refusing to surrender his title and kingdom, was eventually kidnapped by Lord Roche and the Lord Deputy, Sir Henry Sidney, in 1565 and taken to Elizabeth I's court in England. Under duress he was made to acknowledge the English Crown and become Earl of Clancarthy and Baron of Valentia. But Donal was astute enough not to surrender his title as MacCarthy Mór, which carried the in-built recognition of his royal status. Once back safely in Desmond, he declared himself still king, sending ambassadors to the Pope and the King of Spain, raising the standard of resistance.

From 1569 to 1572 he was fighting the attempt by Elizabeth to conquer Desmond. Elizabeth's generals eventually took the upper hand. Donal's son, Tadhg, Lord of Valentia, was taken hostage in 1578 and held in Dublin Castle as a guarantee of Donal's good behavior. Donal even wrote to Elizabeth I on May 23, 1583, seeking the boy's release. In the letter he also reveals that Elizabeth was holding his wife hostage in Cork. Elizabeth had Tadhg taken to England to be taught English ways, language, law and customs. However, the boy was soon back in Dublin Castle. From there, with the help of William Barry, he managed to escape to France. He died abroad in mysterious circumstances before July 1, 1588. The conclusion was that he probably died at the hands of the agents of William Cecil, Lord Burghley (1520–98), Elizabeth I's chief advisor and lord treasurer, who had organized a "secret service" that had assassinated several Irish aristocrats who had fled to Europe. It has even been speculated that Florence MacCarthy, the son of MacCarthy Reagh, had a hand in the matter as he had much to gain by it.

Donal, who was still referred to as Earl of Clancarthy but consistently used the title MacCarthy Mór, was now left without a legitimate son to name as his tanist. He had a daughter married to Florence MacCarthy, a son of Donough MacCarthy Reagh. Donal IX also had an illegitimate son, also named Donal, who emerged as a considerable military commander. Even during the worst times, Donal continued to lead his men as guerrilla fighters in the Kerry mountains, and, with Eóghan MacRory O'More, was an architect of the Earl of Essex's famous defeat in March 1599 at Bearna na Cleitidhe (The Pass of Plumes) near Ballyknocken Castle, four miles southeast of Portlaoise.

Long before his death in 1596, however, faced with the terrible devastation of Munster by the Elizabethan conquests—conquests that had, to all extents and purposes, transformed the kingdom into a desert—not to mention his personal tragedies, King Donal had retreated into his castle at Killarney, where he became more involved in religion and poetry. He was buried in Muckross Abbey where his tomb, bearing his arms, may still be seen in the chancel. Nearby are tombs of other Eóghanacht nobles—O'Donoghue of the Glens, MacGillycuddy of the Reeks and O'Sullivan Mór.

The war was carried on after his death, mainly by his illegitimate son, Donal. But the succession of the title was dispute. Donal has been described, at his meeting with Aodh Ruadh O'Neill, as The MacCarthy Mór. He certainly had considerable support for that claim from the Desmond nobles. Reports that O'Neill could create a MacCarthy Mór and did so, recognizing at different times both Donal and Donal IX's son-in-law, Florence MacCarthy (popularly, but incorrectly, referred to as Florence MacCarthy Reagh of Carberry), are fanciful. The O'Neill had no legal right to interfere in such a matter. Although Donal fought at Kinsale and joined O'Sullivan Beare in the aftermath of that defeat, a lifetime of fighting had exhausted him. He retired to his estates and dropped his claims to the title. His son, also illegitimate, did not pursue those claims either, and his descendants are said to have left for America in the nineteenth century.

The other claimant who flirted with The O'Neill for recognition as The MacCarthy Mór, Donal IX's son-in-law, Florence (1562?–1640), was the eldest son of Donough MacCarthy Reagh, Lord of Carbery. He had married Ellen, the only daughter and only surviving legitimate child of Donal IX. Florence showed some ambivalence in supporting his father-in-law against the Elizabethan conquest of Desmond. In 1589 he had been taken captive and imprisoned in the Tower of London. When he was liberated in 1591, he tried to negotiate with Elizabeth's ministers, suggesting that he would bring Desmond onto England's side if he were recognized as heir to his father-in-law's titles and estates. The title he was more concerned with was the one that Donal IX had rejected—that of Earl of Clancare (Clancarthy).

When The MacCarthy Reagh died in 1594, it was his nephew, Donal na Pipi (d. 1612), who succeeded under Irish law, and not Florence. He was not, then, The MacCarthy Reagh as has been claimed in some accounts. Rejected by his own people as well as by the English, Florence appealed to O'Neill, who had arrived in Munster with his army in 1600, to recognize him. O'Neill, as a political move, accepted him as The MacCarthy Mór in place of Donal, even though he had no legal power to do so. Once Florence saw that the wind of change was now blowing in England's favor, he promptly surrendered to England, hoping to curry favor. However, he was again committed as a prisoner to the Tower of London in 1601.

From then on he was virtually a prisoner. He had privileges in the Tower and wrote a history of Ireland in the early period dedicated to the Earl of Thomond as well as a treatise on antiquity and numerous letters. As for his claims, however, his cousin, Donal na Pipi, the legitimate MacCarthy Reagh, described him as "a damned counterfeit Englishman, whose study and practice was to deceive and betray all the Irishmen in Ireland." The burial register of St. Martin's in the Fields, London, marks Florence passing on December 18, 1640.

His sons claimed to be The MacCarthy Mór after him. Charles was appointed governor of Carrickfergus Castle by James II. He surrendered it to the Duke of Schomberg, William of Orange's general. He was found hiding in the kitchen of the Duke's headquarters. On being told that, Schomberg remarked: "If he had stayed with his men like a soldier, I would have sent for him, but if he would go and eat with servants in a kitchen, let him be doing." Charles's son died in 1770 and a cousin of his, a major in Clare's Regiment of the Irish Brigade of France, tried to claim the title but died without issue. Thereafter no descendant of Florence made any attempt to seek the title.

The line that did claim the title with more success than others were the Lords of Muskerry. The Lordship of Muskerry had been bestowed by Cormac VI (1325–59) on his second son, Diarmaid. Cormac MacTeige MacCarthy, who succeeded as twelfth Lord of Muskerry in 1571, was, according to the MacCarthy *Genealogie*, granted "542 pardons issued to him from the Crown for such of his subjects as took part in the MacCarthy Mór and Desmond confederacy with Spain." He had surrendered to Elizabeth on May 9, 1589, technically giving up his Gaelic title of Muskerry. Cormac Og resumed the Gaelic title as fifteenth Lord of Muskerry in 1617. But with the new social order he decided to make himself acceptable to the administration, and, on November 15, 1628, the titles of Viscount Muskerry and Baron Blarney were bestowed on him by Charles I. He died in 1640.

It has been argued that the Muskerry line retained the title of The Mac-Carthy Mór "with opposition." Viscount Muskerry's son, Donnchadh, who became the second viscount, fought from 1641 to 1650 and fled to France, joining Charles II's court. He was created first Earl of Clancarthy in 1658. The line of his first son (d. 1665) ceased with his infant grandson, Charles James (1665–1666). His second son, Callaghan, became third Earl of Clancarthy (1666–76). Callaghan's son Donough, the fourth Earl, espoused James II's cause and in 1689 welcomed James II to his house. He was made a lord of the bedchamber and given command of a foot regiment. Defending Cork, he was taken prisoner by the Williamites in October 1690. He was taken to the Tower of London. He managed to escape in 1694 and made his way to St. Germains, where James II had his court in exile. He was appointed as commander of the royal horse guards. He was recaptured by Williamites in 1697 and sent to Newgate to be tried as a traitor. However, William granted him a pardon on condition that he went into permanent exile. He went first to Hamburg. The poet Aodhagán Ó Rathaille wrote:

Darinis (Valentia) in the West—it has no lord of the noble race:
Woe is me! in Hamburg is the lord of the gentle merry heroes:
Aged, grey-browed eyes, bitterly weeping for each of these . . .

His line died with his son Robert, who, under the Jacobite peerage, was fifth Earl of Clancarthy (d. 1769).

It must be pointed out that the current Earls of Clancarty are related to MacCarthys only on the distaff side. This title was re-created in the United Kingdom peerage in 1803 for the family of Le Poer Trench, then holding the titles of Baron Kilconnel (1797) and Viscount Dunlo (1801). The family did claim a female MacCarthy descent, which was why those chose the title. Terence McCarthy claimed that the eighth Earl (who died in 1995) was his referendary general of the dynastic order of the Niadh Nask between 1980 and 1995, but nothing that Terence McCarthy said can be taken on trust. The eighth earl was an active member of the House of Lords and interested in unidentified flying objects. He was the author of seven books on the subject under his family name, Brinsley Le Poer Trench.

The line of the first Earl of Clancarthy, Donnchadh of Muskerry, had continued with Justin MacCarthy (b. ca. 1642, died 1694).[12] His Irish name was Saorbhreathach, but he has become better known under the Anglicized form of Justin. He had entered French service while his family was exiled during the Cromwellian period. In 1689 he took the side of James II and was at Cork to welcome James to Ireland. He was made master-general of artillery and also sat as a member for Cork in James II's 1689 Parliament in Dublin. On May 24 (June 3) 1689 James II created him Viscount Mountcashel. During the decisive battle of Newtown Butler against the Williamite forces, Mountcashel saw the defeat of his troops and personally threw himself at the enemy, hoping that death would exonerate his disgrace. The Williamites, recognizing him, spared his life and took him captive.

He escaped from Enniskillen, where he had been held. A sergeant in charge of his guard was executed for his lapse of vigilance. Mountcashel reached Dublin and was given command of a French regiment under the Duc de Lauzun, the former French commander of James II's army in Ireland. Tirconnell, however, ordered him to France to negotiate for reinforcements. After the initial Williamite victories, Mountcashel took nearly six thousand Irish soldiers into exile. These formed the nucleus of the famous Irish Brigade of the French Army, who were to play the decisive role in the defeat of the English at Fontenoy in 1745. Mountcashel was replaced as Irish Brigade Commander when Patrick Sarsfield, the Earl of Lucan, arrived with more Irish troops following the Treaty of Limerick. Mountcashel died "of wounds" at Barèges while taking the curative waters on July 1, 1694, says the *Gazette de France*. He had received wounds in Ireland, at Moutine and in the Rhineland. He had wanted his body returned to Ireland for burial, but this request was refused and he was buried at Barèges.

Terence McCarthy has claimed that Lord Mountcashel had actually been made Duke of Clancarthy by James II, and, as he was childless, he adopted his cousin Florence Callaghan MacCarthy as his heir, leaving him the title as well as estates in an elaborate will. Terence argued that the French king had recognized Florence as the second Duc de Clancarthy. He also claimed that the dukes survived until the time of the seventh Duc and that these Ducs de Clancarty-Blarney asserted the rights and prerogatives of MacCarthy Mór and the right to bestow the dynastic order of the Niadh Nask. All this was fabricated history (see chapter 12), for no such title existed in France.

It is true that during the eighteenth century there were at least two branches of the royal dynasty in France. The house of the Comtes MacCarthy Reagh de Toulouse was founded by Justin MacCarthy, born in Springhouse, County Tipperary, in 1744. The family was descended from Donal-na-Pipi, Prince of Carbery (d. 1612). Justin settled in France, having decided to quit

Ireland until religious liberty was restored. He had an "immense fortune" and became a naturalized Frenchman, receiving letters patent in September 1776, which elevated him to the French nobility. He married in 1765 to Marie-Winifride Tuite, daughter of Lord Tuite of Westmeath. He also bought what became known as the Hôtel du MacCarthy in Toulouse, a palatial eighteenth-century house. In 1868 the ownership passed to the old Toulouse family Courtois de Viçose, who still own it.

In the library, which Samuel Trant McCarthy mistakenly thought had been sold off by 1923, is a book entitled *Généalogie de la Maison Mac Carthy* (Paris, 1835), which does state that Justin MacCarthy was considered as Mac-Carthy Mór (*le double titre de Mac-Carthy-Mòr et Mac-Carthy Reagh*). Samuel Trant McCarthy, however, dismissed the Comtes MacCarthy Reagh as "a minor branch" of the family.

A second titled MacCarthy established the fortunes of his house at the same time. This was Denis MacCarthy, who had been admitted to the ranks of French nobility in 1756 as Comte MacCarthy de la Marliére, "*seigneur de Beaju, Fondival et Marlière.*" He had proved his noble lineage and founded the Mac-Carthy businesses at Bordeaux. He opened a trading house and a vineyard at Château MacCarthy that still exists today producing, under that name, an excellent St. Estèphe wine. Hôtel MacCarthy still exists in the Cour de Verdun in Bordeaux. The current owner of Château MacCarthy is the firm of Henri Duboscq & Fils.

By the early nineteenth century, the firm was one of the richest wine makers and exporters in France. It was known as MacCarthy Frères, even though one of the brothers, Daniel, who had been a member of the États-General (French Parliament) during the time of the Revolution, had been imprisoned during "The Terror" of 1793 and died from his experiences. The line continued from his brother John, who married Cecile O'Byrne of Château Houringue, to Comte Nicholas MacCarthy de la Marlière, who died without issue in 1925.

The fact remains, notwithstanding the books and essays written by Terence McCarthy, the soi-disant MacCarthy Mór of 1992 to 1999, with his claims of continuity among the adopted descendants of Lord Mountcashel from the eighteenth century still bestowing the dynastic order of the Niadh Nask, no MacCarthy Mór was ever legally invested under Irish law or recognized by a significant portion of the McCarthy family to warrant consideration. Now and then people claimed the title, but no claimant was ever taken with any degree of seriousness. It was in 1906 that Sir Arthur Vicars, Ulster King of Arms, examined and registered the pedigree of Samuel Trant McCarthy of

Srugrena Abbey, Cahersiveen, County Kerry, finding that he had descended from Cormac of Dunguil, younger son of King Tadhg na Mainistreach, Mac-Carthy Mór, King of Desmond (d. 1426). Based on research available at the time, Sir Arthur believed that the Trant McCarthys were the senior surviving line of the MacCarthy royal family.

The family had been established at Srugrena Abbey in 1656 by Donal Mc-Carthy. One of Donal's sons, Charles, in 1672 had married Ellen, a daughter of Cornelius McGillycuddy of the Reeks. Charles's brother, Donal Buidhe Mc-Carthy, was the progenitor of the senior line. In 1841 Daniel McCarthy married Ellen, a daughter of Patrick Trant of Waterview, Portmagee, and thus the name Trant was added to McCarthy as a legally adopted surname. Their first son was Samuel Trant McCarthy (b. 1842).

This, as we shall see in a later chapter, was the same family from which Terence McCarthy claimed descent and based his pedigree on. Samuel Trant McCarthy studied law and took up a position in the British Imperial Service in India; he went to Madras as a judge between 1863 and 1890. He married Dorcas Louisa, daughter of Richard Newman. She died in 1894 leaving Samuel with only two surviving children, both girls, Eileen and Kathleen. He married again in 1899 to Ebba, widow of Count Axel Otto de la Gradie of Maltesholm, Sweden.

Retiring to his home in Kerry, Samuel began to study his family history and wrote his famous book, *The MacCarthys of Munster* (1923). Having had his pedigree confirmed and registered by Ulster's Office in 1906, Samuel Trant McCarthy revived the Gaelic title MacCarthy Mór and, moreover, on July 1, 1921, he adopted the title as a name by deed poll.

According to Valerie Bary's *House of Kerry:*

> In 1922, during the upheaval of the Civil War, Samuel Trant McCarthy strangely claimed by Deed Poll, the title of McCarthy Mór [*sic*]. This could have been disputed by two more senior lines, whose members were said to be still extant. In fact, there had been bitter correspondence in a Kerry newspaper, from members of the Srugrena sept, who contested the seniority of Samuel Trant's grandfather.[13]

All the editions of *Thom's Directory* between 1922 and 1927 listed his name in a section "Ancient Irish Chieftainries Claimed by Representatives."

In 1927 Samuel died. Following the revelation of the imposture of Terence McCarthy there are now two claimants for the title. While Samuel's only son had died as a baby, Samuel did have two brothers: Daniel, who died in 1887, unmarried, and William Patrick (1853–1901), who became a solicitor in Killarney and had three sons. These were Donal (1893–1986), a Jesuit priest; Liam (1894–1967), a solicitor in Dublin; and Samuel (1897–1960). Liam was educated at Clongowes Wood College. He joined the 7th Dublin Battalion in 1914, served in Gallipoli, and also served in the Irish Free State Army after independence. He qualified in law and started a practice in Killarney. Then he moved to Dublin and won a reputation as a leading defense solicitor. When he died in November 1967, his death was widely reported in Irish newspapers.

Liam's son Cormac, who died in December 1999, in Moe, Victoria, Australia, was the senior surviving male heir of the family. Cormac had married Gwyneth Elizabeth Woodhead, in what was then Salisbury, Rhodesia (Harare, Zimbabwe), on April 6, 1957. It was her second marriage. There were five children. Liam, the eldest, was born in Salisbury on December 27, 1957; then Maureen (b. in Salisbury 1959); twins Brian and Moire (b. in Zambia in 1960); and Sheila (b. in Ireland 1963).

Liam began his education in St. Andrew's, a Catholic boarding school in Malawi. The family moved to England in 1964, leaving Cormac to follow. He never rejoined his family and is said to have taken a government-sponsored passage to Australia.

Liam, who is an Irish citizen and passport holder, finished his schooling in London and took a course in motor vehicle and design engineering at Uxbridge Technical College. He went to Africa in the early 1980s but returned to England in 1997. He has two children from two different relationships, his second child being a son, Alexander William. He accepts that he has much to learn about the history of his family as well as Irish history. He has applied for recognition from the Chief Herald as the new MacCarthy Mór.[14]

William Patrick's third and youngest son, Samuel, moved to England and finished his working life managing a small transport company.

Samuel, in turn, had three sons and a daughter: Liam Francis (1920–91), who was an RAF squadron leader and then worked on the administrative staff of London University; Father Desmond Donal (1922–95), a parish priest in the Southwark diocese; daughter Mignonne (1930-); and Barry Joseph Trant McCarthy. Barry Trant was born in Balham on June 6, 1931, and qualified as a certified accountant. He married Joy on August 6, 1960, and has a son, Anthony Donal (1961-) and two daughters.

It was in 1997 that Barry Trant McCarthy, alerted to the public posturing of Terence McCathy, wrote to the Chief Herald of Ireland pointing out that he was the great-nephew of the Samuel Trant McCarthy and that his family had no knowledge of any Belfast branch of the family. This set in motion the two-year investigation that resulted in the exposure of Terence McCarthy and the removal of his recognition. (See chapter 12.) Barry Trant McCarthy, then believing that he was the senior surviving male heir of the family, applied for recognition as MacCarthy Mór.

It is amazing that the descendants of Samuel Trant McCarthy were "lost to view" after his death in 1927, thus allowing for the rise of Terence McCarthy. The family of Samuel's younger brother are clearly mentioned in *The MacCarthys of Munster*, and they also appear on the genealogy drawn up by Sir Arthur Vicars. The Will of Samuel, dated July 1927, a copy of which is also in the Irish archives, clearly appoints William, his nephew, as his heir and successor.

What is even more astonishing is that there is held in the Genealogical Office the "Grey Manuscript," dated October 1944, which states that Father Donal, referred to in the manuscript as Daniel, Samuel's eldest nephew, was, in fact, the head of the family in that year and therefore the rightful claimant to the title. "Recapitulation: Mac Carthy Mór, and representative of Tadhg na Mainistreach, last king of Desmond [*sic*]: Donal Mac Carthy of the line of Dunguil and Srugrena Abbey, b. 1893." Terence McCarthy had access to this manuscript, for he quotes from it. Yet the Genealogical Office never checked the manuscript against his claims.

Until the Chief Herald makes a decision on future recognitions, Barry Trant McCarthy's application and Liam Trant MacCarthy's application will be held in abeyance. Whether one or the other of them will be acknowledged as the new MacCarthy Mór is still uncertain. Should either one be acknowledged, he will have his work cut out to repair the damage done to the name and title by Terence McCarthy.

THE O'CALLAGHAN (Ó CEALLACHÁIN)

Don Juan O'Callaghan Casas, The O'Callaghan, Lord of Clonmeen, Chief of the Name and Arms of O'Callaghan, lives in Barcelona, in Catalonia, Spain. He is head of a princely house that descends in unbroken male line from Morrough, second son of Ceallachán Chaisil (Callaghan of Cashel), the forty-second Christian King of Munster, who died in A.D. 952. Murrough was thus the first O'Callaghan. His eldest brother, Donnchad II, was King of Munster (d. 963).

The Eóghanacht King who gave his name to the O'Callaghan princely house was able to control the Norse attempts to dominate Munster in a series of famous victories. These victories are recounted in the *Cathreim Cheallacháin Chaisil* (The Battle-Career of Ceallacháin of Cashel), which was commissioned by Cormac III sometime between 1127 and 1134 and which has been discussed earlier.

For some time following Ceallacháin's death, the lines descending from his two sons, Donnchadh II and Morrough, lapsed into a bitter and prolonged rivalry regarding the succession of the throne of Munster. The conflict lasted for fifty years until, in 1092, Callaghan O'Callaghan (d. 1115) slew his cousins, Muiredach MacCarthy, King of Cashel, and his tanist, Donough MacCarthy, Ríoghdamna (Prince) of Cashel. Eventually the two branches of the Eóghanacht dynasty realized that the only people to benefit from this internecine feud were the Dál gCais (O'Briens) who claimed the Munster throne. Both sides of the family came together under Cenede O'Callaghan, Chief of Pobul I Callaghan, to support Tadhg I MacCarthy (d. 1124) against the O'Briens. This secured the restoration of the Eóghanacht to Cashel.

But, as a result of the partition between Thomond and Desmond in 1118, the O'Callaghans were driven from their ancestral lands, which lay in Thomond, by the O'Briens. They resettled in Clonmeen as vassals of the MacCarthy Kings of Desmond.

The O'Callaghans survived the destruction of Gaelic Desmond during the Tudor Conquests. Donough O'Callaghan, Lord of Pobul I Callaghan, had, in 1543, decided to enter into the surrender and regrant policy of Henry VIII of England. He was then resident at Dromaneen Castle, County Cork, and had married a daughter of Edmund Fitzgibbon, the White Knight. However, the first actual record we have of the Lord of Pobul I Callaghan having surrendered to the Tudors occurs in 1573, when Callaghan, son of Connor, was granted a pardon in September 1577. He was drowned in the Blackwater in 1578. In that same year we find that John Roche, the son of Lord Roche, who had kidnapped King Donal IX and taken him to London in order to force him to surrender his kingdom, was given the wardship of Donough O'Callaghan and also the custody of his lands to hold during the boy's minority. Roche was to bring up the boy in obedience to the English Crown, law and language.

In 1609 the English administration held an inquisition to determine who owned Clonmeen. The court found in favor of Conogher O'Callaghan, lord of Clonmeen, who had "received the rod, the symbol of rule" from King Donal IX with "a certain writing under the hand and seal of" the king dated July 20, 1590. These were shown to the jurors and they, presumably, accepted it as evidence of the right of the former Desmond Kings to bestow that lordship.

Donough O'Callaghan of Dromaneen and afterward of Clonmeen and finally of Mountallen, County Clare, on his majority, was elected as O'Callaghan. He supported the Irish uprising of 1641 and became a member of the Supreme Council of the Irish Confederate Parliament in Kilkenny. He was commissioned into the Irish Army as colonel and fought at the Battle of Clonleigh on August 2, 1642. He and his brother, Callaghan, a former law student, were declared outlaws and had to flee to France. His estate was confiscated and given to Sir Peter Courthorp. Although Clonmeen came back into O'Callaghan hands at the Restoration of Charles II, it was later burned to the ground during the Williamite Wars and the lands confiscated again.

A cadet branch of the family left to escape the Penal Laws and went to Europe in search of religious freedom. They found patronage among the European monarchs. Seán O'Callaghan had become a captain in O'Brien's Regiment of the Irish Brigade of the French Army. He died in 1712 having received the title of Baron in Baden-Würtemburg. His brother Conchobhar (Cornelius) settled in Spain and became an officer in the Ultonia (Ulster) Regiment of the Irish Brigade of the Spanish Army.

The chiefly branch of the family continued to live in Ireland at Kilgorey until Eamonn (Edmund), acknowledged as O'Callaghan, was killed in a duel at Spancil Hill horse fair, County Clare, in September 1791. As he had only daughters, the title went to his Spanish cousin, Don Ramon O'Callaghan (1765–1833). There was no authoritative arbiter to approve the matter as no *derbhfine* met. The Ulster King of Arms could not, of course, recognize a Gaelic nobiliary title. Therefore, the Lismehane branch of O'Callaghans and the O'Callaghans of Spain disputed the title between them.

When the Genealogical Office was established in Dublin, it was decided that Colonel George O'Callaghan Westropp would be recognized as The O'Callaghan. Leaving aside the curiosity of how someone bearing the surname Westropp could be recognized as The O'Callaghan, *Chief of the Name*, Dr. Edward MacLysaght soon realized that an error had been made and that the recognition of Colonel *Westropp* as The O'Callaghan made the office look rather foolish. He soon realized that the genuine heir to the title by both tanistry and primogeniture was Don Juan O'Callaghan. The Genealogical Office appeared in a quandary. The solution was that Colonel Westropp "was allowed by the Chief Herald to retain the title for his lifetime."[15] This, it was hoped, would avoid bringing the office into disrepute. However, the title The O'Callaghan rested clearly, and continues to do so, with the Spanish branch of the family.

The Chief Herald of Ireland finally recognized the right of Don Juan O'Callaghan (1903–79) to the title of The O'Callaghan. Don Juan was an advocate living in Tortosa. He was married to Enriquetta Casas of Tortosa. His son Don Juan O'Callaghan Casas (in Spain, the mother's surname is given last) was born in Tortosa on October 3, 1934.

Don Juan inherited the title on his father's death. He runs his own business as a consultant engineer, having taken his doctorate in electric engineering at Barcelona in 1960.

In accordance with tanistry custom the family has approved his second son as his tanist, another Don Juan, born in Tortosa on June 14, 1963. This Don Juan is also an engineer, holding doctorates from Barcelona and Wisconsin (in the United States). He is currently a professor at Barcelona University. The O'Callaghan points out that he holds his title under Brehon dynastic law of succession. He feels that the surviving Gaelic Chiefs do have a role to play in the modern world in relationship to the Irish state in creating a better awareness of Ireland's Gaelic past.

The O'Callaghan is a regular visitor to Ireland and took his seat on the Standing Council of Irish Chiefs and Chieftains in 1994. While he is a Spanish citizen, he would, if allowed by law, like to hold an Irish passport by virtue of his lineage and title. He is liberal in religion and, while a Catholic, says that: "In my opinion, any modern state must be secular and all the religious options must be accepted (except violent sects). Human rights must be fully guaranteed."

THE O'CARROLL OF ELY
(Ó CEARBHAILL ÉILE UÍ CHEARBHAILL)

The House of O'Carroll of Ely descends from Ailill Olom, King of Munster in A.D. 300, through his son Cian, from whom descends Cearbhaill, the petty king of Éile, a territory consisting of north County Tipperary and northwestern County Offaly in eastern Munster (Ormond). Cearbhaill was killed fighting the Danes during battle of Clontarf in 1014.

The current Chief claims to be the thirty-fourth generation in direct line from King Cearbhaill and is the only U.S. citizen to sit on the Standing Council of Irish Chiefs and Chieftains. However, like several other Chiefs, he now finds himself placed in an invidious position. The Chief Herald has announced a review of his pedigree which, in 2001, was put "on hold." The results and a decision confirming or withdrawing his "courtesy recognition" might still be years away.

Frederick James O'Carroll was born in Redding, California, on January 2, 1933, and was educated at Modesto College and the Ambassador College, Pasadena, majoring in theology. In 1953 he enlisted in the U.S. Navy where he was a cryptologist in naval intelligence. He served in Korea and left the Navy in 1957, but was called up again in 1966–1970 during the Vietnam War to deal with intelligence and communications.

The petty kingdom of Ely was under the lordship of the MacCarthy kings of Cashel, to whom the O'Carrolls paid tribute. Mánach, who succeeded Cearbhaill, was the first to take the surname of Ó Cearbhaill (O'Carroll). He was slain in 1022.

Under the patronage of an O'Carroll King of Ely, Tadhg (Thaddeus) O'Carroll (d. 1152), one of the great works of Irish art was produced. This is the Shrine of the Book of Dimma, now in Trinity College. An inscription of the shrine, a *cumdach* or ornamental box for the manuscript book, says that Tadhg Buidhe had commissioned the work. Alas, how Ireland forgets its kings! A recent catalogue, referring to the inscription of Tadhg Buidhe, merely says it "refers to Thaddeus O'Carroll, who died in 1152" without mentioning who or what he was.

For many years after the Norman invasion, due to its geographical location, the O'Carroll kingdom acted as a buffer zone against the Norman expansion. King Domhnall Fionn, defending his territory, was slain by the Normans in 1205. The *Annals of the Four Masters* record that the English sustained a great defeat by O'Carroll in 1318. But the English also had their victories, and, in 1407, Tadhg of Ely, regarded as one of the great benefactors to the Irish church and clergy, was also slain. Other O'Carroll princes, such as another Tadhg, tried to make their kingdoms more secure by marriages into the families of some of the great Anglo-Norman lords, such as the Butlers, who had settled in *Urmumhu* (east Munster), hence Anglicized as Ormond. Theobald FitzWalter had been created "Chief Butler" of Ireland by Henry II in 1177, hence the surname Butler. The Butlers settled in east Munster and soon received the title Earls of Ormond.

O'Carroll women were very prominent. "Mareague" O'Carroll (called Margaret), daughter of the Tadhg who had been a beneficiary to the church, summoned the learned people of all the Irish kingdoms to a meeting on the feast day of Da Sincchell (March 26, 1451), at Killeigh, County Offaly. The Chief Brehon of the kingdom, Gille-na-Naemh, recorded the names of the 2,700 *ollamhain* present at the gathering.

Her daughter, Fionnguala, had become wife first of The O'Donel and then of Aodh Buidhe O'Néill. She was regarded as one of the most distinguished women of her time. In 1447 she entered the monastery of Killaghy, where she died forty-six years later, her death being recorded on July 25, 1493.

The O'Carrolls tended to use the title "Prince of Ely" after the death of King Donnchadh in 1377. In 1532 the annals record the death of Prince Maelruna, whom the English regarded as having "ever been one of the King's greatest enemies, and done most hurt to the King's subjects." The Irish view is different, of course. The *Annals of Loch Cé* record him as: "The noblest and most illustrious Gael in Leth Moga." They continue:

> O'Carroll Maolroona, the most distinguished man of his tribe for renown, valour, prosperity, and excellence, to whom poets, travellers, ecclesiastics, and literary men were most thankful; and who gave most entertainment, and bestowed more presents than any other who lived of his lineage, died. He was the supporting mainstay of all persons; the rightful, victorious rudder of his race; the powerful young warrior in the march of tribes; the active triumphant champion of Munster; a precious stone, a carbuncle gem; the anvil of knowledge; and the golden pillar of Ely; and his son, Feranaim, was appointed his successor.

Curiously, Feranaim means *Fear gan Ainm* (man without a name). There was a dynastic dispute within the O'Carroll *derbfhine*, and Fear gan Ainm was challenged by the sons of Seán O'Carroll. Gerald FitzGerald, eighth Earl of Kildare, who was Fear gan Ainm's father-in-law, came to his aid in this internal O'Carroll dispute and besieged the O'Carrolls in Birr Castle. It fell to him. Soon after the Earl of Kildare was imprisoned in the Tower of London, suspected of plotting against the English King. In 1498 he was back as Lord Deputy. Henry VII of England said: "If all Ireland cannot rule this man, let him rule all Ireland." In 1513 he died of wounds he received fighting the O'Carrolls of Ely once again.

However, Fear gan Ainm continued as Prince of the O'Carrolls of Ely. It was on June 12, 1538, that he concluded a treaty with Lord Leonard Grey, the Lord Deputy, that he would cease to be "prince" and thenceforth style himself as "Captain of the Ely O'Carroll, and pay feudal tribute to the English Kings." The treaty outraged Fear gan Ainm's *derbhfine*. In 1541 he was assassinated in Clonisk Castle, near Shinrone. He was supposed to have been elderly and blind by this time and living in seclusion. If so, he would not have continued in office under Brehon law, for he would have been excluded by physical impediment as well as by reclusive habits.

Yet such stories make entertaining reading. It is told that Fear gan Aimn's nephew, Tadhg, was able to gain entrance to the castle through his uncle's trust and then proceeded to slaughter the old man and twelve of his servants who tried to protect him.

Tadhg certainly succeeded his uncle. In May 1543, Henry VIII allowed Tadhg to be recognized as "captain of his nation" to ensure his "good behavior." Tadhg did not behave as the English wanted. In 1548 he led a rising in his territory. Sir James Ware curiously called him "the one eyed O'Carroll." It is curious inasmuch as a physical impediment would have excluded him from office under the law. Tadhg initially managed to rout the English troops and drive them from Ely. Where the Tudors could not succeed in warfare, they resorted to diplomacy and guile. Inviting Prince Tadhg to come to Dublin, to attend a court and discuss ways of resolving the conflict, they simply seized him and imprisoned him in Dublin Castle. After they secured from Prince Tadhg a promise of good behavior under duress, he was released and, in 1552, he was not only pardoned but made a knight and bestowed with the title Baron of Ely.

In 1554 Liam Odher O'Carroll, Tadhg's younger brother, supported by the *derbhfine* who, once again, objected to the surrender by their Chief, challenged Tadhg. Liam Odher now found himself The O'Carroll. But he also found that the Tudor politicians were not so easily dealt with. He allowed himself to be knighted and then recognized by the English administration as "Captain of His Nation." It was, however, only a means of buying time. He finally rose up and fought an "awful war" and met his death in 1558 at Kincor.

The English now used their "influence" to ensure that the new O'Carroll would be more sympathetic to their policies. Liam O'Carroll of Lemyvanane was installed as The O'Carroll of Ely. On July 28, 1578, he formally recited the surrender ritual, in which he agreed to give up the Irish language, laws, titles, and his estates. In return, a portion of the estates were regranted on a feudal basis and he was made a knight. He accepted primogeniture, securing the succession of his properties to his four sons, John, Tadhg, Calloghe and Donoghe, to the exclusion of the rightful heir, his brother Donoghe Koghe O'Carroll, who had been named tanist by the *derbhfine*. Laim became "Sir William," accepting the English title in 1579, the year after his surrender of the title.

The opposition by the *derbhfine* to Sir William's English law successor resulted in a blood feud. The English administrations supported the sons of Sir William. Several O'Carrolls of the *derbhfine*, such as the sons of Fear gan Ainm, who put forth their claims under Brehon law, were assassinated.

However, it proved impossible to impose English law on the O'Carrolls. When Cahir (Calvach), a son of Liam Odher, was appointed The O'Carroll in 1582, it was clear that Brehon law still prevailed. He was initially courted by the Tudor administration and knighted by Sir John Perrott in 1584 in Dublin. He played a waiting game for several years until, with the defeat of the English at Yellow Ford, Cahir decided that the time had come to join his forces to those of the other Irish princes. Troops from O'Neill's army, under Eóghan MacRory O'Moore, had moved south and were joined by troops under the command of Donal MacCarthy, son of the late Donal IX. The O'Carroll took part with them in the famous victory over the Earl of Essex at the Pass of Plumes in

1599, where the O'Carroll battle cry "*Seabhac a bu!*" (The Hawk to Victory!) is said to have panicked Essex's soldiers. Cahir returned to Lemyvanane after the battle. He had given hospitality to a company of MacMahons from Oriel (Monaghan), some one hundred men, who had fought with O'Carroll against Essex. Cahir now refused to pay them a promised sum for expenses. One thing led to another, and hasty words were exchanged. The story is that Cahir led some of his men to where the Oriel warriors were sleeping that night and slaughtered all of them.

The following year when Aodh Ruadh O'Neill Mór was marching southward, the Ulster king took it upon himself to punish Cahir for this crime. He devastated the countryside and left a garrison of his own men in it. He recognized the appointment of Mulroony O'Carroll as The O'Carroll. In July 1600 Cahir was assassinated by a group of O'Carrolls and O'Meaghers. The *Annals of the Four Masters* seemed generous in recording Cahir as "a strong arm against the English and Irish neighbours."

Mulroony, the new Chief, was actually knighted by Sir George Carew at Dublin Castle in 1603, the day of the coronation of James I in London. Now the concept of the old Ely kingdom was completely gone. The O'Carrolls were soon to become merely Anglicized knights with large landholdings. Indeed, Thomas O'Carroll left the estates to settle in Dublin, becoming Lord Mayor. He was knighted by Sir Arthur Chichester and given the Abbey of Baltinglass as his seat.

The family seemed to have adhered to the Stuart cause for a while, being compensated by Charles II for the losses of their estates during the Cromwellian confiscations. Eóghan O'Carroll represented County Offaly in James II's Dublin Parliament of 1689.

The line of the princely house continued in a new guise, still producing strong leaders such as Antoine Fada (Long Anthony), who was one of Patrick Sarsfield's commanders in the Williamite Wars. He was owner of Emmell Castle. At his headquarters in Nenagh, hearing of the approach of the Williamite troops, he burned the town and force marched his troops to Barna. The Williamite soldiers were ambushed by him there and slain to a man. The battle became known as Bloody Togher.

It was Long Anthony's great-grandson, Richard O'Carroll, who lost the remaining lands secured by his family. He indulged in lavish hospitality and was generous to the point of foolishness.

There were many lines of descent of the O'Carroll princely family. One of the most fascinating was the branch founded by Charles O'Carroll, who settled in Maryland, in America, in 1688. He was a direct descendant of King Tadhg, who had endowed the Irish Church. He had managed to obtain a commission, from King James II, appointing him attorney general of Maryland. He married a daughter of Colonel Dernall, a kinsman of Lord Baltimore, who appointed him as "agent and receiver general" of the colony. Charles's grandson, another Charles, of Carrolltown, signed the American Declaration of Independence. This Charles was born in Annapolis in 1737, educated by Jesuits, and studied law in Paris and London. He was thirty-six when he became active in politics and published a series of arguments against the administration, establishing himself as a leading member of the American independence movement. Early in 1776 he was sent by the American Congress, together with Benjamin Franklin and Samuel Chase, to the northern colonies (what is now Canada) to argue the case for independence. He was elected to Congress for Maryland.

He also worked on the Maryland State Constitution and served in the upper house of the state legislature. He worked both in the United States Senate and the Maryland Senate, retiring from public life in 1800. He died at age ninety-four in 1832 and was buried at Doughoregan Manor, near Elliott City. He was regarded as the richest man in the country. Charles left a line that provided a governor of Maryland in the person of John Lee Carroll.

William O'Carroll of Arabeg, Birr, was regarded as the senior representative in 1915, and the genealogy of the various lines of Arrabeg, Kilfada and Emmel, with certified copies of wills and deeds, were held by him. However, the current Chief traces his line from the Litterluna branch of Daniel O'Carroll, whose great-great-grandson, James Carroll (born about 1815) emigrated with his son, also James (born 1840), to the United States in 1851. James, who died in 1921, had a son Michael Frederick. He was born in 1864 and lived in New York, where he died in 1938.

His son, the current O'Carroll's father, Winfrey Frederick O'Carroll, was born in 1909. The family settled in Tehama, California. With the death of Winfrey Fredrick in 1969, his son Frederick James, then aged thirty-six, sought recognition for himself as The O'Carroll of Ely. He was finally given "courtesy recognition" by the Chief Herald of Ireland on January 22, 1993.

However, other branches of the family have claimed the title. These include O'Carroll of Athgoe Park, who traced their descent from Seán, The O'Carroll of Ely (d. 1489). They were living in Wicklow in the 1930s, and their pedigree appeared in *Burke's Landed Gentry of Ireland*. Another claimant to be The O'Carroll was the Carroll family of Killiner House, Drogheda, County Louth, who traced their descent from the O'Carrolls, Princes of Oriel, and The Carrolls of Culcredan of Louth. In the 1930s they were still resident in their seat at Killineer House, with an entry in *Burke's Landed Gentry of Ireland*.

The current O'Carroll, after his career in the U.S. Navy, became an executive for the West Mark Tank Trailer Company. He retired in 1987 and became involved in the establishment of the Clan Cian Services, a company chartered in 1982, promoting the Clan O'Carroll. The Clan Cian indicates the descent from Cian, son of King Ailill Olom. The O'Carroll also supports the Roscrae Heritage Society, in Roscrae, County Tipperary. Like other members of the surviving Gaelic nobility, The O'Carroll is anxious that Ireland's Gaelic identity should not be lost. He endorses the state's proclaimed policy to restore the Irish language and its constitutional place as the first official language of the state. He takes his role seriously:

> I feel the Chiefs and Chieftains should be allowed consideration for their titles within the future political scope of modern Ireland. Since 1982 I have been actively involved with representation, promotion of Irish culture, instructive at activities in regards to Irish heritage, primarily in the United States with visits to Ely O'Carroll territory.

O'Carroll says: "I currently hold a U.S. passport. If allowed I would wish to hold an Irish passport. I consider my relationship to the Irish Republic as an Irish American seeking restoration of my family to the republic."

The O'Carroll first married Agnes Heimstra, on March 1, 1958, a descendant of the Butlers of Ormond. They were divorced. He is currently married to Gracy Ann Block. His son by his first marriage, Frederick Arthur James O'Carroll (b. July 9, 1968), is The O'Carroll's tanist. Frederick Arthur is also married with two sons, Michael Frederick James (b. 1991) and Seán Arthur James (b. 1993), and a daughter.

The O'Carroll looks on the promotion of his heritage very much as a family business. He personally believes that his title descended by primogeniture. He was only one of two Chiefs out of the twenty who initially took this line. He explained:

> I feel Gaelic titles and the right of succession should remain meaningful today, even without the Brehon laws, in the modern Irish Republic. My title is acknowledged through a line of hereditary descent through the Kings of Éile of the Litterluna branch of O'Carrolls originating with Brehon times.

This is not an argument accepted by scholarship or by his fellow Chiefs. The reiteration of the basis of Gaelic titles being founded on Brehon law of succession by the Standing Council on January 9, 1999, has not been challenged by O'Carroll.

THE O'DONOGHUE OF THE GLENS, LORD OF GLENFLESK (Ó DONNCHADHA AN GHLEANNA)

The current O'Donoghue of the Glens is Geoffrey Vincent Paul O'Donoghue, born on July 19, 1937. The origin of the O'Donoghue line, like that of other Munster princely families, resides in the Eóghanacht royal house of Munster descending from Coirpre Luachra, one of the seven sons of King Conall Corc, whose descendants became known as the Eóghanacht Locha Léin—Lough Leane being the largest of the Killarney lakes in County Kerry. The family produced several kings of Munster, the last being Olchoba mac Cináeda (d. A.D. 851). The patronymic came from Donnchadh, who was head of the family in the twelfth century. The numerous islands in Loch Léin were the main strongholds of the Ua Donnchadha or O'Donoghues. Ross Castle, on the shores of the lake, was granted to them as their principal residence by the Mac-Carthy kings after the famous victory over the Anglo-Normans at Callan on July 24, 1261.

It was around this time that a legend sprang up around Donall, a grandson of Donnchadh, who was then The O'Donoghue Mór. Two agnomens were attached to his name. One was *na nGeimhleach* and it has been argued that this means "of the fetters." The alternative form *na gCaoil-each* means "of the slender reeds." No one really knows the correct form. A corpus of legends stretching back to the sixteenth century concern him and are very traditionally Celtic. Supposedly Donall fell into an enchanted sleep and rests in a hidden cavern beneath Loch Léin. Every May Day morning he may be seen at dawn riding his horse, shod with silver shoes, across the waters of the lake. He also can appear at other times in order to protect the people against their oppressors.

The senior line of the O'Donoghues was that of The O'Donoghue Mór, a line that appears to have become extinguished during the Tudor Conquests. Céitinn, in his *History*, mentions that The O'Donoghue Mór and The O'Sullivan Mór were the two princes who were allowed to perform the ceremony of inauguration for The MacCarthy Mór. Pardons had been granted to Rory O'Donoghue, given in the Letters Patent as "alias the O'Donoghue More," and his son, another Rory, during the 1570s. In a grant of the former O'Donoghue estates at Ross to Nicholas Browne, which appears under a Lord Deputy's warrant of March 7, 1600, no mention is made of what had happened to The O'Donoghue Mór, just that the estates and lordship had been granted to him by King Donal IX MacCarthy Mór, referred to as "Earl of Clancar." With Donal being dead, the English Crown felt it could confirm the grant of the estates.

The O'Donoghue of the Glens, a cadet branch of this family holding the lordship of Glenflesk to the southeast of Killarney, also having received pardons at the end of the Tudor Conquests, managed to survive the turmoil of the conquests and confiscations. It is a moot point whether The O'Donoghue of the Glens might be considered, in addition to his title, the heir to the title of The O'Donoghue Mór. Note that the family has no such intention; this is merely a hypothesis on the author's part.

The history of the family is fascinating. The name Seafraidh (Geoffrey) has become a popular name among the holders of the chiefly title. Seafraidh, The O'Donoghue of the Glens, died in May 1601, before the disastrous defeat at Kinsale. His brother, Ruaidri (Roger or Rory), had been executed by the English in 1585. That the O'Donoghues still managed to retained their lands in Glenflesk, Gleann Fleisce—the valley of the hoop—in Kerry might have been due to their natural fortifications in the Derrynasaggart Mountains.

Seafraidh's son, Tadhg, had married the daughter of Donal MacCarthy Reagh. Their son Seafraidh was born in 1620. Seafraidh succeeded his father to the title in the middle of the Cromwellian devastations in 1655. His father had been holding out against the Cromwellian General Ludlow in Killaha Castle. Whether Tadhg's death was from natural causes or the result of the siege is not clear. Certainly, General Ludlow reduced the castle that year. The thirty-five-year-old new Chief was already active in the war against the English. His brother Tadhg had married Griobha, daughter of Sir Phelim O'Neill, leader of the 1641 insurrection. Sir Phelim had been executed in Dublin two years before the new Chief was elected.

Seafraidh Ó Donnchadha an Ghleanna appears as one of the most romantic of Chiefs at this time. He was not only a remarkable guerrilla leader but was one of the most respected poets writing in the Irish language. Besides writing poems in a courtly, traditional style known as the *dán díreach* meter, he wrote political poems, laments and elegies, including a poem on a pet spaniel killed while in pursuit of a mouse. His work has been edited in *Dánta Shéfraidhh Uí Dhonnhadha an Ghleanna* by Pádraig Ua Duinnín (Dublin, 1902). As a man of action as well as a poet, O'Donoghue of the Glens was able to make good use of the natural fortifications of Glenflesk, which became a place of refuge for people from the conquered areas. In 1654 the Irish population was ordered into a reservation consisting of Connacht and County Clare, territory on the west bank of the River Shannon. Any Irish found on the east bank without a permit after May 1, 1654, was liable to immediate execution. Tens of thousands of men, women and children were rounded up and shipped to Barbados and other New World plantations as enforced labor. Glenflesk lay outside this allotted "reserve" but was still holding out; it did so until the Stuart Restoration in 1660. Although the castle and the estates of The O'Donoghue of the Glens had been confiscated on paper, no one had courage actually to enter Glenflesk to enforce the confiscations. Most of the Irish landholders thought the Stuart Restoration would mean a return of their confiscated lands. It did not. Seafraidh wrote a bitter poem:

'*s barra ar an gcleas* . . .

This caps all their tricks, this statute from overseas
That lays the switch on the people of Eber Fionn
A crooked deal has robbed us of our claim
And all our rights in Ireland are swept away.

The Gaels are stripped in Ireland at last
And now let the grave be dug of every man.
Or let them get their pass and cross the waves
And promise to stay gone to their dying day.
He ends, however, with a hopeful verse.

Although the English are stronger now than the Gaels
And though their fortunes are better than for some time here:
Relying on their titles, they will not yield a field.
On their backs God's anger will pour down in streams.

Seafraidh died in March 1678 before he could witness what further tricks and burdens Ireland was to suffer. He was buried in the chancel of Muckross Abbey and is also commemorated on a monument in Killarney, confusingly under another Irish version of the name Geoffrey—Goffraidh.

In spite of Seafraidh's anguish at the failure of the Stuarts to rectify the confiscations of Cromwell, his son Donal, the new Chief, supported James II. Donal and his brother Florence joined with MacCarthy Mór, then recognized to be Lord Clancarthy of the Muskerry line. After the Treaty of Limerick, Donal remained in Ireland hoping that the English would keep to the treaty, and he even applied for a portion of his former Kerry estate in 1700.

His brother, Florence O'Donoghue, was not so trusting of English intentions and became one of those who, in the words of his father, received "their pass and cross(ed) the waves." He became Chevalier Florence O'Donoghue, commander of the Bodyguard to Queen Mary of Modena. Florence's second son, Geoffrey O'Donoghue, became an officer in the army of the French Republic. A descendant of this line achieved fame in the Irish Brigade of the Spanish Army. He was Lieutenant General Juan O'Donoju (the Spanish phonetic of the name). Juan (1755–1821) was appointed Viceroy of Mexico in order to negotiate Spanish withdrawal. He devised the *Plan de Iguala*, which gave Mexico its independence in 1821, and thus an O'Donoghue takes his place in history as Spain's last Viceroy in Mexico.

The family of The O'Donoghue of the Glens managed to survive the Penal Law period and all attempts to eradicate them. They were one of those aristocratic families who "went underground" during this period, known and respected by local people but, to the English administration, merely one more family bearing the name "Donoghue." They lived quietly, refusing to change their religion for political gain, until those pernicious laws were repealed in the nineteenth century. They then reemerged to take an active part in public life. Charles James, The O'Donoghue of the Glens (b. 1806–ca. 1833), died in Florence on a trip to Italy. The family was living at Summerhill, Killarney. His son Daniel O'Donoghue became The O'Donoghue of the Glens, and set out to place the family once more on the historical map of Ireland. His cousin was a maternal aunt of the Irish republican revolutionary advocate and theoretician of the 1848 insurrection—the Young Ireland leader, Thomas Davies. Educated at Stonyhurst, Daniel became a Whig Member of Parliament for Tipperary from 1857 to 1865 and later for Tralee from 1865 to 1885.

Daniel attracted a lot of publicity and he was not reticent about using his Gaelic title. Even the London *Times* accepted its use and always referred to him as The O'Donoghue. While the English law could make no recognition to those Gaelic Chiefly titles abolished by statute and common law, *Thom's Directory* now published listings of those claiming such titles and The O'Donoghue was one of the first titles to be so listed during the Victorian period. However, when *The Times* (London) referred to The O'Donoghue, it was not without disdain and bitterness. A *Times* leader of February 25, 1862, stated:

> The O'Donoghue has been making one of those exhibitions which can only be made in just such a place as the British Parliament, and at just such a time as this middle of the nineteenth century. With the perfect certainty of no unpleasant consequences, he has been able to tamper with his allegiance to defy his Sovereign and finally to insult his opponent on the floor of the House of Commons. In the reign of Queen Elizabeth singular personages appeared in the streets of London under quaint Irish denominations, with bands of retainers in barbaric accoutrements. The Court connived at a breach of the law that

would not have been tolerated in any rational Englishman, and which only amused the rabble, for there was no surer way to lay the ghost of Irish independence than to let it show itself in the streets at midday.

Apparently, The O'Donoghue of the Glens, as a "Home Rule" Member of Parliament, had addressed a meeting in Dublin's Rotunda. According to the London *Times*, he and his followers had "denied the Queen's flag to be the Irishman's flag, they denounced Englishmen as their natural foes, they claimed sympathy with the Irishmen in the American Federal Army, and they invited Irishmen to size the opportunity of shaking off the English yoke." In the course of a debate in the House of Commons, this meeting was referred to, and the Chief Secretary for Ireland, Sir Robert Peel, said that it consisted of "manikin traitors" who sought to imitate the "cabbage garden" proceedings of 1848. This was a reference to the fiasco of the Young Ireland uprising of July 1848, when some of the leaders, including William Smith O'Brien, brother of Sir Lucius of Dromoland Castle, a direct descendant of the High King Brían Bóroimhe, were surrounded by troops in Widow McCormack's farmhouse at Ballingarry and, after a skirmish, forced to surrender. It was later disparagingly called the skirmish in Widow McCormack's "cabbage patch."

The exact words of Sir Robert Peel's speech from the Parliamentary Report were: "A meeting was then held in the Rotunda, at which a few manikin traitors sought to imitate the cabbage garden heroes of 1848; but I am glad to say they met with no response. There was no one to follow. There was not a single man of respectability who answered the appeal."

Sir Robert Peel's reference to The O'Donoghue as one of the "manikin traitors" was considered by The O'Donoghue to be a personal insult. His friend the Member of Parliament for Limerick, Major G. Gavin, later explained the subsequent actions to the Commons.

> I thought over those expressions, and I arrived at the conclusion that they were words that no gentleman should rest under. I had the honour of being in the army for twenty-four years, and I am quite certain that no such language would be tolerated in that honourable profession.

Indeed, The O'Donoghue felt so strongly that he asked Gavin to "act as his friend," a euphemism in those days for a second in a duel, and Gavin called on Sir Robert Peel to ask him to withdraw the words he used. Sir Robert said "he would adhere to the words in their integrity." Major Gavin then asked him to refer him to a friend, conveying The O'Donoghue's challenge. Sir Robert told Gavin that he would need a letter outlining the challenge. Gavin wrote a note:

My dear Sir Robert—As the explanation given by you to me regarding the words you made use of towards The O'Donoghue last night in the House is not satisfactory, and as the matter cannot possible remain in its present position, I must request you at once to refer me to a friend.

Sir Robert told Major Gavin that he would refer the matter to his "friend."

The friend turned out to be Lord Palmerston, the Prime Minister. Palmerston brought the matter up in the House of Commons on February 24, accusing The O'Donoghue of a breach of privilege by challenging Sir Robert Peel. The Prime Minister had absolved Sir Robert from backing out of an "affair of honour" by telling him that it was his duty to decline the challenge: "It is our privilege to say whatever we think right in Parliament and it is a breach of the privileges of this House that what any Member says in this House should be questioned out of this House by any person whatsoever."

Instead of receiving an apology from Sir Robert Peel for his insulting remarks, The O'Donoghue was now ordered by the Speaker to apologize to Sir Robert and the House. The O'Donoghue commenced his speech by saying that he deeply regretted if he had violated the privileges of the House. He was cut short by the Speaker when he referred to Sir Robert Peel's words and pointed out that they were personally insulting. Peel accepted the apology and assured the House that the matter would proceed no further. It did. Rather spitefully, Sir Robert removed The O'Donoghue from his position as a Justice of the Peace for Counties Cork and Kerry.

The people of Tipperary demonstrated their support for The O'Donoghue by giving a sumptuous banquet in his honor in April 1862. With the ending of the Civil War in America and the demobilization of tens of thousands of Irish veterans who had taken an Irish Republican Brotherhood oath, there now began a period of unrest in Ireland leading to the suspension of habeas corpus in February 1866.

The Times in London began to describe him as "a defender of Fenianism." The IRB's sobriquet was Fenians, naming themselves after the Fianna, the élite bodyguard of the High Kings of Ireland. In a debate on the "disturbances" in Ireland, on February 9, 1866, *The Times* reported that

The O'Donoghue . . . proceeded to point out the causes of this disaffection. The chief of these, he said, was the Act of Union, which had deprived the people of the right of self-government and prevented them from redressing the evils of which they complained. He denied that Fenianism had produced this disaffection; the Fenians, on the contrary, had found everything ready to their hands, and the foundations of Fenianism, with which he warned the House the majority of peasantry deeply sympathised, was an impression that all the ills which afflicted the country were the result of English misrule.

Against the Fenian attempt to seize the munitions store at Chester Castle in February 1867 and then the insurrection, mainly confined to Dublin, Cork, Limerick, Tipperary and Clare, during March, *The Times* castigated the speeches of The O'Donoghue.

On February 12, 1867, *The Times* was able to report another speech by The O'Donoghue in which he boldly stated: "English rule in Ireland was synonymous with oppression and tyranny." The O'Donoghue's outspokenness in the cause of Irish independence caused Dr. David Moriarty, the Catholic Bishop of Kerry (1856–77), to publicly censure his conduct. Not daunted by an attack from the prelate, The O'Donoghue replied in a letter in *The Times* telling the bishop that his admonition that Ireland must be subservient to the interests of England was not in accordance with the spirit of the Irish people.

With the defeat of the Fenian insurrection and the total clampdown on republican activity followed by the emergence of Isaac Butt's Irish Party to pursue domestic self-government in Westminster, The O'Donoghue, who was very much an individual, found several matters in the party policy to disagree with. The London *Times* immediately started to lavish praise on him, claiming that he had done a "public service" by not joining the Irish Party.

In May 1874 The O'Donoghue wrote a letter explaining his apparent change of heart towards Irish self-government. "I have not joined in the agitation for a separate legislature not, as you seem to think, because I am opposed to Irish rule in Ireland, but because I believe the Irish members can govern Ireland in the Imperial parliament." The O'Donoghue seemed to adopt the theory that a reform of Parliament with a stronger emphasis on Irish Members concluding domestic Irish business without the majority of English Members of Parliament being allowed to vote on these matters was the answer for better government. However, he soon realized that the majority, English Members, would not allow this "ideal" to happen. When in 1879 Charles Stewart Parnell took over the Irish Party, he became its active supporter.

The O'Donoghue was a man of extremes. At the same time as apparently explaining the Fenian cause he took a commission as a major in the Kerry Militia. He married the daughter and coheiress of Sir John Ennis of Ballinahoun Court, Athlone, Westmeath, and that became his seat. But it seems he was a spendthrift, squandering his money. In 1870 he was in the Court of Bankruptcy and the hearing became a cause célèbre. His bankruptcy was annulled in 1871.

In 1881 another bankruptcy hearing was begun; again the findings were annulled in 1882. This colorful O'Donoghue died in 1889.

His eldest son, Geoffrey Charles Patrick O'Donoghue, succeeded to the title at the age of thirty. Like his father he was educated at Stonyhurst. Unlike his father, he preferred a more quiet life. He married the daughter of a Surgeon General in the British Army, Anne Charlton of Clonmacnoise House, Offaly. When he died in 1935, his son Geoffrey Charles Patrick Randal O'Donoghue succeeded as The O'Donoghue of the Glens.

Geoffrey had been born in 1895 and also went to Stonyhurst, which was becoming a family tradition. From school he went to Sandhurst and was commissioned, in January 1915, as a second lieutenant in the Connaught Rangers. By the end of 1915 he was a full lieutenant, serving in the 3rd Battalion. He was sent to France. In later years he revealed that one of his fellow officers in the Connaught Rangers was the actor and film star Stanley Holloway. Stanley Holloway did, indeed, see service as a lieutenant in France with the Connaught Rangers.

Geoffrey O'Donoghue was wounded early in 1916 but, after a spell of convalescence, rejoined his unit. In this day and age we know something about post-traumatic stress disorder. Those soldiers executed between 1914 and 1918 by firing squad for "cowardice" and recently accepted to have been cases of shell shock, which was not then admitted as a physical trauma by the British Army, have now been "pardoned" and rehabilitated in the service records. Whether such a trauma arising from his wound was the cause of Geoffrey's subsequent attitude to continued service in his front-line battalion is a possible explanation to the fact that he seemed to go to pieces. His conduct led to a Court of Inquiry and a subsequent General Courts Martial on March 2, 1917, at Locre, resulting in him being cashiered.

Geoffrey, even before the verdict was confirmed, had enlisted as a private in the South Irish Horse, and some months later transferred to the Royal Dublin Fusiliers. He served until February 1919, officially being discharged in January 1920, with the rank of lance-corporal. The day after his discharge he reenlisted as a private in the 1st Battalion of the Royal Dublin Fusiliers and was sent to India. One wonders if he was spurred on by the thought of redeeming himself for being cashiered.

Speaking on Radio Éireann some years before his death in 1974, The O'Donoghue told how he was stationed in Multan (Multoon) in the Punjab. It was here that he heard the news during June 1920 that soldiers from the 1st Battalion of his old Regiment, the Connaught Rangers, hearing of the atrocities of the English "Black and Tans" and "Auxiliaries" in Ireland, had run up the Irish republican flag and refused to take orders from their officer. The incident happened at the battalion bases at Jullundur and at Solan. Eventually only one soldier was executed out of the sixty men who were sentenced to death; the others had their sentences commuted to terms of penal servitude. The British Army as well as the politicians had been keen to "hush up" news of the mutiny, and too many executions were liable to bring the matter to public attention. The consideration was not simply the effect such news would have in Ireland during the continuing conflict; there was the question of the reaction in India to consider. This was only a year after General A. E. Dyer had ordered his troops to fire into a crowd of several thousands, including women and children, attending a peaceful protest meeting in Jallianwala Bagh, a square in the middle of Amritsar. Casualties were 379 dead and over 1,200 wounded. Subsequently, General Dyer had ordered public floggings and forced Indians to crawl on their hands and knees through certain streets in the city. The situation in India as well as Ireland under the *pax Britannia* was volatile.

The O'Donoghue, in his radio broadcast, recalled how he and three companions named Kirwan, Fitzpatrick and Murray had hoisted an Irish republican flag over their base in Multan on St. Patrick's Day, 1921, to commemorate the event. There is no regimental record of any such incident in the official diaries of the Royal Dublin Fusiliers, but within seven months of his arriving in India, Fusilier O'Donoghue was discharged from the army, his "services no longer required." The story occurs also in the O'Donoghue entry in *Burke's Irish Family Records* of 1976. After returning to the newly established Irish Free State, Geoffrey became a captain in the Free State Army.

The current O'Donoghue of the Glens succeeded to the title at the age of thirty-six on the death of his father. Breaking with the previous tradition, he was educated at the Christian Brothers School in Enniscorthy, County Wexford, living for a while in Westmeath before making his home in Tullamore, County Offaly. He is a widower; his wife, Frances, a school teacher, was killed in a road accident in 1984. He has three sons and four daughters. He runs a small engineering business, having previously served as a noncommissioned officer in the Irish Army Air Corps. As an aviation engineer he later worked for the British Aircraft Corporation on the development of the VC10, TSR2 and Concorde.

The Irish *Who's Who* has called him "a low profile chief." He accepts that his title has a real meaning only if passed down through the Brehon laws of tanistry succession that created it in the first place. Therefore it is not his eldest son Conor (born 1964) nor his second son Donagh (born 1970) who will succeed him as The O'Donoghue of the Glens, but his youngest son Geoffrey

Paul (born 1971). He has already been appointed as tanist and heir to the title. Geoffrey Paul is a graduate of Trinity College, Dublin, and holds a degree in computer science.

While The O'Donoghue of the Glens is inclined to the belief that Gaelic titles might be seen as something of an anachronism in a democratic republic, he believes that they can have validity only if they are a link with Gaelic culture and law and not re-created in an English primogeniture system. He considers that only the Irish of the "diaspora" show any real interest in the old Gaelic nobility. "Most Irish people in Ireland do not forget that many of the Gaelic nobility fled abroad leaving the ordinary Irish people to face the devastations and Penal Laws of the English conquest." He feels that Irish people are generally unaware of the old Gaelic aristocracy and would not understand if they were now given any role in the modern Irish state. He thinks, perhaps, that subsequent generations of Chiefs might overcome this lack of knowledge.

The O'Donoghue of the Glens is a mild-mannered man, passionately interested in studying Irish history in what time he can spare from running his business concerns. He is an enthusiast about County Offaly history and is very exhilarated at having made his home in a county that is full of so many fascinating memorials of past events. His ambition is to ensure that there is an awareness among Irish people of the history of the Gaelic aristocracy. He also hopes that the Irish language will be preserved as "it is an important link with the past and without it there can be no understanding of that past." His late wife was Irish speaking. Although he is a Catholic, he does not agree with any special role between church and state that had been given in the 1937 Constitution. "The old Gaelic tradition was not religiously exclusive. It is time for Ireland to accept that it is a secular state."

Although there is a point in O'Donoghue's view that most Irish people today view the families of the old Gaelic aristocracy as, somehow, "deserters," who fled as refugees to Europe with what finances they could to leave the ordinary people to suffer the consequence of the English conquests, it is not an accusation one can level against his Chiefly line. Until modern times there was always an O'Donoghue of the Glens living if not in Glenflesk itself, then close by in County Kerry. Now the Chief lives in County Offaly. The O'Donoghues have suffered equally with their people from the results of the conquests and played no small part in fighting those conquests. Additionally, they have played their part in the continuing struggle for independence. No consideration of the War of Independence (1919–21) can be made without reference to the various historical studies of Florence O'Donoghue (1894–1967), from Rathmore, Kerry, who fought in Cork No. 1 Brigade of the Irish Volunteers as Brigade

Adjutant and Intelligence Officer. He also served in the Defence Forces (1940–45). And no general review of Irish literature can ignore the diversity of the poems of their most romantic Chief, Seafraidh Ó Donnchadha an Ghleanna. The history of The O'Donoghues of the Glens is truly reflective of the struggle for existence of Gaelic Ireland.

THE O'DONOVAN OF CLAN CATHAIL
(Ó DONNDHUBHÁIN)

The O'Donovan Chiefs are of princely origin, and the family stems from one of the royal Eóghanacht houses of Munster. The family take their name from Donnabháin, a son of Ceallacháin mac Buadacháin, King of Munster (d. A.D. 954). Donnabháin settled near Limerick where his father had defeated the Danes who had established a city-state there. His name meant "black" or "swarthy headed." About A.D. 977 Donnabháin's son Crom Ua Dhonndubháin (O'Donovan) adopted the patronymic form, then becoming popular in Ireland. The name then became variously given in Irish as Ó Donnabháin and Ó Donndubhán. Crom settled in Castle Croim, on the bank of the Maigue, County Limerick, which became a seat of their power.

They were eventually driven from their ancestral lands by the expanding new power of the Dál gCais who were not only dominant in north Munster (Thomond) but were to wrest the throne of Munster from the Eóghanacht. The Uí Dhonnabháin and their followers moved south to settle in the area of Glandore Bay and Skibbereen, in southwest Cork, where the current Chief still resides.

Crom's son Cathal O'Donovan, who became the head of his family, gave his name to the clan, which became the Clan Cathail. The head of the O'Donovans was originally called the "Lord of Clan Cathail," but the current O'Donovan points out that this suffix has not been used by his family for a considerable time. Another branch of the family became the Clan Loughlin. Both branches paid feudal dues and were installed by the MacCarthy Reagh, who, in turn, served their kinsmen, the MacCarthy Kings of Munster.

Dermot, The O'Donovan of Castle Donovan, three miles north of Drimoleague, County Cork, received a pardon from Elizabeth in May 1577 and surrendered his title and estates. The last acknowledged Lord of Clan Cathail to be installed under the Brehon system, receiving the white wand of office from the MacCarthy Reagh in 1591, was Donal O'Donovan of Castle Donovan. Even the English administration, in the person of the Lord Chancellor, Archbishop Adam Loftus, recognized him as "captain of his nation," the euphemism for a senior Gaelic noble, on February 12, 1592. Dr. John O'Donovan found an inauguration ode in Irish written by Maldoni O'Morrison, which he translated in a personal letter to The O'Donovan dated September 15, 1841:

> Who is the prop of the name of the West
> Of the Princes of the Race of Fiaha?
> It behoveth one like me
> To point out the Chief of the Name,
> The one of Donal Fragon of Tonn Cleena
> Is the representative of the hereditary name . . .

Donal (called Daniel by the English) finally surrendered his title and territory in the reign of James I to Sir Nicholas Welsh, the English President of Munster, in May 1601. In 1608 he is reported to have received a regrant of the entire estate, having agreed to convert to the Anglican Protestant faith and become English in speech and culture and accept English law. He was, however, not rewarded with a title and is referred to as "Gent." His Gaelic title had been abolished under law.

The Irish scholar, John O'Donovan, a member of a cadet branch of the family, wrote to The O'Donovan in 1841: "I am satisfied that none of the name of O'Donovan ever had [an English] title; never! not even that of knight! . . . It does not appear that any of that family ever got a title under the Crown of England except Sir Owen who fought at Kinsale 1601–2."

A confirmation of the pardon for "Daniel O'Donovan Gent. of Castle Donovan" was made on October 27, 1607.

Donal's son Donal (also referred to as Daniel) was stripped of his estates during the Cromwellian devastations. His son, also Daniel, managed to have them restored by Charles II. An adherent of the Stuarts, Daniel served in James II's Dublin Parliament of 1689 as Member for Baltimore. He became a colonel in the Jacobite army. Having commanded Charlesfort at Kinsale, he was forced to surrender to the future Duke of Marlborough, John Churchill. He had the foresight to obtain honorable terms from Churchill, who secured him in his estates in spite of the Williamite Confiscations.

It was with another Daniel O'Donovan (whose will is dated 1770) that his direct line ceased. In his will O'Donovan named his heir a Morgan Donovan, of the city of Cork, described as "a kinsman." This demonstrates that the Brehon concepts were not dead among the O'Donovans, because Daniel had two sons. So this kinsman Morgan, with family approval, was to inherit the residue of the estates in order "to preserve them with the Chiefship of the sept." However, Morgan died before Daniel's own son Richard, and so the inheritance went to him.

General Richard O'Donovan (born 1768) served in the 6th Dragoon Regiment of the British Army in Flanders and Spain. He was married but without issue, and his brother had died unmarried. Richard left the estate of Clan Cathail to his widow and his remaining property to his cousin, the son of the kinsman Morgan who had been named in his father's will. This son, the Reverend Morgan O'Donovan, rector of Dundurrow, County Cork (1769–1839), became The O'Donovan. He married Alicia, a daughter of William Jones, of the Bence-Jones family.

His son Morgan William O'Donovan (1796–1870) succeeded to the title followed by his brother Henry Winthrop O'Donovan (1812–90). Henry was High Sheriff of the county and married a daughter of Gerald de Courcy O'Grady, who was The O'Grady of Kilballyowen. It was Henry who made a particular point of reviving the old Gaelic title. His son, Morgan William O'Donovan, became a colonel in the Royal Munster Fusiliers and served in the South African War, commanding the regiment's 4th Battalion from 1903 to 1914. He also served as High Sheriff of Cork before he died in 1940.

His successor was Morgan John Winthrop O'Donovan, who followed his father into a military career, serving in the Royal Irish Fusiliers during World War I, winning a Military Cross in 1917 and being mentioned in dispatches. As a brigadier he commanded the 1st Battalion of the regiment from 1937 to 1940 and retired to finish the war serving with the Red Cross. He died in 1969 to be succeeded by his son.

As with several other Chiefly titles, The O'Donovan title has not been without its recent challengers and, until the 1960s, the O'Donovens of Clerahan styled themselves as The O'Doneven. The family were descended from Hugh Óg O'Donovan, who sailed with the remnants of his regiment to exile in France after the defeat of the Irish in 1691. They served in the Irish Brigade of the French Army. In 1843, Lieutenant Colonel Rhoderick James *O'Donoven* (the spelling showing the French influence), of the 87th French Infantry Regiment, was allowed to take up residence in Ireland at Clerahan, near Clonmel. His wife was also descended from Irish exiles, being Marguerite Lally-Tollendale. The family maintained the title The O'Doneven through the years of exile and after they had resettled in Ireland until the 1960s, when the title was challenged as not being recognized by the Chief Herald of Ireland under the new primogeniture rule.

Lieutenant Colonel Ernest O'Donoven (b. 1895) was a leading member of the Irish Genealogical Research Society and Military History Society of Ireland, signing his articles "Lieutenant Colonel, The O'Doneven."

The current O'Donovan points out that among the famous members of the clan was Diarmuid (Jeremiah) O'Donovan Rossa (1831–1915), born in the family territory at Rosscabrery. His first language was Irish, and he ran a small business in Skibbereen. He became a leading organizer of the Irish Republican Brotherhood (the Fenians) in 1858. He became business manager of *The Irish People*, the journal of the movement, but was arrested in 1865 and sentenced to life imprisonment for treason. In 1869, while still in prison, the people of Tipperary elected him as their Member of Parliament. He was badly treated in English prisons and wrote a classic account of his ill-treatment, published in New York in 1874. He was released in 1871 due to the public outcry about this treatment and exiled to America.

He remained politically active through his newspaper *United Irishmen*, urging the continued struggle for an independent republic in Ireland. He died in 1915 and his body was brought back to Ireland to be buried at Glasnevin in Dublin. Pádraic Pearse gave his famous graveside oration, which wound up with the prophetic words:

> The Defenders of this Realm have worked well in secret and in the open. They think that they have pacified Ireland. They think that they have purchased half of us and intimidated the other half. They think that they have foreseen everything, think that they have provided against everything; but the fools, the fools, the fools!—they have left us our Fenian dead, and while Ireland holds these graves, Ireland unfree shall never be at peace.

Within the year the Easter uprising had taken place in Ireland.

Another member of the family was the renowned antiquarian and scholar John O'Donovan (1809–61), whose works are legion, making pioneering translations and editions of many of the ancient manuscript books of medieval Ireland. His son, Edmund O'Donovan (1844–83), became a famous war correspondent. In 1883 he went with the army of Hicks Pasha to the Sudan as a representative of the *Daily News*. On November 1, 1883, General William Hicks's 10,000 troops were ambushed at El Obeid by the troops of the Mahdi. Three days later not a man had survived and O'Donovan was never heard of again.

The current holder of the title, Morgan Gerald Daniel O'Donovan, was born in Pau, France, on May 4, 1931, where his mother, Cornelia, daughter of William Bagnell of the Royal College of Surgeons, Dublin, was also born and partially brought up. Daniel, as he is known, was educated at Stowe and at Trinity College, Cambridge, where he received his master's degree in 1954. In 1959 he married Frances Jane, the only daughter of Field Marshal Sir Gerald Templer. His son and heir is Morgan Teige Gerald (b. 1961), educated at Harrow. He is a barrister in London and is also married.

The family seat is still in the ancestral lands. The current O'Donovan settled his family in Skibbereen, County Cork, on the death of his mother in 1974. He had been a company director in an engineering business and was managing director of Waters & County Ltd. He turned from engineering to farming and farmed his estate for ten years. Then he decided to rent the unusable acreage and improve the accommodation of two lodge houses and two more houses for tourist accommodation. He serves on the General Synod of the Church of Ireland, is a governor of Middleton College, Cork, and serves on the Standing Council of Irish Chiefs and Chieftains, being elected to serve as chairman in January 1998 until 2000.

He accepts, but with qualification, that Brehon law succession is the only meaningful way to inherit a Gaelic title.

> I claim that my being Chief of the Name is indisputable. My family being fortunate in that Dr. John O'Donovan produced after lengthy research, and as a footnote to his great work in translating *The Annals of the Four Masters*, my family pedigree, the historical veracity of which has never been scholastically challenged or at any rate refuted. Possibly I beg the definition of "meaningful" but since primogeniture has pragmatically been appealed to since the Brehon Law of Succession (i.e., by election, even though always within a confined definition of democracy) ceased to be adhered to for the pragmatic reasons expounded by Edward MacLysaght and others, it must be regarded as valid. Probably I would be Chief of the Name had Brehon Law have been scrupulously followed, but I fear that it could only be a matter of conjecture, in my case, and I can't help thinking, in that of all Chiefs and Chieftains.

The O'Donovan holds both Irish and United Kingdom passports. He does not agree with some of his fellow Chiefs that the holders of the ancient Gaelic titles could realistically have any other role in the modern Irish state than they do already. "The Senate would be the only body which realistically might have representation but this country's constitutional views on titles makes the possibility remote at this moment."

He is interested in Irish history but in particular his own family, "possibly of a greater interest to O'Donovans outside rather than inside Ireland."

> It would be a tragedy were the [Irish] language and its literature be lost, but I consider that preservation as the result of generous scholarships would be more effective than compulsory learning of the language by official decree, which probably kills a high proportion of potential enthusiasm as well as being manifestly wasteful of resources and talents.

Although a member of the Synod of the Church of Ireland, The O'Donovan did not wish to see the removal of the clause in the Constitution that gave a special recognition to the Roman Church. He reasons:

> I might object to the Constitutionally supported position of the Roman Catholic Church, particularly as the Government of the country has on occasion unquestionably been influenced thereby. But Roman Catholicism, though like all religions in this age, waning in its influence, is the church of the vast majority of Irishmen, and as a Christian I dislike the notion of a secular state. So my answer is a qualified "yes" in support of special position.

THE O'LONG OF GARRANELONGY, LORD OF CANOVEE (Ó LONGAIDH)

It is a common mistake today to regard anyone with the name Long in Ireland as being of English origin. The name belongs to a family that is one of the oldest branches of the Eóghanacht royal dynasty of Munster.

Oengus Mac Nad Fróich, the first Christian King of Munster (d. A.D. 490/492), had a brother named Cass. Cass was the great-great-great-great-grandfather of Prince Longadh, living around A.D. 640, who was the patriarch of the Clan Longaidh, the O'Longs.

The present O'Long, Denis O'Long, was born in 1930, and believes he is the thirty-sixth generation in unbroken male line descent from Longadh, and fortieth from Oenghus, who was said to have been baptized by Saint Patrick and St. Ailbe on the Rock of Cashel. His early genealogical heritage survives in a poem attributed to the seventh century entitled *Duan Cathain*, preserved in *An Leabhar Muimhneach*. By the time of the Anglo-Norman invasion, the O'Longs were already well established in their present territory in Muskerry, mid-county Cork—the lands of Canovee, Moviddy, Kilbonane, Kilmurry and Dunisky, straddling the River Lee.

From an early period the O'Longs were closely associated with the Catholic Church, and references to them can be found in the *Calendar of Papal Letters* during the time of Innocent VIII in 1484. Donatus O'Longay was designated to the vicarage of Canovee and Magourney. In 1459 another O'Long priest named Gilbert is referred to in the parish of Aglish. Further papal documents mentioned other O'Longs in priestly office, such as John O'Long in the parish of Moviddy in 1490, and Donal O'Long was referred to in the parish of Kilmurry next to Canovee.

The O'Longs paid feudal rents to the MacCarthy Lords of Muskerry amounting to some £4 10s annually.

That the O'Long chiefs, like all Gaelic chiefs of Munster, resisted the Elizabethan conquest is borne out by the fact that the then-Chief "Donogh Rua O'Longe of Kanavoy" had to receive pardon from Elizabeth I on November 21, 1576, for having fought for Donal IX MacCarthy Mór. Donal's heir, Dermod, received a similar pardon on February 17, 1600. Numerous members of the family received pardons in 1602 and 1603 in the wake of the Irish defeat at Kinsale. We have reference to a Dermot O'Long in 1602 fighting with Don Juan de Aquila, commanding the Spanish forces, at Kinsale. Dermot fled into exile in Spain. The title of The O'Long was then abolished, and certainly the old Gaelic territorial lordship of Canovee was no longer admitted by the English administration. Presumably, although the records do not appear to show it, the O'Longs had made formal submission, surrendering the title and land in return for receiving a portion of the estate back in regrant under feudal conditions.

When Dermot O'Long of Canovee died on March 2, 1623, an inquisition was held on September 24, 1624, and found that he held lands in Canovee and several adjoining estates. It was ordered that, on the payment of £106, the O'Long heir could resume the ownership. The heir was John FitzDermot (the *Fitz* substituted for *Mac*) O'Long, born around 1598/99. He was twenty five and married. The O'Longs were ordered to render military service to the English crown as part of the rents due on their lands.

For a short time, the O'Longs enjoyed a period of comparatively settled conditions. In 1636 John Long—for the administration required the dropping of the Gaelic "O" and "Mac"—a son of Thomas Long, who had been educated at the University of Paris, was given permission to build the manor of Mount Long on a thousand acres of land near Oysterhaven. In 1641 this John Long of "Rynynyan," a cousin of the claimant to the title of O'Long, became High Sheriff of County Cork, and with the rising of 1641 he formed the "rebel camp" at Belgooly near Mount Long. In 1642 this was attacked by the English and dispersed. Mount Long was abandoned. John Long was taken prisoner, and, in 1652, John Cooke was sent by Parliament to preside at his trial in Cork. Cooke had been the solicitor for Parliament at the trial of Charles I. Long could expect no mercy nor was he given any. Cooke himself, as a regicide, was to be executed in London at Charing Cross on October 16, 1660. The ruins of Mount Long still stand and are now the property of the Irish state.

John Long was not the only member of the family to fight during the wars from 1641 and pay the supreme penalty. The O'Long himself fought alongside Donnchahdh an Chúil, Viscount Muskerry, head of the MacCarthys of Muskerry, against the English Parliamentary forces. For this, following Cromwell's victory, the O'Long estates were confiscated. The O'Long died in 1653.

At the time of the Restoration, Donough MacCarthy, the new Earl of Clancarthy, was able to use his influence to get Charles II to restore all the Muskerry lands under his lordship. Therefore the estate of Canovee returned to the O'Longs in the person of another John O'Long. He held the ancestral home bearing the name Garranelongy (grove of the Longs), which had been renamed by the English settlers as Bellmount.

Darby O'Long, the successor to the chiefship, was actually appointed a judge of the law courts in 1687. He held the office of Recorder of the city of Cork and sat in James II's Dublin Parliament of 1689 representing Old Leighlin, County Carlow. In the same parliament, distant kinsmen Dermot and John Long represented Middleton. For his support of James II, Darby O'Long was outlawed in 1691.

By some means, he seems to have reconciled himself with the new Williamite administration and returned to his estate. The confiscations and devastations and Penal Laws of William's conquest passed Darby O'Long by for a few years. Then, in 1711, the estates of Canovee were passed into the ownership of Joseph Damer. Perhaps Darby O'Long's experience in law helped him for he was able to retrieve the ownership.

When the Anglican Bishop Dive Downes of Cloynes later made a tour of his diocese, he noted in his journal that the church at Canovee was in ruins. "Counsellor Long's lands bound upon it—the Earl of Clancarthy had, and Counsellor Long has, an estate in the parish. No other proprietors." The O'Longs had saved their ancestral home at Garranelongy.

Darby's son, Darby II (d. 1786), who is buried at Kilmurray, succeeded to the estates. The Gaelic gentry now began to be reduced by the oppressive Penal Laws of the Williamite Conquest to a social level barely indistinguishable from that of many small tenants. They were forbidden by law to any form of education, practice of professions or even the purchase of freehold interests in land. The heirs to many of the Chiefly houses drifted into exile in Europe or simply changed their faith, language and culture to become indistinguishable in the ordinary people's eyes from their conquerors.

The O'Longs remained in Canovee and Garranelongy, enduring and surviving quietly. Their only genuflection to the new order was the Anglicization of their name and the excising of the "O." However, maintaining their Catholic faith, they were excluded from office and bounded by disabilities. But because no Catholic could own lands under the Penal Laws, a member of the family had to convert to the Anglican faith in order to maintain them. The Longs were still acknowledged as members of the Gaelic nobility of Muskerry.

In 1706 Ellinor, the daughter of Darby I O'Long, married Daniel FitzGerald, son of John, the thirteenth Knight of Kerry and his wife, the daughter of Viscount Clare. Their son Maurice became an officer in the regiment of Lord Clare in the Irish Brigade of the French Army. Their eldest son married Mary Butler, eldest daughter of Theobald, seventh Lord Cahir of Cahir Castle. In 1789, James, The O'Long, married Johanna Sweeney, one of the Mac Suibhnes who had been Lords of Mashanaglass.

With the easing of the Penal Laws and the allowance of Catholics to join the professions, life changed for the O'Longs. Like other Irish Catholics, they were now free to follow what careers they chose. They could also reassert the "O" in their name. Denis O'Long (b. 1886) was educated at the Christian Brothers College in Cork and qualified as a surgeon at the Royal College of Surgeons in Dublin. He succeeded his father, William, in 1908 as The O'Long and married Elizabeth, daughter of John F. Corkeran, a Justice of the Peace, of Blarney, County Cork.

His son is Denis Clement Long, the current Chief, born in 1930. Like his father, he was educated at the Christian Brothers College in Cork. He is also a Knight of Honour and Devotion of the Order of Malta. In 1971 he married Lester Jean O'Rorke Clarke and has two sons. His tanist is James Stephen Long, born on May 21, 1973, who followed the tradition of an education at the Christian Brothers College Cork and later took an honors degree at University College, Cork, in 1994. He is now director of his father's company, D. C. Long Ltd.

The O'Long has been chairman of the Blarney Pigs Company from 1972. He became managing director of D. C. Long Ltd. in that year also. His hobbies are hunting with the Muskerry Foxhounds, sailing with the Royal Cork Yacht Club and, of course, the study of Irish history. He has written and lectured about his own family history. He has been patron of the Kilmurry History Society, Honorary Secretary of the Canovee Historical and Archaeological Society and a council member of the Cork Historical and Archaeological Society.

When the Chief Herald of Ireland, Donal Begley, granted "courtesy recognition" to his title, endorsing his pedigree, in 1989, The O'Long organized an O'Long Clan Rally, which was held on August 25, 1990, and was officially opened by the Irish Minister of State for Culture (now the Ministry for Heritage), Denis Lyons TD. The Chief Herald was there to present the documentation along with Gene Fitzgerald, Member of the European Parliament, and a collection of dignitaries including O'Conor Don, The O'Brien (Lord Inchiquin) and The O'Grady.

The O'Long considers that the Irish Chiefs ought to have representation in the Irish Senate and other Irish institutions by virtue of their titles. He is a strong supporter of Gaelic culture and of the attempts to preserve the Irish language in Irish life.

He is a Catholic and agrees with the Irish Constitution recognizing the special position, within the state, of the Holy Catholic and Apostolic and Roman church as a guardian of the faith, as amended on December 7, 1972. "I do not feel that the Irish State should become a secular State."

Although The O'Long recognizes that his title must, in reality, have meaning only if held under the Brehon law of succession and feels that he does hold his title with the approval of his *derbhfine*, he adds the caveat: "I still must have regard to and respect for the laws of the land as a citizen of the Republic of Ireland, which must have a part in the equation too."

In the wake of the MacCarthy Mór revelations, O'Long was another Chief who found his pedigree under attack from Seán Murphy, who runs his own, one-man Centre for Irish Genealogical and Local Studies. On May 9, 2000, on his website, Murphy quoted the Deputy Chief Herald, Fergus Gillespie, as making the following statement: "There is no registered pedigree of O'Long at this office. O'Long has never had arms granted or confirmed to him by any Chief Herald." Even Murphy found this "startling." Indeed, it was highly damaging to the reputation of O'Long. On May 17 the Chief Herald, Brendan O'Donoghue, confirmed the statement.

> I can confirm that there is no Registered Pedigree for O'Long and no grant or confirmation of arms. Besides, I regret to have to tell you that we have been unable to locate a file relating to his recognition as Chief of the Name.
>
> In case there may be any confusion, I should add that Registered Pedigree has a particular meaning in Genealogical Office terms, well known to Seán Murphy who made the specific original enquiry to Fergus Gillespie. Secondly, grants or confirmations of arms are those dealt with formally by letters patent and included in the Arms Registers kept at the Office. There is, of course, an entry for O'Long in *Clár na dTaoiseach*, and this contains what might be called a simple pedigree and a painting of arms, but these do not amount to a Registered Pedigree or a grant/confirmation of arms.[16]

The Chief Herald added: "As of now, we have no proposals to re-open O'Long's case for recognition."

But within a few months the situation had apparently changed due to publicity engendered by Seán Murphy in the press and media. Murphy denounced O'Long's pedigree as bogus and called for an inquiry. The Office, sensitive after the "McCarthy Affair," announced a review of O'Long's pedigree. This, like the other reviews, is currently on "hold."

However, The O'Long, even before the announcement of a review, was shocked by the accusations and employed a reputable genealogist, Paul Gorry. Gorry had discovered the McCarthy fraud after being employed by the Chief Herald's Office to examine his pedigree. O'Long also asked for the help of medievalist Dr. Kenneth Nicholls of Cork University to examine the material pertaining to that period.

While the Genealogical Office could not find the registered pedigree of The O'Long, O'Long was in possession of copies of correspondence and documentation with the Genealogical Office dating from March 1978. At that date Eileen O'Byrne had set about drawing up an O'Long pedigree which was completed at the Office in January 1985. On August 1, 1989, The O'Long's Patent and Arms were duly recognized by the Office. In October 1993, Eilish Ellis completed a new, lengthier O'Long pedigree, which was placed in the Office in January 1994, bearing the Office stamp. More important, *Iris Oifigiúil*, the official Irish Government Gazette, of February 18, 1994, published the official courtesy recognition given to The O'Long by the then Chief Herald. On May 17, 2000, The O'Long was invited to meet with the Deputy Chief Herald to show him copies of those documents which had been "mislaid" by the Genealogical Office. Yet, on the same day, the Chief Herald placed in writing his confirmation that the Office did not have the documentation.

This appears to reflect the apparent chaos into which the Genealogical Office had now been thrown by the "McCarthy Affair." Like the other Chiefs "named" by Seán Murphy on his website, it seems that the review of The O'Long's pedigree and claim to his title will take some time. In the meantime, The O'Long, who has a reputation for punctilious honesty, is financing his own review through a reputable genealogist and historian.

THE MACGILLYCUDDY OF THE REEKS, LORD OF DOONEBO (MAC GIOLLA MOCHUDHA)

The house and title of MacGillycuddy, Lord of Doonebo (the appendage "of The Reeks" was a nineteenth-century one) is a comparatively new arrival by Irish standards. The MacGillycuddys originated as a distinct line in the sixteenth century, having previously been a cadet branch of the house of the O'Sullivan Mór. In turn, the O'Sullivans were a branch of the Eóghanacht royal dynasty of Munster. Súileabháin (the hawk-eyed), flourished in A.D. 950, and traced his ancestry back to Eóghan Mór (d. A.D. 192). Buadhach, Súileabháin's successor, was the first to use the patronymic Ó Súileabháin. The senior prince of this house became, in Anglicized terms, O'Sullivan Mór, whose stronghold was in Kenmare Bay in Kerry. A second branch occupied the Beara Peninsula, straddling Kerry and Cork, and took the title O'Sullivan Beare.

The territory of MacGillycuddy was on the Iveragh Peninsula, more popularly denoted these days as the Ring of Kerry. Ireland's spectacular mountain range, containing Ireland's highest mountain, Carrantuohill (3,414 feet), is called MacGillycuddy's Reeks. It is here that "The Reeks" mansion at Beaufort still stands, home of the MacGillycuddy of The Reeks family until it was sold in 1985.

A popular first name among the O'Sullivans from the thirteenth century became Giolla Mochuda, *giolla*—meaning servant—of Mochuda, the pet form of St. Carthach of Lismore (d. A.D. 653). In 1563 Conchobhar (Conor) Giolla Mochuda Ó Súileabháin slew his kinsman Donal, the O'Sullivan Beare. The fact is mentioned in the *Annals of the Four Masters*. It was from this time that his line became known as Mac Giolla Mochuda.

The MacGillycuddys had already been given a territorial lordship by the MacCarthy Kings of Desmond and were Lords of Doonebo. Sir Warham St. Leger, reporting to the Privy Council of Elizabeth I said, "The eighth [lordship] is the country of MacGillicuddy. It containeth 46 ploughlands. He [Donal IX MacCarthy Mór] claimeth there rising out, the giving of the rod, the finding of 30 gallowglasses, and the value of £30 a year in spending."

In other words, the MacGillycuddys were not allowed to take office unless they were handed the white wand or rod of office by The MacCarthy Mór. They also had to provide him with military service, which included thirty gallowglass—mercenaries originally from Scotland.

There is little known of the details of the early MacGillycuddys. One was described by the poet Aonghus Fionn Ó Dálaigh (c. 1599) as hating mankind "as a daisy hates the night." Domhnall Geraltach MacGillycuddy was slain in the fight against the Tudor Conquest in 1595. Some of his estates were confiscated and granted to Edmund Barrett. John MacGillycuddy was pardoned in 1600, but in 1615 other sections of the MacGillycuddy lands were confiscated and granted to Sir Charles Wilmot and Walter Crosbie.

Donough MacGillycuddy of Carnbeg Castle supported the Irish uprising in 1641 and the establishment of the Irish Confederate Government in Kilkenny, which returned the estates. With the Cromwellian conquest, the MacGillycuddys suffered confiscation again. On the Restoration of Charles II, in 1661, Donough MacCarthy, the new Earl of Clancarthy, certified the good service of The MacGillycuddy against the Parliamentary forces and Charles II confirmed the restoration of the estates. Donough thereby became Sheriff of County Kerry and obtained a grant of arms from the Ulster King of Arms.

With the conflict between James II and William of Orange, the MacGill-cuddys thought it prudent to have members of the family supporting both sides. The lessons of the previous wars had been taken to heart. Donough's son Conor (Cornelius) MacGillycuddy secured a commission in Lord Slane's Regi-ment of the Jacobite Army. Another member of the family fought in Limerick during the siege in 1691. Yet another MacGillycuddy was Governor of Cork and had to surrender it to John Churchill, the future Duke of Marlborough. But Donough, The MacGillycuddy, was to take the oath of allegiance to William and Mary in November 1694. Denys MacGillycuddy, his great-nephew, had taken a commission in William's service, and his immediate family served William of Orange in various military capacities.

It would appear that the family now fully accepted the Tudor conditions of surrender and embraced the Anglican faith, English law and language, and through these means they were able to retain ownership, influence and power over part of their former estates in Kerry long after the collapse of the Gaelic aristocracy.

They continued to aspire to high office in County Kerry. Richard (b. 1750) not only became High Sheriff but in 1793 was deputy governor of the county. As it became fashionable to reassert the old Gaelic titles in public, the MacGillycuddy also reassumed his title. In spite of the entries in *Burke's Irish Family Records*, it was only in the nineteenth century that "of The Reeks" was added to the title. The *Kerry Evening Post*, in June, 1866, reported the death of Richard MacGillycuddy (b. 1790) in these terms:

Obituary of Eminent Persons
The M'Gillycuddy

Richard M'Gillycuddy, called, as chief of his sept "The M'Gillycuddy of The Reeks," died on the 6th instant, at his temporary residence, 6 Upper Pembroke Street, Dublin, after a protracted illness. He was the eldest son of Francis M'Gillycuddy Esq by his wife Catherine, widow of Darby M'Gill Esq, and third daughter of Denis Mahony Esq of Dromore Castle, and was nephew of The M'Gillycuddy, his predecessor. He was born January 1, 1790, and inher-ited November 19, 1826, the chieftainship and the considerable property and much influence possessed by the family in Kerry of which county he was a mag-istrate and Deputy Lieutenant. He was High Sheriff of Kerry in 1823.

The obituary continues in glowing terms, demonstrating the acceptance of the newspaper and its readers of the Gaelic title. Referring to the ending of the Gaelic order, the report adds: "Since that period down to now the M'Gillycuddy's have, by high alliances, constant loyalty, and honourable conduct, maintained a prominent position among the leading gentry of Ireland."

The same newspaper, ten years later, was able to report the return of the MacGillycuddys to their estate having been absent from it.

> Madam M'Gillycuddy (after an absence of two years in England) and The M'Gillycuddy, her son, arrived on Monday evening last at the family mansion as permanent residents. The tenants and people of the neighbourhood generally made it the occasion of rejoicings and festivity. A large bonfire blazed in front of the principal entrance as well as several on the surrounding mountains round which the people assembled, amused themselves and vindicated the national character for hilarity by dancing to the enlivening strains of the bagpipes. Triumphal arches spanned the approached to the house with "Welcome" "*Cead mile failte*" and other suitable devices in flowers and evergreen.

The *Kerry Evening Post* ended its enthusiastic report with the comment: "It would be well if all the landed proprietors of Ireland deserved and returned the invariable kind and cordial feelings that have always existed between the tenants and this ancient family."

The family's Kerry estate still consisted of 15,518 acres of land by the end of the nineteenth century.

Perhaps the most influential of The MacGillycuddys was Ross Kinloch MacKillycuddy, born in 1882 and educated in Edinburgh. He pursued a military career in the British Army, joining the Dragoon Guards. By the end of World War I he was a colonel of the Royal Irish Dragoon Guards holding the Distinguished Service Order and Legion d'Honneur. He had served with Lawrence of Arabia and is credited with designing the tripod fixing of the Lewis machine gun. In June 1921 he retired from the British Army and returned to an Ireland full of enthusiasm as talks were taking place that, it was hoped, would finally bring Irish independence after the hundreds of years of conflict. Yet within six months the country was teetering on the brink of civil war as an unfavorable settlement was forced on the country.

Ross MacGillycuddy's father Donough, The MacGillycuddy, who had arrived at "The Reeks" as a young boy with his mother, had died at the estate. Ross, as the new MacGillycuddy, arrived with his wife and family to take charge of the family property.

The Irish Civil War seemed to pass the family by, even though Kerry was to suffer greatly from the fighting between Free Staters and Republican forces and witnessed some of the most appalling atrocities of the war. Ross concentrated on getting the estates in order, building up a herd of pedigree

Kerry cattle. His wife, Helen, engrossed herself in the gardens, flower as well as fruit and vegetable. A new wing was added to the house and more furnishings were bought.

With the end of the Civil War and the emergence of the Irish Free State, Ross entered local politics and was elected to Kerry County Council. He then stood as an elected member for the Irish Senate in 1928, being nominated by Lord Landsdowne, but was defeated. That same year came another opportunity to stand for the Senate; this time he was elected, supporting Cumann na nGaeheal, the Free State party that had won the Civil War. In 1933 this party became Fine Gael.

The Senate at this time was dominated by anti-Republicans, mainly representatives of the old ascendancy families. Ross was to write:

> When De Valéra came into power, the opposition (Cumann na nGaedheal) still had a majority in the Senate and used their power on several occasions to hold up legislation. This led to the temporary abolition of the Senate, but not long after a new Senate was set up by decree to be elected by the Dáil and County Councils. . . . My years in the Senate left very definite impressions on my mind. Those who control modern Ireland, whatever party they belong to, are bitterly jealous of those who came before them and are glad to be rid of them. This attitude will take many years to change and meanwhile the standards of the new order are going from bad to worse.[17]

He remained a Senator until 1943 but in 1939, with the outbreak of World War II and Ireland's policy of neutrality, The MacGillycuddy of The Reeks believed that the neutrality was a political mistake. He volunteered for active service in the British Army, although he was fifty-seven years old. He rejoined one of Britain's Irish regiments but had to retire in 1942 at the age of sixty. Curiously, although serving in the armed forces of a country that had become belligerent in the war while his own country remained neutral, MacGillycuddy felt that he should not resign from the Senate, and he continued to sit during the period of his active service and for a year thereafter. This is something no seriously neutral country could have tolerated, but, as Enno Stephan has demonstrated in his book, Ireland was neutral in name only and served the Allied cause better in its neutral capacity than as an official belligerent.[18]

According to records, some 183,000 Irish citizens with addresses in the Free State served in the British forces. It has been pointed out that, due to neutrality, many recruits were deemed "British" on the muster rolls and a more realistic total figure of 250,000 Irish citizens was more likely—excluding Northern Ireland. An Irish Brigade, consisting of three battalions, of the volunteers from "neutral" Ireland was formed. It was designated the 38th but its Irishness was never stressed due to the neutrality situation.[19] Similarly, due to large numbers of Irish pilots serving in the Royal Air Force, British Prime Minister Winston Churchill wanted to form a "Shamrock Wing."[20] However, this unit was not formed and, like the Irish Brigade, no publicity was given to it because it was deemed a breach of neutrality under international law. It was perhaps ironic, though, that the Commander in Chief of Fighter Command RAF immediately after the war was a much-decorated Galway man named Basil Embry. Citizens of the "neutral" Irish Free State, serving in the British forces, won 780 decorations for valor, including eight Victoria Crosses, Britain's highest decoration for valor. This was almost as many as the officially belligerent Canadian forces with three times as many service personnel. Once again, the figure given does not include similar awards to personnel from Northern Ireland. Many more Irishmen and women were to be found in the forces of the United States as well as Canada, Australia and other Commonwealth countries.

The point is that the strange position of MacGillycuddy as Senator of a neutral country while an officer in the army of a belligerent state has to be seen in the context of how Ireland exercised its "neutrality." The popular joke goes that when being informed that the country was neutral in 1939, an Irishman in the street replied: "Good. Who are we neutral against?" Historian Joseph T. Carroll maintains that Senator MacGillycuddy was in regular contact with Lord Rigby (John Mahaffy, Britain's representative in Dublin), informing him of matters within the Irish Senate with respect to the policy of Irish neutrality.[21]

He finally retired from public life and devoted himself to his estate in Kerry. He was deerstalking in Muckross Forest, near Killarney, in 1949 when he suffered a severe heart attack. This confined him in his room until his death in April 1950.

It was Ross who started the tradition of having his sons educated at Eton. His son John Patrick, who was a major in the Northamptonshire Yeomanry during World War II, wounded twice and mentioned in dispatches, succeeded his father. He made little impression as MacGillycuddy and died in 1959.

The current MacGillycuddy of The Reeks is Richard Denis Wyer, born on October 4, 1948. He was educated at Eton College and then at Aix-en-Provence University. He is married to Virginia Astor, daughter of the Honourable Hugh Astor. They have two daughters—Tara (b. 1985) and Sorcha (b. 1990). After living in France for twelve years, where he was an executive in a real estate business, and during which time the County Kerry estates were sold off, MacGillycuddy returned to Ireland and now lives in Westmeath.

His tanist, or heir-apparent, is Donough MacGillycuddy, his first cousin, who currently lives in Northamptonshire in England. MacGillycuddy takes his role as a member of the Gaelic aristocracy and holder of an ancient title seriously. He is an active member of the Council of Chiefs. He has presided over MacGillycuddy clan gatherings. The clan society is run by distant cousins, Rosemary and Nicholas MacGillycuddy, who live in Baltimore, County Cork. Rosemary has written *A Short History of the Clan MacGillycuddy*. Her husband is a descendant of John "Jackgillycuddy" of Flesk Castle, who was High Sheriff of Kerry in 1894. In 1884 the sister of "Jackgillycuddy," Agnes, married Dr. George Stoker, a younger brother of the famous Dublin writer Bram Stoker, best known for his classic Gothic novel *Dracula* (1897). George, who had studied with "Jackgillycuddy" at Trinity College, Dublin, went on to become a Licentiate of the Royal College of Physicians. In 1876 George Stoker volunteered to join the Turkish army as a surgeon, accompanying the Turks in their campaign through the very areas where the historical Vlad Dracula lived and fought. On his return he wrote a book of his experiences, *With "The Untouchables" or Two Years campaigning in European and Asiatic Turkey*, which was published in Dublin (1878) by the same publishers who had published his brother's first book. George became a well-known medical expert on the treatment of wound traumas.

Another branch of the family who settled abroad produced Cornelius McGillycuddy, born in East Brookfield, Massachusetts, in 1862. Cornelius McGillycuddy informally shortened his name to "Connie Mack" and became a famous baseball player, manager and club owner for whom the Connie Mack Stadium (formerly Shibe Park) in Philadelphia was named. He died in 1956, not long after his sons forced him to sell his club for $3.5 million. His grandson, also Cornelius McGillylcuddy, was Connie Mack III, who became a Republican U.S. Senator in 1989 for Florida. A Catholic, he was one of the Republican senators who took a prominent role in the impeachment proceedings of President Clinton early in 1999 that ended with Clinton's exoneration.

The present MacGillycuddy, who is a member of the Church of Ireland, would prefer that the state was a secular one in terms of its constitution but, he admits, "in practical terms it has never had any effect on my life." MacGillycuddy and his wife, Virginia, are interested in Irish history and culture and support the attempts to preserve the Irish language. Furthermore, MacGillycuddy believes that the old Gaelic titled nobility, the Chiefs, should have some representation in the Irish Senate. He even looks forward to the day that one of the Gaelic Chiefs might be elected as President of Ireland.

CHAPTER EIGHT

THE KINGDOM OF MUNSTER
(THOMOND)

THOMOND (THUAIDH MUMHAIN), OR NORTH MUNSTER, no longer exists as a geographic territory, only as a historical memory. As a separate kingdom, it came into being in A.D.1118 at the partition of Munster by the Treaty of Glanmire. Historically it consisted of modern County Clare, with portions of County Limerick and some bordering areas of County Tipperary. When the O'Brian royal house was no longer able to claim the High Kingship, after 1119, the O'Conor kingdom of Connacht, then frequently in the ascendant, claimed overlordship of the tiny kingdom. However, the O'Briens assiduously maintained their independence, and the kingdom only vanished in the sixteenth century, after King Murrough O'Brien surrendered it to Henry VIII. It became an English earldom between 1543 and 1741. During the seventeenth-century shiring of Ireland, its territory was reduced to County Clare. The actual estate of the earldom was also reduced in size. From 1800 it was a marquisette which became extinct in 1855 with the death of Admiral James O'Brien, third Marquis Thomond. The O'Briens are unique among the old Gaelic aristocrats as having survived the conquests with their ancestral estate in their ownership, and having a continuous history as kings, earls and marquises but still remain bearing their subsidiary titles as Barons of Inchiquin, the name coming from the place (*Inse Cúinne*, water or island nook) in County Clare and as baronets. Yet, above these English titles, the head of the family still boasts the ancient Gaelic title of The O'Brien, Prince of Thomond.

The O'Brien, Prince of Thomond,
(Eighteenth Baron Inchiquin in the
Peerage of Ireland and Tenth Baronet)
(Ó Bríain)

The O'Briens, the royal house of Thomond, claim to be descended from Cormac Cas, a brother of King Eóghan Mór (d. A.D. 192), the progenitor of the Eóghanacht. According to scholars, such claims are spurious and the genealogies were forged when the Dál gCais, the people of Cas, tried to justify their claims to the Munster throne and then the High Kingship. Professor Byrne comments:

> Perhaps the most blatant example is the fiction that the Dál Cais, rulers of a petty state in east Clare, were a collateral branch of the Eóghanacht, entitled from remote antiquity to share in the over-kingship of Munster. So deeply rooted were the claims of aristocratic descent that the spectacular rise to power of Brían Bóruma, and the consolidation of that power by the O'Briens, were not sufficient to promote the Dál Cais in the political hierarchy without the spurious lustre of ancestral prestige.[1]

It is accepted by scholars that the warlike Dál gCais with their ruling house were originally the Déisi Becc who had settled in east Clare in the fifth century. According to Byrne:

> A branch of the latter, the Déisi Becc, are said to have conquered Thomond (North Munster) from Connacht in the fifth century, and by the tenth century their ruling dynasty, the Dál Cais, were able to seize the kingdom of Munster almost painlessly from the enfeebled grasp of the Eóghanachta: they justified their success on the patently false grounds that they were not Déisi at all but of common descent with the Eóganachta with whom they had anciently enjoyed alternative rights of kingship.[2]

The Eóghanacht kingdom had been weakened by its wars against the Danish incursions, in which, if we are to believe the twelfth-century *Caithreim Cheallacháin Chaisil*, recounting these wars, the Dál gCais had formed alliances against the Cashel kings.[3] They built up their forces and on the death of Donnchadh II mac Ceallacháin Caisil in A.D. 963, they were able to challenge the Eóghanacht.

The first notable Dál gCais ruler recorded in the annals was Lorcan (ca. A.D. 920). Cennétigh, presumably his son, is mentioned as "Rí Tuathmuman" (north Munster) in 951, and he was slain by King Ceallachán of Cashel in his wars against the Danish threat. It is Mathgamain mac Cennétigh who led the attack on Cashel and seized the throne. It was a tenuous occupation, and in 976 he met his own death at the hands of Maelmuad, a prince of the Eóghanacht Raithlinn, according to the *Annals of Innisfallen*. The throne returned to the Eóghanacht for two more years.

Maethgamain's brother led a fresh assault on Cashel and slew King Maelmuad at the Battle of Belach Lechta in 978. This brother's name was Brían mac Cennétigh, and he would become known as Brían Bóroimhe—the *bóroimhe* being a tax in cows that the kings of Leinster agreed was payable to the High King, a tax that Brían was the first to actually extract.

Brían mac Cennétigh became the catalyst for the ambitions of the Dál gCais, for he not only seized the kingdom of Munster but went on to seize the High Kingship, with the aim of converting the office from a "precedence of honor" between the Uí Néill and Eóghanacht, an office in which the Uí Néill had been more interested in maintaining during the centuries immediately prior to the appearance of Brían, to a centralized power. The Uí Néill seemed concerned with creating a real central power base. Then the Dál gCais had arrived in power with a fine disregard for the laws of regnal succession and a reliance on the power of their swords. As Brian Ó Cuív wrote: "the accession of Brian Bóroimhe to the high kingship marked a break with the past. It paved the way for a strong central monarchy. . . ."[4] It was no wonder that the Dál gCais chose to name their dynasty after, perhaps, their greatest king.

Brían was an aggressive ruler, and soon his armies were ravaging Connacht, Meath and Breifne. He was by no means recognized as legitimate High King; indeed, the Eóghanacht had not even acknowledged his claim to Munster's throne and were still waging war. The Uí Néill High King, Mael Sechnaill, met Brían in 998 at the Abbey of Clonfert and, for the sake of peace, agreed to recognize him as king of the southern half of Ireland, if Brían accepted him as king of the northern half. At this time, in 999, the Leinster king, Donnchadh Mac Domhnaill Cláin (984–1003) allied himself with the Norse-Irish city-kingdoms and denied Brían's authority in that kingdom. Brían inflicted a crushing defeat on them in County Wicklow and occupied the Danish kingdom of Dublin. He married Gormflaith, mother of Sitric, King of Dublin.

Brían was now strong enough to be able to break his agreement with Mael Sechnaill and assert his claim to the High Kingship. Mael Sechnaill, failing to secure support from the northern Uí Néill, surrendered the High Kingship to him. Brían was now High King but with opposition from the outraged, more ancient royal dynasties.

In 1005 Brían marched to Armagh "with the royalty of Ireland," says the *Annals of Ulster*, and left twenty ounces of gold "on the altar of St. Patrick." By this action he was clearly acknowledging Armagh as the primatial jurisdiction of Ireland for the first time. There were two main ecclesiastical seats in Ireland, that of the Comarb (successor) of Patrick, the Bishop of Armagh, and the Comarb of Ailbe, the Bishop of Emly (County Tipperary). Armagh had long demanded, however, that it should be recognized as the seat of the primacy over all Ireland.

In 1006 Brían, when conducting a campaign against the Uí Néill of the north, had obtained some submissions and recognition of his kingship. However, opposition continued, for seizing the kingship without the backing of the law was not acceptable to the kings of Ireland. It was in this context that Brían's *ollamhain*, or scholars, began to devise the genealogy, making them Eóghanacht princes in order to justify the seizure of power.[5]

Brían tried to exert a strong central policy on Ireland, and once more the Leinster kingdom rose up, this time in alliance with the Uí Neill of the north. It was the Leinster King Mael Morda mac Murchada (1003–14) who sought alliances with the Danes, not only those of the Irish city-kingdoms but from the Isle of Man and the Western Islands, Orkneys and even as far as Norway itself. The Norse had their own agenda to dominate Ireland rather than merely help the Irish kings curb the power of Brían. The Uí Néill now stood aloof; although not liking Brían, they also had no liking for the idea of such a strong Norse army being invited into Ireland.

On April 23, 1014, Good Friday, Brían Bóroime defeated the King of Leinster and his Danish and Norse allies at Clontarf. While Brían was slain by his tent by a retreating Norse warrior, his army was victorious. His body was taken and buried at Armagh by the clergy who had seen in him a king who had recognized their claims to the primacy and who was bringing about a centralized Irish kingdom.

Brían's death brought about a weakening of the Dál gCais, who now became the O'Briens. Brían's son Donnchadh (d. 1064) had become King of Thomond but continued to claim the kingship of Munster with opposition from the Eóghanacht. Donnchadh had made a foray into the territory controlled by the Eóghanacht princes in 1013 and had managed to take captive Domhnall of Dubhdabhoreann, the progenitor of The O'Donoghues.

With Brían's death, Donnchadh tried to follow his father's example and began to raid Meath and Leinster. He lost his right hand in a single combat in 1019 and was also wounded in the head. In spite of his debility, which, by law, negated his claim to rule, he refused to give up. He suffered several defeats and even made war on his own kinsman Maelruanaidh, whom he killed. When he invaded Leinster again he found himself ranged against Dermot Mac Mael-namboo of the Uí Cheinnselaig, who routed him in a battle in the Glen of Ark-low. In 1064 he was finally deposed by his dissatisfied *derbhfine* and went off on pilgrimage to Rome. He died in Rome in the monastery of St. Stephen.

He was succeeded by Murchadh, who reigned for four years before being defeated by his kinsman Tairrdelbach in 1064. The next O'Brien king was more in the mold of Brían Bóroimhe. Tairrdelbach, often given as Toirdhealb-hach and Anglicized as Turlough (1009–86), had the same desire to be a strong central monarch. He began to assert his claim to be king of all Munster with strong opposition from the Eóghanacht. Like his grandfather Brían, he was de-termined to seize power by force. He fought with the men of Connacht even against his own kinsman Murchadh an Sceith Ghirr (short shield), a battle in which four hundred men and fifteen nobles are recorded as being slain.

He was only a year into his claim to be King of Munster when he led his warriors into Leinster, which had an alliance with the Déisi Mumhain, who were settled around Waterford and with whom the Déisi Becc, the original Dál gCais, were said to be related. In 1072 Tairrdelbach claimed the High Kingship by force. He sacked the Abbey of Clonmacnoise and marched against the north-ern kingdoms of the Uí Néill, which were able to repulse him. In 1077 he devas-tated Leinster once again. He plundered at will, taking hostages and booty.

It seems that from the looting of the Abbey of Clonmacnoise, Tairrdelbach became ill. Christian scribes made much of this fact. He died on July 14, 1086, at Ceancoradh (Kincorra) in his County Clare homeland.

His son Muirchertach was to become the third and last O'Brien to claim the High Kingship. Muirchertach managed to defeat Donnchad mac Domnaill Remair, the King of Leinster, in 1087, near Howth, County Dublin, but in the following year he himself was defeated and forced back into Thomond. He made several forays against Meath and Connacht and plundered the Abbey of Clonmacnoise, obviously emulating his father. His raids caused even the Arch-bishop of Armagh to intervene. Every year witnessed O'Brien raiding; in one year he is said to have made a circuit of Ireland in six weeks with his army. In 1113 he was badly defeated in the north and fell ill.

During this period, the violence of the Dál gCais King of Thomond shook the political status quo to its core, not just in Munster but throughout Ireland. In 1118 Muirchertach was back campaigning again and found that his hold over Munster was precarious. In 1118 he was facing the army of the Eóghanacht prince, Tadhg MacCarthy, at Glanmire in County Cork. Muirchertach had de-manded, as High King, support from the other kings to crush the "troublesome"

Eóghanacht. The kings of Ireland finally saw their opportunity to place the O'Briens in a position whereby their power base was weakened and they would not be able to continue to threaten the peace of the kingdoms.

The *Book of MacCarthaigh* reports that Tairrdelbach Ó Conchohairr, King of Connacht, Murchadh Ó Mael Seachlainn, of the Uí Néill, and Aodh, son of King Donnchadh Ó Ruairc of Breifne, arrived with their armies as allies of O'Brien and pressured Muirchertach to make a treaty with the Eóghanacht. "It was then that Muirchertach O'Brien was parted from the kinship of Munster and Ireland."

The Treaty of Glanmire formally partitioned Munster into north and south, Thomond and Desmond. Desmond retained the bulk of Munster with its capital at Cashel, restoring the dynasty with Tadhg I (1118–23). Muirchertach O'Brien died the following year on March 10, 1119, probably of pulmonary consumption, and was buried in Killaloe. He had been deposed three times from his kingships, but twice his sword had restored him. He had not been so lucky the third time.

The position of High King was now filled by Domhnall Ua Lochlainn, a branch of Uí Néill of Cenél Eóghain. He was displaced by Tairrdelbach Ua Conchobhair of Connacht, who turned with alacrity from his role of king-maker at Glenmire into claimant for the High Kingship.

The O'Briens had returned to kingship of Thomond, but not without protest. They did not remain passive for long. After the arrival of the Normans, Donnchadh Cairprech (d. 1247) helped the newcomers to raid Connacht. However, in 1235 the Normans turned on Thomond itself, and Donnchadh found himself having to defend it from his erstwhile allies. He founded the Franciscan monastery at Ennis, County Clare, and is said to have been a patron of literature supporting poets like Muiredeach O'Dálaigh, a member of one of the great literary families in Munster, which also had branches in Meath.

His son Conchobhar na Sindaine (1247–68) had some successes in turning back Norman attempts to take over Thomond and was one of the princes who decided to support Brían O'Neill's bid to become High King and unite the country against the Anglo-Normans. He is recorded as having sent a hundred horses to O'Neill as a gift. After the death of his son Tadhg in 1248, Conchohar seldom appeared in public and never attended any official feasts. His people became bitter at his lack of concern for their welfare and showed their displeasure by refusing to pay the royal rents and dues. Conchobhar came out of his seclusion and resorted to his ancestors' method of dealing with matters. He raised an army and began to raid the countryside, even raiding into Eóganacht territory in Desmond.

In 1267 Conchobhar Carrack Lochlainn met Conchobhar O'Brien's army at Belaclugga, County Clare, and defeated and slew him. Conchobhar O'Brien was buried in the monastery of East Burren, which is now the Abbey of Corcomroe. His tomb and full-length effigy wearing a crown are still seen there.

Brían Ruadh (1268–76) was his third son. It is reported that when his title was proclaimed not one of the assembled chiefs in his *derbhfine* voiced any opposition. Their attitudes soon changed. Brían Ruadh began to campaign against the Normans in 1270 and captured Clare Castle. By 1275, however, his military campaigning was proving to be as unpopular as that of his father. His kinsman Sioda MacNeill MacConamara, who had supported him in the first place, now rose against him, declaring that Tairrdelbach Mac Tadhg, the nephew of Brían Ruadh, should now be king.

The conflict came to a major battle at Moygressan in which Tairrdelbhach's ally, the Norman baron Richard de Clare, was defeated. De Clare, however, managed to capture King Brían Ruadh and promptly hanged the unfortunate King of Thomond. Tairrdelbach O'Brien (1277–1306) is remembered in *Caithreim Thoirdhealbhaigh*, a work that was composed during his lifetime and that was discovered in the nineteenth century by the scholar Standish Hayes O'Grady. Tairrdelbach was buried in Ennis Friary, which became the burial place of succeeding Kings of Thomond until Conor Ó Brien was buried there in 1581.

In 1318, at the Battle of Dysert O'Dea, the Normans, under Richard de Clare, were driven from Thomond. But within fifty years the FitzGeralds were moving northward and encroaching on O'Brien territory in east Limerick. Brían Sreamhach, King of Thomond (1369–1400), decided to attempt to check the FitzGeralds. In July 1370 he inflicted a crushing defeat on them at Monasteranenagh, two miles east of Croom, where, in the twelfth century, King Tairrdelbach O'Brien had ordered the building of a monastery (Mainistir an Aonaigh—monastery of the fair) in thanks for his defeat over the Norsemen in 1148. It was a significant sight. His descendant King Brian Sreamhach even captured the third Earl of Desmond, Gearóid Iarla Fitzgerald (ca. 1335–95)—famous for his poetic compositions in Irish. O'Brien brought the earl to Ennis Clonroad. During his imprisonment there, the earl wrote several of his poems.

> The harp of O'Brien at whose playing I drink beer
> The sound of the bell of Ennis to the west
> The wail of the rock as it juts into the sea water
> These are my three constant melodies.

William of Windsor was dispatched from London to curb King Brian Sreamhach's successes over the Anglo-Normans.

The Thomond kingdom survived, sometimes under pressure not only from the Anglo-Normans but from the kings of Connacht, who maintained that they had a right of lordship over it. By 1528 the end of the Kingdom of Thomond was approaching. Conchobhar mac Toirdhealbhaigh Duinn succeeded his father that year. His brother Donogh was nominated his tanist. Donogh died in 1531 and a third brother, Murrough, became heir-elect. Conchobhar (or, in English form, Conor) had become king at a very critical period not only for Thomond but for all of Ireland. Two Anglo-Norman families, the FitzGeralds and the Butlers, were vying for power. Conor was married to a daughter of James FitzGerald (Earl of Kildare) and therefore sided with Kildare. Conor's son Donough, however, had taken the side of the Butlers (Earl of Ormond), having married a daughter of the Earl of Ossory (one of the family). Donough was wounded in a battle but the FitzGeralds were eventually defeated.

Son now turned against father. In 1536 Lord Leonard Grey, the new Lord Deputy, advanced into Thomond with the guidance of Donough. For six months his father, King Conor, held out. At his court, as a refugee, was Gerald Fitzgerald the eleventh Earl of Kildare. As it appeared that the lord deputy would finally defeat Conor's forces. Conor fled Thomond's protection and went to France. In 1537 King Conor surrendered to Lord Grey, and a treaty was made between them at Limerick.

Conor died in 1539/40 to be succeeded by his brother Murrough. It is said that Conor was the last independent King of Thomond.

Upon succession to the kingship, Murrough sought to join O'Neill and O'Donnel in the north in a confederacy against the English. With the arrival of Anthony St. Leger as new Lord Deputy, however, negotiations were opened between them and Murrough was identified as "the Achilles' heel" of Ireland. In February 1541, the Lord Deputy met Murrough at Limerick. He was told the conditions for surrendering his kingship in return for an earldom. Murrough asked for time to consult his *derbhfine*, for, he pointed out, under law, he could not make such a decision by himself. It is hard to believe that his *derbhfine* would have approved a surrender. But by summer of that year Murrough had accepted the terms offered. He sent his representatives to attend the Dublin Parliament called in June 1541 by Henry VIII. Leading the king's representatives was his nephew, Donough O'Brien, the son of the late King Conor, who had been elected as tanist, or heir-apparent. It was at this parliament that Henry VIII's emissaries officially announced that the King of England would was no longer be Lord of Ireland but King of Ireland instead. The Lord

Deputy's report of June 26 makes no mention of the attendance of any other major Irish king, such as MacCarthy, O'Neill or MacMorrough Kavanagh.[6] However, O'Brien's acceptance of the "new deal" was the probable cause for why his former ally, Conn Bacach O'Neill, made his extraordinary early submission in December 1541.

There was a problem, however, in reconciling the new primogeniture law of England with Irish law and succession by tanistry. The English, ever good on political compromise, allowed the O'Brien king to be created Earl of Thomond and Baron Inchiquin for his lifetime. But the title Earl of Thomond would not then go to his son, who would simply become the second Baron Inchiquin. The new earl would be his elected tanist, his nephew, Donough, who, meanwhile, would be known as Baron Ibrickan. After that genuflection to the Gaelic system, the title "Earl Thomond" would descend through Donough's line by primogeniture.

King Murrough arrived in England in June 1543 with the Norman-Irish MacWilliam Uachtar Bourke, who became the first Earl of Clanricade. Murrough went to Greenwich Palace, where he personally surrendered to Henry VIII. He died in 1551 and was succeeded as Earl of Thomond by Donough, who immediately began to prepare the path for the succession of his son Conor by primogeniture. Historian Ivar O'Brien says that Henry had granted personal arms to the Earl of Thomond, which have become the arms of the head of the O'Brien family down to this day.[7] There is no reference to this in the letters patent or in the office of the Ulster King of Arms. One also doubts that the motto "Lamh Laidir an Uachtar" (the Strong Hand Uppermost) was approved when the policy was to eradicate the Irish language. The motto still used today by the Inchiquins is usually "Vigeur de Dessus," an inaccurate translation actually meaning "Strength from Above." Indeed, the tomb of Domhnall Mór Ua Briain (d. 1194) in Limerick Cathedral bears a different coat of arms featuring a lion. There is no sign of the embowed arm holding a sword, which was an Eóghanacht crest until that time.

The outrage felt by the O'Briens and the people of Thomond at the disregard of Brehon law succession quickly erupted into warfare. On April 1553 the second Earl of Thomond died, probably from a wound, while besieged in one of his castles, when the *derbhfine* chose his brother Donell as O'Brien, King of Thomond. The third Earl of Thomond was Donough's son Conor, nicknamed "Groibleach" (or long nailed), but he, too, was denied the Gaelic titles.

His uncle Donell was formerly inaugurated as The O'Brien, King of Thomond, under Irish law and supported by most of the country. His nephew Conor was forced to surrender his central, principal residence at Ennis Clonroad, and he retired into Connacht for safety.

King Donell was now de facto King of Thomond as well as de jure king by Irish law. Yet, curiously, he petitioned the Lord Deputy St. Leger for recognition as the Chief of the O'Briens, which, as such titles had been abolished, St. Leger could not, nor would not, grant. In 1558 Queen Mary, for reasons we have discussed in a previous chapter, ordered her troops to reinstate the ousted third earl of Thomond, and an army commanded by the Earl of Sussex arrived at Limerick. King Donell as well as his brother Teige (d. 1582) and their cousin Donough, of Lemenagh and Dromoland, were proclaimed traitors. King Donell sought refuge with The Maguire, Prince of Fermanagh, while Teige and Donough found sanctuary with Fitzgerald, Earl of Desmond.

With Conor, third Earl of Thomond, back in his Ennis stronghold, Lord Sussex's army withdrew. In 1559 Teige and Donough also returned and once again raised their supporters for Donell, inflicting a severe defeat on the army of Conor and his ally Lord Clanricade. The English had to come to the rescue again. The Lord Justice, Fitzwilliam, intervened and managed to capture Teige, whom he imprisoned in Dublin Castle. Early in 1562 Teige managed to escape and rejoined Donell, who had now raised a formidable army in Thomond. It was clear that Conor O'Brien, the third Earl, was not popular nor did his people recognize the legitimacy of his claims to rule over them by the English laws. He was even forced to borrow artillery from the English.

It took some years of conflict before a war-weary Donell offered in April 1565 to surrender his claims on condition that he receive the lordship of Corcomroe. Although he had been exhausted by the continued conflict, war was allowed to continue. Conor saw victory approaching. The new Lord Deputy, Sir Henry Sidney, arrived in Limerick in April 1567 and made a brief to report to the Privy Council on the Earl of Thomond's "insufficiency to govern." Donell, at last, surrendered his claims on the kingdom and was allowed to retire of his castle, accepting a knighthood. He died in 1579.

Rejected by his own people and despised by the English, the third earl had joined James FitzMaurice FitzGerald, the Earl of Desmond, in his wars against the Elizabethan Conquest of Munster. Forced to surrender by the Earl of Ormond, he fled to the French court. He appeared to the English to be more trouble in France than he was worth, and the English ambassador at the French court, Sir Henry Norris, later Baron Norris of Rycote, reported that he was intriguing with the French. Negotiations were, therefore, opened with him and he was persuaded to return to Thomond, where he made public confession of his treason to England in return for being formally pardoned by the Lord Deputy, Sir Henry Sidney. He surrendered all his lands to Queen Elizabeth. After showing his good behavior, he had a portion of his lands restored in 1573.

Conor was dogged by disaffection among his people and continuing dynastic disputes in Thomond, which was now designated the new county of "Clare." He even asked Sir William Drury to place the territory under martial law. He died in January 1581.

His eldest son, Donough, succeed him as fourth Earl of Thomond while his third son, Daniel, was created first Viscount Clare.

Donough (d. 1624) is called the "Great" Earl of Thomond. He was brought up at Elizabeth's court as a hostage to ensure his family's good behavior and as a way of turning him into an Englishman. He had succeeded as Baron Ibrickand and was still at Elizabeth's court in 1577. He returned to Ireland in 1582, the year after his father died, and was assiduous in support of the lord deputy and English administration. He tried to ensure that County Clare, which was going to be placed under the administration of Connacht, remained as Thomond. He not only attended the Dublin Parliament of 1589 but, during the Elizabeth wars, he commanded troops against the Irish. After campaigning for some years, he went to England and remained there for a while.

The Irish victory at Yellow Ford was followed by the O'Briens and Thomond trying immediately to reassert their own independence from English administration. Teige O'Brien, brother of the "Great" Earl of Thomond, who had not been Anglicized, now entered an alliance with Aodh Ruadh O'Néill, who was to be the last regnant King of Ulster. In 1599 Aodh Ruadh O'Donel (1571–1602), O'Néill's principal commander, fresh from the victory of Yellow Ford, arrived in Thomond with his men. Teige's youngest brother, Donal (Daniel), who supported the English, was made a prisoner. Teige was killed when his own brother, the Anglicized "Great" Earl, pursued his forces in 1599. The "Great" Earl of Thomond had returned from England with fresh English troops and invaded Clare and laid siege to the Irish strongholds. He hanged captured Irish soldiers and civilians on trees at Dunbeg after they had surrendered. During 1599 the Earl of Thomond accompanied the Earl of Essex in his attempt to invade Desmond and suffered defeat with him at the Pass of Plumes. Lord Thomond was appointed governor of County Clare on August 15 that year and a member of the Privy Council in the following month.

Lord Thomond remained a staunch supporter of the English administration. In 1600 he was wounded when he, Sir George Carew and Lord Ormond had to cut their way out of an ambush. During the remaining years of the war he fought against O'Donel and The O'Neill. He appears to have been fond of hanging and ordered sixteen men hanged at Limerick in one Assize. He went to England but returned in 1601 to bring reinforcements to Kinsale. He was also at Dunboy, the castle of The O'Sullivan Beare, when its garrison surrendered. He immediately hanged fifty-eight survivors of the siege after they had surrendered.

Elizabeth was so grateful for his services that she ordered that his name should always be placed next to those of the Lord Deputy and Chief Justice in Commissions of Oyer and Terminer and Gaol Delivery. On May 6, 1605, he became President of Munster and a leading advocate of the Protestant party. He died on September 5, 1624, and was buried in Limerick Cathedral.

Approved of by English as "the most influential and vigorous of Irish loyalists," Lord Thomond's own people saw him as nothing less than a traitor or, at best, not even Irish, having been raised at the English court as an Englishman. He had two sons, Henry, the fifth earl, who died without issue in 1639, and Barnabas, the sixth Earl.

Before following the fortunes of Barnabas, reference should be made to the line of Donal (1577?–1663). He had been left to defend the estates of his brother, the "Great" Earl, while the latter was in England. Donal was attacked in his Castle of Ibrickan when his younger brother, Teige, had joined the Irish army of O'Donnel. Donal had been wounded and taken prisoner. On his release he accompanied his brother, Lord Thomond, to Elizabeth's court. In 1604 he was knighted for his services to England.

Afterward, Donal (now called Daniel) decided to switch his religion from Protestant back to Catholic. He attended the Dublin Parliament of 1613, but his actions caused him to be summoned to England to account for his conduct. In 1641 he joined the Irish insurrection and became a member of the Confederation Parliament at Kilkenny. He vigorously supported it and was elected to its Supreme Council. During the Cromwellian period he had to flee to France, but on the Restoration he returned to his estate and in 1663 he was created Viscount Care. His grandson Daniel, the third viscount, was Lord Lieutenant of Clare under James II and raised a regiment of dragoons and two regiments of infantry to fight against William of Orange. This Daniel died in 1690.

The Clares went into exile in France following the Williamite conquest. Clare's Dragoons were to enter Irish folklore. The famous victory of France over England at Fontenoy in 1745 was due to the conduct of the Irish Brigade of the French Army; its six regiments were commanded by Charles O'Brien, sixth viscount Clare and ninth Earl of Thomond.

Barnabas, sixth Earl of Thomond, proved another firm adherent of English government in Ireland. He succeeded in 1639. He was Lord Lieutenant of Clare but when the insurrection of 1641 broke out, he tried to remain neutral. However, in 1644 he opened negotiations with the English Parliament, allowing a Parliamentary force to take over Bunratty Castle. He went to live in

England, where he abruptly changed politics to court the Royalist cause. He joined Charles I at Oxford and was created Marquis of Billing (Northampton-shire). He died in 1657 and was succeeded by his son Henry.

The line of the Earls of Thomond passed down to Henry, the eighth Earl (1688–1741), who was also created Viscount Tadcaster in the English peerage. When he died the Earldom of Thomond was claimed by the Jacobite Viscounts Clare. Charles, the sixth Viscount Clare (1699–1761), claimed entitlement to be ninth Earl of Thomond. His son, Charles (ca. 1774), the seventh viscount, also claimed to be tenth Earl of Thomond in the Jacobite Peerage. However, in England, Percy Wyndham (ca. 1713–74), the nephew of the eighth Earl and son of Sir William Wyndham Bart, took the additional name of O'Brien and was created Earl of Thomond in 1756. He died unmarried and the title again became extinct.

Curiously, that was not the end of the story. In 1936 a descendant of the Wyndham family, calling himself Raymond Moulton-O'Brien, managed to obtain a judgment decree from a court in Juarez, Mexico, stating that he was Earl of Thomond. The German government ratified the decree in December that year; Luxemburg and France followed in 1937. Moulton-O'Brien applied to the Ge-nealogical Office in Dublin for a recognition as "The O'Brien." In 1944 he con-cocted an elaborate charade to get evidence for his claim by trying to get the Registrar of the High Court to register a claim for damages against a nonexistent person on the grounds that this person had claimed that he was not The O'Brien.[8]

In spite of the fact that Donough O'Brien, the sixteenth Baron Inchiquin, had already been given "courtesy recognition" as the rightful O'Brien, Moul-ton-O'Brien managed to get an official Vatican document in 1948 that con-ferred blessings on his son as "the Catholic heir to the Principality of Thomond in the person of His Highness Prince Turlough the Strong, *a seaghan*, Baron of Ibrickan." Moulton-O'Brien even managed to get a transfer of lands to his son registered with the Registry of Deeds, signing himself as "Colonel His Highness Raymond Moulton Seán, by the Sovereign authority of the Roman Pontiff Prince O'Brien of Thomond, The O'Brien Prince of the Dalcassians of Thomond, Earl and Count of Thomond, Baron of Ibrickan, of Castle Clare, Co. Clare."

Moulton-O'Brien set up his own "Most Honourable Dalcassian Order of the Princely House of Thomond," maintained his own "embassy" in Dublin and was, surprisingly, actually listed in *Thom's Directory* for 1950. His entry was deleted in subsequent editions, although he registered the birth of his daughter as "Her Highness Princess Grania Bebhin." Refused recognition by the Ge-nealogical Office as well as by the College of Arms London and Lord Lyon

King of Arms in Scotland, Moulton-O'Brien conducted a campaign against "The Arch Communists of The Kremlin and their dupes at the Genealogical office, Dublin Castle" who, he claimed, were plotting against him. He died in Dublin on March 31, 1977, but was buried in Birmingham, England, on April 6.

Was there some presage or even inspiration in the career of the soi-desant O'Brien and the rise of Terence McCarthy, who began his correspondence with the Genealogical Office one month after the death of Moulton-O'Brien?

In 1741, with the death of the eighth Earl of Thomond, the chiefship was deemed to have passed to the next senior line, that of King Murrough's son, who had taken the title of second Baron Inchiquin. This title had been passed down to Murrough, the sixth Baron (1614–74).

Murrough is one of the "bogeymen" of Irish history known as Murchadh *na dTóitheán* or "Murrough of the Burnings." Like the Thomonds, he was ardently supportive of the English in Ireland. His grandfather had been killed at the Erne fighting for Queen Elizabeth. He was brought up as a ward of William St. Leger, as an Englishman, but in 1636 he was in the service of Spain fighting in Italy. He returned to Ireland in 1639 and was made Vice President of Munster, sitting in the Earl of Strafford's Dublin Parliament. He even approved of Strafford's scheme to colonize County Clare with English settlers, removing the local population.

When the insurrection broke out on October 23, 1641, Baron Inchiquin devoted his energies to fighting the Irish. Like his cousin, the Earl of Thomond, whom he had fought for Elizabeth, Murrough was a brutal soldier. All Irish prisoners taken at Carrick-on-Suir were executed. Inchiquin now became Governor of Munster and fought several engagements. He devastated the counties of Cork and Waterford, looting and executing those he deemed guilty of "rebellion." When Ormond concluded a peace deal with the Irish Confederation on September 15, 1643, Inchiquin signed his approval, but obviously unwillingly.

He took his regiments to England and went to Oxford to see the king. It seems during this time that King Charles gave him a warrant, creating him as first Earl of Inchiquin. He did not use it and indeed was discontented. In July 1644 he urged King Charles to make peace with the English Parliament so that troops could be released to fight in Ireland. He was so vehement that he began to be thought of as a supporter of Parliament. It was also fact that the English Parliament made him President of Munster. In August he ordered the expulsion of all Catholics from the towns of Cork, Youghal and Kinsale, allowing them to take only what they wore.

Inchiquin's devastations in Munster are still notorious among Irish people. He gave no quarter to any Irish and destroyed abbeys and monasteries, such as the Franciscan friary of Adare, in County Limerick. On September 12, 1647/8 he attacked the ancient royal capital of Cashel. He slaughtered everyone, including thirty priests and friars. According to eyewitnesses, Inchiquin put on the archiepiscopal mitre during these proceedings to mock those about to be slaughtered. A few months later he changed sides from Parliament to Royalist.

When Cromwell landed in Ireland on August 18, 1649, Inchiquin chose to remain committed to the Royalist cause. In 1650 he fled to Brittany and joined the court of Charles II. In May 1654 he was confirmed in the earldom. Incredibly, in view of his past actions, he became a convert to Catholicism. He was made Governor of Catalonia in French service. He went to England in 1663 after the Restoration and became Vice President of Munster. He was restored to all his honors and given an estate of 10,000 acres with £8,000 compensation for his losses. He ended his days at Rostellan, Cork Harbour, where he died on September 9, 1674.

The Irish people may see an irony in the fact that "Murrough of the Burnings" had a sister Mary O'Brien, who married Michael Boyle, Anglican Archbishop of Armagh and Lord Chancellor of Ireland (d. 1702). From their line, eight generations later, was born Elizabeth Bowes Lyon, daughter of the fourteenth Earl of Strathmore, who is now the Queen Elizabeth, the Queen Mother, mother of Queen Elizabeth II of England.

Murrough's son, William, the second Earl (d. 1691), had also gone into exile, serving Charles II, and was later vice admiral of Tangier and then Governor of Jamaica. His grandson, the fourth Earl Inchiquin (d. ca. 1777), became the head of the O'Brien family in 1741. His son, another Murrough (d. 1808), became the fifth Earl Inchiquin and first Marquis of Thomond. The line ended with James (d. 1855) who was third Marquis and twelfth Baron Inchiquin.

Once more the chiefship of the O'Briens moved to another branch of the family. The next senior surviving line was that of the youngest son of King Murrough, the first Earl of Thomond. This was Donough of Lemenagh and Dromoland. His heirs had been bestowed with knighthoods when the earldom passed to his cousin. It was only with Donough (d. 1717) that the line were created baronets. The chiefship of the O'Briens passed to Sir Lucius, the fifth baronet (d. 1872) who became the thirteenth Baron Inchiquin.

Their residence was Dromoland Castle. The name Dromland is said to denote a ridge of honeysuckle. The castle was originally built in the late fifteenth or early sixteenth century, and King Murrough had left it to his son Donough, who was hanged by the English in 1582 for having been active in trying to retrieve the Thomond kingship for his cousin. This allowed Sir George Cusack, the sheriff, to attempt to appropriate the castle for himself. However, the O'Briens returned.

There was a legal battle between the earls of Thomond and the O'Briens of Dromoland for ownership of the castle. In 1642 Colonel Conor O'Brien of Leamaneh managed to expel the adherents of Lord Thomond from the castle.

Conor was killed in a skirmish with the Cromwellian General Ludlow's troops on July 25, 1651. His widow was one of the famous women of Irish history, Máire Rua O'Brien (1615–86).

Máire Rua was probably born in her parents' home of Bunratty Castle, County Clare, the daughter of Torlach MacMahon and Máire, the daughter of the third Earl of Thomond. She was wealthy in her own right, being the widow of Daniel Neylon of Neylon Castle, Dysert O'Dea. Her second marriage to Conor O'Brien of Leamaneh produced eight children. Máire was thirty-six when Conor O'Brien was killed fighting the Cromwellians.

In 1653 the Cromwellian administration announced the confiscation of all her property, but Máire Rua, it seems, contracted marriage to a Cromwellian officer named John Cooper. Cooper, therefore, became the "legal" owner in English terms of the property. Soon after the marriage he conveniently died. Folklore has it that Máire Rua killed him once he had served his purpose to safeguard the property. Indeed, murder charges were brought against her. She finally received a royal pardon on December 31, 1644. She had reared her son Donough, by Conor O'Brien, as a Protestant, and he moved into Dromoland, becoming the "richest commoner in Ireland."[9]

Sir Donough became the first baronet of the line and entertained the Duke of Berwick, James II's illegitimate son, who commanded the Jacobite troops at Limerick in November 1690.

The tradition of the family of Lemenagh and Dromoland was more radical and sympathetically Irish than the other branches of the family. In fact, the brother of Sir Lucius, who inherited the title of Baron Inchiquin and the chiefship as O'Brien, was one of the leading figures of the Irish Republican uprising of 1848. William Smith O'Brien (the Smith taken from his mother, Charlotte Smith) was born at Dromoland in 1803, the son of Sir Edward (d. 1837), the fourth Baronet. Educated at Harrow and Cambridge University, he became a Conservative Member of Parliament for Ennis in 1825 and then for County Limerick in 1835. But his views changed as he saw the suffering of the Irish people. He sought first the reestablishment of a parliament in Dublin, the Repeal of the Union as it was called, but moved on to becoming convinced that the answer lay in a sovereign republic. He became a leading member of the Young Ireland movement.

In March 1848, after four years of an artificially created famine, in which Ireland lost, in real terms, two and a half million of its population, he urged the formation of an Irish National Guard with the example of the Paris Revolution in mind. With other Young Ireland leaders he sought to make preparations for an armed uprising. In July 1848 a "War Directory" consisting of O'Brien, the lawyer John Blake Dillon, lawyer and politician Thomas Francis Meagher and Thomas D'Arcy McGee was formed. While on an excursion to organize the movement, O'Brien and his companions were cornered by police and soldiers in Ballingarry, County Tipperary. The skirmish ended any hopes of an uprising. O'Brien escaped but was later arrested at Thurles. He was tried at Clonmel and found guilty of High Treason. The death sentence was commuted to life transportation to southwest Australia.

His health broken, he eventually he received a pardon in 1854 on condition that he should not set foot in Ireland nor, indeed, any part of the United Kingdom. He settled in Brussels, and eventually his pardon was made unconditional. He died at Bangor in Wales on June 16, 1864, and his body was returned to Ireland. His coffin was escorted by the radical students of Trinity College across Dublin and put on a train for his ancestral home in Dromoland. Among those students, and describing the event later in his autobiography, was writer Alfred Perceval Graves (1846–1931), sadly perhaps better known now as the father of the poet and novelist Robert Graves (1895–1985) than for his own considerable body of poetry and prose.[10]

After Irish independence, Sir Lucius, fifteenth Baron Inchiquin, and his family continued to live quietly at Dromoland Castle. His son the sixteenth Baron took his duties as the O'Brien seriously and organized a major O'Brien Clan gathering on St. Patrick's Day, 1936. In 1937 the government of Eamon de Valéra was passing a new state constitution and had used the abdication of Edward VIII in 1936 to distance themselves from the English Crown as head of state. Between 1922 and 1937 Ireland had three Governors-General who replaced the office of Lord Lieutenant or Viceroy. De Valéra decided to abolish the Governor Generalship and replace it with a President of Ireland as titular head of state.

It was the year that the Gaelic Monarchist Party was supporting O'Conor Don as a potential "King of Ireland." *The Cork Examiner* announced that Lord Inchiquin was a more suitable choice for president:

> If heredity counted, he would be first favourite, for he is in the direct descent from Brian Boru who, whatever his faults, was the strongest ruler Ireland ever had. If he had survived Clontarf he might have established the O'Brien dynasty so firmly that the present Earl [*sic*] would be King of All Ireland and there would be no Irish problem to be solved—unless in the meantime the

O'Neills had asserted the independence of Ulster, as they probably would try to do; which brings us back to the fact that there was an Ulster problem nine hundred years ago as well as today.[11]

According to the daughter of the sixteenth Lord Inchiquin, Grania R. O'Brien Weir:

> Donough had been approached about accepting the Presidency of Ireland on 13th December, 1937 when Captain Charles Spring Rice, "representing certain influential people in Ireland" came to ask if he would accept it, if it were to be offered to him. He was asked to go to Dublin for discussions. Donough's reply was in the negative.[12]

There was little doubt whom Charles Spring Rice was representing. Spring Rice was the family name of the old Jacobite Barons Monteagle of Brandon who own estates in County Kerry and in Foyles, County Limerick. Charles (1887–1946) was to succeed as the fifth Baron Monteagle on December 22, 1937. His notable cousin was the daughter of the second Baron, the Honorable Mary Ellen Spring Rice (1880–1924), who was an enthusiastic member of the Gaelic League, an Irish speaker and committed nationalist. She took part with Erskine Childers in the gun-running operation for the Irish Volunteers in 1914, when the *Asgad*, Childers's yacht, landed guns near Howth. Captions to the famous picture of Mrs. Erskine Childers handling the guns aboard *Askard* often do not state that her female companion is the Honorable Mary Ellen Spring Rice. Also what is not so well known is that there were two other yachts engaged in bringing arms to the Volunteers—the *Chotah*, skippered by Sir Thomas Myles, and the *Kelpie*, skippered by Spring Rice's cousin, Conor O'Brien. Mary Ellen was also active in the Society of United Irishwomen, and during the War of Independence she served as a nurse for the Volunteers. When she died, her health having failed during the War of Independence and the subsequent Civil War, she was only forty four. She was given a full republican burial at Loghill, Foynes. Her family had close connections with De Valéra and the leading members of the Fianna Fáil Government.

Oddly enough, the same Lord Inchiquin was also approached in 1958 about being patron of another newly formed "Irish Royalist Group," according to Grania O'Brien Weir. She quotes a London newspaper: "At a secret political meeting in London last month, this group of prominent Irishmen decided to start a movement to restore the monarchy in Ireland."

They were led by a thirty-four-year-old Galway businessman named James Murray. The subject was forgotten until Walter J. Curley, a former United

States Ambassador to Ireland, in a book called *Monarchs in Waiting*, mentioned the O'Briens with the O'Neills and O'Conors, although omitting the MacCarthys, as aspirants to the High Kingship of Ireland.

During Sir Donough's last years, a problem with finances caused the estate to be depleted. Dromoland Castle had been sold off in 1962 to be turned into a luxury hotel by Bernard McDonough. It was once rated by Egon Ronay as having the best restaurant in Ireland. However, the sale caused the breakup of the historic collection of portraits and works of art, including a painting of King Murrough surrendering to Henry VIII at Greenwich, a portrait of the famous Máire Rua, two china statuettes of William Smith O'Brien and his wife and other rare O'Brien paintings and items. Queen Anne (1665–1714) was actually a first cousin to Catharine Keightley, the wife of Lucius O'Brien of Dromoland (1675–1717), and some of her gifts to her cousin were also in Dromoland.

While the castle was sold off, the Dromoland estate remained within the family control. Sir Donough died in 1968.

Sir Donough's brother Sir Phaedruig O'Brien became the seventeenth Lord Inchiquin. When he died on May 20, 1982, the titles and estates were inherited by his nephew, Conor Myles John O'Brien. The new Lord Inchiquin was actually born in Surrey, England, on July 17, 1943. He was the son of the Honorable Fionn O'Brien, the youngest son of the fifteenth Baron Inchiquin. Educated at Eton and having served in the British Army in the 14/20th King's Hussars in the Middle East, Far East and Europe from 1963 to 1975, he retired with the rank of captain. He then ran his own trading company in Hong Kong and Singapore.

Upon becoming the eighteenth Baron Inchiquin and tenth baronet, O'Brien, as he is simply referred to in Ireland, moved to the ancestral estate in County Clare. He lives in Thomond House on the Dromoland estate. He has since turned the estate into a major sporting and leisure center, with various activities including stalking, shooting, fishing, horse riding, eventing, hunter trials, 4 x 4 off-road driving, clay pigeon shooting, archery and other activities. Married to Helen O'Farrell of County Longford in 1988, he has two daughters, the Honorable Slaney O'Brien (b. 1989) and the Honorable Lucia O'Brien (b. 1991). The O'Brien and his wife run Thomond House as a deluxe guesthouse with six guest rooms.

Conor O'Brien is a member of the Standing Council of Irish Chiefs and Chieftains, of which he became vice-chairman in January 2000. He is another holder of an ancient Gaelic title who believes there is a place for him in modern Irish life. He says:

with the tremendous interest in roots and Clans, the Irish Chiefs have a major role that they can play in the Gaelic and cultural heritage of Ireland and in helping the state authorities in the promotion of tourism through the medium of the Clan Associations and Clan Gatherings as well as ensuring that the country recognizes the importance of the link between the old Gaelic culture and our modern-day Republican culture.

However, he does not feel that holders of Gaelic titles should have a permanent representation in the Irish Senate unless it has been achieved by due democratic process.

He was responsible for the formation of the O'Brien Clan Association. The first clan gathering since 1936 was held in County Clare in 1992. A special commemorative book, *The Royal O'Briens*, was issued to mark the occasion. He is actively working on the formation of The O'Brien Clan Foundation as a worldwide organization and launched this in the United States in 1998. He has scheduled other major clan gatherings for the O'Briens, including one in 2002, which will be a Dál gCais Festival in Killaloe, County Clare commemorating the thousandth anniversary of the accession of Brían Bóroimhe to the High Kingship. In fact, O'Brien is an advisor on a prospective film production on the life of Brían Bóroimhe based on the best-selling novel *The Lion of Ireland* by Morgan Llywelyn.

He believes that the holders of the old Gaelic titles have

> a role to bridge the gap between the old Gaelic past and the modern Republic, to foster better understanding of our Gaelic heritage and to play a role in the cultural and literary part of our society. I believe also that the Chiefs should play a role in the economic growth of the country through, in particular, tourism and the promotion of clan gatherings and the return of the Irish Diaspora. Where appropriate and possible we should also play our part in the Northern Ireland peace process.

He believes he is an ambassador for Gaelic Ireland in all senses. He supports the attempts to preserve the Irish language. Like his republican forebear, William Smith O'Brien, he is a member of the Church of Ireland; his branch of the family has been so since Máire Rua brought her son Donough up in that faith in order to protect the family estates. He does not agree in any sect having a special relationship with the state.

> The Church has had too much control since the formation of the state, which in many ways has held back progress and helped with the demise of the

Protestant faith particularly in the rural areas. It is not good to have the monopoly of one Church. I believe that we should become a secular state.

THE O'GRADY (Ó GRÁDAIGH)

The O'Grady chiefly line are a branch of the Dál gCais of Thomond and generally regarded as a cadet branch of the O'Briens. They were princes of the Cenél Dunghaile whose territory was in County Clare. One of their main centers was a fortress on Inis Cealtra (the island of burials, now referred to as Holy Island) in Lough Derg. The island has five churches and the remains of a monastery founded by St. Cainín in the seventh century A.D. O'Grady sites occur all around Lough Derg and there is a Lough Grady, which is one of the smaller lakes nearby.

The family traces its roots to Donal O'Grady, who was killed in battle in 1309. In the same year his son Aodh acquired the lands of Kilballyowen in County Limerick through marriage to the daughter of a neighboring clan's chief (Chief of Anlan Cliath). Kilballyowen remained in possession of the family until 1994, when the estate was broken up. There is, however, still a family connection there.

There seem to have been few members of note in the family in its early period except one of their number, "Johannes," who became Archbishop of Tuam (1364–71).

During the frenetic Tudor period, Donough O'Grady, known to the English as "Dionysius," and referred to as "captain of his nation," followed the example of the King of Thomond. In 1543 he surrendered his title and lands to Henry VIII. He was then accorded the rank of an English knight and allowed his lands at Kilballyowen back on feudal tenure. Since then there has been a tendency to support the English administration in Ireland. In July 1582 Donough's son Seán went further by taking the name John Brady as a means of becoming English. His brother, Hugh Brady, was to become the first Protestant Bishop of Meath. He was also the progenitor of the Bradys of Raheen, County Clare.

However, the chiefly line seems to have quickly resumed the more phonetical Anglicized form of O'Grady.

In 1633 Darby O'Grady married the daughter of Sir Thomas Standish of Lancaster; thereafter the name Standish has appeared often among the names of the O'Grady family. In fact, a grandson of a John O'Grady of Kilballyowen, recorded as marrying in 1698, was Standish O'Grady (1766–1840), who was raised to the English peerage as Viscount Guillamore of Cahir and Baron O'Grady of Rockbarton in 1831. He won notoriety as the Attorney General who prosecuted the Irish revolutionary leader Robert Emmet in 1803. He was succeeded by his brother, whose son became one of the great Irish historians and novelists—Standish James O'Grady (1846–1928). Standish James studied at Trinity College, Dublin, and was called to the bar, but his interest in Irish history was aroused by O'Curry's *Manners and Customs of the Ancient Irish*. O'Grady was assured by a professor at Trinity College that the native Irish "had no history" and that the High King Brían Bóroimhe was a mythological character.

His most famous work was *The History of Ireland: Heroic Period* (1878–80). His writings awakened his contemporaries to a creative sense of Ireland's epic past, and he has often been called "Father of the Irish Literary Revival." O'Grady's influence is acknowledged by W. B. Yeats and AE (George Russell), as well as Katharine Tynan and Aubrey de Vere. He is, however, often confused with his cousin Standish Hayes O'Grady (1832–1915), who was the son of Admiral Hayes O'Grady. Standish Hayes became a leading Irish language scholar who made a *Catalogue of Irish Manuscripts in the British Museum*. His compilation of tales from early Irish manuscripts published as *Silva Gadelica* (1892) was an important contribution to understanding early literary endeavor in ancient Ireland.

In 1751 John O'Grady married the Honorable Mary Elizabeth de Courcy, eldest daughter and coheiress of the fourteenth Baron Kinsale. The de Courcy family was among the first Normans to settle in Ireland during the twelfth century. John de Courcy led the first Norman expedition into Ulster and even claimed the title "Princeps Ulidiae," having defeated the Uí Néill king. Therefore de Courcy also appears as a name among the members of the O'Grady family.

The generations of the O'Grady chiefs seemed to have led uneventful and quiet lives, according to *Burke's Irish Family Records* (1979). During 1879 and 1903, the Land War took place in Ireland, a struggle to break the insidious system of absentee English landlordism, the still-feudal relationship of landlord to tenant, which had been the cause for many terrible famines in Ireland. Famine was a common feature of Irish life in the eighteenth and nineteenth century. Between 1728 and 1845 records show no fewer than twenty-four "famines." It is not strictly correct to call any of these events "famines," for a famine implies a scarcity of food in the country. That was never the case in Ireland. Ireland produced enough foodstuffs to feed its population many times over. What was happening was, in fact, starvation of the poorer section of the population by the arrogance of the colonial landlord system.

In the "famine" of 1740, it was estimated that 400,000 people died. In the 1822 famine about 100,000 people died. The English social reformer William Cobbett, in his *Political Register* in July 1822, commented:

Pray observe this ... the food is there [in Ireland] but those who have it in
their possession will not give it without the money. And we know that the food
is there; for since this famine has been declared in parliament, thousands of
quarters of corn have been imported every week from Ireland to England.

Even after An Gorta Mhór (the Great Hunger) of 1844 to 1848, which saw
the loss, in real terms, of two and a half million from the Irish population, there
were still "famines." Hundreds of thousands of Irish rural poor died unneces-
sarily due to the uncompromising colonial landlord system.

With the deterioration in agriculture, due to a fall in world prices for produce and large-scale agricultural improvements in the United States, Irish
farming was adversely affected. Between 1875 and 1879 prices for produce fell
by 75 percent, yet landowners still expected their tenants to continue to pay
rents in accordance with previous production figures. When they could not,
they were evicted, often to starve by the side of the road. Between 1878 and
1886 some 130,000 families were turned out of their homes. Ireland, at this
point, was owned by 20,000 landlords, of whom just 750 owned half of the
acreage in the entire country. The Land League initially sought fair rents and a
fixity of tenure, but, in the face of the intransigence of the landlords, the
League began to develop a philosophy of overthrowing the great feudal estates.
During this time the O'Grady property in Limerick was the site of grim scenes.

In 1887 Thomas de Courcy O'Grady (1844–98), who freely used his title
The O'Grady, according to the *Times* (London) of August 17, announced that
he would be evicting any of his tenants who obeyed the Land League's call not
to pay the rents demanded by landlords if they were unreasonable. O'Grady's
tenants believed that O'Grady's rents were unreasonable. Some days later 70
men of the 2nd Battalion, Leinster Regiment, with 130 men of the Royal Irish
Constabulary, commanded by Inspector Moriarty, marched from Kilballyowen, the residence of The O'Grady, where they had been encamped, and
began to evict those tenants who refused or could not pay. The first tenant to
be evicted was John Carroll, near Herbertstown. Within days some forty-two
tenants on The O'Grady estate were evicted in spite of demonstrations by protesters. Many of the protesters were arrested, including three women.

By March of the following year the action of the tenants, organized by the
Land League, was beginning to hit the landlords in their pockets. The Land
League had forged a new weapon. Captain Charles Cunningham Boycott
(1823–97) was land agent for Lord Erne's estate at Lough Mask, County Mayo.
His name was given to the new weapon. Instead of being subject to attack, as
they had been in the eighteenth century, the landlords and their agents were

boycotted, their crops left to rot or harvested at great expense by laborers brought in under military protection.

The O'Grady now offered to sell the holdings to his tenants, but at a sum comprising the total of eighteen years' worth of rents. This was a price no tenant farmer could afford. Later that year O'Grady took the confiscated cattle from his evicted tenants' farms and shipped them to Liverpool for sale. He was immediately denounced, and through Land League pressure he was unable to find a buyer. His cattle were boycotted.

A. G. O'Donnell, the High Sheriff of the county, was obviously a supporter of the Land League and is reported in the *Times* (London) of December 24, 1888, as stating: "It was simply disgraceful to the city of Limerick that any man in it should be found mean enough to give assistance to The O'Grady against his oppressed tenantry."

The conflict between O'Grady and his tenants continued and was reported in the *Times* (London) of February 11, 1889. Thomas Wallace Russell (1841–1920), the first Earl Russell, had defeated William O'Brien (1841–1920) of the Land League as Member of Parliament in 1886 in South Tyrone, standing as a Unionist. Yet, after 1900, he switched his support to Home Rule for Ireland and lost his seat, though he won the North Tyrone seat in 1910. Russell wrote an extraordinary, two-and-a-half-columns long letter in the *Times* (London) in support of The O'Grady.

Referring to John Dillon MP and William Smith MP, leaders of the Land League and the League's activities against The O'Grady, he said: "The O'Grady is as Irish as either of these gentlemen and certainly more Irish than Mr. Parnell. He is one of the old stock; and is the 17th in direct succession to the family estate during the past 400 years."

He could not, of course, make the same claim against O'Brien. Referring to the Land League, Russell said: "If there be a place in all Ireland where this wicked combination should be fought with outright, where the most heart and loyal support ought to be given to the landlord, Kilballyowen is the place and The O'Grady is the landlord."

This O'Grady, however, was to see the Land Purchase Acts and other measures provide against arbitrary eviction, prohibit the unilateral raising of rents and commence the establishment of peasant ownership by state laws. With the passing of the Wyndham Act of 1903, the end of the feudal system of landholding in Ireland was assured. In thirty-six years some 13 million acres, divided into 400,000 smallholdings, were purchased by the tenant farmers.

Thomas's brother William de Rienzi O'Grady (1852–1932) succeeded him in 1898 as The O'Grady. In turn, a cousin succeeded both to the estate and title in 1932. This was Gerald Vigors de Courcy O'Grady (1912–93), who had joined the British Army serving as aide-de-camp to the commander in chief in India (1939–40). He won the Military Cross in 1945 and left the service with the rank of lieutenant colonel, having commanded the Oxfordshire Yeomanry and been an instructor at Sandhurst.

He returned to his estate, becoming the president of the Irish Grassland Association. He was an outspoken man and vehemently criticized the fact that the Genealogical Office had added "of Kilballyowen" to his title. He is reported to have said: "I am *The* O'Grady, where I live is irrelevant to my title." He was enthusiastic when the Standing Council of Chiefs was established. His first marriage had been dissolved in 1961 and his widow, Madam Mollie O'Grady of Maryland, the United States, still lives on the estate. He died on January 7, 1993.

His son, Brian de Courcy O'Grady, was born in 1943, went to his father's old school of Wellington and studied at the Northampton College of Agriculture. However, he went into the insurance business and made his home in Sussex. He took an interest in his heritage and participated in the activities of the Standing Council. He spoke several times with the author, but it soon became evident that he was fighting cancer. He died on May 7, 1998.

In turn, he was succeeded by his son Henry Thomas Standish O'Grady, born on April 17, 1974. He was educated at Harrow. At Bristol University he took a master's degree in engineering and French, with a year studying in Toulouse University. He then did a second master's degree in Oxford and in Paris in European business management. He now lives in Paris and works as a consultant for a French management consultant firm.

As he is not married, his tanist, or heir-apparent, is his cousin, Donagh Philip Standish O'Grady, born in Kuala Lumpur in 1960, the son of Colonel Philip O'Grady of Askeaton, County Limerick. Donough, too, went to Wellington College and Oxford and Brisbane Universities. He farms in Limerick.

The O'Grady is taking his title seriously. "I am honoured to have a seat on the Standing Council of Irish Chiefs but, given my lack of experience of its workings, I feel it would be inappropriate at present for me to comment on either its role, or the role of the O'Grady family."

An O'Grady Project has been set up by the East Clare Heritage Centre to refurbish the O'Grady Castle at Tuamgraney as an O'Grady Center. The castle actually belongs to William MacLysaght, the son of the late Edward MacLysaght, the first Chief Herald of Ireland. It is hoped to incorporate a museum. The cost, in 1998, was estimated at IR£300,000. It is envisaged as an important center that will be a focus for all members of the O'Grady and Brady clan as well as the chiefly family.

CHAPTER NINE

THE KINGDOM OF CONNACHT

CONNACHT, SOMETIMES SPELLED CONNAUGHT, is a western province of
Ireland having, for the greater part, the River Shannon as its eastern boundary.
It now includes the counties of Galway, Mayo, Sligo, Leitrim and Roscommon
and consists of some 6,610 square miles. The Irish name Connachta is said to
have derived from the name of Connmac, one of the sons of the fabulous
Queen Medb whose royal residence was at Cruachain, now Croghan, County
Roscommon. She features prominently in the saga the *Táin Bó Cuailnge* (the
Cattle Raid of Cooley). This epic was certainly already known and popular in
the late sixth century when Seanchán Tórpeist (ca. A.D. 570–647), a Munster
poet who became Chief Bard of Ireland, was said to have saved the manuscript
from destruction by having the only known copy returned from Brittany. The
earliest complete version of it survives in the twelfth-century *Leabhar na hUidre*
(Book of the Dun Cow). The scholar R. A. S. Macalister described the *Táin*, in
his book *Ancient Ireland*, as "a literature which comes down to us right from the
heart of the La Tène period" (ca. 500–100 B.C.).

A Gaelic dynasty certainly arose at an early period with its capital at Cruachain. Connacht was initially associated with the land of the Fir Bolg of Irish
myth, who are often claimed as a pre-Gaelic people. After the defeat of the Fir
Bolg at the first Battle of Magh Tuiredh (Moytura), Connacht was given as a
peace settlement to Sreng, a Fir Bolg who had cut off the arm of Nuada, the
leader of the Tuatha Dé Danaan, the gods and goddesses of the Gaels.

The ruling dynasty of Connacht trace their line back to Brión, a brother of
Niall of the Nine Hostages, and therefore the royal dynasty of Connacht became

known as the Uí Briúin, descendants of Brión. More particularly they descend from the line of the Uí Bríon Aí. Most of their pedigrees start with Eochaidh Moydedon (A.D. 358–366), a King of Connacht who claimed the High Kingship and is said to have reigned thirteen years and died peacefully at Tara.

The dynasty then took, as their patronymic, the name Ó Conchobhair from Conchobar (Anglicized as Conor), who died in 973. He was the son of Tadhg of the Three Towers (d. 956), who was said to be eighteenth in descent from Duach Galach, the first Christian King of Connacht (d. 438), who was converted by St. Patrick. The first to use the O'Conor patronymic was Cathal, who reigned for thirty years, acknowledged Brían Bóroimhe as High King and finally abdicated in favor of his son Tadhg to become a monk for his remaining years. Tadhg "of the White Steed" reigned until 1030.

It was Tairrdelbach Ua Conchobhair, who came to the throne of Connacht in 1106, who finally made the O'Conor dynasty a power in all Ireland. His father, Ruaidri na Saide Buidhe, had been blinded by an O'Flaherty in 1092 and had to abdicate. Ruaidri ended his days in a monastery in 1118. His son Domnall was deposed from the kingship in 1106 and, coincidentally, also died in 1118. And it was in 1118 that Domnall's brother Tairrdelbach found himself in the role of kingmaker, forcing the O'Brien High King to accept the Treaty that partitioned Munster.

Tairrdelbach became supreme in Connacht. He is regarded not so much as a warrior but as a statesman, although he fought and won a famous battle at Moin-mór near Emly in Tipperary in 1151, where he shattered the forces of Tairrdelbach O'Brien, the King of Thomond (d. 1167). The O'Briens having shown how the High Kingship could be simply seized by the sword, Tairrdelbach Ua Conchobhair commandeered the office on the death of the Uí Néill king, Domnall Ua Lochlainn, in 1121. Like the O'Briens, the O'Conor High King became a centralizing monarch, best remembered for building stone bridges, improving the road network, building castles and organizing a strong naval force, based in the mouth of the Shannon. His greatest naval victory was against the fleet of the Kingdom of the Isle of Man and the Isles in 1154. He also maintained a mint producing silver coins and was especially remembered as the king who commissioned the magnificent professional Cross of Cong, about 1123, which was said to have enshrined a relic of the True Cross that had been sent from Rome in 1112. The famous High Cross of Tuam was also erected during his reign. Even the usually independent Norse city-states, such as Dublin, acknowledged his suzerain rule.

He died in 1156 and was buried in the church of St. Ciaran at Clonmacnoise. For all his achievements, Tairrdelbach's period as High King was opposed by many of the other Irish kings, and the kingdoms of Desmond, Thomond, Leinster as well as the Uí Néill kingdoms were ranged against him. But his policy was to divide and rule; where he could not do so, he brought the weight of superior force to bear. As he grew older, however, the Uí Néill began to gain the upper hand. Muirchertach Ua Lochlainn emerged as the "front runner" for the High Kingship. He forced Tairrdelbach's dutiful subking, Tiernán Ó Ruairc, the King of Breifne, to submit to him in 1150 and support his claim. In fact, from this time, Muirchertach was referred to as High King and was able to consolidate that position by weakening the Kingdom of Midhe (Meath), which had, through its King Murrough Ó Maoil Sechlainn, been an ally of the O'Conor king. The kingdom was divided into three; a third was allowed to O'Conor, a third to Ó Ruairc and a third to The O'Carroll of Oriel, while Maoil Sechlainn was sent into exile.

Muirchertach Mac Lochlainn controlled the High Kingship for the next ten years.

Tairrdelbach's son Ruaidri Ua Conchobhair had become King of Connacht on the death of his father in 1156 by the simple process of blinding the eldest of his three brothers, who was thought to be the most accomplished and qualified for the kingship. He immediately challenged Muirchertach Ua Lochlainn for the High Kingship. In 1159 Muirchertach defeated his armies in a battle at Ardee. After two years of prevaricating, Ruaidri formally acknowledged Muirchertach as High King.

Yet, with the inevitably of the outcome of a Greek tragedy, other forces were gathering. The personalities, politics and intrigue are brilliantly told in Nicholas Furlong's study *Dermot, King of Leinster and the Foreigners*, which tells the events that led Muirchertach, the High King, to commit "high crimes and misdemeanors." Growing paranoid about the security of his support from the Uí Néill princes, he demanded the son of each prince as a hostage and then put them to death in the spring of 1166. This act was considered so extraordinary and heinous a crime that Muirchertach was denounced by the Church, regarded by the Brehons of Ireland as unfit to be High King any longer. Finally, isolated and alone, he was hunted from bog to bog like a beast and run to ground in the Fews (*Feá* = woods) of Armagh called Leitir Luin. The *Annals of Ulster* are triumphant: "A great marvel and wonderful deed was then done; to wit, the King of Ireland to fall without battle, without contest, after his dishonouring the successor of Patrick, the staff of Jesus and the successor of Colmcille, and the Gospel of St. Martin and many clergy besides."

Muirchertach's one remaining ally, Dermot Mac Murrough, the King of Leinster, chased from his kingdom, set out to get mercenary assistance from the Angevin emperor, Henry II, setting in train a series of events that still re-verberate in Ireland today.

Ruaidri Ua Conchobhair, with his close ally Tiernan Ó Ruaric, now made straight for Dublin, to fill the power vacuum. He was inaugurated as High King "as honourable as any king of the Gael was ever inaugurated," says the *Annals of the Four Masters*. In spite of the kingdom of Desmond remaining aloof, the Uí Néill being in utter disarray and the King of Leinster having left the country, Ruaidri's reign started auspiciously. In 1168 Ruaidri seemed popu-lar, and his great festival at Taillteann symbolized the new unity of Ireland. But by 1169 King Dermot had returned with the first of the Norman adventurers, the mercenary knights of Richard de Clare, Earl of Pembroke. The next year more armed adventurers followed with the earl at their head, and soon the Angevin emperor himself came to claim lordship over all Ireland.

Ruaidri fought from 1169 to 1175, in spite of truces and submissions, by which time his exhausted army had taken up positions on the western shore of Lough Derg. Ruaidri knew he could not sustain the war any longer. He opened negotiations with Mylor FitzHenry and envoys were sent to Henry II at Wind-sor. These were Ruaidri's chancellor, Archbishop Lawrence O'Toole of Dublin, Bishop Cadhla Ó Dubhthaigh of Tuam and "Cantordis," Abbot of Clonfert. They agreed to sign what became known as the Treaty of Windsor in October 1175. This recognized Henry as Lord Paramount of all Ireland. Ruaidri was to hold his kingdom of Connacht as a vassal king to the Angevin emperor.

Many forget certain points about this act. Ruaidri did not agree to the Treaty as High King, which office he had automatically forfeited under Brehon law, once he had admitted defeat. Even when he had held the office, it had been held with "opposition" from the Uí Néill of the north, the King of Leinster, and the King of Desmond and King of Thomond. He agreed the Treaty only as King of Connacht, and therefore the treaty was not binding on any other Irish king. Also, under Brehon law, his own people of Connacht were not bound by the surrender and; indeed, there was much dissension in the king-dom. His own sons rebelled and drove him into Munster. Henry II had de-manded hostages for Ruaidri's good behavior, including one of Ruaidri's own sons. They were sent to the Angevin court at Anjou in France in 1180. Ruaidri now tried to strengthen his bond with the Norman conquerors by marrying his daughter to Henry II's viceroy, Sir Hugh de Lacy. In 1186 Ruaidri was forced to abdicate as King of Connacht and did so in favor of his son Conor Moin. Ruaidri then entered the Monastery of Cong, where he died in 1198. Some thirty years after his death, his remains were transferred for burial to Clonmac-noise, being placed alongside his father, Tairrdelbach.

Ruaidri is misremembered in history as last High King of Ireland. He was not even the last native High King, for an Uí Néill aspired to that position, albeit with opposition. This was Brían O'Neill, whose brief term of office was between 1258 and 1260, when he was slain by the English. And, of course, the last de facto High King was the Norman Scot, Edward Bruce, brother of King Robert I of Scotland, invited by certain of the Irish princes, including Felim O'Conor, King of Connacht, to take that position. However, it is true that the concept of the office of High King had diminished. With the settlement of the Norman lords, paying tribute to the Angevin Empire, the centralizing movement of the High Kingship ceased and power devolved back to the constituent kingdoms.

There was a period of instability in Connacht following Ruaidri's abdication, and his son and his uncle took the crown in swift succession. Yet in the three years that Conor Moin was king he did manage to inflict one major defeat on the Normans, who were commanded by the viceroy, John de Courcy. Conor Moin was able to throw off Norman supremacy until 1189, when he was assassinated.

Then in 1201 Ruaidri's half brother, Conor's uncle, Cathal Crobhderg (Cathal of the Wine Red Hand) was inaugurated as king at the traditional site of Carnfree. His reign lasted twenty-three years. He did much to stabilize the kingdom, marrying Mór, daughter of the King of Thomond. He endowed the building of twelve abbeys in his kingdom, including the famous Abbey of Ballintober, which illustrates the change of architecture from Irish Romanesque to Gothic form. He also built the Abbey of Knockmoy. Cathal met King John of England, whose misrule had reduced most of the Continental Angevin Empire and brought the center of the Norman kings from France to England. Cathal acknowledged John as his suzerain lord.

On the death of Cathal in 1224 his son Aodh (Hugh) became king, though not without opposition from the surviving sons of Ruaidri. In 1228 Aodh was killed by a Norman knight in a fit of jealousy.

It was 1235, while Fedlimid mac Cathail Chrobhdeirg, brother of Aodh, was king, that Maurice Fitzgerald, the Justiciar (or viceroy), crossed the Shannon with an army of Norman knights and men-at-arms and laid waste the kingdom. The Justiciar allowed the Normans to seize part of the kingdom for their own estates, breaking the treaty with Ruaidri and his successors. However, many of these Norman adventurers settled down and intermarried so that families such as the Joyces, the de Burgos and the de Lacys, within a few generations, had become more Irish than the Irish, adopting the language, laws and customs of the indigenous people.

As previously mentioned, among the Irish kings who invited Edward Bruce to come to Ireland as High King was King Fedlimid mac Aeda of Connacht. It is interesting that the request of the Irish princes had gone to Robert Bruce. The Scottish King's reply is still on record, demonstrating the Gaelic kinship felt between the two countries:

> Whereas we and you and our people and your people, free since ancient times, share the same national ancestry and are urged to come together more eagerly and joyfully in friendship by a common language and by common custom, we have sent over to you our beloved kinsmen, the bearers of this letter, to negotiate with you in our name about permanently strengthening and maintaining inviolate that special friendship between us and you, so that with God's will your nation may be able to recover her ancient liberty.[1]

Edward Bruce was crowned on May Day, 1316. Fedlimid mac Aeda fought at the Battle of Athenry on August 10, 1316, facing the armies of Richard de Burgo and Richard de Bermingham. The battle was a great defeat for the Irish, and fifty-six leading members of the Gaelic aristocracy were killed, including King Fedlimid. Fedlimid was succeeded by his brother Tairrdelbach, who had married the daughter of The O'Donel, Prince of Tirconnell. The famous "Remonstrance of the Irish Princes to Pope John XXII" was drawn up in 1317 under the instigation of Domnall O'Neill, King of Ulster (1283–86 and 1295–1325) in which the princes listed their grievances. On October 14, 1318, King Edward Bruce was killed at the Battle of Faughart.

Fedlimid became the ancestor of a branch of the family which took the title Ó Conchobhair Ruadh (O'Conor Roe) while his brother Tairrdelbach became the ancestor of the Ó Conchobhair Donn (O'Conor Don). At this point in time there were three distinct branches of the O'Conor royal dynasty in Connacht.

O'CONOR SLIGO (IN ABEYANCE)

The Uí Chonchobhair Sligigh, or O'Conor Sligo, princes had descended from Brían Luigheach, one of the sons of the High King Tairrdelbach Ua Conchobhair. After the abdication of his brother Ruaidrí in 1186, Brían had retired from Connacht politics to concentrate on maintaining his castle and estates and raising his cattle. His family were Lords of Carbury and Sligo, and later the head of the house bore the title O'Conor Sligo. They intermarried with many of the great Norman families who had settled in their area. They showed an unusual disposition to be of service to the Anglo-Normans. Cathal Óg allowed them a strategic foothold in Sligo. O'Conor Sligo was one of the first to surrender his Gaelic title to Henry VIII.

Patrick O'Connor says:

> In pursuit of this policy they induced Irish Chiefs, by profuse gifts of dignities and of money, to renounce their Irish titles and accept English lordships or other titles instead; to surrender their Brehon tenures and customs and to take back their lands as grants from the [English] King on the usual condition of English landed estate; and, in general, to exchange their Irish status, with its dependence on their septs, for an English status, resting on and supported by the authority of the Crown.[2]

Donal O'Conor, The O'Conor Sligo, also surrendered to Elizabeth I of England through auspices of her Lord Deputy Sir Henry Sydney in 1565. On November 8 he traveled to Hampton Court to personally pledge his allegiance to Elizabeth. The account of his visit says that he came

> ... and there, in his Irish tongue, by an interpreter, declared that the chief causes of his coming was to see and speak to the powerful and illustrious Princess whom he recognises to be his Sovereign Lady, acknowledging that both he and his ancestors had long lived in an uncivil, rude and barbarous fashion, destitute of the true knowledge of God, and ignorant of their duty to the Imperial Crown of England.[3]

He made a solemn promise that he would raise his clan against any of his own countrymen fighting the English. For this Elizabeth was pleased to give him a knighthood. The Tudors recognized his authority from Ballyshannon to Sligo and from Sligo to the Curlew Mountains. Sir Donal O'Conor died in 1588, still a firm ally of the English. Donough, his nephew, succeeded him but not without great opposition from Sir Richard Bingham, the Elizabethan commander who had been made "President of Connacht" and who saw Sligo as "the key of the door of Connacht" by which he could invade and conquer the kingdom. Bingham did not trust Donough and felt he needed total control of Sligo to achieve his purpose.

However, Donough continued his uncle's policy as a staunch ally of England and devoted himself with the greatest zeal to promote the English interests throughout his country. At the outbreak of the renewed war led by Aodh Ruadh O'Néill as King of Ulster, O'Neill's general Aodh Ruadh O'Donnel, Prince of Tirconnell, was besieging O'Conor Sligo's castle at Colloney. Now, with an eye for the main chance, and the defeat of the English army at the Yellow Pass through the Curlews, which had been Donough's hope for relief, O'Conor Sligo decided to join the Irish side. Aodh Ruadh O'Donnel was always mistrustful of this alliance and in 1601 finally accused him of being a spy for the English authorities, which undoubtedly was true. Donough O'Conor Sligo was, therefore, imprisoned on an island on Lough Esk for two years until the Treaty of Mellifont of 1603 ended the war.

Sir Donough O'Conor reemerged as a firm ally of England once again and married Lady Eleanor Butler, Countess of Desmond, receiving a knighthood in 1604. He died in 1609 and was succeeded by his half brother. The son of this half brother was Charles O'Conor, created a baronet in 1622.

Twenty years after this, three brothers of Tadhg, the new O'Conor Sligo, broke away from his English allies and led the Sligo men in the insurrection of 1641. With the early successes of the Irish forces, Tadhg decided to join his brothers and was given command of the garrison and town of Sligo. In 1645, however, Sir Robert Stewart forced him to surrender. Tadhg O'Conor Sligo was executed in Boyle in 1652. His estates were confiscated and divided.

Tadhg's grandson, Martin, claimed the estates during the Restoration and supported James II, but, with the Williamite Conquest, the O'Conor Sligos lost all hope of recovering anything. Martin's son fled to Europe and subsequently became a general in the Austrian service. He died in Brussels in 1756, regarded by historians as "the last O'Conor Sligo."

O'CONOR ROE (IN ABEYANCE)

Tairrdelbach Ruadh, who became King of Connacht from 1384 to 1425/6, is also referred to in the annals from 1385 as Ó Conchobhair Ruadh (O'Conor Roe). He was the grandson of King Fedlimid mac Aeda, who fell fighting for Edward Bruce as King of Ireland in 1316. He is mentioned as Ó Conor Roe or Ruadh (foxy or red haired). His cousin Tairrdelbach Óg, grandson of Fedlimid's brother, who was King of Connacht three times, from 1317 to 1345, became known as Tairrdelbach Óg Donn from about 1392. It has been argued whether Tairrdelbach was nicknamed *donn* meaning brown haired to differentiate him from his cousin *ruadh* or whether the name had another significance. It has been suggested by John O'Donovan that the word *don* could have implied a rightful king as an ancient word did indicate "kingly" or "princely." The personal arms of The O'Conor Don actually bears the symbol of a mystic oak tree, associated with royalty in the ancient Celtic world, and the motto *O Dhia! Gach Cú Cabhrach*—O God! Every hero's protection.

The two related houses of O'Conor Roe and O'Conor Don could not agree on succession, and the kingdom of Connacht was divided between them. The division was not without enmity. Tairrdelbach Óg O'Conor Don was killed in 1406 by Cathal Dubh, son of O'Conor Roe. When Tairrdelbach O'Conor Roe died in 1426, there seems to have been a reunification. The O'Conor Roe was styled as King of Connacht and not "half King," as previous O'Conor Roes and O'Conor Dons had been. However, a few years later the internal warfare erupted again, and the O'Conor Roe and O'Conor Don went their separate ways, dividing the kingdom in two again.

In 1585 Tadhg Óg O'Conor Roe subscribed to the Composition of Connacht, abolishing all Gaelic titles in the former kingdom. His seat was at Bealnamulta (Bealonemilly). He had surrendered his Gaelic title and lands in 1568 and had been recognized as "captain of thee country of Clountie." In 1617 Balinfad, County Roscommon, was, according to the records, held by Cathal O'Conor Roe as his family's chief seat. During the seventeenth century the family was forced into exile. Roger O'Conor, who was governor of Civita Vecchia, Italy (ca. 1734), is regarded as the last O'Conor Roe.

THE O'CONOR DON, PRINCE OF CONNACHT (Ó CONCHOBHAIR DONN)

Tairrdlbach Óg, the first O'Conor Don, submitted to Richard II at Waterford on April 29, 1395. Tairrdelbach claimed total sovereignty over Connacht, as did his cousin, The O'Conor Roe. The annalists reconciled the counterclaims between the cousins by calling them both "half kings." This submission to Richard II angered some sections of his people, and he was inveigled into the house of a Burke kinsman and attacked. He was killed by Cathal Dubh, son of O'Conor Roe, on December 9, 1406. The O'Conor Don line maintained their "half kingship" until the time of Cairbre mac Eóghain Chaoich (1475–1546). According to O'Conor Nash: "in 1543 the O'Connors like the O'Neills and O'Brians nominally surrendered their titles and agreed to adopt English customs and laws and to obey the precepts of the English Crown, promises they had no intention of keeping but preserving their hereditary lands."[4]

Cairbre's son Aodh mac Eóghain Chaoich succeeded but was deposed after four years in 1550. His brother Diarmuid, who married Dorothy, the daughter of Tadhg Buidhe O'Conor Roe (1519–34), succeeded as "half king" in 1550. When he died in 1585 it could be said that he was the last O'Conor King of Connacht for, notwithstanding his father's nominal surrender, he was the last to exercise jurisdiction, with opposition from his brother-in-law, Tadhg Óg mac Taidhg Buidhe, O'Conor Roe, over Connacht. In 1570 Sir Edward Fytton had been made "President of Connaught" to oversee the English administration of the newly surrendered country. The state papers record that he took troops through Connaught burning churches and expelling the religious. In 1571 he demanded a meeting with King Diarmuid and gave him safe passage to come to his headquarters. As usual, safe passage did not mean much to the Tudor administrators. Sir Edward took Diarmuid captive to use him as a hostage to provide leverage for his people's good behavior.

Diarmuid's son Aodh together with the son of Diarmuid's brother-in-law, O'Conor Roe, led a daring rescue bid, which succeeded in releasing the king from Fytton's Castle. On February 14, 1571, Fytton wrote to Lord Cecil: "O'Conor Don, the ancient King of Connaught, lying pledge for his whole sept, escaped very presumptuously by night." Fytton immediately marched on Diarmuid's main castle and captured it.

Diarmuid, with other Connacht nobles, such as MacDermot of Moylurg, organized an army and recruited 1,200 Scots gallowglasses (mercenaries). Diarmuid was indicted for High Treason when he attacked the English garrison at Athlone, the seat of the English administration in the region, and destroyed it. The Connacht King continued a war that lasted until 1576.

Even as late as 1582, Diarmuid's son Aodh was still conducting guerrilla warfare against the English with the aid of the Ó Ruairc, Prince of Breifne. King Diarmuid had become feeble as the war and his age took its toll. The new Lord Deputy, Sir John Perrot, appointed a governor of Connacht in the person of Sir Richard Bingham. The Irish sources abound in reports of Bingham's cruelty and injustice. Bingham was a brutal man who showed no humanity, either to his own men or to the Irish. Perrot himself was little better. The Lord Deputy organized a Parliament in Dublin and, according to the *Annals of Loch Cé*, invited several leading Irish nobles to attend it. He then promptly hanged those he deemed the most troublesome.

In September 1585 King Diarmuid died. The annals accord him thirty-five years of sovereignty. He was buried in Roscommon. That year, of course, was the year of the Composition of Connacht, which finally abolished all Gaelic titles in Connacht.

Aodh, now The O'Conor Don, finally surrendered to Lord Deputy Perrot. This coincided with the removal from office of Sir Richard Bingham, whose massacres, hangings and confiscations in Connacht were finally realized as being nonproductive. Bingham was sent to Flanders. The English administration began to look forward to the fruits of their conquest.

After a period of quiet unease, Aodh Ruadh O'Neill, King of Ulster, rose up. The victory of the Irish at Beal an Atha Buidhe (Yellow Ford) annihilated the English army commanded by Marshal Sir Henry Bagnal. The news from the north brought Aodh O'Conor Don back into the conflict, in support of O'Neill. There was even mention of O'Neill becoming the new High King once the English were totally defeated. In 1599 the Earl of Essex arrived with a new English army. For no apparent reason, Aodh O'Conor Don abruptly decided to throw in his lot with Essex, for which the grateful earl bestowed a knighthood on him. Essex was later to answer charges about his indiscriminate bestowal of knighthoods on all and sundry.

Sir Aodh O'Conor Don joined forces with the army of Sir Conyers Clifford, the new governor of Connacht, and was at the Battle of the Curlews. When O'Donel, Prince of Tirconnell, won this battle, O'Conor Don fled but was soon made a captive of the Irish forces. Apparently after the Earl of Essex entered negotiations with Aodh Ruadh O'Neill, part of the agreement was O'Conor Don's release.

With the end of the war and the flight of many of the leading heads of the Gaelic aristocratic families in 1608, a parliament was summoned in Dublin in 1613. O'Conor Don was returned to this parliament as "first knight of shire" for Roscommon. He married the daughter of Brian O'Rourke, Prince of Breifne. Sir Aodh had received a regrant of some of his estates in 1617 from James I. These were centered at Ballintober Castle, which became a refuge for persecuted Catholic clergy. O'Conor Don seized the chance to take a civil oath, allowed by James, rather than an oath of supremacy, which would have required him to have to convert to the Protestant Church of England.

When he died in 1627 he left four sons. The third son, Cathal Óg, inherited the estate and assumed the title O'Conor Don. Cathal (Charles) (1584–1655) married Mary, daughter of Tadhg na Loing (Theobald of the Ships), whose mother was the celebrated Gráinne (Grace) O'Malley (1530–1603), called "Grainuaile" because she wore her hair close-cropped like a boy's. She was an O'Flaherty noblewoman who had fought the English both on sea and on land and even went to negotiate with Elizabeth I at Greenwich on equal terms. There is a famous picture of the two women in conversation.[5] Elizabeth was said to have had an Irish phrase book printed for the occasion so that she could speak a few words to Gráinne in her own language. Certainly such a phrase book in Irish, English and Latin does survive, compiled for Elizabeth by Lord Delvin.

Records indicate that Cathal Óg actually continued to regard himself as "King of Connacht," issued proclamations from Ballintober and raised a regular army.

Cathal O'Conor Don joined the insurrection of 1641 and died in 1655 having witnessed the Cromwellian conquest and confiscations. Out of the 6,000 acres of his estate, his widow was allowed to keep 700 acres. His son Aodh or Hugh (1617–69) had been appointed colonel in the Irish Army and was captured in 1642 in the attack on Castlecoote. He was released after seven months and rejoined the Irish forces. In 1652 he was forced to surrender to Cromwell's forces. He was declared an outlaw when he managed to flee to France, where he joined the Duke of Gloucester's regiment in Charles II's army. On the Restoration Hugh, now O'Conor Don, appealed for the restoration of his father's estate. Decisions were delayed until his death in 1669.

His son, also Hugh O'Conor, succeeded him, and in 1676 he finally regained some 1,100 acres of the original acreage of the estate. He died unmarried in 1686, and the estate went to an uncle Charles with the remainder going to his cousins, the O'Conors of Castlerea and Belanagare, County Roscommon. This uncle, Charles (d. 1699), gave his land at Ballintober to Colonel Burke in payment for a debt. He died without issue.

Andrew O'Conor, a grandson of Charles (d. 1655) became the next O'Conor Don. His father had fled into exile after the Cromwellian Conquest and remained in Spain until the Restoration. Andrew's mother, however, had managed to retain some 440 acres of profitable land and some unprofitable bogland with a house at Clonalis. Clonalis House is still O'Conor property. Andrew died in 1718 to be succeeded by his son Daniel (1718–69). He was succeeded by a son Dominick (1769–95), who died without issue. Dominick's brother Alexander (1795–1820) then succeeded but also died without issue.

The line passed to the O'Conors of Belanagare, who descended from a son of Cathal Óg's third son, Sir Hugh (d. 1632). Owen (1632–92), Cathal's first son, was declared an outlaw and fled to France. He became a major in the same regiment as his cousin, the Duke of Gloucester. During the Williamite Conquest he was captured and died a prisoner in Chester Castle in 1692. The line of Belanagare descends from his brother, who was convicted of treason and died in 1696. His son Donough Lia (1674–1750) and Donough's sons converted to the Anglican religion and thus managed to restore some 800 acres of the ancestral estates. However, while theoretically Anglican to maintain ownership, they also secretly adhered to the Catholic church.

It was Charles O'Conor of Belanagare (1710–90), a son of Donough Lia, who became the famous historian whose principal work was *The Dissertations on Irish History* (1753). His grandson was Dr. Charles O'Conor, a Catholic priest and ecclesiastical scholar who wrote *Rerum Hibernicarum Scriptores*, in four volumes. He appeared to suffer from dementia in later life and returned to Belanagare in 1827 and died there on July 29, 1828.

Other members of the family were more political, such as Charles of Mount Allen (1736–1808), the grandson of Charles the historian of Belanagare. He became much involved in politics and was a close friend of John Keogh, a leading spirit of the Catholic committee to get the repressive Penal Laws repealed. He became one of the first people in Connacht to join the United Irishmen in November 1791. His application to join was seconded by James Napper Tandy. In a letter of December 1, 1791, he referred to Theobald Wolf Tone, the republican leader, as "our friend."

He was elected to the Catholic convention in Dublin with Myles Keogh as representing Leitrim. The MacDermot, Prince of Coolavin, represented Sligo while Owen O'Conor represented Roscommon. Charles's son Thomas (1770–1855) also joined the United Irishmen. The Right Honorable Charles Owen O'Conor Don tried to water down his ancestors' commitment to the republican movement of his day by curiously claiming "Whilst Charles O'Conor and his friends thus joined heartily with the founders of the Society of United Irishmen, they never contemplated going outside the constitution or having recourse to means inconsistent with their loyalty to the [English] Crown."[6]

In the wake of the failure of the 1798 uprising, Charles O'Conor and his son, Thomas, fled to the United States. Charles's other son, Denis, was already settled there. Tom became a journalist, and during the 1812 War with England he edited weekly newspapers, *The War* and then *Military Monitor*. He also edited *The Shamrock* and *The Globe*. His major work was *A History of the War* (of 1812 to 1815).

Thomas's son Charles (1804–84), born in New York, became a Democratic lawyer, and at the end of the American Civil War was senior defense counsel for Jefferson Davis, former president of the Confederate States. In 1872 he was the Democratic candidate for the presidency of the United States but lost out to Ulysses S. Grant, attributing his failure to his Irish Catholic background. In his house on Nantucket Island, he built a library of 18,000 volumes. He was vice president of the New York Historical Society.

Owen O'Conor of Belanagare (1763–1831) became head of the family in 1820, on the death of his cousin Alexander O'Conor Don. Owen became a tireless worker for Catholic Emancipation and became a close friend and associate of Daniel O'Connell—"The Liberator." Before that he had joined the Irish Volunteers and been a delegate to the 1793 Catholic National Convention. Wolfe Tone wrote approvingly of his "political fiery ardour" in his diary. He seems to have been on intimate terms with Tone, Keogh and Byrne and other republican leaders but left the United Irish movement in 1795. He joined Daniel O'Connell's party to pursue Catholic Emancipation by constitutional methods. He was on its committee from 1811. He was elected to serve as a delegate from the Catholics of Ireland to England. Following the repeal of the last of the Penal Laws in 1829, when Catholics could at last take public office, he was elected to Parliament for County Roscommon. It is worth commenting that Sir Hugh O'Conor Don had represented County Roscommon in the Dublin Parliament of 1613.

Denis O'Conor (1794–1847) succeeded his father in 1831 as O'Conor Don and also as Member of Parliament for County Roscommon. He became Lord of the Treasury. With the restrictions on Catholics now gone, his second son not only became High Sheriff for County Roscommon but Member of Parliament for Sligo (1868–83).

His eldest son, who inherited the title, was Charles Owen O'Conor (1838–1906) and perhaps is the best known of those bearing the title O'Conor Don. He had been educated at Downside by Benedictines and studied at London University, becoming a doctor of law. He was elected Liberal Member of Parliament for Roscommon in 1860 and held the seat for the next twenty years until defeated by an Irish Party candidate from the Parnellite wing.

In the London Parliament he became a leading spokesman of Catholic opinion and urged reform of the land tenure in Ireland and also supported "home rule." He was interested in education, penal reform and reform of work practices in factories and workshops and served on royal commissions in those areas. He was supportive of the Irish language and was President of the Society for the Preservation of the Irish Language, being instrumental in procuring the introduction of the Irish language into the curricula of the Intermediate School Board. He was a friend of Douglas Hyde, who in 1893 founded Conradh na Gaeilge (the Gaelic League) and who was to become President of Ireland from 1937 to 1947. The O'Conor Don was also president of the Royal Society of Antiquaries of Ireland and of the Royal Irish Academy.

Unfortunately, in spite of his activities for self-government and the restoration of the Irish language to its rightful place in Irish society, The O'Conor Don is still remembered in Ireland for his appearance at the coronation of Edward VII in 1902 when he walked in the procession in Westminster Abbey carrying a banner described as "The Standard of Ireland." This was a flag with a harp symbol that had been hastily devised for the occasion. A double-page picture of the event appeared in a special issue of the *Illustrated London News* on August 14, 1902.

It was incorrectly reported that the O'Conor Don family was the direct line from the last High King of Ireland. Of course, not only was Ruaidri Ua

Conchobhair not the last High King of Ireland, but the O'Conor Don branch descended from Ruaidri's brother Cathal Crobhderg, who was only a King of Connacht after Ruaidri. The claims seemed to have annoyed some people at the time. It was thought that O'Conor Don was claiming some sort of legitimacy to speak for all the Irish nobility to endorse Edward VII's recognition as lawful monarch of Ireland and not ruler by right of conquest. The fact that the artificial standard was carried by someone whose title had been "utterly abolished and made extinct forever" by the same English monarchy that was using him to endorse its own titles left a nasty taste in many Irish mouths. The positive actions that he had made in support of the Irish language and other matters appeared forgotten. Charles died in 1906.

At a time when the struggle for Irish independence was growing, his ill-advised action was compounded when his son Denis Charles Joseph O'Conor appeared as The O'Conor Don in the coronation procession of George V in 1912 bearing another "Standard of Ireland." This time the standard with the harp symbol had been replaced by the equally artificial banner of St. Patrick. This red saltire cross had been devised, on the lines of Scottish saltire, following the Union of 1801. The "Standard of Ireland" is still displayed in the hall at Clonalis House. Denis, who died in 1917, was a Privy Councillor and served as both Lieutenant and High Sheriff of Roscommon. He died unmarried and his brother Owen Phelim O'Conor (1870–1943) succeeded him.

In the 1930s a Monarchist Party emerged in Ireland. In 1937 a report appeared in the newspapers with a portrait of Owen Phelim under the headline "May Become King of Ireland." The report announced that he was "the direct descendant of Roderic O'Conor, last monarch of Ireland [sic], who may be invited to become King of Ireland by the Monarchist Party."

Unfortunately, no other trace of this Irish Monarchist Party has come to light. Owen Phelim had no male issue and therefore his cousin, Father Charles Denis O'Conor, became The O'Conor Don between 1943 and 1981. Father Charles was a provincial of the Jesuit Order in Ireland and was prohibited from calling himself "The O'Conor Don." His sister Gertrude Mary married Group Captain Rupert Nash of the Royal Air Force. Their son Pyers O'Conor Nash is the current owner of Clonalis House, which houses the O'Conor archives, library and memorabilia.

After father Charles's death in 1981 the title passed to Denis Armar O'Conor. He had been born in London in January 1912, the son of Charles William O'Conor, nephew of Charles Owen (d. 1906). He was educated at Downside, where most of the family had received their schooling, and went to Sandhurst military academy in 1931. He was commissioned in the Lincolnshire

Regiment and served with the British Army in India and China. He was injured in a training accident and so never saw active service. He returned with the rank of major and moved to Roundwood, County Wicklow, where his father had a farm. He became a company director and, due to his love for animals, an inspector with the Society for the Prevention of Cruelty to Animals.

In 1936 he married Elizabeth Marris, a clergyman's daughter, but the marriage did not outlast the birth of their son, Desmond. After the divorce, Elizabeth married the famous British journalist, broadcaster and author James Cameron (1911–1985), who won more international awards than any other newspaper reporter.

Denis O'Conor then married Rosemary O'Connell-Hewitt in 1943. She was a great granddaughter of Daniel O'Connel, "The Liberator." They had two sons, one of whom, Kieran O'Conor, an archaeologist, later acquired the runs of Belanagare, the home of his ancestors, with a view to its restoration. Because of his divorce, Denis was precluded from following the family tradition of becoming a member of the Catholic Order of Malta. He did become Grand Prior of the Irish Priory of the Ecumenical Order of St. Lazarus of Jerusalem.

As The O'Conor Don, he became the recipient of various decoration from foreign governments. He was president of the Dun Laoghaire Historical Society where he lived, and a master of the Delgany Beagles, a hunting pack, having bred beagles and trained horses in his time. He was active in the early years of the Standing Council of Irish Chiefs and Chieftains and tried to bring his title into higher profile. Doubtless inspired by the success that Terence McCarthy was having with his reinvented Niadh Nask, he was advised that the Royal House of Connacht ought to have a similar order (to be discussed in chapter 13). Denis, The O'Conor Don, died on July 10, 2000 and even the London *Daily Telegraph* of July 21 devoted an entire half page to an obituary under the heading, "The O'Conor Don."

As he became elderly and stalked by ill health, certain of his affairs, including matters pertaining to his title, began to be handled by his eldest son, Desmond, who was named as his tanist, or heir-apparent. Desmond had been born on September 22, 1938 and had been brought up by his mother and stepfather, James Cameron. Based in Sussex, England, he had been a corporate finance director of Dresden Kleinwort Benson, with special responsibility for Latin America and Iberia. He retired in September 1998. A fluent speaker of Spanish and Portuguese, he has lived in Guatemala, Honduras, Peru, and Brazil and was chairman and vice chairman of his company's subsidiaries in Latin America and Spain.

Although Desmond holds Irish citizenship, he continues to live in Sussex and is married to Virginia Williams, daughter of Sir Michael Williams KCMG. They have three children, including a son, Philip Hugh, born on February 17, 1967, who now becomes tanist to his father.

Speaking to the author before the death of his father, Desmond O'Conor, the new O'Conor Don, expressed decided views on his role:

> It would, in a republic, in my view, be unconstitutional for any Irish Chief or Chieftain to hold any unelected political position unless he were elected like any other Irish citizen. In theory, I suppose, there could be a nomination to the Senate, but this would probably also need a Constitutional change. I definitely do not think that Chiefs or Chieftains should have *by right* any such position. In my view they would have to earn it and most likely then only by election.
>
> Every holder of the title should, in my view, do what he can for Ireland, but inevitably (and it was my father's case) this is likely to be confined to supporting, wherever and whenever, Irish culture. If he also happens to be a businessman, then support and help, particularly to help create employment, seems to me to be a good use of one's legacy. One may also add to this the promotion of tourism.

The new O'Conor Don, like his father, completely supports encouraging and sustaining the use of the Irish language. He points out:

> My ancestors have a distinguished history in this regard, particularly Charles O'Conor Don of Bellanagere (1710–90) and Charles Owen O'Conor Don (1826–1906), who was the first vice president for the [Society for the] Preservation of the Irish language and largely responsible for the Irish language being included in the schools' curriculum.

THE O'KELLY OF GALLAGH AND TYCOOLY (EIGHTH COUNT O'KELLY OF THE HOLY ROMAN EMPIRE) (Ó CELLAIGH)

The pedigree of The O'Kelly is traced back to Maine Mór of Connacht, who is recorded in A.D. 457 as a prince or petty king of a territory known as Uí Maine, often given as Hy-Maine, stretching from South Roscommon into East Galway. His descendants, as princes, were hereditary marshals to the Kings of Connacht. The surname is taken from Cellagh, meaning "bright headed," who is listed as the twelfth Prince of Hy-Maine, whose son Tadhg Mór was killed in the Battle of Clontarf in 1014 when the High King, Brían Bóroimhe, defeated a Leinster and Danish alliance.

It is a tradition that the crest on their coat of arms—"on a ducal crest—coronet or an enfield passant vert"—has been borne since the time of Tadhg Mór because, so the story goes, this fabulous animal arose from the sea to protect the body of the O'Kelly prince from the Danish warriors until it could be recovered by his comrades and removed from the field of battle.

The O'Kellys became one of the most prolific clans in Ireland, spreading at one time into eight different branches, but the senior branch was that of Gallagh or Uí Maine. They produced an Archbishop of Tuam who compiled the historic *Book of the O'Kellys*, which some misguided tourists think they are seeing when queuing up in Trinity College, Dublin, to see the ninth-century gospel manuscript—*Book of Kells*.

The O'Kelly princes made good political marriages over the years, marrying into the O'Brien Kings of Thomond and the O'Conor kings of Connacht and the kings of Moylurg and Princes of Coolavin. Donough, the son of Mealachlan O'Ceallagh and Finola, daughter of King Tairrdelbach O'Conor, King of Connaught, is given as the twenty-fourth O'Kelly prince of Hy-Maine in most genealogies.

The O'Kelly princes had a reputation for hospitality. In 1351 Uilliam Buidhe (William Boy), who built the castles of Callow and Gaile, invited all the bards of Ireland to a Christmas feast. His chief bard was Seán Mór Ó Dugabhán (d. ca. 1375), whose work is still extant today. His long genealogical poem *Ríoga sil Eibhir* (The Kings of the Race of Eibhear), written about 1370, and translated by Michael Kearney in 1635, was edited and published by John Daly in 1847. Ó Dugabháin's work on topography was published and edited by Dr. John O'Donovan in 1862.

The O'Kellys initially fought against the Elizabethan Conquest but Conor O'Kelly, known as Conor na Garroghe O'Kelly of Gallagh, was forced to surrender and seek pardon. On September 10, 1578, he was granted the Castle of Gallagh with ten "quarters" of land called "Twonepallice" in Galway, to hold forever by the service of a twentieth part of a knight's fee. In November 1581 he also surrendered his Gaelic title. In return, not being considered a significant aristocrat, he was granted the office of "seneschal of the barony of Kylconnell." He was to hold this "during pleasure as fully as Mellaghlen m'Eabbe O'Kelly held it." A few weeks later "William m'Mellaughlen m'Enabbe O'Kelly" was recognized "to be tanist or second person of the Kellies country beyond the river Suck in the province of Connaught." The Fiants, or Letters Patent, show that the princes had now become merely seneschals in the new English order of aristocracy.[7]

The O'Kelly's made more political marriages with the Anglo-Norman Burke family, the Earls of Clanricade. However, William O'Kelly, the O'Kelly, fought during 1641 to 1649, was exiled in Spain and returned at the Restoration. He then became a colonel in James II's army in Ireland while his kinsman Charles O'Kelly (1621–95) sat in James II's Dublin Parliament of 1689. In spite of Charles's advanced age, he commanded his regiment under Patrick Sarsfield, the Earl of Lucan, until the surrender in 1691. He was imprisoned on Inisbofin. He was finally allowed to retire to a small estate at Aughrane where he wrote an account of the Williamite War from the Jacobite viewpoint. As Ireland was under Williamite occupation, he wrote it in Latin, using ciphers for people and places. He presented it as an account of the conquest of "Cyprus": *Macariae Excidium; or the Destruction of Cyprus containing the last War and Conquest of that Kingdom* (1692). He also wrote his personal memoirs but the manuscript has been lost.

William O'Kelly, The O'Kelly, fared little better after the great defeat of Aughrim in 1691. He was driven out of Gallagh Castle by the Williamites and found a refuge in Tycooly. It was his second son, Festus, who succeeded him to the Gaelic title and, by Imperial Letters Patent of November 25, 1767, Emperor Joseph III created him *Reichsgraf* (Count) of the Holy Roman Empire with remainder to all descendants male and female in the male line, the females to bear the title until their marriage. The honor was granted because of the services to the Holy Roman Empire by Festus's son, Dillon. Dillon John O'Kelly, the son of Festus, was not only a distinguished soldier in the Imperial Army but was also Imperial Chamberlain and Minister Plenipotentiary to the Empress Maria-Theresa in 1755. His brother Connor succeeded to both Gaelic and Austrian titles.

The Holy Roman Empire came to an end in 1806 following the triumph of Napoleon Bonaparte. No attempt was made to resurrect it, and Emperor Francis II called himself Emperor of Austria.

Many of the family had been killed during the Williamite Conquest while others went into exile in Austria, Spain, Germany and the Low Countries. John James O'Kelly-Farrell was created a count by Louis XV in 1756. Marshal William O'Kelly was created a count of the Holy Roman Empire in 1767. Dionisio O'Kelly became a Knight of Santiago in Spain in 1772, while Lorenzo O'Kelly de Galway became a count in Belgium.

In more liberal times in the nineteenth century, Cornelius Joseph O'Kelly of Gallagh Castle, the fifth Count, became High Sheriff of Galway and a Justice of the Peace. He had been educated at Trinity College, Dublin.

Among the distinguished members of the family was James J. O'Kelly (1845–1916) who joined the Irish Republican Brotherhood in 1860 while, at the same time, joining the French Foreign Legion to gain military experience. He fought in Mexico when Napoleon III of France made his ill-starred attempt to set up a Hapsburg prince as emperor of Mexico in 1864. O'Kelly was a member of the Irish Republican Brotherhood's Supreme Council. He later became an Irish Party Member of Parliament for North Roscommon and was imprisoned for his Land League activities. He supported John Redmond as leader of the Irish Party after the death of Parnell in 1891.

Equally prominent was Count Gerald Edward O'Kelly de Gallagh (1890–1968), born in Portumna, County Galway, and educated at Clongowes Wood College and University College, Dublin. After the general election of 1918 that swept Sinn Féin into power with the Irish Declaration of Independence in January 1919, Count Gerald was sent by the de facto Irish government, after the United Kingdom government had declared it to be an illegal assembly, to present the Irish case to the League of Nations. He then became the Irish emissary to Belgium. He served abroad in diplomatic positions during the War of Independence (1919–21).

After the Civil War (1921–23) and the establishment of the Free State, his talents were ignored because of his republican sympathies, but when De Valéra came to power, he was appointed ambassador to France in 1929. During World War II he acted as special counselor to the Irish mission to France and managed to negotiate the release of many Irish citizens interned by the German occupation forces. In 1948 he was chargé d'affaires in Lisbon. He died in Lisbon in 1968 while still serving the Irish Republic as chargé d'affaires.

The current O'Kelly, and eighth Count, Walter was born on July 17, 1921. He was educated at Stonyhurst and Trinity College, Dublin. He took degrees in engineering. He served in the British Army during World War II as a captain in the Royal Engineers. Returning to Ireland after the war, he had a career as an executive with the Bord na Mona, a state company formed in 1946 to develop the country's energy resources. The O'Kelly lives in Dalkey near Dublin. He has one son and three daughters. His heir is his son Robert O'Kelly, who can, according to the Imperial Letters Patent, also use the style Count Robert O'Kelly. He lives in County Kildare.

As regards his Gaelic title, the O'Kelly takes a rather different view from most of his fellow Chiefs. Although he accepts that English law has abolished and made extinct his title and that the Irish Republic has inherited English law, he still believes that the state can give "courtesy recognition" to his Gaelic title under the English laws of inheritance.

> In 1585 it was agreed that the chieftainship of the county called O'Kelly's country or Hy-Many (Uí Maine), all elections and Irish divisions of land be

utterly abolished and extinct forever. These and other items brought an end to the Gaelic Order that had existed for centuries in Hy-Many.

The lands of Hy-Many, already much reduced by the inroad of Norman families, were allocated to various branches of the O'Kelly clan on the special condition that they bind themselves and their heirs, that they shall henceforth behave themselves like subjects, bringing up their children in the English fashion and in the use of the English tongue, hence my title The O'Kelly is a courtesy title.

The O'Kelly certainly does not believe that the surviving holders of Gaelic titles should have any position in public life because of their titles: "Ireland is a democracy and those in public life are elected by public ballot."

While he is a Catholic and agrees in principle with Ireland giving a special place to the Catholic Church within the state, he says: " . . . however, all faiths should be catered for satisfactorily. I support ecumenism and would like to see a Catholic Church or Cathedral with chapels covering the recognized faiths or religions of those believing in one God."

The O'Kelly is supportive of Irish cultural endeavors, which he sees as the main function of bearing a Gaelic title. "I favor bilingualism. However, being now part of Europe perhaps English is more useful together with other European languages. But in no way should the Irish language be lost."

His personal aim is to promote the O'Kellys and Kellys both at home and abroad. There is an O'Kelly Clan Association (Muintir Uí Cheallaigh) of which he is patron. Her Serene Highness, the late Princess Grace of Monaco (the former film star Grace Kelly) supported the association. The association is run by Seán Ó Ceallaigh, who owns a firm of Dublin solicitors. It produces a regular newsletter and holds clan gatherings.

Perhaps the most famous member of the O'Kelly clan was Seán T. O'Kelly (1883–1966), the first President of the Irish Republic (1949–59). He had fought in the GPO in 1916, was elected as Sinn Féin Member of Parliament in 1918 but became Speaker over the breakaway Irish Parliament, the Dáil, in 1919. He acted as a delegate to the Paris Peace Conference. He rejected the Anglo-Irish Treaty and was sent as an envoy to the United States during the Civil War. He later had a distinguished career in the Fianna Fáil governments between 1932 to 1945, when he became president. He died in 1966.

THE MACDERMOT, PRINCE OF COOLAVIN (MAC DIARMADA)

The princely house of MacDermot of Coolavin is fairly unusual in that, like that of The MacSweeney Doe, during the worst excesses of the Penal Laws, they remained suffering with the people of their former kingdom. In spite of the penury to which they were reduced, the people around Loch Gara still acknowledged them as princes. The English traveler Arthur Young, in his *A Tour in Ireland* (1776–79), notes: "Another great family in Connaught is MacDermot, who calls himself Prince of Coolavin. He lives at Coolavin in Sligo, and though he has not above one hundred pounds a year, will not admit his children to sit down in his presence."

The family traced their original descent from Brión, brother of Niall of the Nine Hostages. From Brión came the Uí Briúin, who divided into three main branches: the Uí Breifne, ancestors of the Ó Ruairc; the Uí Briúin Seola, ancestors of the Ó Flaithbheartaigh (O'Flahertys); and the Uí Briúin Aí, ancestors of the Ó Conors and the MacDermots.

The MacDermots trace their line especially from Muiredach Mullethan, who was King of Connacht from A.D. 697 to 702. The successors of King Tadhg of Three Towers, King of Connacht (925 to 956), were King Conchobar (966 to 973) and Conchobhar's brother, Maelruanaidh Mór, who became king of a substantial division of Connacht encompassing Sligo, Roscommon and parts of Mayo. The ancient name for the kingdom was Magh Luirg (Moylurg), the Plain of the Tracks of The Dagda, the Good God of the Tuatha Dé Danaan. The Moylurg subkings, of course, acknowledged that they were a division of the authority of Connacht.

The principal seat of the Kings of Moylurg was The Rock of Loch Cé (Loch Key). In 1184 the *Annals of Loch Cé* record a curious event. On the Friday after Shrovetide the palace of King Conor MacDermot was struck by lightning. The *Annals of Ulster* and the *Annals of the Four Masters* give the date as 1187. As Conor did not succeed as king until 1186, we can accept the latter date as correct. We are told that Conor's wife and his granddaughter and fifteen of the nobility, along with six or seven score of their retainers, were killed and, it seems, not just by the lightning strike but by panic; the annals say "every one of them who was not burned was suffocated in this tumultuous consternation in the entrance of the place." King Conor and a few others managed to escape. Conor reigned until 1197.

Conor's son, Tomaltach na Cairge (of the Rock), succeeded his father. He is remembered for building the first stone castle on the Rock of Loch Cé and because his first wife died in a lightning strike. It became known as MacDermot's Castle.

The Norman invasion did not impinge on the political situation in Connacht immediately. The Connacht King Ruaidri Ua Conchobhair had lost the High Kingship but retained power over Connacht. His daughter married King

Cathal MacDermot of Moylurg (1207–15). It was only in 1235, during the reign of King Cormac MacDermot (1218–44), that Richard de Burgo with five hundred mounted Norman knights and men-at-arms set out to conqueror the kingdom of Connacht and its subkingdoms.

The last military engagement of the campaign was when the army went to Port na Cairge on Loch Cé, which was the MacDermot capital. A fleet of ships with galleries and perriers, or catapults, came into the loch, and the catapults were used to fling boulders at the king's palace. The palace was set afire and the Irish came out to surrender. King Cormac asked for terms. Justiciar Maurice FitzGerald, who had joined de Burgo, granted them; the terms were recognition and payment of feudal dues to Henry III as Lord of Ireland.

However, under successive kings, Moylurg never lost the opportunity to exert its independence, and the sporadic campaigns by the Normans and, later, the English failed to bring it to absolute obedience.

The Moylurg kingdom continued into Tudor times. Ruaidri MacDermot became king in 1538 but, in a situation not unusual under Brehon law, he shared the kingdom with his kinsman Aodh Mac Dermot, Abbot of Boyle. The abbey was a short distance from Loch Cé on the Boyle River. When the abbot died in 1549, Ruaidri was the sole king. He is renowned for his largess and the invitation he gave to the leading scholars of Ireland to attend his court during the Christmas of 1540. He and his wife, Sadhbh, distributed gifts to the poets and professors at the Rock of Loch Cé (Castle MacDermot). His wife died there on Holy Thursday, 1542, and is buried at Athenry.

In 1543 when Lord Deputy St. Leger called the Gaelic nobles to attend a council in Dublin to sort out their submission to Henry VIII, newly proclaimed King of Ireland, we find King Ruaidri in attendance. He took the opportunity to purchase the confiscated churchlands of Clonshanville and Kilnamanagh from the Anglican archbishop and gave them back to the people. One might presume that, merely by his attendance, Ruaidri surrendered his title "king" and agreed to the other terms, but this does not appear so. In 1549 Ruaidri summoned another great Christmas gathering of scholars to his court and again distributed gifts and patronage. Certainly much of his reign was then spent in conducting a defensive warfare to keep his kingdom secure from English incursions. He died on Maundy Thursday, 1568, and his obituary in the *Annals of Loch Cé* described him as the last King of Moylurg. He was eighty years old.

He was succeeded by Tairrdelbach (Turlough) MacDermot (1568–76), who was inaugurated king with due process under Brehon law, with the consent of church, laity and *ollamhain*. Tairrdelbach was the son of Eóghan MacDermot, Ruaidri's brother, who had been king in 1533/4. Ruaidri's third son, Brian, married to Medbh, daughter of The O'Conor Sligo, was angry that the *derb-hfine* had not elected him to the kingship. Brian began courting the English as the Tudor wars of conquest clearly swung in their favor. Brian did not immediately succeed in his ambition of becoming King of Moylurg, for the Tairrdelbach's successor was Tadhg (1576–85).

With the Composition of Connacht, which finally made clear the abolition of all Gaelic titles and Irish methods of landholding throughout Connacht, we find that Brian was deemed by the English to be "captain of his nation." Brian and The O'Conor Sligo, his brother-in-law, had already submitted to the English and been rewarded with knighthoods. In 1577 they had joined Colonel Sir Nicholas Malby, deemed even by English writers as a "tough and formidable man" and now appointed military governor of Connacht. He assembled an army on the borders of Sligo and Donegal to fight the O'Donel, Prince of Tirconnell. In 1578 Brian was at a great council in Dublin. He surrendered the Moylurg kingship, which he was not qualified in law to do, as Tadhg was still king. Brian was then appointed by the English on June 6, 1578, to "the office of seneschal of the barony of Moylurg in the province of Connacht."

Thus the kingdom had been eliminated in English eyes. Brian died on October 31, 1592.

Brian left nine sons but his *derbhfine* still cleaved to Brehon law succession, and he was succeeded by his cousin Conor Óg MacDermot, as MacDermot (1592–1603). After the devastating English defeat at Yellow Ford, an Irish renaissance was taking place. On August 15, 1599, O'Donel, Prince of Tirconnell, was besieging England's ally, Sir Donough O'Conor Sligo at Collooney Castle. Sir Conyers Clifford had marched from Roscommon town with an army in an attempt to rescue his ally. They came to the Yellow Pass through the Curlew Mountains, on the western side of Moylurg. O'Donel's men ambushed them. Spearheading the attack was Conor Óg MacDermot and Brian Óg Ó Rourke of Breifne. The English commander, Sir Conyers, was among those killed in the attack. The English, in retreat, refused to send anyone to recover his body, which the Irish were willing to return. Sir Conyers was buried on Trinity Island on Loch Cé by courtesy of the MacDermots. Conor Óg commanded a contingent from Moylurg to Kinsale. He died in 1603 after the defeat of the Irish forces.

Brian MacDermot, the son of the Brian "named as seneschal of the barony of Moylurg," had been brought up as a ward of court under the plan, conceived under the Tudors and carried on by the Stuarts, to take all the sons of the leading Gaelic nobles and raise them as Englishmen in speech, culture and in the Anglican religion. Brian died in 1636 and his son Charles was styled "Cathal Ruadh Chief and Prince of Moylurg." Following the Irish uprising of 1641, when Ó Conor Don had raised a Connacht army, MacDermot took troops from Moylurg to join it. However, they were routed by English forces at Ballintober in 1642. Cathal Ruadh's son Eóghan was one of the Irish company who captured Sligo Castle. He was married to Sinéad Plunkett. Cathal Rua's estates were confiscated during the Cromwellian administration. He was allowed to remove to an estate called Coolavin, by the shores of Loch Gara in the western part of the former kingdom. The name came from Cuil o'bhFinn (the corner of the Fionns) because it had been inhabited by a clan called the O'Finns. At the Restoration Cathal Rua was restored to his lands, but after the Williamite Conquest the family was forced back to Coolavin.

Cathal Ruadh's son Terence had sat in James II's Dublin Parliament in 1689, and other members of the family had held seats in it. They also held several commissions in the Jacobite Army, including command of a regiment raised by them and called MacDermot's Regiment. Its commander was Colonel Brian MacDermot. Hugh MacDermot was now called the Prince of Coolavin, a title that arose by the popular choice of the people who remembered that the family had once been Kings of Moylurg. Hugh garrisoned Sligo at his own expense in support of the Jacobites. He was captured at the Battle of Aughrim "of the Slaughter" in 1691 and died in 1707.

The MacDermots refused to leave Ireland as some of the other Irish nobility were then doing and submitted themselves to William of Orange. Perhaps they, as others, believed that conditions of the Treaty of Limerick, which had guaranteed civil and religious liberties, would be maintained. When the provisions of the Treaty began to be broken by William, in 1699, no less than ten leading members of the MacDermot family were indicted and outlawed for High Treason. For some reason Hugh of Coolavin was not among them.

The family had settled quietly at Coolavin. As Sir Charles MacDermot wrote: "When I was young, the family tradition was that our ancestors were penniless princes who sat by the shores of Loch Gara reading the Latin classics. There is some truth in this." In writing about the adoption of the title "Prince of Coolavin," Sir Charles admits it arose by popular usage and was not the original Gaelic title.

In the Composition of Connacht of 1585 . . . the Irish chieftains agreed to renounce their Irish titles. . . . When the MacDermots were compelled to leave their estates in Moylurg and find a new home in the barony of Coolavin, they could not thereby be divested of their royal antecedents. They continued to regard themselves as princes and which is more important, to be called princes by the people among whom they lived. This local custom, which continues into the present day, can be regarded as a survival of the respect held in ancient times for persons who were, by hereditary, "*Rígdamna.*"[8]

Indeed, when the Genealogical Office in Dublin gave "courtesy recognition" to the Gaelic title "MacDermot" it also, in the official government publication, recognized the title "Prince of Coolavin."

Some members of the princely family did go to Europe to seek education and professional status away from the constraints of the Penal Laws, but they always returned home to Coolavin. Roger MacDermot was an officer in the Hibernia Regiment of the Irish Brigade of the Spanish Army, receiving his full commission in 1753. He often returned home on leave to Coolavin. Others went to India. However, wherever the members of the family went, the member designated "Chief and Prince" remained at Coolavin. As knowledge of Brehon law succession faded, with the eradication of the Brehon and the destruction of their law texts, the title was handed down by senior son inheritance.

Among the more fascinating of these Princes of Coolavin was Hugh MacDermot, who had pursued medical studies in Paris and Edinburgh. He returned to Ireland in 1782 at age twenty-six, having qualified as a doctor. He was a cultured and learned young man given to a voluminous correspondence. He also wrote a play entitled "Litigation," which was turned down by The Drury Lane Theatre in London although a copy still survives at Coolavin. When his father, Myles, Prince of Coolavin, died in January 1793, Hugh succeeded to the title. However, he always preferred to call himself "Dr. Hugh" rather than MacDermot or "Prince of Coolavin." In July of 1793 he married his cousin Elizabeth, the daughter of Denis O'Conor of Belanagare.

Like the O'Conors, Hugh joined the United Irishmen. He managed to avoid the attention of the authorities during the insurrection and so, unlike his O'Conor cousins, was not forced to flee to America. In fact, so "respectable" did the former United Irishman become that he was appointed Deputy Governor of County Sligo on August 30, 1830, and one of his sons, Henry, became a District Inspector in the Royal Irish Constabulary. The Irish Constabulary had been formed in 1836; the "Royal" was prefixed in 1867.

Henry's son, Henry Roderick MacDermot (1849–1915), also became a County Inspector of the Royal Irish Constabulary. With one of those ironic twists of Irish history, County Inspector Henry's eldest son, Rory (1893–1942), was a member of the insurgent garrison in Dublin's GPO during the 1916 uprising. He survived the War of Independence but took the Pro-Treaty side during the Civil War to become a captain in the Irish Free State Army.

"Dr. Hugh's" grandson had no problem using the title when he became The MacDermot. In fact, he was styled the Right Honorable Hugh Hyacinth O'Rorke MacDermot, Prince of Coolavin, a Privy Councillor (1892), Queen's Counsel, and Solicitor General for Ireland in 1886 and Attorney General in 1892. He was born in July 1834, educated at the Catholic University (now University College, Dublin), and died in 1904.

His youngest son was Frank MacDermot (born 1886), educated at Downside and Oxford. Frank became a barrister and went into the British Army during World War I (1914–18) and then worked in a merchant bank in New York. After returning to Ireland in the late 1920s, he was elected to the Dáil for Roscommon in 1932 as an Independent. He joined James Dillon in forming the National Centre Party, which won eleven seats in the following year. Right wing in politics, the party grew close to Cumann na nGaedheal and the Blueshirt (Irish Fascist movement). Frank MacDermot brought about a merger of these parties into Fine Gael in September 1933, of which party he became vice president. However, when Fine Gael supported Mussolini and his invasion of Abyssinia (now Ethiopia) in 1935, Frank MacDermot resigned both from the party and his seat. He became a Senator on the nomination of Eamon de Valéra and served until 1942, when he returned to journalism. He wrote a lengthy and somewhat biased biography of the Irish republican leader of 1798, Theobald Wolfe Tone, published in 1939.

The eldest surviving son of the Hugh Hyacinth, Charles Edward, succeeded in 1904 to the title. He also went into law. He was born in 1862 and became a barrister and Justice of the Peace. He died in 1947. Charles Edward's eldest son, Hugh, had been killed in Gallipoli in 1915, and so a younger son, Charles John, succeeded. Charles John was born in 1899, educated at Stonyhurst and Trinity College, Dublin. During World War II he had been assistant manager of a rubber plantation in Malaya and was an officer in the local defense corps. He was a prisoner of the Japanese from 1942 to 1945.

As he died without issue, Charles John's brother Sir Dermot Francis MacDermot KCMG, CMG, CBE (b. 1906), educated at Stonyhurst and Trinity College, Dublin, became Prince of Coolavin. He was in the British Diplomatic Service from 1929 to 1965, having been minister to Romania (1954–56) and ambassador to Indonesia (1956–59) and to Thailand (1961–64). Sir Dermot MacDermot spent many years researching his family history. When he died he left a manuscript that was edited and published, in 1996, by the current Chief's brother, Conor, at Drumlin Publications, County Leitrim. It is a 544-page volume of high academic quality.

The current MacDermot, Prince of Coolavin, Niall Anthony MacDermot, was born in Yokohama, Japan, in 1935—in the British Consulate where his father was posted. He was educated in St. Gerard's, Bray, and Downside. He served in the Royal Air Force, retiring with the rank of squadron leader. He is now chief executive of Coolavin Systems Ltd. (County Kildare), his own computer software company. Married to Janet Frost, he has a very active tanist in his son Rory, born on July 29, 1960. Rory and his sister Siobhán run the MacDermot Clan Association, of which The MacDermot is patron. It has its own journal and is on the Internet. A clan rally is held every three years.

The MacDermot accepts that his title has been handed down by eldest son inheritance since the seventeenth century but, like the other Chiefs on the Standing Council, admits it has its basis in Brehon law and that there is no legal authority to change that succession. However, he states:

> Under the old law, and within the strictly defined rules of eligibility, a Chief occupied his position by consent and not by right of descent. Recognition by an official of the state, however grand his title may be, does not therefore establish the *bona fides* of the Chief of an Irish Gaelic clan. If one is to apply the spirit of the Brehon Law, one would need to be able to show three things: acceptance of the Chief as such by the population of the old territory, reasonably continuous occupation of the land and a general recognition within the family of one's preeminent position. It is worth noting that the MacDermot has lived in Moylurg continuously for the past thousand years and that my princely title is still recognized by the people in and around Boyle, the center of the old kingdom.

He does not see any official role for holders of old Gaelic titles in the modern Irish state by simple virtue of their titles.

> If one of us were to become influential politically, it would be by virtue of his own personal capabilities not his title. . . . As MacDermot, Prince of Coolavin, I feel that I have a considerable responsibility, shared by my immediate family, for preserving our own ancient Gaelic heritage and, where possible, to promulgate and publish relevant information to all and sundry but most particularly to MacDermot descendants wherever they may be.

He believes that the government should have no hand in trying to preserve the Irish language. "If the poor thing were left alone, it might yet revive itself. Even people in the various Irish-speaking parts of the West are pessimistic about its eventual survival."

The MacDermots are mostly Catholic, although the current Madam MacDermot is a member of Church of Ireland.

Many of us feel quite strongly that Ireland needs to free herself from the oppressive domination of our people by the Roman Catholic hierarchy. The country is fundamentally very strongly Christian and, God willing, it will remain so but we need to espouse ecumenism more wholeheartedly and put a bit of charity into our dealings with other parts of Christ's flock.

The MacDermot is an active member of the Standing Council of Irish Chiefs and Chieftains.

THE Ó RUAIRC, PRINCE OF BREIFNE (Ó RUAIRC)

Geoffrey Philip Colomb O'Rorke, The Ó Ruairc, Prince of Breifne, is the thirty-second in male line descent from Tigernán, King of Breifne (d. A.D. 888) and is recognized as head of the ancient princely house of Uí Briúin Breifne. The Uí Briúin are descended from Brión, brother of Niall of the Nine Hostages and father of Daui Tenga Umi (d. A.D. 502), the first Uí Briúin King of Connacht, who was the common ancestor of the Uí Briúin Breifne (Ó Ruairc) and the Uí Briúin Aí (O'Conors of Connacht and MacDermots of Moylurg).

At its greatest extent, during the twelfth century, the kingdom of Breifne stretched from the coast on the Leitrim-Donegal border, southeastward to the Abbey of Mellifont and nearly to Tara in Westmeath. This was when the High King, Muirchertach Mac Lochlainn (d. 1166), forced the division of the Kingdom of Midhe (Meath) into three and gave one-third to Breifne.

Ruarc, the son of Tigernan, was King of Breifne and died in 893. The first Ó Ruairc was his grandson "Sean" Fergal Ua Ruairc (Old Ferghal), King of Connacht. He was killed in A.D. 966/67. It is claimed that the name Ruarc is a derivation of the name Ruaidri. "Sean" Fergal, in fact, was the first of the Uí Briúin Breifne to be elected King of Connacht after generations of Uí Briúin Aí (ancestors of the O'Conors) held the kingship. A conflicting claim by the two Uí Briúin houses resulted in many bloody clashes. Domhnal Ó Ruairc (d. 1102) was the last King of Breifne to also be King of Connacht. The annals claim that he was a man of peace, but this did not stop him from being killed by his own people.

His successor, as King of Breifne, was Aodh Ó Ruairc, who was given the unusual nickname of Gilla Sronmael (flat-nosed man). He was one of the kings who refused to accept the authority of Muirchertagh Ó Brian as High King. Muirchertagh invaded his territory twice, in 1109 and 1111. In 1118, however, Aodh Ó Ruairc pretended to be the High King's ally and joined his army in

Munster, by which the O'Brien hoped to eliminate the Eóghanacht threat to his power base. Aodh Ó Ruairc then joined Tairrdelbach Ua Conchobhair in withdrawing support and forcing O'Brien to agree to the Treaty of Glanmire, which partitioned Munster.

According to the annals, however, this Aodh Ó Ruairc was a plunderer of monasteries and churches and in one attack even killed the Abbot of Kells. That could not be tolerated, and in 1122 Aodh met his death at the hands of the King of Midhe (Meath), Murchadh Ó Maoil Seachlainn (sometimes given as Ó Maelachlann) with the support of the ecclesiastics. Murchadh Ó Maoil Seachlainnn supported Aodh's cousin, Tigernan, in his claim for the kingship of Breifne. Tigernan had married Murchadh's daughter Dervorgilla (1108–93) who is sometimes called "the cause of the Norman invasion of Ireland."

Dervogilla, or, to give her correct Irish name, Der bForgaill, meaning "daughter of Forgal" (Forgall was an ancient Irish god), certainly was one of the most fascinating people in Irish history at a time when one of the most important events was about to happen. In 1152 Dermot MacMorrough of Uí Cheinnselaig, the King of Leinster, who was then sixty-one years old, arrived in Breifne, and Dervorgilla, forty-three years old, eloped with him. To add insult to injury, she took her belongings and her cattle herds.

Tairrdelbach Ua Conchobhair, kinsman to Ó Ruairc, had become High King. He lost no time in taking an army into Leinster and attacking King Dermot's fortress at Ferns, burning it and taking Devorgilla back to her husband. Fines and compensation were demanded from King Dermot. In 1157 King Tigernán Ó Ruairc and Dervogilla are recorded as attending the consecration of the church at Mellifont Abbey, the first Cistercian Abbey in Ireland. Also in attendance were the Comarb of Patrick, archbishop of Armagh, seventeen bishops with the Papal Legate, the High King and King Donnchadh Ó Cearbhaill of the Uí Néill petty kingdom of Oriel. Dervorgilla presented a spectacular chalice to the Mellifont. In the very year that her former lover, King Dermot, was inviting Norman mercenaries into Ireland to help him regain his throne in Leinster, she endowed the building of the Nuns' Church at Clonmacnoise in County Offaly. Clonmacnoise was one of the great monastic settlements, founded by St. Ciaráin on January 25, 545, on the east shore of the Shannon. It was a focus of early Irish Christian art and literature. The *Leabhar na hUidri* (Book of the Dun Cow) was compiled there about 1100. Seven High Kings were buried there. It was not abandoned until its sack by English troops in 1552. The priceless *Leabhar na hUidri* disappeared after being stolen by Cromwellian troops. It was found in the hands of a Dublin bookseller, George Smith, in 1837.

Dervorgilla went on a pilgrimage to Mellifont and decided to end her days there. She died in 1193. Her husband, King Tigernán, had been killed in 1172, fighting against the Normans. He was slain by one of Henry's commanders, Hugo de Lacy. Aodh, grandson of Tigernán and Dervorgilla, now became King of Breifne. He recognized Conchobhair Maenmaige (d. 1189), King of Connacht, as his overlord.

The Kingship of Breifne then passed by Brehon law to the descendants of Tigernán's brother Cathal. Apart from various minor squabbles, during the next 150 years, which saw the rise to a more powerful position of the Ó Raighilligh (O'Reilly) of East Breifne, there seem no rulers worthy of comment. In 1213 the chronicles record that Ualgharg Ó Ruairc, King of Breifne, died while on a pilgrimage to the River Jordan. Unfortunately they do not elaborate.

By the early fourteenth century the Connacht O'Conor kings still claimed lordship over Breifne. But Breifne was fast becoming a chaotic border country in which various Norman and Gaelic factions were fighting to control sovereignty of the land. The annals are full of raids and battles, and a new power arose: the Norman de Burgo's (Burkes), who were busy carving out their own kingdom. In 1316 Fedlimid O'Conor became undisputed King of Connacht, being acknowledged by the Ó Ruaircs of Breifne, albeit with some reluctance. Fedlimid, however, at the age of twenty-three, was slain at Athenry. Ualgharg Ó Ruairc quickly formed an alliance with Maelruanaidh MacDermot, King of Moylurg, and married his daughter Derbhail. He later married the daughter of The O'Brien, King of Thomond, as a means of obtaining some balance of power. It is uncertain what happened to his first wife.

In the crucial Tudor period, Brian Ballach Mór became King of Breifne. He was inaugurated in 1536, according to the *Annals of Loch Cé*, and died in 1562. He built Leitrim Castle in 1540 and formed various alliances to keep English incursions in check. He is generally regarded as the last regnant King of Breifne, although the *Annals of the Four Masters* clearly record that his son Aodh Gallda was inaugurated as king. Two years later "he was maliciously and malignantly slain by his own people in Leitrim."

There was some dispute about succession until Brian na Murtha (of the Defense), knighted by the English in return for surrendering his Gaelic title and lands, became "Lord of Breifne." Brian was not a good English subject, however. Sir Nicholas Malby, the English Governor of Connacht, wrote to Elizabeth's Secretary of State, Sir Francis Walsingham, that: "Ó Rourke thinks himself too great a man to be a subject—Ó Rourke is the proudest Irishman of them all."

In 1584 Ó Ruairc (O'Rourke and O'Rorke now became Anglicized forms of the name) was forced to hand over his fifteen-year-old son Brian Óg as a hostage to ensure his good behavior. Brian was sent to New College, Oxford, to be brought up as an Englishman. His father, however, was keeping the English on tenterhooks as to whether he was on their side or still forming alliances with the other Irish princes. Four years later Ó Ruairc made clear his intentions.

In 1588 Sir Richard Bingham, the notorious Governor of Connacht, wrote to the Lord Deputy: "Sir Brian Ó Rourke hath written to the Spaniards in the north to join him." This was in the wake of the destruction of the Spanish Armada, a fleet of sixty-five heavily armed galleons, twenty-five store ships and thirty smaller vessels, which carried an invasion force to England. Buffeted by high winds, harried by experienced English seamen, the fleet was dispersed and, in an attempt to return to Spain, sought a route north around Scotland and Ireland. Several ships were wrecked along the Irish coast; Bingham reported that no less than twelve were wrecked on the shores of Connacht. He reported:

> The men of these ships all perished, save 1,100 or more who were put to the sword, amongst whom were officers and gentlemen of quality to the number of fifty and whose names have been set down in a list. The gentlemen were spared until the Lord Deputy sent me specific directions to see them executed— reserving alone de Cordova and his nephew.⁹

Bingham then clearly blames the Lord Deputy, Sir William Fitzwilliam, for the massacre of the Spanish shipwreck survivors on the shores. "I spared them . . ." he writes, "But the Lord Deputy Fitzwilliam came to Connacht and ordered all killed except de Cordova and his nephew who were at Athlone."

Later propaganda by the English administration tried to put the blame on the "barbaric Irish" for the slaughter, doubtless in the hope of driving a wedge between the natural alliance of Spain and Ireland. Some five thousand Spaniards were massacred in this fashion, being clubbed, shot, stabbed and hanged once they had managed to reach the shore. Contrary to the propaganda put out by Elizabeth's officials for Spanish consumption, many Irish nobles placed their lives in jeopardy by aiding the Spaniards, offering them food and shelter and securing them passage back to Spain. Foremost among these was Brían Ó Ruairc of Breifne. We have the testimony of Captain Francisco Cuellar of the *San Juan de Sicilia* wrecked off the coast of Sligo. He survived the wreck and, trying to find shelter, came across two fellow Spanish shipwreck survivors, one badly wounded. They had just escaped from where English soldiers had killed hundreds of their companions. The three of them hid and, after the English soldiers passed on, they counted four hundred bodies. Among the shipmates Cuellar recognized were several senior officers, such as Don Diego Enriquez.

Cuellar encountered an Irishman who managed to communicate with him in Latin and directed him to Ó Ruairc's stronghold. Cuellar called Ó Ruairc Lord de Ruerge. Ó Ruairc provided clothes, food and shelter and asked an account of Cuellar's adventures. "Had it not been for these people not one of us would now be alive," wrote Cueller. Ó Ruairc passed Cuellar and his survivors on to a chieftain called Mac Fhlannchaidh (MacClancy), "always great enemy of the Queen and never loved anything that was hers, nor would he obey her, and therefore the English Governor of this part of the island wanted very much to take him prisoner." Governor Bingham eventually achieved his ambition. He caught MacClancy in an ambush, with MacClancy breaking an arm in the skirmish. The Irish noble was taken to Sligo and beheaded. Bingham reported: "He was a most barbarous creature; his country extended from Grange to Ballyshannon: he was O'Rourke's right hand; he had fourteen Spaniards with him, some of whom were taken alive." [10]

Fortunately Captain Cuellar had already passed through MacClancy's hands and reached Spain in safety to write the truth of what had happened.

In 1589 the Ó Ruairc's son Brian Óg had escaped from England and was back in Breifne. His English indoctrination had been in vain. He joined his father in raids on the English and their allies. In 1590 his father decided to go to James VI of Scotland to seek aid for the Irish cause. It was a mistake. King James, whether blackmailed by Elizabeth or not, handed Brian Ó Ruairc to her officials. There is a mysterious comment in a letter from James VI to Elizabeth: "Remember what you promised by your letter of thanks for the delivery of O'Rourke." [11] Had Elizabeth promised that in exchange for Ó Ruairc she would raise no objection to James being appointed her successor to the English throne?

By May 1591 Ó Ruairc was imprisoned in the Tower of London, and in November 1591 he was executed at Tyburn. The *Annals of the Four Masters* record in that year: "The death of this Brian was one of the mournful stories of the Irish, for there had not been for a longtime any one of his tribe who excelled him in bounty, in hospitality, in giving rewards for panegyric poems, in sumptuousness, in numerous troops, in comeliness, in firmness, in maintaining the field of battle to defend his patrimony against foreign adventurers; for all which he was celebrated until his death on this occasion."

Brian Óg, who was now called Brian na Samhthach (of the battle axes), was forced to seek shelter with the Maguire, Prince of Fermanagh, while the English were devastating Breifne in search of him. He took a prominent and active part in the full-scale wars that followed, acknowledging the leadership of Aodh Ruadh O'Neill, King of Ulster. After the Irish defeat of Kinsale, he returned to Breifne to find that his half brother Tadhg had secured the title as "Lord of Breifne." He wrote to James I asking him to reinstate him in his father's title and inheritance. It was not surprising that James refused. The English had seized all of Breifne. Brian wandered Ireland and finally settled in Galway, where another half brother, Andrew, was a merchant. Brian Óg died on January 28, 1604, thirty-five years old, in the Franciscan abbey of Rosserrilly, County Galway.

Tadhg (Teige) Ó Ruairc, as head of the Breifne Ó Ruairc, was knighted by the English, but they did not trust him. He died in mysterious circumstances in 1605 at only twenty-eight years of age. His son Brian, then only six years old, was immediately taken to the Tower of London as a "Ward of Court." It was reported by Sir Oliver St. John to the Earl of Salisbury in 1611: "The inhabitants of O'Rourke's country, the heir of which is His Majesty's ward, a country very wild and apt to stir, take pleasure to declare themselves in troublesome and disorderly times." Young Brian was sent under strict supervision to Dublin and made a student at Trinity College. Then, in 1617, he was sent to Oxford and there to the Middle Temple Inns of Court. In 1619 he was confined again and ended his days as a prisoner in the Tower of London in 1641, at age forty-two years. His petitions for his freedom over the years are still extant and make heartrending reading. His last petition was dated January 8, 1641; he died a week later. The Burial Register of the Tower of London records: "Brian O'Rorke, Irish prisoner. buried the 16th day of January, 1641."

His younger brother, Aodh, had managed to escape to join the service of Spain. The territory of the Breifne Ó Ruairc was confiscated and divided into the shire or county of Leitrim, to prepare the way for the a new colonization.[12]

Although the title of the Ó Ruairc had now been abolished under English law, Ó Ruaircs still survived. We find Owen Mór, son of Tigernan Bán, tanist of Breifne, and brother to Brian na Murtha, given a commission as colonel in the Irish army in the uprising of 1641. His son, Owen Óg, was a captain. They managed to survive the wars and the Cromwellian Conquest and were exonerated after the Restoration of Charles II.

Eóghan (Owen) Óg's son Donagh had a son Seán whose son Tadhg (Teige) became a parish priest of Killanumery near Dromahair. He was lodging with his cousin Elinor at Rathbaun, Killanumery. Elinor was daughter of Farrell O'Rorke of Carrowcrin and also the widow of John Gallagher, by whom she had three children. The Gallaghers had conformed to the Established Church. In 1770 Father Teige did likewise; he caused a great scandal not only by his conversion from the Catholic priesthood but by then marrying Elinor Gallagher. The couple moved to Galway, where Teige emerged using the Anglicized form of his name as the Reverend Thaddeus O'Rorke. Not only had he converted; he had taken Anglican holy orders to become curate of Ballinlough and Kiltullag between 1785 and 1798 and then curate of Cong, County Mayo, until his death in 1799. Two of his sons became clergymen in the Church of Ireland.

From then on, the Ó Ruairc chiefly line have been Anglican, or Church of Ireland, as it is now. It is from this line that the current Ó Ruairc, Prince of Breifne, descends.

Other cadet lines of the family threw up remarkable branches. O'Rourkes served the Austrian empire. An Eóghan O'Rourke became the Austrian ambassador to St. James's Court. Count John O'Rourke, who also styled himself "Prince of Breffy," (*sic*) served the Russian tsar and the French kings and was made Count O'Rourke.

Perhaps the most famous O'Rourke of the princely house is the one whose portrait hangs in the Heroes' Gallery of the Hermitage, in St. Petersburg, Russia. This is General Count Joseph Kornilievitch O'Rourke of Breifne. He was one of the "Russian" generals who defeated Napoleon in his invasion of Russia in 1812. At the age of forty-eight he was, in fact, General-in-Chief of the Russian Army and married to a Polish lady. Settled in Poland, his descendants fled the German invasion in 1939 to England. One of the O'Rourkes, Count Illinskim, served as a fighter pilot with the Royal Air Force's Polish Squadron but was killed in action in 1943. Other members of the family moved on to Canada.

The current Ó Ruairc, Prince of Breifne, was the first of his family to be born in England, on January 20, 1943. He was educated privately and is a member of the International Stock Exchange. In 1981 he married Penelope Barclay, who is the sister of Peter Barclay of Towie Barclay, Chief of the Scottish Clan Barclay. Although based in London he maintains his Irish passport and is a frequent visitor to his relatives in Ireland.

The Ó Ruairc points out that since the execution of his ancestor Brian Ó Ruairc and the imprisonment of Brian's sons by the English monarchs at the beginning of the seventeenth century, no one in his family, of the legitimate princely line, had ever publicly claimed the Gaelic title. He recalls that members of his family had long maintained that they had a legitimate claim to it, including his father, who had never officially pursued it. During the 1980s, Ó Ruairc presented his lineage to the Genealogical Office in Ireland, having, with family (*derbhfine*) approval, made public his claim to the title. The claim was given official "courtesy recognition" by the Chief Herald of Ireland in 1991.

However, in 2000, the Chief Herald announced that his pedigree and claim to the title was to be the subject of a review, along with several other Chiefs. This came in the wake of the "McCarthy Affair" and public criticism of the Genealogical Office by Seán Murphy. At the moment, it may be years before this review sees completion.

Ó Ruairc agrees with other members of the Standing Council of Irish Chiefs and Chieftains that this title stems from Brehon law and no legal authority outside of the *derbhfine* can change that form of succession.

> The essence of a Gaelic title must depend on the Brehon law of succession. However, in practice, most of the current recognised Chiefs hold their titles de facto by primogeniture.
>
> My claim to the title of Ó Ruairc was recognised by the Chief Herald some ten years ago on the basis of the genealogical evidence that I provided. Up to that point there had been no recognised Ó Ruairc since the mid-seventeenth century.
>
> I should prefer to pass on my title under Brehon Law concepts. I have no son and the primogeniture heir is my nephew. However, under Brehon law tanistry, I would name my first cousin as a more suitable Chief.

He foresees representatives of the old Gaelic aristocracy as having a more prominent part in Irish state affairs.

> Our Council has, thus far, eschewed any political role, though I could see a case for the Chiefs of, say, the five major Gaelic kingdoms having a permanent representation in the Irish Senate and, possibly, influence with the Office of Public Works. In the non political field I think one major role should be to foster much more awareness of our Gaelic history and culture.

In this respect he wants to see the Irish language preserved and encouraged.

The President of the Irish Republic, Mary Robinson, receives some of the survivors of the old Gaelic aristocracy at Áras an Uachtaráin, the presidential residence in Dublin, in October, 1991. Left to right, back row: John Joyce, head of the Joyce family; The O'Donovan; Patrick Joyce; The O'Conor Don (d. 2000); The Ó Ruairc of Breifne; The MacGillycuddy of The Reeks. Middle row: Chevalier Gerard Crotty; The O'Morchoe; The O'Grady (d. 1993); The O'Brien; Mr Nicholas Robinson; The O'Neill of Clanaboy. Front row: Terence McCarthy (at the time, recognized by the Irish State as The MacCarthy Mór), The Donoghue of the Glens; Admiral Pascual O'Dogherty (brother of The Ó Dochertaigh of Inishowen); The Maguire of Fermanagh; Irish President, Mary Robinson; The MacDermot, Prince of Coolavin; The O'Long; Chief Herald Donal Begley and a representative of Bord Fáilte (the Irish Tourist Board).

Leopoldo O'Donnell, Duke of Tetuan, and heir to The O'Donel, Prince of Tirconnell, receives an honorary doctorate from the National University of Ireland in 1954. Eamon de Valéra, the Prime Minister of the Irish Republic and eventually to become President, looks on.

Above Hugo O'Donnell, Duke of Estrada, heir to the Duke of Tetuan, being greeted by King Juan Carlos of Spain in 1997.

Right Dr. Ramon Salvador O'Dogherty, The O'Dochertaigh of Inishowen, at an inauguration ceremony. He carries the sword of his ancestor Caothair, who was carrying it when he was slain in ambush by English troops in 1608.

Left Conor O'Brien, The O'Brien, Prince of Thomond (also 18th Baron Inchiquin and 10th Baronet in the Peerage of Ireland)

Right Desmond O'Conor, The O'Conor Don

Frederick James O'Carroll, The O'Carroll of Ely

The late Brian de Courcy O'Grady, The O'Grady (d. 1998)

William Butler Kavanagh, The MacMorrough Kavanagh, Prince of Leinster

Count Walter O'Kelly, The O'Kelly

Above   David Niall Creagh
O'Morchoe, The O'Morchoe and his
wife Margaret

Right   Geoffrey Philip Colomb
O'Rorke, The Ó Ruairc, Prince of
Breifne

Left Thomas MacSweeney,
The MacSweeney Doe

Right Count Randal
MacDonnell, The
MacDonnell of The
Glens

Terence Maguire, The Maguire, Prince of Fermanagh. His lineage is now under suspicion due to his relationship to Terence McCarthy.

Morgan Gerald Daniel O'Donovan, The O'Donovan

Denis Clement Long, The O'Long of Garranelongy

Douglas John Fox, The Fox

Don Juan O'Callaghan
Casas, The O'Callaghan

Above   The late Denis, O'Conor Don (d. 2000) with Conor, The O'Brien.

Right   Terence McCarthy. At this time the Irish State had recognised him as The MacCarthy Mór (Prince of Desmond) and he received numerous international recognitions and honours before he was stripped of his title in 1999.

Embarrassment in retrospect. Terence McCarthy welcomes Irish President, Mary Robinson, and her husband, Nicholas, in his role as The MacCarthy Mór, Prince of Desmond, to Cashel, the capital of the ancient MacCarthy Kings, in 1996. Three years later the Irish State announced he was a fraud.

The Standing Council of Irish Chiefs and Chieftains meeting at Cashel in 1994. Front row, left to right: The O'Brien, The O'Morchoe, The Maguire, Terence McCarthy, The O'Callaghan. Back row, left to right: The Ó Ruairc, The O'Donoghue of the Glens, Chevalier Gerard Crotty (Heraldic Adviser to the Council), The O'Long of Garranelongy, The O'Grady (d. 1998) and The MacGillycuddy of The Reeks.

CHAPTER TEN

THE KINGDOM OF ULSTER

ULSTER IS THE PROVINCE OF IRELAND THAT OCCUPIES the northern part of the island. The province consists of the counties of Donegal (the most northerly county in Ireland), Derry, Antrim, Fermanagh, Tyone, Cavan, Monaghan, Armagh and Down, covering 6,486 square miles. On December 7, 1922, the day after the Irish Free State came into being, Unionists, who constituted an electoral majority in only four of the Ulster counties, petitioned King George V of England to allow a territory consisting of six of these counties—Armagh, Antrim, Fermanagh, Derry, Down and Tyrone—which constituted only 52.3 percent of the total Ulster territory, to withdraw from the Irish Free State and remain within the United Kingdom as "Northern Ireland." The arbitrary border was imposed by force to include the two counties (Fermanagh and Tyrone) that had Republican majorities. The democratically elected councils and local government bodies were removed at gunpoint by the Belfast regime, and elected members were imprisoned. The name "Ulster" is now often erroneously applied merely to these six counties.

At the start of the Christian period the territory was ruled by the Uí Néill. Like that of the Eóghanachta of Munster, Uí Néill was not a patronymic but a dynastic appellation applied to several families sharing a common remote ancestry. This fact is often confused, as the senior royal house of the Uí Néill became known as the O'Neills. The dynasty is, with the Eóghanachta, one of the two oldest and most powerful dynasties in Ireland. The Uí Neill trace their kingship descent in an unbroken line, if we are to believe the ancient genealogies, back to Eremon, son of Milé Easpain, who arrived with his brothers and followers in Ireland at the end of the second millennium B.C.

The early Christian scribes in Ireland, as did the scribes serving other European dynasties at the time, embellished the genealogies of the Uí Néill so that the line of Eremon could be traced farther back, father to son, through to the Biblical characters of Baath, son of Magog, son of Japeth, son of Noah and from there the nine more generations back to Seth, son of Adam. While it was necessary in Christian times to trace such an ancestry for a king, certainly the Celtic peoples would have done this in pre-Christian times as well, but their genealogies linked back to Celtic gods and goddesses. Feinius Farsaidh, given as son of Baath, is the first to appear in the genealogies with a Celtic name. According to the *Lebor Gabhála* (Book of Invasions), he was present at the Tower of Babel during the Biblical separation of the languages of the world. He alone retained a knowledge of them all. His son Niul went to Egypt and married the pharaoh's daughter, and their son Gaedheal Glas fashioned the Irish language out of the seventy-two languages in existence. Feinius appears to be the same word as Féni, a name for Ireland's earliest Celtic inhabitants, hence Brehon law is technically the Law of the Fénechus.

It is thirty-seven generations from Adam and twenty-three from Feinius Farsaidh that we encounter Eremon and his brother Eber Fionn, the sons of Míle Easpain (or Golamh, to give his proper name). Having conquered Ireland, the brothers, as we have discussed in previous chapters, divided Ireland into two sections. This has been variously dated as between 1498 B.C. (*Annals of the Four Masters*) and 1029 B.C. (*Annals of Clonmacnoise*). The border between the two sections of Ireland was a continuous line of low gravel hills stretching from Dublin to County Galway and called Eiscir Riada. The two sections were named as Leth Chuinn, Conn's Half, in the north, and Leth Mug Nuadat, the Half of the Servant of Nuada, in the south.

A quarrel arose between Eremon and Eber over the right rule all Ireland and it continued through their descendants. Eremon and Eber, so legend had it, originally made a wager on which of them would reach Ireland first. Realizing that Eber was about to reach the shore before him, Eremon is said to have cut off his hand and thrown it onto the shore, claiming to have won the bet. Thereafter the O'Neill kings adopted a symbol of a Red Hand. But a hand reaching forth is a symbol of kingship, and the severed hand is a fanciful tale. However, by one of those ironies that fill Irish history, the Red Hand is now the symbol of the Ulster Unionists who deny the Gaelic heritage.

It is an interesting fact that apart from the Eóghanacht descendants of Eber and the Dál gCais, the other royal dynasties in Ireland are branches of the line claiming descent from Eremon.

Fifty-three generations down the line from Eremon, the northern Uí Néill High King was Niall Naoi-Ghiallach, known as Niall of the Nine Hostages (d. ca. A.D. 405), from which the Uí Néill dynasty takes its name.

By this time Ulster—Uladh is the Irish name to which the Norse *stadr* (or ster), meaning "a place," has been added—had been divided into three major kingdoms. That of Uladh, or Ulidia, was confined to Antrim and Down. Oirghialla, or Oriel, was south of this. Tir Eoghain (Tyrone) covered the northwest and must not be confused with the modern county of that name. Tir Conaill was a subkingdom of Tir Eoghain in the extreme northwest.

The exact dates of the reign of Niall Naoi-Ghiallach, historical King of Tara and progenitor of the Uí Néill, are, like most things, the subject of debate. An examination of chronologies leads to the conclusion that he died around A.D. 405, a date that Francis Byrne accepts.[1] The name Niall is thought to come from the word *nél*, meaning "cloud," indicating an affinity with some religious sky god origin. Naoi-Ghiallach means "having nine hostages" and symbolizes his power and success as a ruler.

Niall was the son of Eochadh Muighmheadhon, whose seat of power was in Connacht. Niall's brother Bríon is the progenitor of the Uí Briúin Kings of Connacht. The role of Niall in the political history of early Ireland is crucial, but the literature devoted to his life is interwoven, in traditional Celtic style, with much fantasy and religious symbolism.

We do know that he was given to conducting military expeditions outside of Ireland. He is said to have gone to Gaul and also to Italy and to have conducted sea raids around the coast of Britain. Although annalists accord him the High Kingship of Ireland, Professor Ó hÓgáin has pointed out that "it is unlikely that Niall's power extended far into the south of the country, but this did not prevent the medieval writers from describing how he gained the overlordship of Munster also by a speedy invasion of that province."[2] Niall's *ollamh* and chief bard was Torna Eisgeas (fl. A.D. 400). Torna appears in three of his own poems as an ambassador or mediator between Niall and the Munster king.

Niall's death was the stuff of sagas. In one account we learn that when visiting Alba (Scotland) he was shot with an arrow by Eochu, son of the Leinster king Enna Cennsalach, whose kingdom Niall had ravaged. A variant account has the location for this action in the Alps. As both *Alba* (Scotland) and the *Alps* derived from the same Celtic word being "high country," confusion is understandable. A third tradition has become even more popular, that he was slain by Eochu in a sea battle in what is now the English Channel (*muir Iocht*). Sources agree that the body was returned to Ireland and that he was buried at Ochann

(Faughan's Hill, near Navan, County Meath). On hearing the news, Torna is reported to have fallen dead from grief.

By the time of Niall's death, his brothers and his sons had established their dynasties in various kingdoms even as far south as Leinster. Long before Niall's period, a kingdom called Midhe (Meath) had been established as "the middle kingdom." It must not be confused with modern Meath and Westmeath for it also incorporated tracts of Counties Offaly, Longford, Louth and Dublin. The chronicles claim that this was the seat of the High Kings and that it had been created by Tuathal Techtmar (the Legitimate) in the second century B.C. as the estate of the High King so that he would not be prejudiced toward his native province when ruling. Whatever the reality, the Indo-European concept of five kingdoms with the center being in the fifth kingdom certainly survived in Ireland. As we have already discussed, each kingdom was known as "a fifth" (cóiced). In some later texts, such as Leabhar na gCeart, a king was referred to as nipsa cenn cáidh cóigedhach (the venerable head of a fifth). Today, in modern Ireland, while there are only four provinces, the modern Irish word for a province remains cúige (a fifth).

By the time of the Christian period, the Uí Néill were also in control of the kingship of Tara, or Midhe. The southern and northern Uí Néill branches vied for the office of High King. In practice during this period, the High Kingship meant no more than being King of Meath at Tara instead of power over all Ireland. The Eóghanachta no longer participated in a recognition of this precedent of honor. The High Kingship would not begin to mean a centralized power in Ireland until the rise of the Dál gCais.

Archaeology and mythology identifies an eighteen-acre hill fort site at Navan, County Armagh, as Emain Macha, the court of the Ulster kings made famous by the stories of Conchobar Mac Nessa and the Red Branch knights in the Ulster Cycle. These are also the tales featuring the Ulster hero Cúchulainn, tales that scholars have described as belonging to an age several centuries before Christ. We know that the epic Táin is referred to in written form by the seventh century while other tales were being transcribed in the eighth century. However, these tales, copied by Christian scribes, underwent a certain bowdlerization and a sanitization to eradicate the more outrageous affronts to the new faith.

Among those who ruled at Emain Macha was Macha Mong Ruadh, Macha of the Red Tresses (d. ca. 377 B.C.), who is said to have established the first hospital in Ireland, called Bróin Bherg (house of sorrow). By comparison, the Hindu Annals of Charake tell us that the Indian Emperor Asoka (ca. 273–232 B.C.) established the first hospitals in India. It was not until St. Fabiola (d. ca. 399 A.D.) that the first hospital in Rome was set up.

Whether myth or not, we know that the Brehon laws provide strict rules on the running of hospitals. All who needed curative treatment, sick maintenance and allowances could obtain them no matter their financial or social position. And the laws also governed the qualifications of doctors, providing rules against the practice of unqualified doctors.

The Uí Néill kingdoms soon felt the effects of the Normans' arrival in 1169. The Norman knight John de Courcy moved northward and established himself as "Conquestor Ultoniae." He established an earldom of Ulster, with its territory partly in north County Down and partly in south County Antrim. With the Irish renaissance at the end of the thirteenth century, however, the O'Neills could still claim to be kings of an Ulster that we can recognize as, more or less, the modern province.

THE O'NEILL, PRINCE OF TYRONE
(MARQUES DE LA GRANJA Y DEL NORTE, CONDE DE BENAGAIR IN THE SPANISH PEERAGE)
(Ó NÉILL, THÍR EÓGHAIN)
AND THE O'NEILL, PRINCE OF CLANABOY
(Ó NEILL, CHLANN AEDHA BUIDHE)

It was during the fourteenth century that the O'Neill royal house separated into two distinct branches—the O'Neill of Tyrone and the O'Neill of Clanaboy. Their common ancestor was the Aodh Macaemh Toinsleag (the Lazy Arsed youth), who was the Uí Neill King of Cenél Eoghain, or Tir Eóghan (Tyrone), the major part of what is now called Ulster. He had avenged his father who had been murdered during the excesses of the High King Muirchertach Mac Lochlainn (d. 1166). By 1176 he had become supreme ruler of Cenél Eoghain in the north of the country. A Norman French poem records that he and three thousand of his warriors came to aid of the High King Ruaidri Ua Conchobhair against Henry II. Aodh was killed in battle against the Normans in 1177.

He left four sons. His eldest was Aodh Meth "the Fat" who became king (1196–1230). His brother Niall Ruadh is recorded as "King of Uladh," succeeding Aodh Meth but reigning for only one month. He was the progenitor of the line of O'Neills of Tyrone. However, immediately he was succeeded by a son of Aodh Meth, his nephew, called Domhnall Óg, who ruled between 1231 and 1234. Domhnall Óg's son Aodh Buidhe (1260–83) was the last to whom the then archaic title of King of Aileach was given. It was from this Aodh Buidhe that the name Clann Aodha Buidhe (the people of Aodh the Yellow) or Clanaboy takes its name.

The kingship descended as usual in Brehon law with the candidates chosen from both branches of the family. However, the predominant number of kings of Ulster came from the line of the O'Neill of Tyrone. The O'Neill of Clanaboy line produced only two more kings.

Niall Ruadh's son Brian O'Neill, King of Ulster from 1241 to 1260, also became the last native High King of Ireland (1258–60). His supremacy in the north was unchallenged. He joined an Irish confederacy to drive the Anglo-Normans out of Ireland in 1256. A meeting of the Irish kings and princes, with the notable exception of the Eóghanchta of Munster, but including the O'Brien of Thomond, Ua Maoil Seachlainn of Meath, the O'Conor of Connacht and lesser members of the nobility, acknowledged Brian as High King in 1258.

In 1260, at Catha an Duin, the Battle of Downpatrick, Brian was defeated and killed by the Anglo-Normans. His head was sent to London to be exhibited. Ulster's chief bard, Giolla Brighde "Albanach" Mac Conmidhe (ca. 1180–1260), composed "The Lament of King Brian O'Neill" just before his own death. He was nicknamed "Albanach" (Scotsman) not because he was one but because he went to Scotland to recover the famous harp of Donough Cairbreach O'Brien, King of Thomond. He also went to Palestine between 1218–21, probably as a pilgrim, and returned with poems about the hardship of his journey. The Kings of Thomond, Connacht and Ulster patronized him, and his work has been studied and discussed by several scholars during this century.

Brian's son, Domnall, was King of Ulster between 1283 and 1286 but was deposed by the Normans. Restored by the Irish in 1295, he continued to reign until 1325. He decided, in the interests of Irish independence, to renounce the claims to the High Kingship based on his father's short rule, and invited Edward Bruce, brother of King Robert of Scotland, to come to Ireland to be High King. Supported by other Irish kings, Edward was duly crowned, but the resultant military campaign against England ended in Edward's defeat and death, along with that of many of the Irish nobility. Domnall survived, and his name heads the famous "Remonstrance to Pope John XXII" signed by the Irish princes in 1317.

The Clanaboy line was able to claim the kingship after the death of King Domhnall in 1325. Henry, as Prince of Clanaboy, had not supported his kinsman in acknowledging Edward Bruce as High King. He and his father were, in fact, allied to the Normans' "Earl of Ulster" against Brian and his son Domhnall, and had used the opportunity to expand and consolidate their own power base east of the river Bann and south of Lough Neagh, establishing a kingdom that was fairly independent of their O'Neill kinsmen. However, assisted by the

Justiciar, Sir Ralph d'Ufford, Henry was able to prevent the succession of Domhnall's son Aodh and establish himself as King of Ulster between 1325 and 1344. In 1344 he was deposed by Aodh Ramhar ("The Stout"), Domhnall's son. Henry died in 1347.

Aodh Ramhar ruled as King of Ulster between 1344 and 1364. Aodh's seals bear the inscription "ODONIS Ó NEIL REGIS HYBERNICORUM ULTONIE" and the famous Red Hand emblem of his dynasty. He died in 1364.

The O'Neill of Tyrone line then held the kingship of Ulster with only one interruption, when the grandson of King Eóghan (1432–55), Art (1509–1514), became King of Ulster. His father Aodh (d. 1475) was named as the tanist of Cenél Eoghain and had, in 1435, extended his rule over the Fews (*féa* = a wood) in Armagh, an area "full of woods and impassable fens, a long ridge of mountainous waste." Aodh's son Art was an ally of his cousin King Conn Mór O'Neill against the English in 1487 and succeeded him as King of Ulster from 1509 to 1514.

Art's son Fedlimid Ruadh became known as Lord of the Fews. When the line of the last King of Ulster, Aodh Ruadh (Red Hugh), known to the English as the second Earl of Tyrone, died out on the Continent, the descendants of the line of the Lord of the Fews became represented by Don Arturo O'Neill, first Marques del Norte (1736–1814).

Conn Mór O'Neill, King of Ulster between 1483 and 1493, was noted as founding a Franciscan Friary near Dunganon in 1489. His second wife was the daughter of the Lord Deputy of Ireland, Thomas Fitzgerald, seventh Earl of Kildare. His son Art Óg became King of Ulster between 1514 and 1519.

Art Óg was succeeded by his brother Conn Bacach "the Lame." Conn Bacach is often wrongly regarded as the last King of Ulster. Certainly, in 1542, he submitted to Henry VIII and surrendered his kingship. For having promised to change his religion, method of holding land, laws and language, he was rewarded with an English title, Earl of Tyrone. His eldest, although illegitimate, son Ferdorcha, whose name was promptly converted to Matthew in English records, became first Baron of Dungannon.

Within weeks of Conn Bacach returning to his Ulster kingdom, his *derbhfine* were in revolt at his betrayal. As an anonymous poet wrote:

> The O'Neills of Aileach and Navan,
> The King of Tara and Tailltean,
> In foolish submission,
> Have surrendered their kingdoms for
> the Earldom of Ulster!

Conn Bacach immediately wrote to Henry VIII seeking help to put down his own people but was driven into exile in the Pale, the English-dominated area around Dublin, as a refugee. He died there shortly afterward in 1559. Conn Bacach's youngest son, Seán an Díomais (Shane the Proud) was inaugurated as The O'Neill and King of Ulster in his father's place. Ferdorcha (Matthew), Conn Bacach's eldest son, the first Baron Dungannon, was not even considered. Ferdorcha did not accept the decision lightly and rebelled against his brother. He was finally killed in 1558, the year before his father died. He had two sons, Brían, the second Baron of Dungannon, killed in the continuing dynastic quarrel, and the famous Aodh Ruadh. Brían, although he did not use the title, technically inherited his grandfather's earldom and was the second Earl of Tyrone.

For the next few years the new king, Seán the Proud, having rejected the earldom and restored the kingdom, was at war with the English administration and the Lord Deputy, the Earl of Sussex. During Elizabeth's reign a tenuous peace was agreed. Seán the Proud actually went to London to discuss the situation with Elizabeth I. It is recorded that he tried to explain to her the successional laws of Ireland. He married Catherine, daughter of The MacDonnell of The Glens, chief of the MacDonnells of The Glens of Antrim, whose ancient lineage was one held in common with the Uí Néill. They had two sons. His second marriage was to Catherine of Lachlan MacLean of Duart, chief of Clan Gillean, who could speak five languages. He had two more sons. Seán, in maintaining control over his kingdom, had defeated the army of the MacDonnell of The Glens, capturing him and his brother, Somhairle Buidhe (Sorley Boy) MacDonnell, Lord of the Route in Antrim. He was later invited to a conference by the MacDonnell of The Glens on June 2, 1567, and assassinated.

Tairrdelbach Luimneach O'Neill, the grandson of Art Óg, King of Ulster (1514–19), was now installed at Tulach Óg as The O'Neill, King of Ulster. Walter, the Earl of Essex (not to be confused with his more flamboyant son, Robert, who became one of Elizabeth I's favorites), sent to bring Tairrdelbach to submission, found him an astute general and politician. After a battle in June 1575, it was the Earl of Essex who was forced to come to terms with King Tairrdelbach. The Ulster king was then left in peace to consolidate his kingdom. Lord Essex, Earl Marshal of Ireland, died of dysentery in Dublin in 1576.

Seán the Proud's eldest son, Seán Óg, was killed in 1592. A son, Henry, was imprisoned in Dublin Castle with his half brother Art. They escaped in 1592 with Aodh Ruadh O'Donel, the Prince of Tirconnell. Art O'Neill died of exposure in the Wicklow Mountains.

Ferdorcha's only legitimate surviving son was Aodh Ruadh, Red Hugh, and he was inaugurated on the royal stone at Tulach Óg. Aodh Ruadh, born in

Dungannon in 1550, had, at the age of nine, been taken to England as ward of the former Lord Deputy, Sir Henry Sidney, and raised in Ludlow (Shropshire,) at Penshurst (Kent) and in London to be an Englishman and Anglican. "Red Hugh," as third Baron Dungannon and third Earl of Tyrone, returned to Ireland in 1568 and proved loyal to his English foster parents. He commanded a troop of Elizabeth's horses against Donal IX, the MacCarthy King of Desmond, during the war there. He even hanged Aodh Geimleach, the surviving son of Seán the Proud, in 1590.

Aodh Ruadh married several times. The most tempestuous marriage was to Mabel, the daughter of Sir Henry Bagenal, commander of the English Army in Ireland. Mabel left him after a few months and made public complaint against him. Aodh Ruadh began to retract his allegiance to England. Whether there was any relevance in the stormy ending of his marriage is a conjecture that may be left to novelists. By 1593 Aodh Ruadh had become the "darling of Ulster" and the old king, Tairrdelbach, even abdicated in his favor. Aodh Ruadh was still regarded as Earl of Tyrone by the English. However, he had rejected the English title and was installed at Tulach Óg with due ceremony as The O'Neill, King of Ulster. For this act, in June 1595, he was proclaimed a traitor by the English colonial administration. In Irish records he is recorded as "the last and one of the greatest of Gaelic Kings."

His defeat of Sir John Norris's army at the Battle of Clontibert in the year of his inauguration began a war that did not end until the defeat of the Irish at Kinsale. With the defeat of Marshal Sir Henry Bagenal's army at Yellow Ford near Armagh in August 1598, the biggest defeat ever suffered by an English army in Ireland, Aodh Ruadh began to be regarded virtually as High King. In panic, in 1599 Elizabeth I sent her favorite, Robert, Earl of Essex, with an army of twenty thousand fresh troops to Ireland. She gave him unlimited power to deal with the situation. The first setback Essex received was his defeat by forces led by Donal MacCarthy, son of Donal IX of Desmond, and Eoghan MacRory Moore at the Pass of Plumes, near Portlaoise, when he attempted to invade Desmond. He then turned north. In September Aodh Ruadh offered him a parley. Essex and Aodh Ruadh met in the middle of a river near Dundalk and agreed a cessation of hostilities until May 1, 1600.

When Essex returned to England, Elizabeth was so enraged at his actions that his disgrace and execution soon followed. Charles Blount, Lord Mountjoy, was sent to Ireland to reconquer it. Mountjoy was a past master at *divide et impera,* and he managed to split some of the Irish forces. O'Neill and his right-hand man, O'Donel, Prince of Tirconnell, were lured to Desmond, a kingdom still in a state of confusion following the death of Donal IX. Four thousand

Spanish allies commanded by Don Juan del Aguila had landed in Ireland. But, on December 24, 1601, at Kinsale, the Irish forces were defeated.

O'Neill retreated to Ulster, harried by English forces. In March 1603, at the very time Elizabeth I was on her deathbed, O'Neill decided that he had no alternative but to submit to Mountjoy. Hearing that the English planned to assassinate him and other leading Irish aristocrats, he fled into exile. This has been called the "Flight of the Earls," for the Prince of Tirconnell went with him. From the Irish perspective, it should be named the "Flight of the Princes." Aodh Ruadh, the last King of Ulster, died in Rome on July 20, 1616. His tomb may still be seen in the church of San Pietro in Montorio, in the Via Garibaldi, in front of the High Altar. The inscription describes him as a "Prince of Ulster."

Aodh Ruadh's son Conn had died from wounds in 1601. Conn's son, Ferdorcha, accompanied his grandfather into exile. Aodh Ruadh's next son Hugh, fourth Baron Dungannon, died unmarried in Rome in 1609, and his third son, Henry, third Conde de Tyrone, died childless in 1610. His fourth son John, fourth Conde de Tyrone, was killed near Barcelona in 1641, leaving a son Hugo, known as Eugenio, styled Prince of Ulster and fifth Conde de Tyrone, but he died childless. His fifth son, Conn na Creige, died in the Tower of London 1622. His sixth son, Brian O'Neill, was murdered in Brussels by English secret agents in 1617 at the age of thirteen. Aodh Ruadh also had eight daughters.

Ferdorach, the son of Conn Bacach, had left an illegitimate son Ferdorcha, Art "Mac Baron" (d. 1618). His line produced the famous Eoghan Ruadh O'Neill, who became Lord General of the Irish Army in 1642, defeating the army of General Munro at Benburb in 1649. His son Henry Ruadh was beheaded by the Cromwellians. His grandson was styled as seventh Conde de Tyrone Knight of Calatrava, Colonel of an Irish regiment in Spanish Service. The last Conde de Tyrone was Eoghan (Eugenio), ninth Conde, and colonel of the Tyrone Regiment of the Spanish Army. He died sometime after 1689, and from then on another O'Neill branch in France assumed the title. The last of the French family styling themselves Comte de Tyrone was Augustus Eugene Valentine O'Neille of Martinique, a politician. When he died toward the end of the nineteenth century, he left only three daughters. One of them, still styling herself Viscomtesse de Tyrone, died in France in 1932. However, the daughters, by a family pact that we will discuss shortly, agreed in 1901 that Jorge, The O'Neill of Clanaboy, then a peer of Portugal, was the senior male heir. This was a rather dubious agreement because daughters had no rights under Brehon law or even primogeniture as it then stood to bequeath such rights. However, in 1989, a François Henri O'Neill of France, claiming to be senior male heir of the Comte de Tyrone, repudiated this pact. He maintained the daughters of the last "Comte de Tyrone" "were unaware of what they were doing and the seriousness of their act."[3]

According to the genealogist Sir Iain Moncrieff of that Ilk, with the extinction of Aodh Ruadh's line at the end of the seventeenth century, the title of The O'Neill, which Moncrieff gives as "O'Neill Mór of Tyrone," a title hotly disputed by the current O'Neill of Clanaboy, was vested in the next senior branch of the line of the Lord of the Fews.[4] But we do not know what happened to Aodh Ruadh's grandson, Ferdorcha, who had accompanied his grandfather into exile. Was he, in fact, the progenitor of the French O'Neill line of the "Comtes de Tyrone"? And, before examining the lines of the Lord of the Fews, we should consider two members of the family who also have earned their own place in Irish history. Sir Feidlimid (Phelim) O'Neill (1604?–53) was the leader of the 1641 uprising, and Eoghan Ruadh O'Neill (1690–49) commanded the Irish armies between 1642 and 1649.

Sir Phelim O'Neill was descended from Seán, son of Conn Mór, King of Ulster (1483–93), by his second wife. Seán became tanist of The O'Neill of Tyrone but died in 1517. Phelim was the eldest son of Turlough O'Neill (d. 1608). He had been cheated out of his estates by Sir Arthur Chichester. He studied law at Lincoln's Inn in London and was elected to the Dublin Parliament in 1641. It is claimed that he had been inaugurated at Tulach Óg as O'Neill, Prince of Ulster, although the ancient Uí Neill inauguration stone had been smashed to pieces by Lord Mountjoy.

He organized and led the Irish uprising of 1641, which started on October 22. As Lord General of the Irish Army, Sir Phelim captured Charlemont Castle, a place of considerable strategic importance, commanding the Blackwater on the great northern road. When his kinsman Eoghan Ruadh (Red Owen) arrived in Ireland in 1642, Sir Phelim immediately went to Lough Swilly to meet him and escort him by way of Ballyshannon to Charlemont. He at once yielded the command of the Irish forces to Eoghan Ruadh. This is curious for Phelim was a legitimate son, heir of Ulster kings, whereas Eoghan Ruadh was the son of the illegitimate son of Ferdorcha, who, in turn, was son of the deposed King Conn Bacach. Could Phelim, if he had been legitimately endorsed as O'Neill, Prince of Ulster, simply abdicate his rank as well as his command to his distant cousin? He could not have claimed the Gaelic title under Brehon law or even by primogeniture.

Eoghan Ruadh had entered Spanish service in 1610 and had a distinguished military career. With the uprising in 1641, Eoghan Ruadh sailed for

Ireland and landed at the end of July 1642. His most famous victory was the defeat, on June 5, 1646, of the Scottish general, Robert Munro, at Benburb on the Blackwater.

Whereas Eóghan Ruadh sought a free, independent Ireland, Phelim gradually drew to the side of those fighting against the Cromwellians for the Stuart King Charles. There was a confusion of interests, and when Eoghan Ruadh died in November 1649, Phelim was bitter not to be returned as his successor in command of the army. With the victory of the Cromwellian forces he went into hiding on an island in County Tyrone. On August 23, 1652, a reward of £300 was offered for his apprehension. He was betrayed by a kinsman, Philip Roe MacHugh O'Neill. He was taken to Dublin and brought to trial on March 5. Several times he was offered a pardon if he would admit that Charles I had given him a commission to start the uprising. He refused. On March 10, 1653, he was executed as an traitor in Dublin.

Eóghan Ruadh's nephew Hugh O'Neill (fl.1642–60) had been born in the Spanish Netherlands and appointed a major general in the Irish army. In February 1650 he was appointed governor of Clonmel with twelve hundred troops. He faced an overwhelming force commanded by Oliver Cromwell. Cromwell opened the attack on the town on April 27, having besieged it since February. Never had Cromwell met with greater resistance. Although he breached the wall, the attackers, when they poured through, were caught in a trap by O'Neill's men and pushed out again. Cromwell is reported to have lost two thousand of his "Ironsides." It is claimed that Seathrún Céitinn (Geoffrey Keating, ca. 1570–1650), the Tipperary-born historian and doctor of theology, educated at the Irish College in Bordeaux, was killed in the attack on Clonmel. His magnum opus was *Foras Feasa ar Éireann* (History of Ireland), which he began while hiding out in a cave in the Glen of Aherlow during a previous penal period.

When it was obvious that Clonmel would fall, O'Neill and his surviving soldiers slipped away in the dead of night with instructions for the mayor to agree to terms with Cromwell. Cromwell was outraged when he realized that he had been outgeneraled and counted Clonmel one of his worst military disasters. However, he kept his treaty with the city but wanted to learn what he could about his opponent. O'Neill arrived in Limerick and was given command of the city against General Ireton's siege of it. His luck did not hold and he was forced to surrender the city. He was taken captive in October 1659 and eventually sent to the Tower of London. He arrived on January 10, 1652. As O'Neill had been born under Spanish jurisdiction, the Spanish ambassador, Alonso de Cardenas, applied for his release as a Spanish subject. He ended his days in Spain sometime after 1660. In October of that year he had sought to claim the title Earl of Tyrone from Charles II. That title had been held by his kinsman, John O'Neill, who died in 1641. But Hugh O'Neill, like his uncle Eoghan Ruadh, was a descendant of an illegitimate son of Baron Dungannon.

Sir Iain Montcrieff believes that the title of "O'Neill Mór" [5] now resided in the descendants of Feidlimid, Lord of the Fews, son of King Art (1509–14). In this line, Tairrdelbach (Turlough), Lord of the Fews, was transplanted to Mayo during the Cromwellian confiscations and died in 1676. His son Conn, also transplanted, had a daughter who married a distant cousin, Henry O'Neill, brother to "French John" O'Neill who had managed to retain ownership of Shane's Castle in Antrim. Conn's son Henry served in the Jacobite Army from 1689 to 1691, and his grandson, Henry Ruadh, studied law in France during the Penal Years. He married Isabel, daughter of Don Tadhg O'Sullivan, Conde de Berehaven, Knight of Santiago.

Henry Ruadh's son Don Arturo (1736–1814) became the first Marques del Norte. He had served in South America and the West Indies, was Governor of Pensacola (1781), Captain-General of Yucatan, Governor of Merida and a member of the Spanish Supreme War Council in 1803. As a general in the Spanish Army he played a prominent part in the Peninsular War against Napoleon's forces. His nephew, Don Tulio, who succeeded him, was a lieutenant general in the cavalry and won many decorations for his gallantry in the Peninsular War at the sieges of Salamanca, Pamplona and Bayonne. The King of Spain presented him with a ceremonial sword of honor. He married the Marquesa de la Granja.

Their son, Don Juan Antonio Leuis O'Neill, inherited his mother's family titles in 1857, becoming the eighth Marqués de la Granja and the Conde de Benagiar. The direct line of the Spanish O'Neills continued to the current Marqués, Don Carlos O'Neill y Lastrillo, whose titles are listed in the current edition of the Spanish nobility guide *Elenco de Grandezas y Titulos Nobiliarios Españoles*, Madrid, 1997. He is Marqués de la Granja and del Notre y de Villaverde da San Isidro, Conde de Benagiar, O'Néill Mór, Licenciado, Maestrante de la Réal de Silla. He is married to Doña María de Orutea y Gatan de Ayala and they have six children. His heir is Don Carlos O'Neill y Orutea, born in San Sebastian in 1970. The family lives on their estate in Seville. Don Carlos is the twelfth Marqués de la Granja and the fifth Marqués del Norte.

Although the Marqués states his title as "The O'Neill Mór" in the Spanish nobility guide, he will not comment on whether he wishes to continue to pursue recognition of the Gaelic title from the Chief Herald of Ireland. There is a Royal O'Neill Clan Society to which he has given some patronage. The society is run by Don and Kathleen O'Neill from Belfast and in 1998 held its seventh international rally. The Marqués has made no official application to join the Standing Council at the time of writing.

There is another O'Neill Clan Society, supported by The O'Neill of Clanaboy, which, by one of those curious ironies of history, has as its chairman Raymond Arthur Clanaboy O'Neill, fourth Baron O'Neill of Shane's Castle in Antrim. The irony here is that Lord O'Neill's ancestor, the first Baron O'Neill, was actually a Chichester, descended from Sir Arthur Chichester (1563–1625), architect of the Ulster Plantation, who was instrumental in driving the O'Neills from their ancestral kingdom. Arthur Chichester was Lord Deputy of Ireland (1604–14). The Ulster historian Cyril Fall wrote: "While to uninstructed Irish Nationalists Cromwell is the English villain of Irish history, the better read reserve that place to Chichester."[6]

Chichester pursued a ruthless policy of what would now be called "ethnic cleansing." He wrote to Lord Burghley, Elizabeth I's chief advisor: "I have often said and written it is Famine which must consume them [the Irish]; our swords and other endeavours work not that speedy effect which is expected for their overthrow. . . ."[7] That policy took on a grim reality in the eighteenth and nineteenth centuries when, between 1728 and 1890, there were no less than twenty-seven artificially induced famines in Ireland costing several millions of people their lives.

Arthur Chichester, more than any other administrator, was the instrument of the suppression of the Brehon laws and Irish social system and the destruction of Gaelic aristocracy. How, then, can a descendant of Chichester be called an O'Neill and be chairman of an O'Neill clan society?

Brian O'Neill, Prince of Clanaboy, had surrendered to Sir Henry Sidney and exchanged his title for a knighthood. He had even welcomed the Earl of Essex (Walter Devereux) to Ulster with three days of feasting in Belfast. In payment, the English slaughtered two hundred of his people, including women and children, and carried off Clanaboy and his wife in chains. In 1575 he was hanged, drawn and quartered. His son Seán was set up as Chief by Marshal Sir Henry Bagenal, desperate for allies in his fight against O'Neill of Tyrone. Seán was unable to hold Clanaboy and retreated to the north by Kellswater. His alliance was worthless, for Sir Arthur Chichester confiscated 600,000 acres of Clanaboy lands while Seán, known as Shane to the English, was allowed to keep only the ancestral seat of Edenduffcarrick Castle, which became known as Shane's Castle, in County Antrim. He died in 1616.

His son Henry O'Neill of Shane's Castle had been created a baronet by Charles II in 1666 and retained some of his personal estate. He had married to the sister of Lord Deputy Richard Talbot, Earl of Tirconnell. His son Sir Niall

(1658–1690) fought for James II at the Boyne, defending the crossing at Rosnaree with his dragoons. He died of his wounds. His brother Sir Daniel did not suffer an act of attainder and kept Shane's Castle. He died in 1700. His son Charles had a son, John O'Neill (1740–1798), born at Shane's Castle. Matriculating from Christ Church, Oxford, this John O'Neill was elected to the Irish Parliament three times for Randalstown.

In 1793 he was raised to the Irish peerage as Baron O'Neill and then became Viscount O'Neill. He was also governor of Antrim. During the 1798 republican uprising, O'Neill was leading the "loyalists" against the insurgents, and was mortally wounded. He was succeeded by his son Charles Henry St. John O'Neill (1779–1841), who became the first Earl O'Neill for his support for the Union of Ireland and the United Kingdom of Great Britain in 1801. O'Neill became Lord Lieutenant of Antrim and Grand Master of the Orange Order. When he died unmarried the earldom became extinct and the viscountship devolved on his younger brother, John Bruce Richard O'Neill, third Viscount (1780–1855). He died of gout and influenza at Shane's Castle. He had no sons and his daughter Mary had married the Reverend William Chichester, a descendant of the same Sir Arthur Chichester who had driven the Uí Neill royal dynasty into exile.

On April 18, 1868, William Chichester, who had now inherited Shane's Castle through his wife Mary, was created a Baron. He decided to change his name to O'Neill and so became Baron O'Neill of Shane's Castle. It is to this O'Neill family that Terence Marne O'Neill, who was Prime Minister of Northern Ireland 1963–69 (later Lord O'Neill of the Maine), belonged. Also, from the same family came James Chichester-Clark, who succeeded his cousin as Prime Minister of Northern Ireland 1969–71 and became Baron Moyola.

The current Lord O'Neill of Shane's Castle is Raymond Arthur Clanaboy O'Neill, fourth Baron, who inherited the title at the age of eleven when his father was killed, in 1944, serving in Italy. The links, therefore, to the O'Neill royal house of Ulster by this family through one distaff connection descended from the Clanaboy line in the nineteenth century is very tenuous indeed.

The last of the Clanaboy line to be King of Ulster was Henry (1325–44), and his sons took the title Princeps Cloinne Aodha Buidhe (Princes of Clanaboy). Although stemming from an elder son of the preceding king, the Irish law system applied succession so that a younger son could be deemed the rightful successor.

Moncrieff states: "Niall Óg 'the Young,' O'Neill, king of Ulster 1394–1403, styled The Great O'Neill, or Ua Neill Mór (the title used by his branch to distinguish them from their rivals of the senior or Clanaboy branch, whose chief was styled The O'Neill Buidhe, is called 'le grand O'Nel' by Froissart. . . ."[8] Even Hugo O'Neill of Clanaboy, writing to the author, has accepted that "the style of Ua Neill Mór meaning O'Neill the Great" was adopted by Aedh Reamhar and his descendants.[9] But he denies the right of the Marqués de la Granja to bear it, believing that he should be regarded as head of all the O'Neills.

The Princes of Clanaboy did not succeed to the kingship nor were either recognized as The O'Neill Mór or O'Neill of Tyrone, which styles implied chiefship of Cenél Eoghain after that date. Indeed, there were dynastic struggles within Clanaboy itself, with Aodh claiming chieftainship from his cousin Murtough in 1548 and hiring seven thousand Scottish mercenaries to back his claim. Although the English backed Aodh, Murtough (Muirchertach Doibhlenach; 1548–52) was the last Prince of Clanaboy who was properly inaugurated according to the Irish laws.

His grandson, Conn Buidhe, initially received a grant of several thousand acres of the land seized from Aodh Ruadh after he had fled in 1608. But this was confiscated when he took part in the plot to rescue Aodh Ruadh's son, Conn, from Charlemont Castle. He died in 1630. Sir Arthur Chichester tried to set up his own candidate to be "captain of Clanaboy." This was Conn of Castlereagh, whom Chichester actually "installed" in 1601. Conn was an alcoholic and a spendthrift who was quickly tricked out of his estates by colonial adventurers such as James Hamilton (who became first Viscount Clandeboye) and Hugh Montgomery (first Viscount Montgomery of Great Ardes). He died in 1619. Chichester commented cynically that if the Irish had hanged his candidate to the chieftainship, the world would not miss him.

Conn's sons were of a different hue. Domhall became a major-general in the army of Charles I, fought at Marston Moor and Naseby and escaped from the Tower of London disguised as a woman. On the Restoration he was Postmaster General. The second son, another Conn, fought as a colonel in the Irish army in 1641 but was captured and murdered by a Protestant minister who had promised him quarter at Clones in 1643.

However, the genuine line of the Princes of Clanaboy continued with Feidhlimidh Dubh (Black Phelim), who took part in the Irish uprising in 1641 and distinguished himself under the command of his kinsman, Eoghan Ruadh O'Neill. His grandson was fighting for James II and took part in the siege of Derry, fought at the Boyne, at Aughrim and then in defense of Limerick. He sailed with his regiment into French service and was killed on September 11, 1709, while fighting with the Irish Brigade against the English at Malplaquet.

His son, however, was living in Dublin and married Cecilia, a daughter of Captain Felix O'Hanlon, who had descended from a sister of Aodh Ruadh

O'Neill. Their son Seán (João) settled in Portugal in 1740 and bought an estate on the Tagus, opposite Lisbon. In 1756 he had his genealogy set down on parchment by the family's *ollamh* in Latin, which was attested by Michael Reilly, Archbishop of Armagh; Anthony Gawey, Bishop of Dromore; John MacMullin, the Proto-Notary Apostolic; and Brother Bernard MacHenry OP, Vicar of Ulster and ex-Provincial.

His son Charles (Carlos) was educated at St. Omer in France and became a Knight of the Order of Christ and a friend of the Portuguese Royal House. He entertained King John VI of Portugal at his château at Setubal. He died in 1835.

José Maria O'Neill (1788) was Consul General of Denmark at Lisbon and entertained Queen Maria II and King Ferdinand at his house at Setubal. His eldest son José-Carlos (1816–89), also played host to King Pedro V and Luis I at the O'Neill estate called Quintas das Machadas near Setubal. His youngest son became Visconde de Santa Monica, grand officer of the Royal Household of Portugal and Minister of Justice (1821–89). The second son Jorge Torlades O'Neill, (1817–80)—a friend, incidentally, of Hans Christian Andersen—received many Portuguese, Danish and Brazilian orders.

His eldest son, Jorge, began to reassert his Gaelic title as "The O'Neill, hereditary Prince of Ulster and of Tyrone and Clanaboy." Jorge (1848–1925) was a Peer of Portugal, Knight of Malta, Knight of the Grand Cross of the Papal Order of St. Gregory the Great, Grand Cross of Isabella the Catholic of Spain, officer of the Legion of Honor of France and Grand Officer of the Royal Household to the King of Portugal.

As mentioned previously, although a French branch of the O'Neill family assumed the title "Comte de Tyrone" and claimed descent from Sir Phelim Roe O'Neill, the pedigree of this branch has never, so far as is known, been proven. However, at the death of Augustus Eugene Valentine O'Neille, "Comte de Tyrone," a Martinique politician, he was succeeded by three daughters. Jorge O'Neill of the Clanaboy branch in Portugal organized a meeting in Paris in 1901 before an attorney, M. Kastler. It was not, however, attended by the Spanish branch of the family, the Marqués de la Granja y del Norte, nor by a branch settled in Majorca that had descended from Turlough, The O'Neill of Tyrone (1567–93). A family pact was signed and notarized by which the daughters of this "Comte de Tyrone" recognized that the O'Neills of Clanaboy were the senior branch and entitled to the style of Count of Tyrone. Despite the many rights enjoyed by females under the Brehon Law, disposing of Gaelic Chiefly titles was not one of them, nor could the daughters of late Comte dispose of what was essentially an English title stemming from "Earl of Tyrone," abolished by James I fully three centuries earlier.

The claim also had the implication that the head of the Clanaboy family was also recognized as head of the Cenél Eoghan, therefore as The O'Neill, Prince of Ulster. But with the existence of the line of the Marqués de la Granja in Spain, apparently, according to Sir Iain Moncrieff, having a direct descent to the last Ulster Kings, such a claim was arguable. In 1989 François Henri O'Neill of France, claiming to be an heir male of the French Comte de Tyrone, argued his primogeniture right to be senior heir, although primogeniture is not valid in Gaelic titles. François believed that the daughter of the last French "Comte" had signed away their birthright without knowing the implications and declared his intention to pursue his claim.

Hugo, the current O'Neill of Clanaboy, who lives in Setubal, Portugal, and who dislikes being addressed by the Portuguese courtesy title of dignity, *Dom* Hugo has firm views on the matter. He dismisses the claim of the Marqués de la Granja y del Norte to be The O'Neill Mór, Prince of Ulster. It has been argued that, in spite of Moncrieff using this form of title, the O'Neills of Tyrone called themselves simply "O'Neill." However, we have the clear statement from Jean Froissart (in his *Chroniques*) that the Tyrone branch *did* call themselves O'Neill Mór to distinguish themselves from the Clanaboy branch. Hugo's argument for his seniority relies on primogeniture for its basis. While it can be admitted that the Clanaboy line was a senior line of the Uí Néill house by such descent, that was not the method by which the kingship descended and the Clanaboy line had not held the kingship of Ulster since the fourteenth century. According to O'Neill of Clanaboy:

> I do not believe that O'Neill Mór is necessarily synonymous to being the head of the Cenél Eoghain. . . . Mac Uí Néill Buidhe chiefs were never subjects of O'Neill Mór and, as heirs of Aedh Bhuidhe, they always considered themselves to be the rightful heads of the Cenél Eoghain. This was the attitude of my forefathers and mine is not different. I also believe that judging by the way tanistry was applied in our sept there cannot be any qualified candidate to the title O'Néill Mór.[10]

O'Neill of Clanaboy believes he will be proven correct once the *Leabhar Cloinne Aodha Bhuidhe* (The Book of Clanaboy) is examined by scholars, translated and contextualized. "I am sure it will bring new light and will help to understand better the role of the two branches of the Cenél Eoghain in the fourteenth and fifteenth centuries." In this, his expectations might be disappointed. Although *Leabhar Cloinne Aodha Bhuidhe* has not been published in English translation, it is available in an Irish-language edition, edited by Dr. Tadhg Ó Donnchadha, and its content has been known to scholars for many years.[11]

O'Neill of Clanaboy continues:

> At the risk of being judged a vain fool who dares challenge the views of the most reputed scholars in Irish history and succession laws, I support the view that in the case of the Cenél Eoghain, the tanist was as a rule the eldest surviving son of a former chief and elected from the four generations of the *derbhfine*.[12]

When Jorge O'Neill submitted his genealogy to Sir Arthur Vicars, Ulster King of Arms and H. Farnham Burke, Somerset Herald, they issued certificates confirming that he was "a lineal descent and representative of the Royal House of O'Neill, Monarchs of Ireland, Kings of Ulster and Princes of Tyrone and Clanaboy." The genealogy and the arms and motto which bears the words "*Lamh Dearg Éireann*" (Red Hand of Ireland) were registered as being that of O'Neill of Clanaboy.

It must be said that scholarship does not agree with the claims of the Portuguese O'Neills that the Clanaboy line is the senior claimant of the titles of the Royal House of Ulster family. Nor would scholars endorse the claim that the line of the O'Neill of Tyrone usurped the Ulster kingship from the descendants of Henry (d. 1344). We have to keep reminding ourselves, in this day and age, that primogeniture was not the basis of successional law. Yet the argument will doubtless continue. It is one that has its roots in the fourteenth century and has generations of tradition and doctrine on both sides.

After 1901, the King of Portugal offered to make Jorge a Portuguese count bearing the title Count of Tyrone, but he declined this. He was formally addressed, however, as The Most Serene Prince and Count of Tyrone and Clanaboy by both Pope Leo XIII and Pius X as well as recorded as such by the Registrar of Portuguese Nobility with the sanction of the High Chamberlain and Great Master of the Household in Portugal. By this Jorge was accepted as a former sovereign prince. The current O'Neill, Prince of Clanaboy, is happy being addressed simply by his Gaelic title.

Jorge O'Neill, in fact, contributed significant financial support to the cause of Irish independence, sending money to help arm the Irish Volunteers in 1914. He became a close friend of Sir Roger Casement, executed in 1916, who wrote him a letter thanking him for that support, now in the National Library in Dublin. Earlier, writing from the Union Club, Belfast, on October 25, 1904, Casement wrote: "My dear O'Neill—you see I give you your Irish title. . . ." He had visited O'Neill in Portugal and commented: "The doctors say my very severe attack of internal pain in Portugal was appendicitis and they wished to operate on me but I have decided to forego the surgeon's knife which, seemingly, is not essential to long life."

Casement was trying to get a school built on an island at Tawin, at the head of Galway Bay, which would teach through the medium of Irish. The village consisted of fourteen families, all Irish speaking. The school would need to provide accommodation for forty pupils, and it was estimated that its construction would cost £244. Casement had already donated £20 and Douglas Hyde £2. At the time Casement was writing, a further £35 had been received. Jorge O'Neill also contributed to this cause.

Jorge's eldest son was Hugo Joseph Jorge Ever (1874–1940), who entered the Portuguese Royal Navy. His wife, Julia, could trace her descent back from Charlemagne, the Holy Roman Emperor of A.D. 800 to 814, and through emperors and kings to King John VI (1816–26) of Portugal. Hugo Joseph ensured that he employed an Irish governess for his children. His son Jorge (b. 1908) was given "courtesy recognition" as O'Neill of Clanaboy by the Chief Herald of Ireland. He presided at the first International Gathering of the Clan O'Neill at Shane's Castle, County Antrim, in June 1982. A ceremony of inauguration was performed at the castle.

The current O'Neill, Prince of Clanaboy, Hugo, succeeded in 1992. He was born in Lisbon on March 7, 1939. He took his degree in Lisbon and in 1962 married Rosa Maria Empis, a descendant of the fifth Marqués de Valenca, premier marqués of Portugal. From 1978 to 1986 he was chief executive of an industrial conglomerate, and he now runs his own company as a financial and corporate consultant. His eldest son, his tanist, Jorge Maria Empis O'Neill, born August 6, 1970, is a junior consultant in the office.

Hugo's interpretation of the native Irish law system is:

> The maintenance of the Brehon Law of succession and of the values and life style of Gaelic leaders, compelled Ireland to remain throughout the XI to the XVI a conglomerate of small ultra conservative tribal nations, unable to face the clash of the Anglo Norman invasion and succumbing in the end when challenged by Tudor imperial England.

Having made the caveat, Hugo firmly believes that his Gaelic title has always descended by Brehon law. "It is obvious my forefathers never accepted the English domination of Ulster and the enforcement of English law," he points out. "My branch of the family has never surrendered to English rule."

> If, from a political viewpoint, I think that Gaelic values were bad for Ireland, I cannot be more proud to descend from a long line of great men who were prepared to pay, and most times paid, with their lives, to challenge and be challenged, who generously dedicated themselves to provide glory and well being

to their people, who had to be without blemish and fit for war, who were great lovers and masters of cunning, who were artists and protectors of art.

Hugo is a man of strong opinions:

I think that it is most unfair that the dispossessed Irish aristocrats (who up to the end of Gaeldom in the sixteenth century were Ireland itself) forced to leave the country after the Treaty of Limerick, have to remain exiled from their country now that it has been freed from English domination. They should be asked to hold an Irish passport and I have pointed that out to the former President of Ireland (a famous constitutionalist) during her state visit to Portugal [Mrs. Mary Robinson].

It must be said that in my case the territory which formed our *tuatha* is not part of the Irish Republic.

Hugo even prepared a recommendation to U. S. Senator George Mitchell, chairman of the Ulster peace talks, suggesting that a referendum be held on the proposal to recreate an independent Ulster run by a constitutional monarchy, based on a restored O'Neill dynasty.

Hugo believed

This makes sense from an historical and also from a political point of view as Ulster was always an independent nation and politically an independent Ulster would help to save the face of the two contending communities in their search for a lasting peace. It is however certain that such a suggestion will be never accepted as it goes against the interests of all those who are party to the talks.

In that respect Hugo was perfectly right, and political events in Northern Ireland have now passed on. However, he suggested in his envisaged rebirth of a Kingdom of Ulster a two-chambered parliament, with the Ulster Gaelic nobility sitting with the Anglo-Irish Peers, who would be prepared to sever their ties to the Crown of England and accept the restoration of the Gaelic O'Neill monarchy. Obviously, if O'Neill of Clanaboy was proposing himself as head of the Royal House of O'Neill, such a suggestion, had it been seriously considered, might have soon floundered on the dynastic rights issue.

Regarding the rest of Ireland, Hugo thinks that all Gaelic aristocrats who live in the Irish Republic should be allowed to sit in the Irish Senate.

He describes his own role as the holder of a Gaelic title in this way:

Apart from a political role and from a participation, in association with his peers, the promotion of Gaelic heritage, the role of a modern Chief is to be the effective head of his sept or his Clan.

As a consequence of the Irish Diaspora clans have most of their members dispersed around the world. Present-day data processing and telecommunication resources enable one to communicate easily and cheaply with millions of others wherever they are. It becomes therefore possible for an Irish Chief to "go global" and bring virtually together his clan members around the world, for instance using the Internet World Wide Web. . . .

Hugo is a firm believer in this technology, and the revival was important to him:

What I propose to do as O'Neill was put forward in the speech delivered at the ceremony of my presentation to the Clan held in June of 1992 at the Grian an Aileach, the prehistoric fortress conquered by the founder of the Cenél Eoghain, Eoghan son of Niall. . . .

Let us therefore try to revive the O'Neill Clan by making it instrumental in reconciling O'Neills with their true heritage, in soothing the hardship of O'Neills in friendship and in fostering those blessed with natural abilities to ease their way in today's competitive world, in short, helping each one of us to enjoy our lives better than if left just to ourselves. . . .

In practical terms:

The Irish language should be preserved as a patrimony of the ancient Irish culture. Yet it is my firm belief that the reconciliation of the Irish of today with their true historical heritage is more important for the consolidation of an Irish national identity than the learning of the Irish language.

Most of the cultured Irish persons I have met don't know the history of their country or have just a very romantic view about some of its episodes. Irish history can and needs to be made intelligible to the Irish of Ireland and to the Irish of the rest of the world, but the Irish language will just be spoken by the very few that use it as a mother language or by a handful of academics who take pleasure in communicating that way. Language is above all a communication tool and English became the international language adopted everywhere in the world, hence losing its former significance as a symbol of British imperialism. I see the mastering of the English language by the Irish (who provided the best modern writers, poets and playwrights in English literature) as a very important asset that helped Ireland become one of today's European business leaders and centres of artistic creation. I think therefore that although Irish should be preserved and revived, English should remain Ireland's basic language.

Hugo believes that the best role he can play with regard to cultural endeavors is to support the serious research of Irish history. His idea is that a more uniform view of the history of the Irish kingdoms could be presented. He has been in touch with certain Irish academics to assist in contextualizing an English translation of the *Leabhar Cloinne Aodha Bhoidhe* (Book of Clanaboy).

MACDONNELL OF THE GLENS, A PRINCE OF DÁL RIADA AND THE ISLES COUNT MACDONNELL IN THE PEERAGE OF THE HOLY ROMAN EMPIRE (MAC DOMHNAILL NA NGLEANN AGUS CLANN IAIN MHÓIR)

The Count Randal MacDonnell succeeded his father as MacDonnell of The Glens, Chief of His Name, in 1984. Specifically, he is Chief of Clan Donnell South, also known as Clann Iain Mhóir. He also holds the title of Count of the Holy Roman Empire (Austria), which was first bestowed on his collateral ancestor, James MacDonnell, on April 12, 1738, in recognition of his service to Austria, having been Imperial Chamberlain and Inspector General of the Army. Although Count James died in 1766 without issue, the patent allowed the title to pass on through "heirs male general."

"The Glens" of the MacDonnell title are, of course, The Glens of Antrim, and the family is unique among the old Gaelic nobility in that it ruled in both Gaelic Ireland and Gaelic Scotland. The ancient genealogies acknowledge that the MacDonnells, like the other noble families, descend from Golamh (Míle Easpain) who led the progenitors of the Gaels in Ireland before 1000 B.C. The MacDonnells share their early ancestry with the Uí Néill, from Míle's son Eremon down through such notables as Conn of the Hundred Battles and Cormac Mac Airt to Colla Uais, regarded as the eighty-eighth generation in line from Míle. He was High King of Ireland, and died in A.D. 337. According to Seathrún Céitinn's famous seventeenth-century history, *Foras Feasa ar Éirinn*, Collais Uais secured a major settlement in what was to become Argyll (Airier Gáidheal, the seaboard of the Gaels) in what is now Scotland. The early name for this clan was the Clan Cholla.

The current MacDonnell of the Glens prefers to think of himself as only one of the princes of Dál Riada, rather than, as some of his fellow Chiefs, the prince of a specific area. Historically, of course, there were two parts to the Dál Riada kingdom. The first was the original Irish lands north of Slemish (Sliabh Mis), the mountain on whose slopes St. Patrick was a shepherd. The second part of Dál Riada was in Scotland, corresponding to Argyll and Kintyre. For centuries they were a single kingdom ruled over by a united dynasty.

The ancient Irish kingdom over which the ancestors of the MacDonnells ruled had its origins back in the mists of time, when Eochaidh Riada established it in what is now County Antrim. Dr. John Bannerman points out that we cannot be historically sure when the Irish of The Glens of Antrim crossed the few intervening miles to establish their second kingdom.[13] However, in about A.D. 470, Fergus Mór, the Dál Riada king and brother of Muirchertach, High King of Ireland, founded the kingdom in Argyll and Kintyre. Fergus Mór was also said to have taken the famous Lia Fáil (Stone of Destiny), now commonly called the Stone of Scone, as the sacred coronation stone of his dynasty. This is the same stone that was looted from Scotland by Edward I of England and that remained as an integral part of the English coronation ritual, kept in Westminster Abbey, before being returned to Scotland in the 1990s as a sop to rising Scottish nationalism. By the time of the famous Convention of Druim Ceatt (ca. A.D. 575), the kingdom was fully established. Aedan mac Gabráin, crowned in Iona by St. Colmcille (Columba), who died in 603, claimed to have clinched the fortunes of Dál Riada, which continued to flourish and exert political influence over the other northern Celtic kingdoms, including those of the Picts and Britons that eventually were to unite under the Dál Riada dynasty as Alba or, as it is known today, Scotland.

No short précis could do justice to the extraordinary family of the MacDonnells whose history in Ireland and Scotland, stretching over three thousand years, would fill not one but many volumes. Their history is a mirror of Irish and Scottish history, replete with personalities whose influence was felt not just in these islands but in France, Spain, Austria and many other countries.

That the line of the Dál Riada kings ruled both the Irish and Scottish Dál Riada kingdoms as one united dynasty has been acknowledged by Eoin MacNéill.[14] The line continued down to the emergence of Somhairle, sometimes called Somerled, Tiarna Inse Gall (Lord of the Isles; ca. 1126–64). His actual title was given as Rex Insularum, King of the Isles, and his mother was Norse, giving him the name Sumar-lidi (summer traveler). He actually had been born in Ireland, and his power in Western Scotland, through the isles, including the Isle of Man (he had married the King of Man's daughter) and Antrim, was unassailable. Somhairle, also Anglicized as "Sorley," is credited with the introduction of the hinged rudder on his ships and an attempt to reinstate the Celtic church liturgy and practices on Iona in the place of the newly introduced Roman liturgies. He died before this could be achieved.

A grandson of Somhairle, Domhnall Mac Ragnall, who died about 1250, is said to have supplied the cognomen for the dynasty in Ireland. His son Oengus Mór is said to have been the first Mac Domhnaill and hence the name in its English form MacDonnell. But it was his great-grandson Iain Mhóir Mac Domhnaill, the Lord of Dun Naomhaig (Dunyvaig) and The Glynnes (The Glens of Antrim), whose mother was a daughter of King Robert II of Scotland, who decided to resettle his line in Antrim. There he married, in 1390, Margery, daughter of the Norman de Bysett (Bissett) family, who styled themselves "Lords of The Glens of Antrim." It is from Iain Mhóir that the clan often styles itself Clann Iain Mhóir. He was assassinated in 1427. His son Domhnall Ballach became MacDonnell of The Glens and married a daughter of Conn Mór O'Neill, the King of Ulster. The MacDonnells made several marriages into the family of the Ulster kings. Donal Ballach's sons also married daughters of an O'Neill.

By the time of Donal Ballach's great-grandson, Alasdair (d. 1538), the family connections with Scotland were loosening. Alasdair had eleven children. His father, brothers and grandfather had been betrayed by Mac Iain of Ardnamurchan to their cousin, King James IV of Scots, and they were executed in Edinburgh. Alasdair retaliated by killing Mac Iain, whose daughter (and Alasdair's wife) cursed her firstborn son, Donal, before his birth. Thus, so the story goes, he came into the world blind and was called Donal Mallacht (*mallachtach* = accursed). It was the second son, James, who therefore became the next MacDonnell of The Glens. James was the last MacDonnell to be Lord of the Isles. The change from Rex Insularum to Dominus Insularum—Lord of the Isles— had come about with John MacDonald of Islay (d. ca. 1386), who had resigned his territories to Robert II. The king then regranted them as a lordship in 1372. Tensions between the MacDonalds and the Scottish kings saw the confiscation of the title in 1493 by James IV. Today the Lordship of the Isles is a title used by the British monarchy. The current holder of it is the heir to the throne, the Prince of Wales.

James, The MacDonnell of The Glens, was taken prisoner by Seán an Díomais (Shane the Proud), King of Ulster (1559–67), after a battle in 1565 and died of his wounds. Seán an Díomais was concerned with securing his power base, having deposed his own father Conn Bacach, who had surrendered the kingdom and his title to Henry VIII, contrary to Irish law. Conn had accepted the earldom of Tyrone. Seán, suspicious of MacDonnell's intentions, had marched an army against the clan and defeated them. One story is that James, lying wounded, had been poisoned by Seán. Whether true or not, Seán was murdered in 1567 by James's younger brother, Somhairle Buidhe.

The third son of Alexander, Oengus Uaimhreach (Angus the Haughty), was slain in the same conflict with Seán Mac Díomais.

The fourth of Alexander's sons was Colla Maol Dubh, or Colla na gCapall of Kenbane, County Antrim, who died in 1558 but left no issue. His great-grandson became the famous Irish general of the 1641 uprising, Sir Alasdair mac Colla Ciotach, who is the direct ancestor of the current Chief. Colla was buried at Bunamargie.

But the son who is most remembered by history is the youngest, Somhairle Buidhe, Anglicized as Sorley Boy (ca. 1505–90). He was the ancestor, through his second son, of the earls of Antrim. He was born in Ballycastle, County Antrim, and, after the death of his eldest brother, James, the sixth Chief, he seized the estates of James's infant son, Archibald, who had become the seventh chief. Somhairle also grabbed the lands of another nephew, Gille Easpuig, who was the son of another older brother, Colla Maol Dubh of Kenbane. Gille Ea-spuig's mother was Evelyn Mac Quillan, the daughter and heiress of The Mac-Quillan, the Lord of Dunluce. Through her he was the heir to his maternal grandfather's property. His father, Colla Maol Dubh, had died. Colla's eldest brother, James, the sixth chief, had then appointed their youngest brother, Somhairle Buidhe, as the Lord of the Route, to look after his lands in Antrim during his absence in the Isles. He was attempting to salvage what he could of his Hebridean inheritance following the collapse of the Lordship of the Isles and the encroachment of the Clan Diarmuid (the Campbells) into his territory. Somhairle fought and defeated those MacQuillans who resented the loss of Dunluce through a female heir to Gille Easpuig MacDonnell. No sooner had Somhairle obtained possession of the MacQuillan lands than Gille Easpuig was killed. A bull at his birthday celebrations had gored him, and it was reported that a surgeon sent by Somhairle's family then poisoned him. Whatever the truth of the manner of his death, his widow gave birth to his sole heir, Colla Ciotach, and fled across the Moyle Sea with her child to safety on the Isle of Colonsay, while Somhairle took possession of Dunluce for himself. The heirs of the line of the MacQuillans, who built the Castle of Dunluce, however, are today the line of the current chief. Unlike the McDonnell earls of Antrim, Somhairle is also a descendant of the MacQuillans of Dunluce.

Somhairle Buidhe married the daughter of Conn Bacach who, having been rejected by his people after his surrender to Henry VIII, was chased out of Ulster, and his younger son elected as king. Conn Bacach had died in 1559. Somhairle Buidhe seemed, at first, a crucial obstruction to Elizabeth I's plans to conquer Ulster. She asked her Lord Deputy, the Earl of Sussex, to seek his submission.

It was not until 1571 that Somhairle Buidhe was defeated by Walter Devereux, Earl of Essex, father of Elizabeth I's favorite, near Toome (Tuaim), County Antrim, where the Bann flows out of Lough Neagh. Somhairle Buidhe had sent his wife, his young children and the women and children of his clan to Rathlin Island, off the north Antrim coast, for safety. Essex ordered Captain John Norris to proceed to the island and eliminate them. Essex reported smugly to Elizabeth I that Somhairle Buidhe looked on from the mainland at the rising flames as the MacDonnell women and children were slaughtered. He "was likely to run mad for sorrow," reported Essex to a satisfied Elizabeth, who congratulated him on the outcome. Perhaps this act broke Somhairle Buidhe; he surrendered to Elizabeth on good terms. He died in Dunanyane Castle.

Somhairle Buidhe's new allegiance to the Tudors was not shared by all the leaders of the clan. One of the most famous MacDonnell women at the time was Fionnghuala (Inghean Dubh, the "dark daughter"; b. 1555), who was the mother of Aodh Ruadh (Red Hugh) O'Donel, Prince of Tyrconnel. Her father had been James, MacDonnell of The Glens, who had been killed by Seán an Díomais. Fionnghuala's mother married Turlough Luineach O'Neill, who became King of Ulster after Seán. She brought with her a dowry of 1,200 MacDonnell gallowglasses (mercenaries). Fionnghuala married Aodh Dubh Ó Domhnaill (Black Hugh), ruler of Tyrconnell, in 1570. Under the more liberal Brehon law system she was able to play an active military role as well as a political one, being acclaimed "the head of advice and the counsel of Cenél Conaill." Her generalship won a victory at the battle of Doire Leathan, Donegal, in 1590 and helped her son Aodh Ruadh expel the English from southern Tyrconnell.

The MacDonnell of The Glens during this turbulent period was not Somhairle Buidhe, as some have been led to believe, but Archibald, the oldest son of his elder brother James, who died in 1569. James was the seventh Chief. Archibald's next brother, Angus, followed him as Chief and died in 1613, when his son, Sir James MacDonnell, succeeded him in the chiefship. On Sir James's death in London in 1626, the title was passed to his second cousin Colla Ciotach (left-handed Coll; ca. 1570–1647). Coll Ciotach, who had been born on Colonsay, married his second cousin, Mary MacDonnell, the daughter of Randal MacDonnell of Smerby. He was the younger brother of the seventh and eighth Chiefs and, on the death of Sir James, the ninth chief, his daughter became the heiress to her grandfather. As a consequence of Coll Ciotach's marriage, the present Chief represents both the senior male line of the family and the senior female line of descent from the first Chief, Iain Mhóir.

It was Somhairle Buidhe's second son, Randal Mac Somhairle, who continued to serve the interests of the English monarchy. Randal was created Viscount

Dunluce in 1618 and first Earl of Antrim in 1620 as a reward for helping in the "pacification of Ulster." He agreed to become Anglicized and drop any adherence to the Irish law system. He even joined forces with Arthur Chichester to help "ethnically cleanse" his fellow Ulstermen in preparation for the Ulster Plantation and was appointed Lord Lieutenant of Ulster. Randal Mac Somhairle did not even hesitate to help Chichester eliminate members of his own family. Chichester had no love for the MacDonnell clan and several times marched into its territory to "cleanse" the clan lands. He even advocated starving them out in a letter to Lord Burghey: "I have often said and written it is Famine that must consume them; our swords and other endeavours work not that speedy effect which is expected for their overthrow . . . we kill not multitudes."

Randal Mac Somhairle's son was made a marquess by Charles I in 1644. Randal turned the two sons of his kinsman, Sir Alasdair MacDonnell, and the grandchildren of his Chief, Colla Ciotach, out of his house when he heard that Alasdair had been killed fighting Cromwell in Munster. The children were found wandering and hungry by their uncle, The MacAllister, head of the Clan MacAllister, a separate branch of the Clan Donald, also descendants of Somerled of the Isles.

The Earls of Antrim certainly did not have an enviable history, dispossessing their own family as well as the natives. The fourth Earl (1680–1739), in particular, spent some time even trying to disinherit all of those branches that were senior to him, by reason of their descent from the nine children of Sir James MacDonnell, the oldest brother of his ancestor the first Earl of Antrim. So intense were the attempts to prove legitimacy as the senior line that the current MacDonnell of The Glens found that the family of Count Randal was no longer included in the entry of the Earls of Antrim in *Burke's Peerage*, after 1936, which had previously showed that they were the senior line of the family.

The sixth Earl of Antrim was the last actual MacDonnell to hold that title. In 1785, having no male heirs, he persuaded George III to give him a new earldom of Antrim that he could pass on to his daughters and their male heirs. Thus, on his death in 1791, the original earldom of 1620 became extinct and the new one passed to his eldest daughter, Anne Katherine. She married a Mr. Edmund Phelps who took the surname of McDonnell. She had no male heirs and so the title passed to her sister, Charlotte, who was the wife of Lord Mark Kerr, a younger son of the Marquess of Lothian. On her death the peerage passed to her elder son, Hugh Kerr, who then changed his surname to McDonnell and became the fourth Earl. He had no sons and, consequently, the earldom went to his younger brother, the Honorable Mark Kerr. He also, in 1855, changed his surname to that of McDonnell. Ironically this was shortly before

William Chichester, a descendant of the notorious Arthur Chichester, took the name of O'Neill by Deed Poll to become Baron O'Neill of Shane's Castle, County Antrim, a property he inherited from his wife who was daughter of the third Viscount O'Neill, who had no male heirs. The colonists in Ulster did not hesitate to jump on the Irish titles and few remaining estates when the opportunity arose. Despite this the line of the Earls of Antrim had managed to reduce the grant of some 300,000 acres of MacDonnell land by James I, seized from the senior line of their family, to under 1,300 acres today.

It is important to note that the Chiefship of the Clan did not descend through the line of Somhairle Buidhe, who was only the fifth son, but through his elder brother's line. Indeed, Somhairle Buidhe and his descendants had agreed to renounce the Gaelic laws and accept the English system, which declared all the Gaelic titles to be "extinct forever." The MacDonnell of The Glens had not.

Dr. John McDonnell, the eighteenth Chief, in his book *The Ulster Civil War of 1641* (1879), did his best to correct the myth that is still prevalent in Ulster today that there was a mass movement of Scots into Antrim, which displaced a native Irish population. Dr. John McDonnell points out that Iain Mhóir's descendants still formed the basic population and they were not alien to the Irish "in blood, language or religion." He goes so far as to argue "The Western Highlanders were more purely Celtic than the Irish themselves. The Celtic blood of Ireland had received a considerable infusion of Norman and Saxon blood between 1172 and 1600." Blood is an intangible quality; language and culture are the more substantial factors, which, I believe, Dr. John was attempting to put across.

Indeed, by 1891 The Glens of Antrim, the areas of Cary and Lower Glenarm, still boasted between 10 percent and 25 percent native Gaelic-speaking populations. In the Statistical Survey of 1812 it is recorded that many spoke a Gaelic closer to the Scottish form than to the Irish. The Census of 1851 showed some inhabitants who still did not speak English but Gaelic only. Glenarm, the seat of the earls of Antrim, in the same Census had a 14.9 percent Gaelic speaking population.

Coll Ciotach, The MacDonnell of The Glens, had survived in Colonsay in 1639. He was still Catholic in religion, and, in that year, he refused to sign the covenant condemning Catholicism and claiming that the policies of Charles I supported the Papacy. Because of this he was removed to Dunstaffnage Castle, near Oban in Argyll, where he was kept prisoner. Released in 1644, he declared his support for Montrose and, indeed, for the Irish Confederate government that had been established in Kilkenny in 1642. He was taken prisoner again on

Islay, fighting at the head of the Clann Iain Mhóir (the Clan Donnell South) and hanged near Dunstaffnage.

Due to Coll Ciotach's incarceration, the chiefship lay with his second son, Alasdair MacDonnell (ca. 1605–47), who had become a major-general of the Irish Army. Folktales concerning him, especially his youthful adventures, are numerous in Antrim and Argyll. Like his father, he refused to depart from the Catholic faith. He led the Antrim insurgents in 1641. In 1642 and 1643 he won three devastating victories over the English in Ulster. He joined his army with that of Phelim O'Neill in Derry to face Robert Monroe's Parliamentary forces, newly landed in Ireland. Monroe was victorious and MacDonnell was wounded in the battle and not fit to campaign again until 1644.

The Kilkenny Irish Parliament, needing a diversionary tactic, allowed him to sail from Passage near Waterford on June 27, 1644, in command of a force heading for Scotland. MacDonnell joined forces with the Marquis of Montrose (James Graham). MacDonnell was commander under Montrose at seven battles in Scotland. He is acknowledged as the general who devised the famous "Highland Charge" as a battle tactic. In 1645 he was back in Ireland. He raised fresh troops in The Glens of Antrim in time to take part in the Battle of Dungan's Hill, where his opponent was the Cromwellian Colonel Michael Jones. Four hundred of Alasdair's men were slain and his force defeated. He made his way south where he was appointed Lieutenant General of Munster and on November 13, 1647, joined General Theobald, Lord Taaffe, who was facing Cromwellian forces commanded by Murrough O'Brien, Lord Inchiquin, at Knocknanoss, between Mallow and Kanturk. Alasdair was killed, it was reported, after he had either surrendered or was negotiating a surrender.

There is a story connected with Alasdair that is essentially Gaelic. Alasdair, surrounded by Michael Jones's troops at Dungan's Hill, was rescued from certain slaughter by one of his men from the Antrim Glens. After the battle, he found out that the man had also survived and sent for him. He inquired what the man's name was and invited him to drink with him. "I am only a tinker," replied the soldier. "I am not fit to be named among your nobles."

"*Cá n-uasile duine ion' a céird,*" was Alasdair's reply. "No man is nobler than his deeds."

With the devastating conquests of the seventeenth century, many of the MacDonnells, like other Irish noble families, were forced into exile. Of those who achieved fame abroad, there was a Randal MacDonnell who had left Ireland after the surrender of the Irish at Limerick in 1691. He was the grandson of the third Earl of Antrim. This Randal settled in Spain in whose service he became a distinguished soldier.

His son used the Spanish form Reynaldo, for Randal, and became a colonel of the Irlanda Regiment of the Irish Brigade of the Spanish Army formed in 1709. His son, born in Pontevedra in 1753, was Reynaldo Enrique MacDonnell; his portrait now hangs in the Naval Museum of Madrid.

Reynaldo became a second lieutenant in the Ultonia (Ulster) regiment. However, he applied to transfer to the Spanish Navy. He eventually took command of a ship that was sent to Cuba where another Irish Brigade Regiment, the Hibernia, was stationed. He took part in several naval engagements fighting against the English in support of the newly emergent American colonies fighting their War of Independence.

In 1789 he was sent to Sweden to help in its defense against Russia. In his ship *Oddan* he found himself attacked by seven Russian ships. With all but four guns out of action and a third of his ship's company dead, MacDonnell succumbed to the superior force and was taken as a prisoner to St. Petersburg. The Russians had been impressed with his bravery, and they released him a few months later. Gustav III of Sweden bestowed several honors on him.

He returned to Spain, but, in 1804 Spain was at war with England. MacDonnell was appointed a Rear Admiral and given command of a 100-gun ship, *Rayo*. He was part of Admiral Duque Frederico de Gravina's Spanish ships that joined with Admiral Pierre de Villeneuve clashing with Admiral Horatio Nelson's English fleet at Cape Trafalgar on October 21, 1805. MacDonnell was one of the first into the fight and the last to disengage, finding shelter for the night in Placer de Rota. He had his battle-weary crew work through the night on essential repairs, and at dawn next day they sailed back into the conflict, managing to secure the release of some Spanish ships taken captive by the English. MacDonnell ended his career with the rank of full admiral and died in Cádiz in 1823.

A MacDonnell distinguished himself in the Irish Brigade of France, where Henry McDonnell commanded two battalions, those of Bourke and Wauchop. He died in 1772 in Croatia. Other MacDonnells took service in Austria, such as the first Count James MacDonnell, mentioned earlier, who died in 1766. A branch of the family descended from Somhairle Buidhe's older brother Sir James went to live in County Clare. They married four times into the family of the O'Briens of Dromoland, the ancestors of the present O'Brien of Thomond, Lord Inchiquin, and built New Hall, near Ennis, which today is the home of Joyce of Joyce's Country. Their home at Kilkee is now the site of the town of that name. The Leinster branch produced Richard McDonnell, the Victorian Provost of Trinity College, Dublin, and his son, Sir Richard Graves McDonnell, who was Governor of New South Wales and after whom the great Northern and Southern McDonnell mountain ranges in Australia are named.

The chiefly line, however, remained firmly in Ireland, acknowledged and surviving under the new regime. They continued to display heraldic supporters appropriate to a Chief on their arms engraved on their tombstones in Layd churchyard, near Cushendun in County Antrim. [15]

The sixteenth Chief of the Clan was Dr. James MacDonnell (1763–1845) of Belfast and Murlough, County Down. After growing up in The Glens of Antrim he went to Edinburgh to study medicine, and graduated in 1784. He returned to Belfast and built up a medical practice, which earned him a reputation not only as a skilled physician but as a great benefactor to the poor and needy. MacDonnell was the moving spirit behind the 1792 great Festival of Harpers in Belfast. Apart from his medical pursuits he was a collector of Irish music and an antiquarian.

In politics he was progressive and liberal. When in 1791 the United Irish Society was formed in Belfast, MacDonnell became a firm friend of Theobald Wolfe Tone, to whom he was related by marriage, and many other United leaders, such as Henry Joy McCracken, Hamilton Rowan and Thomas Russell. Wolfe Tone stayed with him several times in Belfast, and it was MacDonnell who proposed that Russell, whom he had invited to live in his house, be made librarian of the Belfast Reading Society, the forerunner of the now-famous Linenhall Library. It was MacDonnell who gave Tone a medicine chest to take on his secret mission to France. Tone in his writings used the sobriquet "the Hypotcrite" for MacDonnell, a play on Hippocrates, who inspired the Hippocratic Oath taken by doctors. It was Tone's method of keeping identities secret in case his papers fell into the wrong hands.

What part MacDonnell played in the uprising of 1798 is hard to say. He survived the persecutions in its aftermath in spite of the fact that a kinsman, Randal MacDonnell of Mayo, had been named Vice President of the Connaught Republic and Colonel John Joseph MacDonnell had commanded some of the insurgent forces. It was Dr. MacDonnell whom Mary Anne McCracken summoned to attempt to resuscitate Henry Joy McCracken after his execution in Belfast.

Out of the turmoil during 1798, MacDonnell founded the Belfast Fever Hospital that became Belfast's first medical school. He also founded the Belfast Harp Society and the first Society for the Preservation of the Irish Language. He died on April 5, 1845, and was buried in Cushendall. His kinsman, the writer Aodh mac Domhnaill (Hugh MacDonnell), published a elegy in Belfast, *Tuireadh an Dochtuir Mhic Domhnaill* (Lament for Dr. MacDonnell), in his memory. This publication was financed by Robert MacAdam (1808–95), an advocate of the Irish language, a collector of old Irish manuscripts and founder and editor of the *Ulster Journal of Archaeology*. Copies of Mac Domhnaill's lament are now rare. Mac Domhnaill was one of the Oriel school of poets who worked as an Irish language teacher under the auspices of the Home Mission set up by the Synod of Ulster. When opposition to the project forced Mac Domhnaill from his employment, MacAdam hired him to transcribe and copy his Irish manuscript collection. Mac Domhnaill was one of many renowned Gaelic poets from The Glens, poets from both Protestant and Catholic communities.

Dr. MacDonnell's successor was his elder son, the Right Honorable Sir Alexander MacDonnell Bart (1794–1875). He was the Commissioner for National Education in Ireland for over thirty years and was made an Irish Privy Councillor and a baronet. He was the principal founder of the Model and National School system in Ireland. Although an ardent Protestant, he stood firmly for allowing freedom of religious worship in Ireland and equality of rights.

His brother was Dr. John MacDonnell (1796–1892), the Irish pioneer of anesthesia. The *Dublin Medical Press* of January 6, 1847, reported a "Case of Amputation of the Arm, performed at Richard Surgical Hospital, without pain" by John MacDonnell MD. The amputation was performed on Mary Kane, age eighteen, a country girl from Drogheda neighborhood. MacDonnell had at first experimented with the anesthetic on himself before he used it on the girl. He was also fascinated by history and was the author of *The Ulster Civil War of 1641* (1879). He married Charity Dobbs of Castle Dobbs, in County Antrim. She was the granddaughter of Arthur Dobbs, Surveyor General of Ireland and Governor of North Carolina.

Dr. John MacDonnell won the warm praise and support of Karl Marx and his daughter Jenny. Part of his duties were as a prison doctor at Mountjoy, and after the Irish uprising of 1867 he was asked to examine the political prisoners. Dr. MacDonnell not only brought to light the maltreatment of the prisoners but revealed the truth about the death of Michael Terbert, a Fenian serving a seven-year sentence, who died in 1870 of mistreatment in prison. Dr. MacDonnell, not being able to get satisfaction from the prison governor, Patrick Joseph Murray, protested to the Chief Secretary, Lord Mayo. The only result was that Dr. MacDonnell was dismissed from his post. Marx and his daughter Jenny wrote several articles in his support.[16]

His second son, Robert (1828–89), was yet another famous MacDonnell surgeon. He became president of the Royal College of Surgeons and the Royal College of Physicians, was the Irish pioneer of blood transfusion and a friend of Charles Darwin. Their exchanges of letters are in the National Library of Ireland. He was born in Dublin, a grandson of Dr. James MacDonnell of Belfast. He was the first doctor in Ireland to give whole blood to a human subject, at Jervis Street Hospital in April 1865. The recipient was a William

Gore of Limerick. Dr. Robert MacDonnell twice refused an offer of a knighthood from Queen Victoria.

When he died, his son Colonel John MacDonnell (d. 1917) became the twentieth Chief of the Clan. On his death, his son Lieutenant Robert Edward MacDonnell was next Chief. Ironically, Colonel's widow refused to allow her son to use the Austrian title of "Count" because, being a Protestant and a Unionist, she thought that the "Holy Roman Empire" had something to do with the Catholic religion and the Vatican. Robert Edward was killed in 1941 and the family seat, Kilsharvan House in County Meath, passed to his sister, who sold it in 1998, having already sold the family's other residence, Drimbawn House on Lough Mask, County Mayo, in the 1960s. The family portraits and other memorabilia are now in the possession of the present chief.

At the death of Lieutenant Robert Edward, the chiefship passed, by family agreement, to his cousin Alasdair Colla MacDonnell, who had been the headmaster of the Portora Royal School and, afterward, a master at Eton College, where he went at the invitation of his brother-in-law, the Honorable Edward Littleton. He died in 1959 without issue. He was the uncle of Count Robert (d. 1984). Count Robert was the great grandson of Dr. John (d.1892) who had been eighteenth Chief. Dr. John's younger son Randal, a Queen's Counsel, was the father of the Irish historical novelist Randal William MacDonnell, who in turn was father of Count Robert.

Randal William MacDonnell was born in Dublin in 1870 and educated at Armagh Royal School and Trinity College, Dublin. He received his master's degree from Dublin University and was assistant librarian at Marsh's Library. He also held a government post. He founded a prize in the Irish language in honor of his godfather, the great Irish scholar Sir Samuel Ferguson and Lady Ferguson, a member of the Guinness family, at Trinity College, Dublin, in 1905. He was best known as a historical novelist with such titles as *Kathleen Mavoureen* (1898), *When Cromwell Came to Drogheda* (1906), *My Sword for Patrick Sarsfield* (1907) and *Ardnaree* (1911). He also published volumes of poetry among which was *The Irish Squireens and Other Verses* (1906). He died in 1943.

Randal's son Robert Jarlath Hartpole Hamilton MacDonnell was born in Dublin in 1909. Count Robert was educated at Belvedere, Clongowes Wood College and Trinity College, Dublin. He joined the British Broadcasting Corporation in 1935 and then Granada Television in 1955, as director of sound. He retired in 1974. He succeeded his uncle as MacDonnell of The Glens in 1959. He, in fact, was the first Catholic to become The MacDonnell of The Glens in nearly two hundred years. A Knight of Malta in 1932 through his mother's bidding, Count Robert was generally ignored by his Protestant Unionist relatives.

Although he was a Catholic, he was not a conventional one. His first two marriages were in Registry Offices, and he was once widowed and once divorced. By his first marriage he had a daughter, Countess Joan, who married Edmond MacDonnell-Alexander, and lives today near Bangor, County Down. She has three children, Peter Randal, Michael and Siobhán. His last marriage, but first in the eyes of the Catholic Church, was to Kathleen Dolan, the daughter of James Dolan, the secretary of the Irish Agricultural Wholesale Society, and his wife Maud Reid. Kathleen Dolan was the head announcer of Radio Éireann and also presented "Hospitals' Requests," the most popular program on Irish radio during the 1940s and 1950s. By this last marriage he had three sons, Count Randal, the present Chief, Count Peter and Count Alasdair Colla (d. 1961). Count Robert was given formal recognition as MacDonnell of The Glens in 1969 by the Chief Herald, Gerard Slevin.[17]

He was succeeded by his son Randal Christian Charles Augustus Somerled Patrick McDonnell, born August 19, 1950. Educated at Stonyhurst, Trinity College, Dublin, and The King's Inns, Dublin, Count Randal is also a Knight of Malta. *Debrett's* gives his career as being twenty-fourth Chief of Clan Donald of South Antrim. His recreations are opera, ballet, rugby, polo, history, parties, genealogy and architecture. He lives in Dublin.

"You've read about us in the history books," he once told the *Irish Times*,

> but we do exist, we're still here. We have been here before there were Caesars in Rome. While the Ascendancy were evicting the Irish and squeezing the life's blood out of them, my family were founding the National Schools, were friends with Wolfe Tone. An ancestor of mine was one of the first to ever use an anaesthetic for operating and another perfected blood transfusion.[18]

To those who claim that the MacDonnells are not really Irish, Randal says:

> My family have lived in Ireland since the late fourteenth century and, consequently, I regard myself as an Irishman. . . . The last of my direct ancestors to own lands in Scotland died in 1647. The family of Clann Domhnaill originated in Ireland. The historical reality of my family's ancestry is that they were anciently Irish, known as the *Siol Cuinn* or the Race of Conn of the Hundred Battles, afterwards they were called Clann Colla after Colla Uais, the Irish King, their ancestor . . . thus when in 1390 my ancestor Iain Mhóir Mac Domhnaill married Margery Bisset . . . he was merely returning to the land where his most remote ancestors had reigned and from where his direct ancestor, King Fergus of Dál Riada, had sailed (all of thirteen miles) across the Moyle Sea to Kintyre.

The Count, like many of his family, is a keen supporter of Irish culture and takes the duties of his chiefship as his priority, attending clan gatherings. He is proud to point out that his great-grandaunt Barbara was a friend of Sir Roger Casement and a patroness of Gaelic cultural activities in The Glens of Antrim. Her father was Dr. John MacDonnell, the eighteenth MacDonnell of The Glens. In 1904 a "Féis na nGleann" was launched in County Antrim with Barbara MacDonnell as first president, the purpose of which was the stimulation of Irish music, language, games and literature. The Honorable Sir Horace Plunkett, the pioneer of agricultural cooperation, son of Lord Dunsany, opened the Féis. Among the celebrities attending was the famous Irish scholar, Professor Eoin MacNeill, who was born at Glenarm, the seat of the Earls of Antrim, and a co-founder of the Gaelic League. It was Barbara MacDonnell's sister who founded the cottage hospital at Cushendall, County Antrim.

Although the father of the current Chief was given "courtesy recognition" by the Chief Herald in 1969, the sensitivities created by the "McCarthy Affair" have caused the Office to announce that The MacDonnell's pedigree will be subject to a review. Like the other Chiefs named by the Office, it may be many years before the results of this are announced. The MacDonnell's tanist is his brother, Count Peter Hamilton MacDonnell KM (b. 1952), who was educated at Ampleforth College and Trinity College, Cambridge. He divides his time between Italy and Venezuela.

The MacDonnell of The Glens is irritated but not concerned about the review. However, he is supportive of Brehon law tanistry succession. "Without the Brehon law we would not exist and I would hope to see that some provision be made by the state to acknowledge the system of tanistry rather than primogeniture, in the strict sense, in respect to the succession of Gaelic titles. Otherwise, the titles become meaningless."

The history of the MacDonnells in Ireland is one of the most colorful, sad and yet, at times, spirited of that of the Gaelic nobles. It is a history of a family determined that their origins and culture should not go down into the abyss to which the imperial ambitions of their neighbors wanted it consigned. In both Ireland, as MacDonnells, and Scotland, as MacDonalds, this clan has produced some of the greatest personalities of the Gaelic world. They have produced formidable Gaelic writers and poets; pioneering doctors; a champion chess-player whose skills were so renown that he won an entry in the *Dictionary of National Biography*. Another descendant of Sir Alasdair MacDonnell (d. 1647) was Captain Charles MacDonnell, "Hero of the 'Roaring Forties,'" a remarkable skipper of a clipper which once made an unparalleled 64-day trip to Melbourne, Australia and returned in 78 days.

His great-great-grandnephew is Dr. Alasdair MacDonnell, a leading spokesman of the Northern Ireland Social Democratic and Labour Party (SDLP), a member of the Legislative Assembly of Northern Ireland and the first Catholic Deputy Lord Mayor of Belfast. Dr. MacDonnell, the current head of the Kilmore branch of the family, is married to Olivia Nugent and has a daughter, Dearbhla. He chose not to use his Austrian title. He lives in Belfast. The last head of the family to live at Kilmore House was Colonel John MacDonnell, who married the Honorable Madelaine O'Hagan, the daughter of the first Lord O'Hagan K.P., the first Catholic to be Lord Chancellor of Ireland since the Reformation.

The family has produced their military men and women as well; their heroes and heroines, famous in song and in story. They have produced their men and women of learning, their doctors, historians, poets and novelists. Their story is one that truly reflects the struggle for the survival of Gaelic Ireland.

THE O'DOGHERTY OF INISHOWEN
(Ó DOCHARTAIGH, INIS EÓGHAIN)

Dr. Ramon Salvador O'Dogherty, born in Cádiz, Spain, in 1919, holds the title of The O'Dogherty of Inishowen. Inishowen is the most northerly of the peninsulas of Ireland, in County Donegal. He is forty-fourth heir male from Niall of the Nine Hostages, King of Ulster and Tara. He is a firm believer in working for his family motto "Ar nDuthchas" (Our Inheritance).

According to the medieval genealogies, the O'Dohertys descend from the Royal House of the Uí Néill through Conall Gulban, son of Niall of the Nine Hostages (ca. A.D. 379–405). The variants of the name, through Anglicized spellings, include O'Doughtery, Doherty, Docherty, Dockerty, Daughterty, Dorrity and several others. This patronymic comes either from Dochtarach, which has been interpreted as "disobliging," or, more likely, from Uí Doire Teagh, Lord of the Oak Houses.

The first reference to an Ó Dochartaigh occurs in the year 1171, in the *Annals of the Four Masters*, when Ó Dochartaigh's death is mentioned. It is uncertain when they became Lords of Inishowen, but in 1413 it is noticed that "Conor O'Dogherty, Chief of Ard Miodhair, and Lord of Inishowen, a man of unbounded generosity and general hospitality to the poor and needy, died."

There are few recorded cases of conflicts between the Ó Dochartaigh family over succession compared to the feuds and conflicts evidenced among the O'Neills and O'Conors.

It seems that Seán Mór Ó Dochartaigh was among the first, with his king, Conn Bacach O'Neill, to surrender his title to Henry VIII, for which he was given an English knighthood in 1541. The family joined the Irish wars against Elizabeth but Seán Óg, the son of Seán Mór, surrendered and received a knighthood in 1585. That year the *Annals of the Four Masters* noted that all the princes of Ulster were ordered to attend a parliament in Dublin under the English administration. Among those who attended was Seán Óg (d. 1601). He was later imprisoned by the Lord Deputy, Sir William FitzWilliam, for giving food and shelter to the survivors of the Spanish Armada ships wrecked on the northern coast of Ireland. He was forced to purchase his freedom after two years of captivity.

In 1600 Sir John Chamberlain, commanding a force of English troops from Derry, entered Inishowen determined to bring the people of the peninsula into submission. Ó Dochartaigh and his troops ambushed Chamberlain's men and defeated them. Seán Óg died on January 27, 1601.

His successor was Caothaoir Ruadh, styled Sir Cahir (Rua) by the English (1587–1608). He was said to be extremely tall and handsome. Caothaoir Ruadh initially made friends with the English. When still only a teenager, he was knighted by Lord Deputy Mountjoy as a tribute to his courage in battle. He also visited the English Court in London. On his return to Ireland he was made admiral of Derry City.

Cahir Rua's uncle, Felim, was Lord of Culmore Castle, on the Isle of Doagh at the mouth of Trawbreaga Bay by Lough Foyle. The castle had been captured by Sir Henry Docwra and English troops in May 1600. Docwra was to become Lord Docwra of Culmore. He became governor of Derry, and he strengthened the castle as a means of controlling the people of Inishowen. It seemed that Caothaoir Ruadh now realized where his allegiances should lie.

At the time of the flight of O'Neill, O'Donnell and other northern aristocrats in 1608, Caothaoir Ruadh became the last Irish noble in the north holding out against the English conquest. In May 1608 he began his resistance by attacking the English garrison at Culmore and recapturing the castle. He then marched on Derry. In the attack, the city's governor, Sir George Paulett, was killed. The city was taken and looted. Caothaoir Ruadh attacked other English fortifications in Derry, Donegal and Tyrone. The English Lord Deputy, Sir Arthur Chichester, offered a reward of five hundred marks for Caothaoir's head.

An army of four thousand troops, commanded by Marshal Wingfield and Sir Oliver Lambert, attempted to trap Caothaoir Ruadh and his men. But they evaded the English forces for some months before Wingfield laid siege to Burt Castle, the main residence of Caothaoir Ruadh, near Lough Swilly. He was not there at the time. Outnumbered and with provisions low, the garrison negotiated a surrender. Wingfield's condition was that their lives would be spared. However, after they had surrendered, he had them all put to the sword.

The outrage put a new spirit of determination into the Donegal men. But on July 18 Caothaoir Ruadh's forces were encamped at a place called Doon Rock, near Kilmacrenan, where the princes of Tyrconell were inaugurated. The English made a surprise attack. One of their number, recognizing Caothoir Ruadh by his stature and plumed helmet, took aim with a musket and shot him dead. His body was sent to Dublin, where it was publicly exhibited. The head was severed and put on a spike at Newgate. His sword and its sheath were taken as trophies and have survived to this day. They are now on public display in the O'Dogherty Castle Museum, Derry. Many of Caothaoir's sub-chiefs and followers were put to death after they had surrendered. Sir Arthur Chichester himself seized the chief's expansive estates and cleared the lands of some six thousand peasants, who were sent off to Livonia as enforced soldiers. A "best-selling book" in England at the time was entitled *Overthrow of an Irish rebel in a late battle: or The death of Sir Cahir Ó Dogherty* (1608).

The family of Caothaoir Ruadh retains a document written in Irish by Seán, brother of Caothaoir, which says:

> After the loss of the unfortunate battle in which my brother Caothaoir fell no tongue could express the misfortunes that ensued. The whole country became the reward of the merciless enemies of this House who spared no one, particularly such as were connected with him by blood or marriage. After the confiscation of my family inheritance in favor of Sir Arthur Chichester my family and I were obliged to live in disguise a mean, wretched vagabond life. My wife sunk and due to her afflictions she left this world for a better one on the twelfth of December, 1637. She left me at her death with five children . . .

However, Seán's grandson Cahir (1639–1714), son of Eóghan, received some land in County Cavan from Charles II in compensation for the devastation of Inishowen. This was in the parish of Enniskean. This Cahir therefore supported the Stuarts and became a major in the army of James II. After the Treaty of Limerick, Cahir was forced to leave with his regiment, first to serve in the Irish Brigade of France, and then to Spain, where he achieved the rank of lieutenant general in the Irish Brigade of the Spanish Army.

Cahir's grandson John (1743–84) had remained in Ireland living the underground life to which the Gaelic nobility were forced under the Penal Laws. His brother Henry (1745–96) studied at the Sorbonne in Paris, was ordained and eventually became Vicar General for the Diocese of Meath. This was a highly dangerous position under the Penal Laws. John's sons, young, ambitious men, unable to abide the constraints of the English Penal laws, decided to leave the country. Their uncle, Henry, had educated his three nephews—Henry

(1776–1803), John (1777–1847) and Clinton Dillon (1778–1805). They applied to become officers in the Royal Spanish Navy, which was then open only to the members of Spanish nobility. Ironically, the Ulster King of Arms, Sir Chichester Fortescue, supported by the Lord Lieutenant, the Earl of Westmoreland, and Lord Hobbard, certified the ancient genealogy and noble rank of the three young men. Indeed, fourteen bishops, an archbishop, the Irish officers of the Ultonia (Ulster) Regiment of the Irish Brigade of the Spanish Army and the Irish residents in Cádiz all certified the nobility of their rank in Gaelic Ireland.

John and Clinton Dillon served as cadets in the Ultonia Regiment while Henry went to sea immediately. He died at sea in 1803 and is buried at Vera Cruz, Mexico. Clinton Dillon O'Dogherty also died at sea in 1805, serving in the corvette *Batidor*, and was buried in Havana, Cuba. In 1797 he had captured an English corvette and, in 1804, he personally led the boarding party that captured the English frigate *Enriqueta* in the River Platte. On the death of Henry, John became the founder of the O'Dogherty family in Spain. He participated in many sea battles and achieved fame for his part in the Battle of Puente Sampayo (1809) during the Napoleonic Wars. In this battle he commanded Spanish troops defending Vigo against the invading French forces. In 1808 he married Maria Josefa Macedo, whose father was shot by the French.

John's grandson, Ramon (1835–1902), served in the Spanish Navy and saw action in Cuba, Santo Domingo and Mexico and was decorated several times. He spent a few years in Ireland and made a legal attempt to get recognition of his title and claims to his family's confiscated Irish estates. The matter came before the Queen's bench and *The Weekly Report* of April 8, 1871, reported the pedigree of his family. However, while the English administration had grown more liberal, it certainly had not become liberal enough to officially recognize a Gaelic title or consider the return of confiscated estates.

Ramon's son, Pascual (1886–1964), had also entered the Spanish Navy but showed a talent for mathematics. He founded the School of Mathematics in San Fernando (Cádiz). A street was named after him there following his death.

Pascual had two sons: Ramon, born in 1919, is the current Ó Dochertaigh, and Pascual is a rear admiral and naval architect. Ramon was educated at the universities of Cádiz and Madrid, and he is a doctor of medicine, specializing in biopathology. He is also a corresponding member of the Royal Academy of Medicine of Palma de Mallorca, a Fellow of the Royal Academy of San Romualdo of Letters, Arts and Sciences and Deputy General Visitor of the Supreme Council of the Royal Institution of Knights Hospitaller of St. John the Baptist. His tanist, or heir-apparent, is his son Ramon, born in 1959, who is a graduate in law from the University of Madrid.

In 1978 Rear Admiral Pascual O'Dogherty was invited to Ireland to attend the cultural festival *Cuirt Ailigh* (Court of Aileach) organized by the people of Inishowen. This led to an active relationship between the Chief and the people of the peninsula through the medium of his brother, Pascual, who speaks fluent English. Because of this, the Standing Council of Irish Chiefs and Chieftains bent their rules slightly to allow Admiral O'Dogherty to represent his brother and his tanist on the Council. The strict rule is that only the Chief or his tanist may attend meeting. The Admiral has written a history of the O'Dogherty Chiefs of Inishowen in English, which is, as yet, unpublished.

In July 1990 there was an O'Dogherty Clan Gathering, and Ó Dochartaigh was invited to attend. During the proceedings he was ceremonially installed at the ancient inaugural stone in Belmont House, Derry, in the manner of his ancestors. The year was a special occasion in that the Chief Herald of Ireland had finally given his title "courtesy recognition." The Ó Dochartaigh had issued a statement in Irish and in English in which he sought a more active role for those bearing Gaelic titles.

During the inauguration ceremony, in which Ó Dochertaigh received the traditional white willow wand of office, he was also handed the sword of his ancestor Caothaoir Ruadh Ó Dochartaigh, killed in the battle at Doon in 1608. The sword was kept in the Guildhall vaults in Derry. The newspapers reported the colorful installation ceremony as being that of the first inauguration of a Gaelic noble in Ulster for four hundred years. They had forgotten the O'Neill of Clanaboy's inauguration ceremony at Shane's Castle, County Antrim, in 1982. Ó Dochartaigh's ceremony was attended by several hundred visitors from Ireland, the United States, Canada, New Zealand, Australia, Holland, Germany and Spain.

However, in late 2000, the Chief Herald announced that Dr. O'Dougherty's pedigree would be subject to a review. Yet again, he was one of a number of Chiefs caught up in the fallout of the "McCarthy Affair." Even so, the thriving O'Dogherty Clan Association, with its newspaper entitled *Ar nDuthchas*, is confident that the Chief Herald will merely confirm the "courtesy recognition." A major gathering of the clan was held in Inishowen in July 2000.

The O'Dogherty Castle still stands on Magazine Street, Derry, on the site of the original sixteenth-century tower house where the arms of the Chief remain engraved on stone above the fireplace in the banquet hall. The castle is now a cultural center and museum. It was originally built by the Lords of Inishowen to protect access to their secluded peninsula.

The Ó Dochartaigh accepts that his title, since the death of Cahir Rua, had been passed down following the principle of senior son inheritance but realizes that it has its base in Brehon Law and dynastic succession governed by tanistry. He is, of course, proud of his Spanish citizenship, but "[a]s a member of the Irish Diaspora, I would be very proud, if it is ever permitted by Irish law, to be given an honorary Irish passport."

He does not see any significant political role for the old Gaelic aristocracy in a modern Irish Republic but believes that the Standing Council of Irish Chiefs "should act as a stimulus to the upkeeping of Irish culture, history, language and traditions." He feels that the holder of an ancient Gaelic title embodies the representation of large numbers of Irish people and "being the direct descendant of the Irish royalty and nobility . . . in this way, a Chief can rally the Irish spirit of all clan members."

THE O'DONEL, PRINCE OF TIRCONNELL
(Ó DOMHNAILL THIR CONAILL)

The O'Donel princely house of Tirconnell, which is now Donegal, represents perhaps one of the most historically eminent of the old Gaelic aristocratic families. They descend from Niall of the Nine Hostages, as do most of the northern aristocratic families, but through his son Conall Gulban, who gave his name to Tir Conaill—the land of Conall. Conall means "strong as a wolf." Conall Gulban was the ancestor of other Donegal families such as the O'Doghertys and O'Gallaghers. As kings of Tir Connell (now Donegal), they were inaugurated on the Rock of Doon, near Letterkenny, and, in Christian times, then proceeded to Kilmacrenan to be blessed by a bishop.

The original name Ó Domhnaill has been Anglicized in many forms from O'Donel to O'Donnell. It seems a matter of fancy. The form O'Donel was given by the Genealogical Office in 1944 for the holder of the title, and this seems as good an Anglicization as any.

The current O'Donel is somewhat of a man of mystery. He is Father Hugh O'Donnell OFM, born in Dublin in 1940, and educated at the Presentation College, Glasthule, and University College, Galway. He also studied in Rome, where he was ordained a priest in 1965. He has served as a missionary in Zimbabwe for the last twenty years and is a parish priest in Harare.

Although he still allows his entry as Chief to appear in *Who's Who in Ireland* and other directories, such as the *Nobility of Europe*, and has his name on the *Clár na dTaoiseach* (Register of Chiefs), he declines to take any interest in the obligations that go with his title, does not attend any meeting of the Standing Council, does not answer correspondence on such matters related to his title and family and expresses a general disinterest in such matters. It has been left to others to promote Clan O'Donel gatherings.

Writing to the author from Rome on May 11, 1998, after much prompting, Father Hugh commented in a brief note: "I made the decision several years ago not to be drawn into any correspondence on the matter. I have personal and family reasons for that decision."

Father Hugh's sister, Nuala Ní Dhomnaill, has argued, on radio and on television, for the succession of the title to go to the female line so that she could claim it for herself and her children. This would be totally contrary to the Brehon dynastic law of succession as well as to primogeniture inheritance. However, the official tanist of the title is Don Leopoldo O'Donnell y Lara, Duke of Tetuan, in Spain. Appearing on an RTÉ program, hosted by Bibi Bascin, with The O'Neill of Clanaboy and The O'Conor Don, Nuala Ní Dhomhnaill, accepting that Leopoldo O'Donnell, Duke of Tetuan, was the heir-apparent, countered: "In this day and age when women are beginning to take their proper place in society, I cannot see any reason to shift the title three hundred years across the sea to Spain." She believed that her children ought to be allowed to inherit as well, and put forward as a justification to her argument her belief that the Duke of Tetuan's title had passed through a female heir. She was, of course, incorrect and was probably confusing the fact that a title of O'Néill Mór, Marques de la Granja, had passed in Spanish law from a female line. But dynastic successional laws, as have already been discussed, cannot be retrospectively altered.

Probably the most famous member of the family was St. Colmcille (ca. A.D. 521–97), born at Garton, Donegal. His father was Fedlimid of Tir Conaill, grandson of Conaill Gulban. He is regarded as the monastic scribe who wrote the *Cathach*, the famous Latin book of psalms, which was carried by the O'Donnells into battle as their rallying symbol. The book has survived and is now in the Royal Irish Academy while its fabulous silver shrine is in the National Museum, Dublin. St. Adamnán, the abbot of Iona (A.D. 626–703), was another member of the family who wrote a life of his kinsman. Colmcille founded monasteries at Derry (A.D. 546) and Durrow (A.D. 553), and the *Book of Durrow* (in Trinity College Library) was said to have been written in his own hand. *The Book of Durrow* was already venerated as a holy relic as early as the tenth century.

It has been argued that Colmcille was responsible for bringing forth the first copyright law and ruling in the world. Colmille went to stay with St. Finnan at the Abbey of Maghbhile (Moville, near Newtownards). Finnan possessed a copy of the Gospel of St. Martin (of Tours), which Colmcille coveted. Each night, unknown to Finnan, Colmcille went to the abbey library and worked on copying the book. Finnan discovered what he was up to and took him before the court of the High King, Diarmaid Mac Cerbhaill (d. ca. A.D.

565). The judgment was "*Le gach bóin a bóinín, le gach leabhar a leabharín*" (To every cow belongs her calf, so to every book belongs its offspring book). Colmcille, being of a princely family, took exception to the ruling and raised his clan to punish the High King for the judgment. The Battle of Cuildremhne (Cooldrevy, in Sligo), in A.D. 561, was a victory for the High King. Colmcille was in peril of excommunication and death. But, instead, he was exiled with some of his followers to the kingdom of Dàl Riada in what is now Scotland. He settled on Iona, which, under his guidance, became a great ecclesiastical center from which many Irish missionaries went to preach and convert the pagan Anglo-Saxon kingdoms. His writings are still a matter of controversy, and a number of works are ascribed to him. Some poems and hymns are authentically his while others are of dubious origin.

Domhnaill—the name means "world mighty," "Rex Tir Conail" (King of Tir Conail)—won a great victory over the mercenary forces of his foster son Prince Congal Claen at Magh Rath (Moyra) in 637. During a six-day battle, he annihilated Congal's forces. The battle is the subject of an ancient poem, which John O'Donovan translated for the Irish Archaeological Society in 1846.

Maeltuanadh, son of Domhnaill (990–1010), became the first to use the surname Ua Domhnaill (O'Donel).

Aodh Ruadh Ó Domhnaill (1461–1505) was responsible for building a castle at Donegal that became the stronghold of Manus Ó Domnaill, Prince of Tirconnell (d. 1563). Manus was a flamboyant man who dressed in the style of Henry VIII of England. He has been described as "very much a Renaissance prince." He was married five times and had nineteen children. He had a great literary talent and wrote love poetry and satiric verse of considerable merit.[19] At his castle at Lifford, he wrote his *Betha Colaim Chille* (A Life of St. Colmcille), completing the manuscript in 1536. It survives in the Bodleian Library, Oxford.[20] It was observed that the book's style is racy and full of humor and gives some indication of what Irish literature might have become if it had been allowed to develop naturally, and if the aristocratic influence had survived. Brady and Cleeve, in their *Biographical Dictionary of Irish Writers*, have commented that one could imagine a twentieth-century Manus writing an Irish *Il Gattopardo* (The Leopard), the novel by Giuseppe Tomasi, Prince of Lampedusa, 1958.[21] The book describes the impact of Garibaldi's invasion of Sicily and subsequent unification of Italy on an aristocratic Sicilian family.

In 1541, however, Manus, followed the example of the King of Ulster, Conn Bacach, and surrendered his title to Henry VIII. As with other nobles who surrendered their titles, there was unrest among the *derbhfine* against the legality of the action. As the anonymous poet of O'Carroll wrote:

Ó Domhnaill Atha Seannaidhnár
ob deabhaidh ná doghraing,
—d'Éirinn fá mór an t-amhghar—
do mheath Maghnas Ó Domhnaill.

[O'Donel of Ballyshannon, who shirked not fight nor hardship, great is Ireland's distress that Manus has deserted her.]

Finally, in 1555, his own son Calbhach (d. 1566), Anglicized as Calvagh and meaning "bald," deposed his father Manus and held him as a prisoner at Lifford Castle, where he died in 1563. It is said that the ambition of Calbhach to succeed was countered by family support for his half brother Aodh Dubh, who was considered legitimate tanist. Calbhach was himself captured and imprisoned by the King of Ulster, Seán the Proud, and died in 1566.

It was, therefore, Aodh Dubh who succeeded as Prince of Tirconnell, but he surrendered his title and received a knighthood in 1567, the year of Seán the Proud's death. Yet he is described by the Donegal poet and biographer, Lughaidh Ó Cléirigh (ca. 1570–1620), author of a biography of Aodh's son, Aodh Ruadh, as "the Achilles of the Irish race."[22]

The abduction of Aodh Ruadh (1571–1602) by the English is one of the great stories of Irish history. The English Lord Deputy, Sir John Perrott, seeking to break Irish resistance to the conquest in the north, kidnapped the seventeen-year-old Aodh Ruadh, along with the sons of two other nobles—Donal Ó Gallchobhair, whose father was hereditary marshal of the army of O'Donel, and Aodh MacSuibhne, son of MacSuibhne na dTuath, with whom he had been fostered, the Irish form of education for a prince. Taking them by boat from Lough Swilly, the English incarcerated them in Dublin Castle.

Here Prince Aodh Ruadh found two sons of King Seán the Proud of Ulster, Henry and Art. English policy was to hold these princes as hostages for their father's good behavior. King Donal IX of Desmond's son had similarly been held in Dublin Castle and the scions of many lesser nobility were also held there. On the night of December 25, 1592, Christmas night, the three young princes, Aodh Ruadh and Henry and Art O'Neill, escaped from Dublin Castle with the help of Aodh Maguire, Prince of Fermanagh. Through one of the coldest winters they trekked across the snow-covered Wicklow Mountains towards Glenmalure, hiding from English patrols. Aodh Ruadh and Art became separated from Henry, and Art died from exposure. More dead than alive, Aodh Ruadh reached Ballinacor, at the head of Glenmalure, the stronghold of Fiach MacHugh O'Byrne (1544–97), Chief of the O'Byrnes of Wicklow, who had been a thorn in the side of the English administration. O'Byrne helped

Aodh Ruadh reach the safety of his father's castle in Ballyshannon in Donegal. Aodh Ruadh had, however, suffered the loss of both big toes from frostbite. A few years later O'Byrne was captured by the new Lord Deputy, Sir William Russell, and instantly beheaded. It is a great saga that has been the subject of books and even a Walt Disney movie entitled *The Fighting Prince of Donegal* (1966) based on Robert T. Reilly's novel *Red Hugh, Prince of Donegal.*

On the joyous return of Aodh Ruadh, and recognizing the talent of his son and the inspiration his escape had given to the people, Aodh Dubh abdicated in his favor. In 1598 Aodh Ruadh had joined his namesake Aodh Ruadh O'Néill, King of Ulster, in his war against England. On August 14, 1598, Marshal Sir Henry Bagenal's army of nearly 4,000 infantry and 329 horses approached the Blackwater from Armagh, at a spot called Yellow Ford. There he found the Irish army, with O'Neill on his left flank and O'Donnell on his right and with The Maguire, Prince of Fermanagh, commanding the cavalry. The battle in which Bagenal himself was killed was the worst defeat ever suffered by the English in Ireland. But a few years later came the reverse at Kinsale. Aodh Ruadh O'Donel immediately went to Spain seeking assistance and was received by Philip III. But in 1602 he suddenly fell ill and died at Simancas. It is clear, from a letter from Sir George Carew to Lord Mountjoy, that a spy in the pay of the English, one James Blake, had poisoned him. He was thirty-one years old. He was buried with regal honors in the church of the monastery of Valladolid.

Ruaidri O'Donnell (1575–1608), tanist to the Prince of Tirconnell, had fought alongside his brother Aodh Ruadh during the war, and after the defeat at Kinsale, during his brother's absence in Spain, he had assumed the chiefship. He was not inaugurated until after his brother's death. For a while Ruaidri and O'Conor Sligo banded together in guerrilla warfare against the English, but in 1603, the war was virtually over, and Aodh Ruadh O'Neill surrendered. In exchange for his surrender, Ruaidri was both knighted and given the English title Earl of Tirconnell. As John O'Donovan wrote in July 1860: "Rory surrendered his princely rank and accepted from England, with the title Earl, the lands over which his ancestors held sway for many centuries."

Like O'Neill, learning that the English were planning the removal of himself and other "troublesome" Irish leaders, Ruaidri joined O'Neill, Maguire and other northern Gaelic nobles to leave Ireland and go into exile. The plan was always to return to free Ireland and never merely to settle abroad forever. He died in Rome in 1608, at only thirty-three years of age, and was buried in the church of San Pietro in Montorio, where the Aodh Ruadh O'Neill was buried when he died in 1618.

Ruaidri's son Hugh Albert, a page to the Infanta of Spain, living in Flanders, was recognized as the Earl of Tirconnell and heir to the chiefship. There are some letters extant from Brussels in which he signs himself "Earl of Tirconnell, Baron of Lifford, Lord of Lower Connacht and Sligo, Knight of the Order of Alcantara, Captain of Spanish Artillery in Belgium." Hugh died in 1642.

There was now the problem of the succession. Although the chiefship was abolished by English law, it was still regarded as important among the people of Donegal. Sir Niall Garbh O'Donnell (1569–1626), Calbach's grandson, had opposed Aodh Ruadh's election as Chief. With some followers, he had installed himself as O'Donnel at Kilmacrenan, just north of Letterkenny. Because he was implicated in the O'Dogherty uprising in Derry in 1608, he was taken captive to the Tower of London, where he languished and died in 1626. His eldest son was also imprisoned in the Tower and also died there. His second son, Manus, was killed at the Battle of Benburb (1646) fighting for Eóghan Ruadh O'Neill.

Hugh O'Donnell (d. 1704), known as "Balldearg" O'Donnel because of his distinctive red birthmark, left Donegal to join the Spanish Army, in which he served as a General. He returned to Ireland to serve in James II's army but arrived after the defeat of the Boyne. He claimed the title Earl of Tirconnell. James II had other ideas. He had given the title to Richard Talbot (1630–91) of Malahide, County Dublin, who had fought against Cromwell in the defense of Drogheda and was a vehement supporter of the Jacobite cause. Talbot came from an "Old English" family in Ireland. A Catholic himself, he was given command of the army in Ireland and became Viceroy in 1687. In July 1688 he was made Duke of Tirconnell.

Balldearg O'Donnell initially commanded a brigade of the Jacobite Army against William of Orange. When things began to go badly for the Jacobite cause he opened negotiations with William's senior commander and agreed terms with him. He even agreed to join the Williamite Army in the attack on Sligo. However, his men mutinied and rejected him, preferring to remain true to their cause. He served William on several missions to Europe, but when William refused to reward him with the earldom of Tirconnell and, indeed, noting the repression of Catholics in Ireland, he retired to Spain with a pension of £500 a year. How long this was paid is uncertain for he rejoined the Spanish Army, eventually retiring with the rank of Major-General. His will was made out in Madrid on April 9, 1674, and he signed it as Earl of Tirconnell. He died in Spain about 1703 or 1704.

Another member of the family who went into the priesthood, becoming a Jesuit Father in Spain, bore his literary ancestor's name—Manus Ó Domhnaill. He attended the University of Salamanca, and in 1694 he translated into Irish the *Lunario* of Geronumus Cortès of Valencia, a treatise of medical astrology. It might be significant that Salamanca was the last European university to have a faculty of astrology (as opposed to astronomy); it finally closed in 1770. The work was rediscovered in Belfast in 1913 and a bilingual text in Irish and English was published by David Nutt of London in 1915.

After the Treaty of Limerick in 1691, Brigadier Daniel O'Donnell went into exile in France, taking the *Cathach of St. Colmcille* with him. It was placed for safe-keeping in a monastery, where it was rediscovered in the 1880s. Sir Niall O'Donnell, a descendant of Daniel, claimed it as a badge of their right to be The O'Donnell, although this was disputed by other branches of the family. Sir Richard Annesley O'Donnell, fourth Baronet of Newport House, placed the priceless *Cathach* in the Royal Irish Academy.

According to John O'Donovan, Niall Garbh's second son, Manus, killed in 1646, had a son Ruaidri who married an O'Donnell cousin. His son Colonel Manus O'Donnel of Newport House had three sons, one of whom was Hugh O'Donnell of Larkfield, who claimed to be The O'Donnell and even called himself Earl of Tirconnell. He died in 1754. His son Conn of Larkfield maintained the Gaelic title, and he married Mary O'Donnell, the sister of Sir Neil O'Donnell of Newport (the first Baronet). Conn died in 1825. His eldest son was an Anglican clergyman in Yorkshire, the Reverend Constantine O'Donnell, who John O'Donovan, writing in 1860, believed to be the rightful claimant to the title.

Father Hugh O'Donnell OFM descends from this line of O'Donnells and is accepted by the Chief Herald of Ireland as such. No O'Donnell asked *Thom's Directory* to list their claims in their early "unofficial" listing of Gaelic titles. However, when the Genealogical Office began to give courtesy recognition to such titles, *Thom's Directory* printed the approved "chieftainries." John O'Donell, born May 23, 1894, was listed as succeeding to the title in 1932 and is styled as "O'Donel of Tirconnell." He married Ellen Reidlinger of Portsmouth. Aodh, the Irish form of Hugh, was born on February 3, 1940, at Monkstown, Dublin. John O'Donel, however, was not one of the first Irish Chiefs to have his claim recognized by the Genealogical Office, and his name does not appear on the first list in the *Éire Iris Oifigiúil.* [23]

It is obvious that from the early seventeenth century no clear succession was made and that no claimant could really justify title under Brehon successional law due to the various dynastic arguments within the *derbhfine*. The later claims under primogeniture, under which the title Earl of Tirconnell was claimed, are also arguable. There were too many branches of the family. Leopoldo O'Donnell is the only representative of the family who has shown the author a detailed family tree, drawn up by qualified heraldic genealogists, with other items showing his line back to the last Princes of Tirconnell.

Many O'Donnells fled abroad in what became known as the Flight of the Wild Geese. Major General Henry, Count O'Donell, was founder of an Austrian branch of the family. His eldest son, Count Joseph (1755–1810), became Finance Minister to the Austrian Government, steering Austria to economic recovery after Napoleon's victory changed the Holy Roman Empire into the Austrian Empire. His son Joseph (1755–1840) was Minister of Finance to Emperor Francis II; his second son, Field Marshal Count Maurice O'Donnell (b. 1780), was father to the famous Major General Maximilian, Count O'Donnell, aide-de-camp to the Emperor Franz Josef, whom he saved from assassination in 1853. The Austrian Counts O'Donnell von Tirconnell are a continuing line in modern Austria.

Joseph O'Donnell (1722–1800), who became a Lieutenant General in Spanish service, had two sons. Both Don José and Don Carlos (1772–1830) became generals in the army. Don Carlos became father of one of the most famous O'Donnells—Don Leopoldo (1809–67). He rose in the army to become Field Marshal, first Duke of Tetuan, Conde (Count) de Lucena, and Visconde (Viscount) de Aliaga. He commanded Spain's successful Moroccan campaign for which he took his title from Tetuan in Morocco in 1860. He was also governor of Cuba for a while. He was then appointed Minister for War and President of the Council of Ministers (basically the office of Prime Minister) in 1858. It is also no secret that he was the lover of Queen Isabella II of Spain (1833–68).

His nephew, also Don Carlos (1834–1903), served as Minister of State and ambassador to the courts of Brussels, Vienna and Lisbon. He became the second Duke of Tetuan as his uncle had no male issue. Carlos's son Don Juan became the third Duke, Count of Lucena and Marques de Altamira as well as Visconde de Aliaga. He was General of Cavalry and Minister for War (1864–1928). He became President of the Convention of the Irish Race in Paris in 1919. This convention, encompassing the Irish of the diaspora as well as from Ireland, endeavored to get U.S. President Wilson's recognition for Ireland's claim to independence. Ireland's unilateral declaration of independence had been made in January 1919.

Through his line has descended the sixth Duque de Tetuan, Marques de las Salinas, who was born on May 19, 1915. He is accepted in all quarters as heir to the title of O'Donel, Prince of Tirconnell. Although he and his family hold many Spanish titles, the Duke of Tetuan is enthusiastic about his Irish links. In 1956 Eamon de Valéra, as Chancellor of the National University of Ireland, conferred an honorary doctorate on the Duke. He is amazingly active for his age, fascinated by Irish history and the history of his own family.

His son is Hugo O'Donnell, Duque de Estrada, Conde de Lucena, Marques de Altmira. He trained as a lawyer and is a retired Minister of Marine under King Juan Carlos of Spain. He is also a historian and corresponding member of the Spanish Academy of History.

The lack of interest by the current holder of the title is more than made up for by the enthusiasm of those who will succeed him. In fact, it has been suggested in some quarters that the current O'Donel should follow the Gaelic custom of abdication in favor of a more suitable Chief. Aodh Dubh, for example, resigned his title when he realized Aodh Ruadh, his tanist, was better fitted for the duties of Chiefship. Certainly the Duke of Tetuan and his son the Duke of Estrada currently show a more healthy interest in O'Donel affairs.

The Spanish O'Donnells are a large family. Their influence is all-pervasive in Madrid, where a principal street bears their name as do shops, commercial houses and even garages. The Duke has said:

> Being in my mid-eighties, perhaps I will not inherit the title of my forebears, nor even my son in his lifetimes. But one of my grandsons doubtless will. Our family, forced to flee from our native land to maintain our own existence, has never really abandoned Ireland, our patrimony nor our people of Tirconnell. We would sincerely wish to maintain their interest in the ancient Gaelic culture that once made Ireland the cradle of civilization during the grim, bleak days of the European "Dark Ages."

THE MAGUIRE, PRINCE OF FERMANAGH
(MAG UIDHIR FHEAR MANAGH)

The Maguires, as princes of Fermanagh, claim a descent from Cormac Mac Airt, High King of Ireland (A.D. 226–28), considered the most learned and wisest of all the pre-Christian kings of Ireland. Cormac has been dismissed by some scholars as a mythical figure as he features as both hero and villain in many of the stories of myth and folklore. Indeed, so much has myth gripped popular consciousness, during recent years Cormac has even featured in comic strips as well as popular fantasy novels. Yet if one accepts the ancient Irish genealogies, there is no reason other than prejudice to dismiss him or his reputation as one of the best pre-Christian rulers.

The Maguire princes trace their descent through Colla, the great-grandson of Cormac. The name Mag Uidhir means "son of Odhar," which is a comparatively rare early name, perhaps meaning "dark, sallow or gray-brown." The feminine form is Ordarnat, a name held by a virgin saint whose feast day occurs on November 13.

Donn Carrach Mag Uidhir (Maguire) was King of Fermanagh between 1264 and 1302. He earned the accolade among the bards as "Ireland's most gracious lord." The current Maguire is twenty-seventh heir male in direct descent from Donn Carrach.

The ancient annals and chronicles of Ireland are filled with praise for the Maguire Kings. It is recorded that they gave good government, endowed churches and monasteries, encouraged the arts and defended their kingdom assiduously.

The Maguire kings were patrons of many well-known bards and scholars and were scholars themselves. For example, Cathal Mac Magnus Mhag Uidhir, Archdeacon of Clogher, compiled in 1498 the famous *Annals of Ulster* from earlier records. There was also Nioclás Mhag Uidhir (1460–1512), Bishop of Leighlin, who was a leading historian of his day. The personal bards of the Maguires were the Ó hEoghusa (O'Hussey) bards of whom Eochaidh (1570–1617) stands out as Chief *Ollamh*. He is often regarded, arguably, as the last of the traditional *ollamhain*. He was certainly one of the two foremost poets of his day. His rival was Tadhg Dall Ó hUiginn. Eochaidh wrote a famous poem describing the campaign of 1599 to 1600 during which Aodh (Hugh) Maguire was fighting with Aodh Ruadh O'Néill against the forces of Elizabeth. Eochaidh's brother or cousin was Gille-Bríghde Ó hEoghusa (1575–1614), who had to flee Ireland and entered Louvain as a Franciscan in 1607. His poems are regarded as classics. He also was the author of one of the earliest Irish printed books in Louvain (1611), *Teagasc Críostaidhe* (Christian Doctrine). Printing in the Irish language was generally forbidden under the English administration, so books on Irish grammar, dictionaries, books on theology and other materials were often printed in France, what is now also Belgium, Italy and Spain.

The annuals record that Pilib na Tuaigh (Philip of the Battle Axes), who ruled Fermanagh (1363–95), controlled an army as well as a navy that "never tasted defeat." His grandson Tomás Óg is noted as having made a pilgrimage to Rome and then to Santiago de Compostella in 1450. He was King of Fermanagh from 1430 to 1471.

The last Maguire recorded as Rí Fhear Manach (King of Fermanagh) was Giolla Pádraig Bán (1538–40). From then on the form of "Prince of Fermanagh" was used. Did the change in title come about because Seán Maguire assisted the English in their war against Seán the Proud, the Maguire overlord? In 1568 Seán the Proud led an army into Fermanagh in revenge and deposed his namesake, helping to establish Seán Maguire's brother "Coconaght" as prince. The name Cú Chonnacht ("hound of Connacht") was much favored among the Maguires and the O'Reillys in the later Middle Ages. On June 1, 1585, he surrendered to

Lord Deputy Perrot. It is noted on that date: "Surrender by Coconaght Mag-wqyre of Innyskillen, captain of his nation; of the whole country of Fermanagh, alias Magwyre's country, in the province of Ulster, with the intention of its being regranted to him." Thus Cú Chonnacht was allowed, in January 1586, to retain some of his estate in return for two knight's fees. Pardon was granted to him and members of his family provided Cú Chonnacht agreed to the usual conditions associated with such surrenders. The Maguires had surrendered first the kingship and then the princedom for the title of an English baronet.

Three years later Cú Chonnacht was dead. His son was made of sterner stuff. He became one of the most famous Maguire princes—Aodh. It was this Maguire who helped Aodh Ruadh O'Donel, Tirconnell and the sons of Seán the Proud in the famous escape from Dublin Castle in 1592. Maguire had traveled to Dublin, ostensibly to be knighted in Christchurch Cathedral as part of the surrender process. It was, however, a cover in order to be on hand and plan the escape of the princes. In fact, while he did receive the knighthood, the three young princes escaped into the snow-covered Wicklow Mountains.

The Maguire was given command of the Irish cavalry at the Battle of Yellow Ford, in August 1598, when Sir Henry Bagenal's English army was annihilated and Bagenal himself was killed. Maguire claimed that he was the first of the Irish nobles to raise the standard against Elizabeth and that he had stood alone for two years before O'Neill and O'Donel took to the field with him. In January 1596 he wrote to Philip II of Spain:

> I was the very first of all in this kingdom, not of my own authority, but through reliance on God's help and your clemency, who had the courage to rouse the Queen of England's wrath. I have incurred infinite losses in consequence, but all these I are little account because of your good will towards me. . . .

Historian Lord Ernest Hamilton observes that "Hugh Maguire was incomparably the best military commander among the Chiefs of the North."

Maguire followed O'Néill south where, in 1600, he is said to have encountered Sir Warham St. Leger in combat and been mortally wounded by him but not before he was able to cleave St. Leger's helmet with a massive blow. The death of Aodh or Hugh Maguire was a severe blow for the Irish cause. He was succeeded by his brother Cú Chonnacht as Prince of Femanagh.

The brother of Aodh, Cú Chonnacht, was endorsed as The Maguire by his people, but the English administration tried to set up a rival leader. Conor Ruadh goes disparagingly into Irish history as "the Queen's Maguire." He was not, at this time, successful in his claims. Naturally, the attempt was unsuccessful as the *derbhfine* and the people gathered behind Cú Chonnacht.

Cú Chonnacht was certainly no friend to the English administration. The northern Irish princes, having surrendered in 1603, learned that the colonial administration had plans to remove them entirely. The Maguire took the initiative and went to Rouen, in France, where he made arrangements for the potential refugees and purchased a ship, bringing it into Lough Swilly. It was from there that The O'Neill, The O'Donel, The Maguire, their families and a hundred loyal followers. left Ireland to go into exile in Europe. It is an event known as "The Flight of the Earls." It has been pointed out that, more realistically, from an Irish viewpoint, it should be "the Flight of the Princes." The current Maguire prefers to call it such and says:

> The "Flight of the Princes" ranks as one of the most important events in Irish history. Its most immediate effect was the clearing of the way for the agrarian settlement known as the Plantation of Ulster which marked the new era and was the most significant evidence of the passing of Gaelic rule.

Maguire, Prince of Fermanagh, was received with great favor by Pope Paul V and given a pension by Philip III, King of Spain. Maguire died in Genoa in 1608 only a few days after arriving there. His brother Brian had survived him but caused no trouble with the authorities, merely obtaining a grant of land at Tempo, County Fermanagh. He was not considered for the succession.

His cousin Conor Ruadh, chieftain of the Lisnaskea branch, came forward again with his claims. Conor Ruadh had supported the English during the war, and for this he was granted 6,480 acres around Lisnaska and a pension of £200 for life. Although, technically, there was no Gaelic title to claim, Conor Ruadh was knighted at Whitehall in 1616. When he died in 1625, his son Brian continued in the English Crown's good opinion and on March 3, 1627/28 he was created Lord Maguire, Baron of Enniskillen. He died in December 1633, leaving four sons.

His eldest son, another Conor Ruadh (b. 1612), succeeded as Lord Maguire. Following the terms of surrender of the Irish nobility, in which they were to Anglicize themselves, he had been educated at Magdalene College, Oxford. He married around 1635 and had a son, also a Conor. Surprisingly, this Conor Ruadh, for all his English education and the pro-English stance of his father and his grandfather, supported the Irish uprising in 1641.

On Wednesday, October 20, 1641, Conor Ruadh set out on horse for Dublin. He had been charged by Phelim O'Neill with seizing Dublin Castle with his men. The attack was to take place on October 23. He was due to be joined by Rory O'Moore and Hugh MacMahon and their men. However, the plan was betrayed by an Owen Connolly, and the three leaders were arrested while in their beds in the early hours of October 23. They were held in solitary confinement for eight months in Dublin Castle and then sent in chains to the Tower of London. Hugh MacMahon was executed a short time before Maguire was put on public trial. Maguire asserted that he was an Irishmen and entitled to fight for his country. He was condemned to be hanged, drawn and quartered. On February 20, 1644, he was taken to Tyburn in London and killed.

A witness, Hugh Bourke, Commissary of the Irish Friars Minors in Germany, disguised among the crowd, wrote this account:

> On February 20, 1644, Baron Maguire to whom the executioner would have shown some favor by leaving him to hang on the gallows until he should be quite dead, and meanwhile the executioner was busy kindling the fire with which his entrails were to be burned after his death, but so inhuman were the officers that they totally denied the Baron the services of one of our Fathers on the scaffold and waited not for the executioner but one of them cut the rope with a halberd and let the Baron drop alive and then called the executioner to open him alive and very ill the executioner did it, the said Baron making resistance with his hand and defending himself with such little strength he had; and such was the cruelty that for sheer compassion the executioner bore not to look upon him in such torment and, to have done with him, speedily handled his knife well and cut his throat.

The title of Baron Maguire of Enniskillen was thereby placed under the subject of attainder.

Lord Maguire's brother Ruaidri commanded the Fermanagh contingents during the 1641 insurrection and was able to drive the English out of the area, except for the garrison in Enniskillen. Ruaidri was in command of a thousand troops under Eóghan Ruadh O'Neill at the battle of Benburb in 1646. He was regarded as one of the most able of Irish commanders.

In spite of the fact that the title had been forfeited by an act of attainder, Conor, the son of the executed Lord Maguire of Enniskillen, assumed the title, as did his son in turn, who died without an heir. The grandson of the first baron, Ruaidri (Rory) Maguire, became a supporter of James II, claiming the title of fifth baron in spite of the attainder of his grandfather. He took a seat in James II's parliament in Dublin and was appointed Lord Lieutenant of County Fermanagh on July 4, 1689. James II seems to have had no problem in styling Ruaidri as Lord Maguire of Enniskillen. Ruaidri also raised an infantry regiment, fought at the Battle of Aughrim and then fought a rear-guard action until going into exile in France. He was proclaimed a traitor by William III. He died at the Court of St. Germains in France in October 1708, age sixty-seven years.

His son Alexander Maguire, known as the sixth Baron of Enniskillen, served as a colonel in the French Army and died in 1719 without issue. He was succeeded by his uncle, Philip (the seventh baron), who had married Mary, a daughter of Sir Phelim O'Neill, the leader of the 1641 uprising. His son, Theophilus (the eighth baron), on succession, married Margaret, the daughter of O'Donel of Tirconnel. Their son, Alexander, the ninth baron, who had been born in Ireland, became an officer in the Irish Brigade of the French Army, serving first in Duke of Berwick's regiment and then in the regiment of the famous Thomas Lally. The ninth baron was created a knight of the Royal French Order of St. Louis, retired from the army in 1763 and died in 1801 in France without issue. He left his entire estate to Comte Justin MacCarthy Reagh of Toulouse.

Although not bearing directly on the Maguires, it is of interest to note that Thomas Lally, in whose regiment the ninth baron served, was the son of Gerard Lally of Tullaghnadaly, County Galway. In 1765 Comte Lally-Tollendal, as he became known, was sent to protect French interests in India. In 1761 he suffered defeat from a fellow Irishman, Eyre Coote of Limerick, commanding the English forces. On his return to France, although warned by MacCarthy Mór (Robert, the fifth Earl of Clancarthy), Comte Lally went to Paris, where he was seized and executed for "losing" India. Voltaire and Madame de Pompadour immediately began a campaign to vindicate him. In 1778 Louis XVI declared that the execution was "without authority." It was not until 1929 that, in a full French Army ceremonial, Comte Lally-Tollendal was publicly exonerated.

Ironically, a place named after him in India has given the English language a quaint expression for being crazy or irrational—"doo-lally." The place was the site of an asylum for the mentally ill, and the phrase entered English by means of the English soldiers who had served in India.

There was now some question as to the successor of the princely line of the Maguires.

A cadet line of Maguires had been founded in Austria in the eighteenth century by John Maguire, born at Ballymacelligott, County Kerry. He became a lieutenant general in the Austrian service in 1751, was awarded the Grand Cross of the Order of Maria Theresa and given the title Graf (Count) von Enniskillen. He died in 1767. Some genealogists believe that any male descendants of this line might have a claim on the title.

In 1834, however, the famous antiquarian John O'Donovan, while visiting Fermanagh, found a hardware merchant in Enniskillen called Thomas Maguire. He not only claimed to be The Maguire, Prince of Fermanagh, but also Baron Enniskillen. O'Donovan wrote cynically to a friend: "He is a hard-ware merchant and, like shop keepers in general, void of patriotic feeling. In-deed it is hard to expect that any man in his situation of life could take any interest in historical research."

However, Thomas Maguire had several things in his possession supporting his claims, including the will of the first Lord Maguire of Enniskillen written in the Tower of London in 1644 before his execution. O'Donovan started to ex-amine the documents and wrote on November 18, 1834, in a letter now held in Linenhall Library, Belfast: "Thomas Maguire of Enniskillen is now The Maguire, as descending from the brother of Conor, who was created Baron of Enniskillen by Queen Elizabeth [*sic*]." Apart from the glaring mistake, for the title Baron of Enniskillen was not created by Elizabeth, O'Donovan had traced the line from Brian, the third brother of the first Lord Maguire of Enniskillen. However, more genealogical research would have revealed that the senior line, as one is tracing the English title of Baron Enniskillen after the death of the ninth baron in 1801, would actually have passed to the descendants of another brother of Conor Ruadh (executed in 1644). This was Tomás, who was older than Brian, whose descendants O'Donovan had uncovered in Enniskillen.

In the 1980s, the Genealogical Office accepted that the male heir after the ninth baron would have been William Maguire (d. 1870), the fifth in descent from Thomas. The family lived in Belfast and had become Protestants. William's father, Daniel Maguire (1760–98), had joined the Lisnaskea Volun-teer Company and held the rank of lieutenant. His insignia and belt buckle is still held by the family. He was present at the "Monster Review" of the Fer-managh Volunteers at Maguiresbridge. Many of the Volunteers, unappeased by the reforms being enacted in the early 1790s, joined the United Irishmen. Daniel Maguire was one of them and was killed during the Battle of Antrim when, on June 7, 1798, Henry Joy McCracken tried to capture Antrim Town for the United Irishmen.

Daniel's son William, a miniature of whom survives, showing his Maguire flaming red hair, which was why so many had the nickname "Ruadh," died in 1870. He was succeeded by his grandson Robert, who had married a Catholic, Rose Morrison, in 1875. Their younger son, James, was raised a Catholic and educated at St. Malachy's College in Belfast. James died in 1937 and his son An-thony (b. 1906) succeeded him. Anthony had one child, Harriett, born on Octo-ber 13, 1931; she married Thomas, the father of Terence McCarthy, in 1955.

The relationship of the current Maguire to Terence McCarthy and the fact that it was Terence McCarthy who undertook the research, in 1981, supporting his maternal great uncle Anthony Maguire's application for recognition at the

Genealogical Office, have cast doubts on the authenticity of the current Maguire, who is the brother of Anthony and also great uncle of Terence McCarthy.

In fact, the question of the authenticity of Terence Maguire's pedigree was raised simultaneously with the question of Terence McCarthy's own fraudulent claim in the Irish Parliament in September 1999. It was not until May 2000 that the Genealogical Office stated that "in light of allegations made and other development, a review of his pedigree and of the basis for recognition in his case is being carried out. Mr. Maguire has been advised of this."[24] A year later the review was "stalled" while the Chief Herald sought advice from the Attorney General of Ireland about certain legal issues raised by The Maguire. Writing to this author on July 27, 2001, the Chief Herald added: "I see no point in opening reviews of others cases from the 1990s until the issues raised by Maguire are dealt with." This, as has already been stated, may take some years. In the meantime, the press and the media, for example, the *Sunday Times*, on January 7, 2001, continue to run stories based on freelance genealogist Seán Murphy's denouncements.

Most damning to The Maguire's case is that Terence McCarthy had published an article entitled "A Brief Genealogical Account of the Maguires, Princes of Fermanagh and Barons of Enniskillen."[25] This article outlined the pedigree on which the claim for the Maguire title is based, tracing his maternal great uncle's family to recent years. The information seems contrary to the genealogy provided by the Earl of Belmore in "Gleanings for Former Fermanagh Articles" in 1897.[26]

At the time of his daughter Harriett's birth in 1931, Anthony Maguire was a laborer living at 28 Tyrone Street, Belfast. In 1955 Anthony Maguire was a glazier. By the time of his death, in 1985, his applications to the Genealogical Office had not been processed.

Following Anthony's death, his brother, Terence James Maguire, born in Belfast in 1924, also forwarded the claim for recognition, prepared mainly by Terence McCarthy. His great nephew pointed out that he was de jure fourteenth Baron Maguire of Enniskillen in the Jacobite Peerage. But this was not a title Terence Maguire wished to claim. He did become a Knight of the Companionate of Merit of the Military and Hospitaller Order of St. Lazarus of Jerusalem. In 1990 the chief Herald announced the courtesy recognition of his title as The Maguire.

It is conceded in several quarters that Terence Maguire is acknowledged as an honorable man, acting in good faith, who inherited the claim to the title on the death of his brother. Terence McCarthy had contributed the initial research for the pedigree and subsequently published some articles on the history of the family. Terence Maguire found no cause to question this research at the time. He telephoned this author to express his personal incredulousness at the news of his great nephew's fraud.

Terence Maguire had left Belfast and continued his education at the University of Witwatersrand in South Africa. He is a Fellow of the Institute of Chartered Secretaries and Administrators, although now a retired company director. He lives in Dublin and is widely traveled, especially in China, to whose people and culture he admits an attachment. As The Maguire, he is patron of the Maguire Clan Society and chairman of the Clan Maguire Trust.

One of his principal interests has been the "Maguire Chalices." As kings of Fermanagh, the Maguires were famous for their endowments to churches, and they presented precious chalices to many churches and religious communities. One of the earliest that survives dates back to 1493 and is now in the National Museum of Antiquities of Scotland. The inscription reads, in translation, that "Katherine, daughter of Neill, wife of John Maguire, Prince of Fermanagh, caused me to be made in the year of the Lord 1493." The Maguire has become an expert on his family chalices and has lectured both in Ireland and abroad on the subject, as well as being the author of *Historic Maguire Chalices*, published in 1996 by Fermanagh District Council. The unique chalices bear testimony to the skills of the Irish craftsmen in gold, silver, copper and wood. At the time when the "McCarthy Affair" had such a devastating effect, Maguire was planning to publish a study on his family history on which he had been working for some time.

If the future sees the withdrawal of recognition from Terence Maguire as The Maguire, there may be some irony in the fact that it was his energies which created the Standing Council of Irish Chiefs and Chieftains in 1990. He is a man of decided views about the future of the Gaelic aristocracy and their role.

> I strongly believe that we should have some say in the future of Ireland, not politically but certainly culturally and economically, as we are, whether we like it or not, the representatives of the Old Gaelic Order and represent a very large number of people worldwide.

He feels that there should be seats in the Irish Senate available for nominated Chiefs. "Were I a younger man I would certainly enter politics for that is where the action is."

> Over the past twelve years or so I have endeavored to play a cultural role in the [Irish] Republic. It was my great privilege and honor to call together, for the first time since Kinsale [1601–2], the Irish Chiefs [October 5, 1991] at Aras an Uachtaráin [the Irish President's residence]. I have been told by my good

friend O'Neill of Clanaboy, that when we formed our Standing Council, after the "Gathering," that it was the 19th Council in our Irish history, the first recorded Council was when the High King Muirchertach Mac Ercae mac Eóghain (d. A.D. 536) formed a Council ca. A.D. 515. It was my great honor to have been elected the first chairman of the Standing Council. . . .

Maguire is a staunch supporter of efforts to expand a knowledge of Gaelic Ireland and maintains that

> The Irish language is of the greatest importance within our culture and I fully support the ideal of a bilingual Irish people . . . at the present our Council is promoting the Irish language through Cork University where it is offering a [financial] prize for an essay in Irish on an Irish event.

Terence Maguire, whatever the future brings, has been one of the most energetic of those Chiefs who, in 1990, attempted to raise an awareness among the Irish people of aspects of their Gaelic history which tend to be overlooked in modern interpretations of that past. Having created and guided the Standing Council of Chiefs and Chieftains through the first years, it could be a sad paradox if he became a further victim of the "McCarthy Affair," and yet independent genealogist Seán Murphy has stated his pedigree to be "based on sentimental family imaginings at best, brazen fabrication at worst." It remains to be seen if Mr. Murphy can substantiate his claims. In the meantime, increasing ill health and the public disgrace of his great nephew has forced Terence Maguire to withdraw from public life.

THE MACSWEENEY DOE, LORD OF TUATH TORY, ROSS GUILL AND CLOGHANEELY (MAC SUIBHNE NA DTUATH)

It is often erroneously thought that name Suibhne, Anglicized as Sweeney, is of Norse origin from Sweyn and that the family were Scottish gallowglasses (*gallóglaigh*, or foreign warriors) who settled in Ireland. In fact, the name Suibhne appears on ancient king lists as well as in the story *Buile Suibhne*, or *Suibhne Geilt* (Wild Sweeney), a fictitious king of the Dál na Araidi who is said to have been cursed or driven mad during a battle. Suibhne Meann (the Stammer) was High King from around A.D. 614 to his death in 628. He was of the Cenél Eógain, a descendant of the Uí Néill and directly descended from Niall Noígiallach himself. The name certainly occurs in the Dál Riada areas of Antrim and in Argylland we may presume that, like the MacDonnells, the MacSweeneys were spread in both Gaelic kingdoms.

The *Annals of the Four Masters* says that the Mac Suibhne, a branch of the Uí Néill, formed three great families in Donegal by the start of the thirteenth century. They were Mac Suibhne of Fanaid, Mac Suibhne of Tir Broghaine (Banagh) and Mac Suibhne na dTuath (of the territories), which is Anglicized as Doe. There is a word play on this name for Mac Suibhne of Doe was also called Mac Suibhne na dTuagh (of the Battle Axes), signifying that they were standard bearers and marshal to the O'Donels of Tirconnell. A branch of the same family had settled in north County Cork by this time, serving as warrior guards to the MacCarthys of Desmond.

The family's line in Ireland is not clearly traced before 1258 when Donal Óg O'Donel arrived in Tirconnell to be proclaimed as Ó Domhnaill. He had been in exile in Argyll, and when he returned he brought with him his wife, Catriona. She was daughter of Eóghan Mac Suibhne, an Argyll chief, who escorted Donal Óg with a band of Argyll gallowglasses.

The *Leabhar Chlainne Suibhne* (Book of the Clan Sweeney), a manuscript dated to 1534 now in the Royal Irish Academy, says that the first Mac Suibhne na dTuath was Donnchadh Mór son of Murchadh Óg, who flourished around 1340, when the Ó Baoigill (O'Boyles) were displaced from the area. Mac Suibhne na dTuath ruled in the clan lands until the conquests of the seventeenth century.

Mac Suibhne survived the dynastic conflicts among the Uí Neill created by Henry VIII's policy. Murchú Mall, who led the clan of MacSweeney Doe in support of Ó Domhnaill against Shane the Proud, during the latter's defeat in 1567, earned his nickname by coming late to the battlefield. Ó Domhnaill is said to have exclaimed: "*Is tú Murchú Mall!*" (You are Murchú the late!). "No," replied Mac Suibhne, "I am Murchú in time!" His fresh troops helped to scatter Seán the Proud's men. In 1570 the Uí Néill had their revenge by murdering Murchú and other Mac Suibhne leaders.

Murchú was succeeded by Eóghan Óg II, his brother, who was Chief from 1570 to 1596.

The Mac Suibhne were not only military leaders but patrons of the arts. Eóghan Óg, for example, was patron of Tadhg Dall Ó hÚiginn (1550–1617), who wrote praise poems on the origins of the clan. Eóghan Óg also supported the poet Eochaidh Ó hEoghusa (1570–1617). He was also foster father to Aodh Ruadh O'Donel (Red Hugh). He is described by the *Annals of the Four Masters* as "influential and generous . . . with a gift of good sense and counsel in peace and war."

Eóghan Óg gave refuge to survivors of the Spanish Armada, protecting them from the English soldiers who tried to kill them as they came ashore from their wrecked ships. Three Spanish ships foundered off Killybegs. One was the 900-ton transport *Duquesa Santa Ana*, with 357 men, including Don Alonzo de Leyva, whose own ship, *La Rata Santa Maria Encoronada*, had been wrecked earlier off the Breifne coast. He and his men had been picked up by the transport. Don Alonso was not the only Spaniard given succor by the Irish. Indeed, the men of Donegal labored alongside the Spanish to help repair the *Gerona* and make it ready for sea for their escape.

Henry Duke reported to the English Lord Deputy Fitzwilliam: "There were 2,400 Spaniards in the country of the MacSweeney. They have left with MacSweeney an Irish friar called James ne Dowrough who went into Spain with James Fitzmaurice." The friar was hunted but he was successfully hidden by the MacSweeneys. Those who consigned themselves to the *Gerona* were driven eastward to the coast of Antrim, where the ship was driven ashore at Duluce, at a point known as Port na Spainneach. Sorley Boy MacDonnell cared for the survivors at Dunluce Castle. When they had recovered, he sent them on their way via Scotland back to Spain.

It was Eóghan Óg II who gave protection to Ó Ruairc of Breifne when the English managed to drive him from Breifne. Eóghan Óg II helped the old prince Aodh of Tirconnell (Chief between 1566 and 1592) fight against an attempted military coup by his son Donal while the old man's other son, Aodh Ruadh, was a prisoner of the English in Dublin. Donal was defeated and slain at Glencolmcille. After his escape, Aodh Ruadh was inaugurated as the Ó Domhnaill, Prince of Tirconnell, at Kilmacrenan in 1592, with the faithful Eóghan Óg in attendance. He died on January 26, 1596, and his nephew, Maolmhuire, son of Murchú Mall, was installed as MacSuibhne na dTuath.

Unfortunately, Maolmhuire chose to support the English for a while and was with Sir Conyer Clifford when they were defeated at the Battle of the Curlieu Mountains. He survived, and when the English appeared to be emerging victorious, he surrendered his title and clan on April 1, 1600. Significantly, although he could write, he did not sign his name, placing an "X" on the document instead. On April 28 certain lands were regranted "to hold forever by service of a twentieth part of a knight's fee, and service of five horsemen and ten footmen at every general hosting, and fifteen beeves [oxen] yearly." On the written instruction of Elizabeth I, dated November 17, 1599, the newly created Sir Myles (Maolmhuire) MacSweeney was recognized as holding lordship over MacSweeney Fanad and MacSweeney Banagh. The Grant of April 30, 1600, is specific:

Grant [under Queen's letter of 17 November, 1599] to Mulmory M'Swyne of Toa knt.; of custody of all manors, lands and hereditaments in the countries of

M'Swyne Fanet and M'Swine Bannet in Tireconnell in the province of Ulster. To hold during pleasure, rendering to the Exchequer the true value according to an extent.

MacSweeney was also granted a large pension of six shillings a day "till he be otherwise provided for."

His loyalty to the English was questionable and, indeed, he was the only MacSweeney Chief from Donegal to accompany "Red Hugh" O'Donel to the fatal battle of Kinsale in 1601. He was pardoned in 1603, but in 1608 he was arraigned for treason. He was in trouble again in 1615, when he was implicated in the failed attempt to rescue Con, son of Hugh O'Neill, from Dungannon Castle. Con O'Neill was seven years old in 1608 and left behind during the flight of the Ulster princes. It was not until 1630 that his lands were once again regranted to him and his heirs. MacSweeney, however, died in poverty, and Donal O'Donnell of Glenties observed that he had drank his estate away.

His grandson Maolmhuire (Myles) Mac Suibhne was not only a delegate to the Kilkenny parliament in 1642 but Colonel of the Tyrconnell Regiment in the army of Eóghan Roe O'Neill. He was forced to surrender to the Cromwellian general Robert Venables, whose army had advanced into Ulster. Maolmhuire's estate at Dunlewy, Gweedore, was forfeited. His son Donogh Óg fought against William of Orange and was at Derry, the Boyne and Limerick. Outlawed in 1691, Donogh Óg was forced to fly to France, where he was killed in a duel.

The current chiefly line descends from Donogh Óg's uncle Edmund, who was also outlawed, went to France and died there.[27] His name was first on the County Donegal Outlawry List of 1691 and his nephew Donagh Óg was third. Edmund was the largest landowner to lose his property at the start of the Williamite Confiscations. His son Donagh Fhergal is said to be the last of the family to hold Doe Castle. It was Donagh Fhergal's son Tarlagh who was the next MacSweeney Doe. Following the confiscations of 1691, the chiefly family chose to walk the roads of Donegal rather than accept land as tenants from the new rulers of Ireland. During the Penal Law years they were given shelter by some members of the extended family and earned a living playing music and working as tinsmiths. It can be argued that the chiefly family did not surrender until the Catholic Emancipation in 1829, when they finally took land as tenants.[28]

The MacSweeney of Doe thereby disappeared into the underground world of Gaelic culture that existed, hidden, from the English colonial administration, although it appears that Captain Hart, the occupant of Doe Castle, knew well the identity of Eamon Rua and his children. According to John O'Donovan:

" . . . Captain Hart told his youngest son that the Mac Sweenie (Swynes) were unjustly deprived of that part of Doe."[29]

It was on September 5, 1835, that the genealogist Dr. John O'Donovan was traveling in Donegal on behalf of the Ordnance Survey. He wrote a letter to his superiors about a surprise encounter with a man walking on the beach with his family. O'Donovan was informed that this was the MacSweeney Doe. After investigating, he was convinced that this was, indeed, the lineal legitimate descendant of the old chiefs of Doe.

The man was Eamon Rua Mac Suibhne, who had become MacSweeney Doe in 1834. He was then about sixty-one years old, a piper and tinsmith. His father Eamon Mór (1738–1834) had also been a piper, and music was a tradition within the family. Eamon Rua supplied O'Donovan with the line of Chiefs back to 1596. The renowned scholar did not realize this, thinking that Eamon Rua was specifying an ancestral line. The direct ancestry was later supplied by Eamon Rua's youngest son, Tarlagh, An Píobaire Mór (The Great Piper). In 1909 Donogh Óg's line ended when he died in exile in France, and the descendants of Donogh Óg's uncle Eamon (Edmund) carried on the line of chiefs in Ireland. Eamon Rua was Edmund's great-great-grandson. One of the proud possessions of the current MacSweeney Doe is the portable tinsmith's anvil that belonged to Eamon Rua, which is now set on an oak stand made by the renowned Irish sculptress Imogen Stuart RHA.

Eamon Rua's son James became a farmer and died in 1883.

By this time the name had been generally shortened to Sweeney. James and two of his brothers rented lands in Derryveigh, part of the Glenveigh Estates, now a national park, which had been the property of Maolmhuire (Sir Myles) MacSweeney. The notorious landlord John George Adair had begun to purchase Glenveigh in 1857. The Sweeneys accounted for one in eight of the 244 people (45 families) evicted from 44 houses in Derryveigh in 1861. Eamon Rua had died just before this. But his elderly widow, Hannah, was one of those put out into the road to fend for themselves.[30]

It had been in July 1859 that the current chief's grandfather, Edward, senior grandson of Eamon Rua, who was then age twenty-one, had been seized illegally in his home in the middle of the night by police. Imprisoned in Lifford jail, he had been marched eighty statute miles forward and back across the countryside in chains to wear down his spirit. Five days after his arrest he was brought before magistrates, but there were no charges to answer.

Edward sought redress because the police had acted without legal warrant merely on the word of Adair, who claimed suspicion of illegal activity. Edward petitioned the Lord Lieutenant of Ireland, the seventh Earl of Carlisle, who refused to take action against the prominent landlord but admitted that "some misunderstanding" had taken place. A few months later Adair sent his agent James Murray to announce changes of status of the Derryveigh tenants. Their status was changed to that of "tenants at will" to clear the way for the evictions. The Sweeneys refused to accept the change imposed by Adair. This further aggravated the hostility that existed between the Sweeneys and Murray, and thus they became suspects when Murray was later killed.

In November 1860 Murray's body was found on a mountainside near Derryveigh. Edward's cousin, Dan Mór, was one of five Sweeneys who were afterward arrested at Adair's behest. Dan Mór had, in fact, decided to leave for Australia and made arrangements to do so, in order to seek work. He left soon after Murray's body was discovered, and Adair insisted the police take out a warrant for his arrest. He was in Liverpool awaiting an Australia-bound ship when he heard the news. Dan Mór, being of the blood of the old chiefs, insisted on returning to Derryveigh. On November 22, 1860, he surrendered in the local police barracks of his own free will. He was tried but acquitted.

The acquittal made Adair furious. On April 6, 1861, he wrote: "I therefore decided . . . to make the people of the district responsible for the crimes committed." He evicted forty-seven families, leveled forty-two houses and cleared eleven thousand acres of land from human habitation. He did to Derryveigh what the Great Hunger had failed to do. In April, 1861, two hundred armed police protected a gang of workmen who were brought into the country to level the houses of the poor Irish tenants. Edward's family was evicted, but the house was not leveled as the police wanted to use it as a barracks. It was a police barracks for the next twenty years and is the only complete original dwelling from the time of the evictions left in Derryveigh today.

Hannah, the elderly widow of Eamon Rua, was also mother of Tarlach (Turlough) Mac Suibhne, who became known as "An Piobaire Mór," the great piper. Tarlach (1831–1916) was acknowledged as one of the greatest pipers who ever lived. He played at the 1893 World's Columbian Exposition (World Fair) in Chicago. His pipes are now in the Donegal Historical Society Museum, Rosnowlagh, County Donegal, as is a fiddle that he played with equal dexterity. One of his own compositions, "Dúlamán na Binne Bui" (Seaweed of the Yellow Sea Cliff), has recently been recorded by Clannad and Altan.[31]

The poet and author Ethna Carbery (1866–1911) wrote:

Play as the bards played in days long ago
When O'Donel arrayed for the foray or feast.
With you kinsmen from Banagh and Fanad and Doe,

With piping and harping and blessing of priest,
Rode out in the blaze of the sun from the East.
O Turlough MacSweeney!

James's eldest son Edward (or Eamon) was not only a farmer but was appointed Justice of the Peace. He died in 1922. His eldest son, James (1874–1958), was a farmer, Peace Commissioner and local district councilor. Dominic (1878–1970) was Edward's second son and was a farmer and also a talented fiddle player. The third son (d. 1970) was Hugh, who joined the Garda Siochána, the new police force of the emergent Irish state when it was formed in 1922. He died a few months before Dominic, and so the title MacSweeney Doe passed to Hugh's son, Tom, the current MacSweeney.

The chiefship of The MacSweeney has, like some of the other Gaelic titles, not been without its challengers. In Rathmullan hangs a curious parchment bearing arms dated September 21, 1979. The arms are surmounted with a golden crown, acting as a crest, although none of the claimants cited below is of kingly dynasties. In one case the colors of the arms are wrong and in another there is a symbol that does not appear in heraldry. However, the parchment reads that the Grand Council of the Clan Sweeney, meeting in Dublin that day, had unanimously resolved that

> it is considered essential for the continuity of the clan organization that the hereditary headship of the three major houses be reintroduced. And whereas the three armigerous officers of the clan have established proof of their descent from each of those houses respectively that the Chevalier Laughlin Joseph Sweeney KLJ shall be the head of the House of Fanad and hereafter known as Mac Suibhne Fanad. His Excellency the Marquis MacSwiney of Mashanaglass KM KCN shall be the head of the House of Doe and hereafter known as Mac Suibhne na dTuatha. His Excellency the Captain Richard Patrick Fortier Mingo Sweeney of Bolgers Park EM DL DCLJ KMLJ be the head of the house of Banagh and be hereafter known as Mac Suibhne Banagh.

This impressive declaration also says that the three lordships would be passed to their heirs under the law of primogeniture. It is signed only by Mingo and Laughlin Sweeney and bears impressive seals. It does not bear the signature of Marquis MacSwiney, who died in 1986. In the seven years from the production of the parchment until his death he apparently did not, perhaps significantly, subscribe his name to it.

However, no MacSweeney chiefship is currently recognized by the Chief Herald of Ireland. A letter from the Deputy Chief Herald, Fergus Gillespie, to

The MacDonnell of The Glens on September 8, 1999, makes the firm statement: "Neither Mingo Sweeney nor Laughlin Sweeney have ever produced proofs of descent from any MacSweeney lord of Donegal." In the same letter, the Deputy Herald points out that the Genealogical Office knew "nothing of any recognition or approval . . . of any *MacSweeney 'pacte de famille.'*" Nor did the Genealogical Office recognize "anyone as honorary commander or constable."[32]

Fergus Gillespie also pointed out that the first house established, the senior MacSweeney house, was Fanad, but if Fanad is extinct then Doe became Fanad and the Arms of Doe became the Arms of Fanad.[33] That the chiefship of MacSweeney Doe resides in the person of Tom Sweeney is accepted by many genealogists and historical authorities as the legitimate descendant of the last acknowledged MacSweeney of Doe. Tom Sweeny has presented his genealogical proofs to the Chief Herald and is awaiting recognition.

Two of the three MacSweeney claimants in the document at Rathmullan had close connections with Terence McCarthy (see chapter 12) and were members of his "dynastic order." Richard Patrick Fortier Mingo Sweeney, a former Canadian army officer, living in Nova Scotia, was an early member of the Niadh Nask and had been a member of the International Commission on Orders of Chivalry in the 1960s. This was the body that gave McCarthy's "dynastic order" credibility by recognition and an organization of which Terence McCarthy later became a vice president and president. Both Mingo Sweeney and McCarthy were also Knights of St. Lazarus and the Order of St. Stanislas.

Mingo Sweeney was instrumental in setting up the Clan tSuibhne Association in 1977. He was named "Commander," Loughlin Sweeney became "Grand Seneschal" and other non-Gaelic officers, such as a "Grand Constable," "Grand Almoner," "Grand Marshal," "Grand Genealogist" and even a "Captain of the Gallowglas Guard," were appointed. McCarthy followed this idea some ten years later. In spite of the fact that the Genealogical Office did not recognize either Mingo or Loughlin Sweeney, nor had they even submitted proofs in claims of their "titles," Laughlin Sweeney sent a letter to members of the Clan tSuibhne Association in 1979:

> The Council decided following discussions with the Chief Herald of Ireland at that time, Gerard Slevin, and the Lord Lyon in Scotland, that the leadership of the Clan should be drawn from armigerous [those with official registered coats-of-arms] representatives of the House of Fanad, Doe and Banagh who could trace a direct connection to these ancient lines, and who would henceforward be known as McSuibhne Fanad, McSuibhne Doe and MacSuibhne Banagh, these ancient titles to pass on by primogeniture.[34]

No record of such an agreement exists at either the Genealogical Office, Dublin, or the Office of the Lord Lyon in Edinburgh.[35] Nor at that time, nor subsequently, had Mingo or Laughlin Sweeney made any official approach to the Chief Herald for "courtesy recognition," and none had been given. The Clan tSuibhne Association, over which they preside, has grown into a worldwide organization. The questions hanging over its leadership, unless answered by a reputable herald, can only damage the association, the clan traditions and the enthusiasm of its membership, as has happened to the MacCarthy Clan societies.

On the more positive side, Tom Sweeney is one of the several heads of Gaelic noble families now awaiting recognition from the Chief Herald but whose applications have been delayed by the events of 1999. He had the misfortune to make his formal application in July 1999. Had the Chief Herald not put a hold on recognitions, then, according to informed sources, Tom Sweeney would already have received courtesy recognition.

Tom Sweeney was born in 1935 and lives in Dublin, where he works for the Department of Education and Science. He trained as a teacher but is also an honors graduate of Queen's University School of Architecture in Belfast. He joined the Irish Department of Education in 1977 as an inspector.

He spent much of his childhood in his father's house, built, symbolically, on an eviction site in Derryveigh. Married in 1963 to Barbara Curran, a teacher and native speaker of Irish from Galway, he has two sons, Piaras and Eamon. Eamon is married to Louise Donnelly, herself a descendant of an ancient Ulster clan whose chief was hereditary marshal of O'Neill's force, and has a daughter Fionnuala. Fionnuala Sweeney became known to millions throughout the world in 1993 for her presentation of the Eurovision Song Contest on behalf of RTÉ broadcasting live from Millstreet, County Cork, to 350 million television viewers in three languages. She is now a presenter on CNN International World News, having worked for RTÉ as both a radio and television reporter and presenter. The family spends much of its leisure time on the family farm in Glendowan, County Donegal, to which Tom's great-grandfather moved in the wake of the Derryveigh evictions.

Tom's mother, Rose Duignan, was a member of a County Sligo republican family and she was wounded on active service in the War of Independence. Her brother Tom, at that time, was a commandant in the IRA who managed to break out of Sligo jail after his capture. It was the last jailbreak of the War of Independence.

Tom takes an active part in the Sweeney Clan Association, which recognized him as The MacSweeney Doe in January 1996, when the association assembled to commemorate the four hundreth anniversary of the death of

Eóghan Óg (1570–96). An Irish speaker, Tom's interests are numerous and varied. Like many of his Sweeney ancestors, he is a musician, and he was the winner of the All-Ireland Ceoil traditional fiddle competition. He is a member of the North-West Donegal Branch of An Taisce and the Donegal Historical Society. He has also lectured widely on craft and architectural heritage and is a member of the Royal Institute of British Architects.

As an Irish speaker, he is fully committed to the restoration and use of the Irish language in a bilingual Ireland. He is a Catholic but was always uncomfortable with the constitution giving a special place to the Catholic Church within the Irish state; he always regarded it as insensitive and was delighted when it was abolished. He supports the office of the Chief Herald and regards it as a valuable and vital bulwark against fraud.

CHAPTER ELEVEN

THE KINGDOM OF LEINSTER

THE NAME LEINSTER DERIVES FROM THE IRISH "Laighin," to which the Norse added *stadr* (place) in the ninth century A.D. Today it is the second largest of the four provinces of Ireland, encompassing 7,850 square miles. It consists of the counties of Carlow, Dublin, Kildare, Kilkenny, Laois, Longford, Louth, Meath, Offaly, Westmeath and Wicklow. However, in its original form, the counties of Meath, Westmeath and parts of Dublin and Offaly were not part of it. They formed the middle kingdom of Midhe. Leinster occupies the middle and southeastern portion of the island.

Leinster has two origin stories. One is that it received its name from Laighne Lethan-glas, a Nemedian, who settled in Ireland before the sons of Míle Easpain. The second origin tale is that it is named after a host of Gaulish Celts who settled there after accompanying the exiled prince Labraid Loingsech on his return home to overthrow his uncle, Cobhthach Caol, in the fourth century B.C. The Gauls were said to have used a broad-pointed spear, called *laighen* because of its blue-green iron color. The story is told in *Orgain Denna Ríg* (Destruction of Dind Ríg). *Lebor na Nuachonghbhála*, popularly known as the "Book of Leinster," written at Glendalough about 1150 under the authority of Bishop Fionn Mac Gormain, dates these events to 307 B.C.

Like the Uí Néill of the north and the Uí Briúin of Connacht, the royal dynasty of Leinster traces its line back to Eremon, son of Míle Easpain. It was Ughaine Mór, fifty-ninth successor to Míle, listed as King of Ireland around 331 B.C. and given a rather fanciful and anachronistic reputation by medieval storytellers, who was the grandfather of Labraid Loingsech.

The royal dynasty of Leinster became known as the Uí Cheinnselaig, from Énna Cennsalach, listed as ninety-second in descent from Míle Easpain, whose son Crimthann (d. A.D. 483) was, therefore, the first of the Uí Cheinnselaig. The genealogies of the family in written form survive from the beginning of the seventh century, and no less than three *forsundud* (genealogical praise poems) survive from the seventh century, written under the patronage of the Leinster kings. According to Professor Francis Byrne, one of the most interesting of the Irish kingship documents is the *Tinna Catháir Máir* (Testament of Catháir Máir), composed in heptasyllabic alliterative verse in about the eighth century. In this, Catháir Mór, eighty-eighth in descent from Míle Easpain, bestows gifts on his ten princely sons who would form the various royal branches of his dynasty. But two Leinster lines are not mentioned in Catháir's Testament—the Uí Garrchon and the Uí Máil—which scholars find puzzling.

From earliest times there were two main royal residences in Leinster. Most famous is the fourteen-acre site of the hill fort of Dún Ailinne, Hill of Allen, near Kilcullen, County Kildare. This appears in the stories of the Fianna, the bodyguards of the High King, and their leader, Fionn mac Cumhail. The stories relate that Finn's father, Cumal, was leader of the Clanna Baoiscne and a King of Leinster. The second royal site is Dind Ríg, on the banks of the Barrow, County Carlow, associated with the story of Labraid Loingsech. The Uí Cheinnselaig dynasty made their court at the site of the alder trees (Fearna), now called Ferns.

All Irish schoolchildren, if they have heard of only one Irish king, will probably know Dermot MacMorrough of Hy Kinsella (Diarmuid Mac Murchada Uí Cheinnselaig), King of Leinster and the Foreigners. "Putrid while living, damned when dead" is the popular expression. It was he who, being driven from his kingdom by the O'Conors and O'Ruaircs, traveled to France in search of the Angevin Emperor, Henry II, and secured what he fondly thought was mercenary help from the Norman barons to win back his kingdom. He thereby precipitated the Norman invasion of Ireland.

Few other Irish kings are so reviled or have had so much written about them. While one cannot argue with the results of his action, the more one examines the reasons behind Dermot's invitation to the Normans the more one can sympathize with him. His story has been exceptionally and sympathetically told by biographer Nicholas Furlong.[1]

Dermot was born in 1110, the third son of the then King of Leinster, Donnchadh MacMurchadha (MacMorrough), the twentieth generation from Énna Cennselach. His father and one of his brothers died in battle in 1115. Another Énna became King of Leinster, but he died unexpectedly in Wexford in 1126.

Dermot MacMorrough had barely reached the age of choice when his *derbh-fine* gathered at the royal residence at Ferna and elected him as king. It has been argued that he was only sixteen, but the Brehon law for the age of maturity, at *aimsir togu* (age of choice), is strict. No one could hold any office or inherit unless he was of age. Nicholas Furlong believes that Dermot has been overly vilified. His achievements are forgotten, his patronage of the arts and his political acumen have all been subsumed by his reputation as the first great Irish traitor who betrayed his country to a ruthless foreign enemy. However, it has to be pointed out that he did live with two wives simultaneously, was responsible for the rape of an abbess and eloped with the wife of Tigernán Ó Ruairc, King of Breifne.

Dermot's kingdom had been under threat for nearly a century from the centralizing ideas of the O'Brien High Kings and then from the O'Conors. Their aggressive policies had made the Leinster kings turn to military alliances, not only with other Irish kingdoms but with the Danes, resulting in the battle at Clontarf in 1014.

In order to protect the kingdom, which had been raided by the O'Conor High King and his allies, Dermot left Ireland in order to seek military aid from the Normans. He went to the court of the Angevin Emperor, Henry II, in Anjou. Henry then issued Dermot with Letters Patent giving permission to any of his Norman knights to help him if they thought fit. Dermot finally persuaded Richard de Clare, nicknamed "Strongbow," the Earl of Pembroke, to give him aid by the expedient of promising him, among other things, his daughter, Aoife, in marriage. He appears to have allowed Strongbow to think that, through her, Strongbow would become King of Leinster after Dermot. Strongbow was not told about the Brehon law of dynastic succession.

An advance contingent of Norman knights landed in Ireland with Dermot in May 1169. Strongbow came in force in August 1170, captured Waterford and married Aoife. Dermot died at Ferns in 1171 according to the *Annals of the Four Masters* "without a will, without penance, without unction, as his evil deeds deserved."

Henry II, realizing his liege men were now doing rather well in Ireland, arrived in Waterford with his own army on October 17, 1171. Henry received the submission of Strongbow at Waterford, who assured him of his continued oath of fealty, and so was promptly granted the lordship of the kingdom of Leinster, with the exception of Dublin, Wexford and Waterford and a coastal strip south of Dublin to Arklow. The rightful King of Leinster, Domhnall Caermanach (1171–75), was already in arms against Strongbow and the Normans. So was the High King, Ruaidri Ua Conchobhair. Henry spent the next six months campaigning in Ireland and thus laid the foundations of what became English rule there and the start of over eight hundred years of conflict between Ireland and England.

Leinster was the first of the Irish kingdoms to fall to Norman domination. In spite of the aspiration of their motto "Siothcháin agus Fairsinge" (Peace and Plenty), the Leinster kings fought on against the conquerors. Domhnall was slain in 1175. Over a hundred years later, in 1281, a successor, King Mortough Mac-Morrough Kavanagh, was slain at Arklow. Little had changed in that time. It seems incredible, but in spite of their early conquest and occupation, as well as the close geographical location to the Anglo-Norman colonies, which occupied several towns in the former kingdom, the MacMorrough Kavanagh kings survived and managed to maintain the allegiance of their people in their war against the Normans. Norman influence remained confined mainly to the port towns.

By the start of the fourteenth century the entire kingdom of Leinster had seen a revival of its fortunes, and many of the old Norman barons, who had settled on estates there—families such as de Clare, de Valence and Bigod—had become extinct or moved off. In 1324 Donall Mac Art MacMorrough was elected King of Leinster and installed to the acclaim of the entire kingdom. He was eventually captured and imprisoned in Dublin Castle, escaped but was slain in 1347.

One of the successful Leinster kings at this time was Art Mór Mac Airt (1375–1417), who is recorded as restoring the fortunes of the kingdom on a scale not unworthy of its pre-Norman days. Art even had annual tribute paid to him by the English colonists. Irish writers extolled King Art's virtues as courageous, liberal and hospitable. He married a Norman, Elizabeth Veele, whose estates were then seized by the English, who claimed that she had forfeited them by her marriage.

Richard II was said to have concluded an agreement with King Art in 1395 restoring his wife's lands and conferring knighthood on him. However, the breaking of the agreement saw Art start hostilities against the English, and in 1399 Richard II arrived back in Ireland with an army. Jean Creton witnessed a meeting between Richard II's emissary, the Earl of Gloucester, and King Art. He describes the king as a fine, large man, marvelously agile, stern and riding on a very swift horse of great value. The discourse lasted some time and led to no agreement. Gloucester demanded Art's surrender to Richard II, to which Art is reported to have replied: "I am rightful king in Ireland, and it is unjust to deprive me of what is my land, by conquest." In fact, King Art, in addition, demanded that Richard II withdraw from his kingdom.[2]

Richard apparently paled with anger on hearing King Art's response and offered a hundred marks for the Irish king alive or dead. He swore he would burn him out of his woods. King Art conducted a war of attrition on the English and, being a good general, refused to enter a major battle in unfavorable conditions. Frustrated and marching back to Waterford, unable to counter the guerrilla tactics of the Irish king, Richard II found grim news awaiting him. His rival, Henry Bolinbroke, Duke of Derby, had returned from exile and raised rebellion against him. Richard II, regarded as the last of the Plantagenet kings of England, sailed home on August 13, 1399, only to surrender to Henry six days later at Flint. After being imprisoned in the Tower of London, Richard II abdicated and Bolinbroke became Henry IV, the first of the House of Lancaster. Richard is said to have met his death by starvation at Pontefract Castle in Yorkshire.

King Art MacMorrough Kavanagh now entered into negotiations with the new English king. Sir John Stanley was the new Lord Deputy in Ireland. Stanley was so great a favorite with Henry IV that he rose to become king of a Gaelic kingdom himself. In 1405 Henry made him "King of Mann and the Isles." The Stanley dynasty lasted on the Isle of Man, with a few interruptions, even after the kingship was changed into a lordship by Henry VIII. This lordship was finally sold to the English Crown in 1765. In March 1400, however, John Stanley reported to his master that King Art was "the most dreaded enemy of the English in Leinster." King Art was so influential that Owain Glyn Dwr (Owen Glendower), trying to restore an independent Welsh kingdom, being a descendant of the kings of Powys, Gwynedd and lords of Deheubarth, was made Prince of Wales. He ruled from 1400 until 1416. He wrote to King Art asking for aid against the English. Glendower's independent Wales finally collapsed the year before King Art died in 1417.

As Edmund Curtis observes of the kingdom of Leinster: "all the country went back to the old race. It was made clear how fatally the Normans had erred in taking over only the richer lands for settlement, and in leaving vast tracts of the hinterland to the Irish, from which in due time they emerged triumphantly."[3]

"The MacMorrough Menace," as the English called the independent-minded Kings of Leinster, was giving such a check to the plans of the colonists that it was felt something had to be done. Sir John de Grey decided that Donnchadh mac Airt Mhoir MacMorrough (1417–abdicated 1455), who had been a hostage of the English, should be returned and set up as king "on certain terms." But within a year after his release Donnchadh was in arms against England, raiding and exacting tribute. King Henry IV finally signed a treaty with him, agreeing to pay Donnchadh an annual tribute of eighty marks for the land under English occupation.

In spite of its proximity to the ports of access from England, Waterford and Wexford, and the Dublin Pale, as well as the consideration that Leinster was the first kingdom in which the Normans settled, the Leinster kings held their kingdom until 1603. There seem to be no record of surrenders until the reign of Caothaoir Mac Airt, who became King of Leinster in 1547 and is recorded as initially being in the forefront of the war against the new Tudor administration. Letters Patent show that many of his followers did surrender and received pardons before the king himself. It is a point of interest that Caothaoir was married to Alicia, daughter of Gerald Óg Fitzgerald, ninth Earl of Kildare, who had been Lord Deputy but died in the Tower of London in 1534 suspected of treason. It was on February 8, 1553, during the reign of Edward VI, that Caothaoir Mac Airt of Leinster came forward and surrendered his kingdom. All he received in return was a barony—he was to be Baron of Ballyanne (Ballian according to the Fiant) in Wexford.

The records of succession show that Caothaoir was regarded as King of Leinster for less than a year after his surrender. He was deposed or abdicated and died around 1557–58 for in 1558 his son Dermot was claiming to be the new Baron Ballyanne by application to Philip and Mary. Another son, Morrough, called Morgan by the English, was claiming to have succeeded his father as the Baron of "Conellelyn" (Coolnaleen, County Wexford). Morrough and another brother, "Keant" Kavanagh, had been imprisoned as hostages to ensure Caothaoir's good behavior at the time he surrendered. It was yet another son, Bryan, who is recorded as succeeding his father as head of his family, although, significantly, not as King of Leinster, and who led the fight against the English colonists.

Murchadh Mac Muiris Kavanagh of Coolnaleen, County Wexford, however, appears as successor to Caothaoir as King of Leinster. There was some confusion as to whether Murchadh was Caothaoir's son. He is described as *Mac Muiris*—son of Muiris and not the son of Caothaoir. Yet we are told that he became Baron Coolnaleen in 1554, the year of his accession to the throne. This is the same title as the one applied for by Murrough, Caothaoir's son. Had the English bureaucrats merely confused the matter in their records through lack of knowledge of Irish and Irish patronymics?

I believe we are talking about two different people because the Letters Patent refer to Murchadh Mac Muiris's family as of "the sept and company of Donell Reagh Cavanagh," who was his grandfather. Murchadh Mac Muiris, having been regarded as King of Leinster between 1554 and 1557, was deposed or abdicated, and died in November 1622. Did the fact that he accepted the title of Baron of Coolnaleen cause the *derbhfine* to depose him?

In 1557 the son of Murchadh Mac Muiris, Criomthann, Anglicized as Crephon in English records, became King of Leinster. Criomthann is listed as King of Leinster until 1582. It becomes significant that, in 1581, several pardons were issued for "Crephon m'Mortagh Kavanagh's people." On July 23

Criomthann was deemed to be principal captain "of the sept and company of Donell reogh Cavanagh . . . with power upon warning from the seneschal or sheriff of County Wexford, to assemble the gentlemen and freeholders of the sept and all others inhabiting their countries, and to govern them according to the laws of the realm."

There is no record of any further Leinster kings until the start of Aodh Ruadh O'Neill's attempt to drive out the English in 1595. Domhnall Spáin-neach Mac Donnchadha, whose name indicated that he had been in exile in Spain, was accepted as king. Domhnall is listed as a grandson of Caothaoir Mac Airt, which would appear to mean that he married his first cousin Elinor, daughter of his uncle Brian Mac Caothaoir. Domhnall commanded the Leinster men, fighting against Elizabeth's forces, but after the defeat at Kinsale and the surrender of O'Neill, he accepted that his situation was untenable. He abdicated his kingship, significantly refusing to surrender on behalf of his heirs and successor nor abandon his royal prerogatives, demonstrating that he acknowledged he could not do so under Brehon law. He abdicated in 1603 and retired with his wife to Clonmullen, where his death was recorded in 1632.

THE MACMORROUGH KAVANAGH, PRINCE OF LEINSTER (MAC MURCHADHA CAOMHÁNACH)

The current MacMorrough Kavanagh, Prince of Leinster, succeeded his father in 1962 at the age of eighteen and is now a retired oil engineer, an Irish citizen, dividing his time between his house in Florida, the United States, and another in Pembroke, Wales. He is planning to relocate to Ireland shortly, where his son Simon lives. His line stems from a younger son of Morgan Kavanagh, The MacMorrough Kavanagh of Borris (1668–1720). This was Hervey Kavanagh of Ballyhale, County Kilkenny (d. 1740).

Confusion about his father's and, subsequently, his own recognition by the Chief Herald was finally cleared up in May 2000, when a missing file was found at the Genealogical Office and an apology was made. "There can be no longer any doubt but that Mr. Slevin recognized your grandfather and, in turn, your father as The MacMorrough Kavanagh," wrote the Chief Herald to Simon MacMorrough Kavanagh, tanist to the Chief.

The line of the MacMorrough Kavanagh Kings of Leinster had descended through Brian, the son of Caothaoir Mac Airt, who became known as The MacMorrough of Borris and Poulmonty. His eldest son was Morgan MacBryan Kavanagh (1566–1636), who married a daughter of Lord Mountgarret, thus making sure he had a good political link with the new colonial order.

The line then proceeded by senior son inheritance.

Thomas Kavanagh, The MacMorrough of Borris (1767–1799), became Member of Parliament for Kilkenny City and subsequently for Carlow, in the Irish Parliament, just before the Union of Ireland with the United Kingdom of Great Britain.

A later generation of the family also entered politics. This was Arthur Kavanagh, The MacMorrough of Borris (1831–89). He was born without arms and legs, only rudimentary stumps, but he showed great resolution in his youth and learned how to ride, shoot, fish and become a fair painter, using his stumps with extraordinary dexterity. He rode to hounds strapped to a chair saddle and even took fences in his stride. His eldest brother, whom he succeeded to the title, was his companion in travels to India, through Russia and Persia, and on a tiger hunt.

Returning to Ireland in 1853, he succeeded his brother to the family estates and to the title. He married his cousin, Frances Mary Forde-Leathley. He was energetic and rebuilt the villages of Borris and Ballyragget and subsidized the local railway from Borris to Bagenalstown. Although the family was by now firmly Anglican in religion, he opposed the disestablishment of the Church of Ireland and he had the New Ross poorhouse provided with a Catholic chapel, the first of its kind in Ireland.

He became High Sheriff of County Kilkenny in 1856 and of Carlow in 1857 and was a Unionist Member of Parliament for County Wexford from 1866 to 1868 and for County Carlow from 1868 to 1880. He was made a Privy Councillor for Ireland in 1886. Surprisingly, he supported the Land Act of 1870, a fact that showed he was out of step with most Unionist and Conservatives. He was also a Justice of the Peace. As an enthusiastic and experienced yachtsman, he sailed his own yacht. In 1865 he published *The Cruise of the RYS Evan*, an account of a cruise along the Albanian coast. He died at his London town house in Chelsea in 1889, and his body was returned to Borris for burial.

He had several children, his third son being General Sir Toler MacMorrough (1864–1950), who served in the British Army during the second South Africa War (1899–1902), in which he won the Distinguished Service Order. For services in World War II he was knighted twice and received several foreign awards. The general's elder brother, the Right Honorable Walter MacMorrough Kavanagh (1856–1922), took the title. He had been educated at Eton and Christ Church, Oxford, and took a commission in the 5th Battalion of the Royal Irish Rifles. He left the army as a captain and followed his father into politics but as a Liberal. He was High Sheriff of County Kilkenny in 1884, and County Wexford in 1893, and a Justice of the Peace. He became Member of Parliament for Carlow from 1908 to 1910. He was also appointed a Privy Councillor. In 1917 he became the representative for Carlow County Council, sitting as a Nationalist in the Irish Convention of 1917–18. He died in July 1922, as Ireland struggled toward independent statehood.

His son, Major Arthur MacMorrough Kavanagh (1888–1953), became The MacMorrough of Borris. Educated at Eton and Sandhurst, he was commissioned in the 7th Queen's Own Hussars and won the Military Cross. Major MacMorrough of Borris died without male issue but with four daughters. The eldest daughter Joane, born in 1915, married twice. Her first marriage was to Gerald, Marquess of Kildare and only child of the seventh Duke of Leinster, by whom she had issue. The marriage was dissolved in 1946. Her second marriage was to Lieutenant Colonel Archibald Macalpine-Downie of Appin. Her son by this marriage, Andrew Macalpine-Downie, became a jockey. He assumed the name MacMorrough Kavanagh by Deed Poll and settled at the family estate at Borris House. When his grandfather died in December 1953, he could not, of course, succeed to the title either in Brehon law tanistry or in primogeniture law. Andrew did claim courtesy recognition, attempting to argue for a retrospective change in successional law inasmuch as modern law now recognizes the right of female inheritance. However, he was informed by the current Chief Herald that his Office was not prepared to depart from its system by which it gave such recognition.[4]

When Major Arthur MacMorrough Kavanagh's title had been recognized, his heir was published as being his brother Sir Dermot. With Irish independence there came another of those ironies that beset Irish history. The lineal descendant of the kings of the first Irish kingdom to be invaded and occupied, Colonel Sir Dermot MacMorrough, was Equerry to George VI of England, Crown Equerry and Extra Equerry to Elizabeth II.

The title, as the family followed a senior male heir practice, technically passed to Sir Dermot between December 1953 and the time of his own death on May 27, 1958. Sir Dermot made no claims and his only child was a daughter. He was the last male line descendant from Morgan Kavanagh and his first wife, France Esmonde.

The next senior branch of the family also descended from Morgan, but through his second wife, Margaret, daughter of Hervey Morres. This was the Ballyhale line started by Hervey Kavanagh, the son of Morgan. Hervey of Ballyhale (d. 1740) had a son Morgan Kavanagh of Ballyhale (d. 1817) who had married Lady Frances Butler, and the name Butler has subsequently occurred as a name in the family. In 1875 Morgan Butler Kavanagh (1845–82) married Katie Shine. Their son Morgan Butler Kavanagh (1876–1919) was born in Dublin and educated at Clongowes Wood College, County Kildare. At the age of twenty, he decided to go to Australia but eventually settled in India as a journalist. His income was apparently augmented by a private allowance from his family. He married to Isabella McKenzie Young in Melbourne in 1906. With the threat of war, he returned to Ireland via the United States where, in February 1914, his son, William Butler Kavanagh, was born in Springfield, Massachusetts. From 1914 to 1918 Morgan served in the British forces. After the war, he returned to India and died shortly after arriving in 1919.

Mrs. Kavanagh and her five-year-old son went to her family's native Scotland to live. William was educated in St. Andrews' University and became a chartered civil engineer, finally settling in Pembroke in Dyfed in South Wales. He became Pembroke Borough Surveyor and in 1939 married Elsie Addis. After the death of his cousin Arthur in 1953, and knowing that Arthur's brother Sir Dermot was elderly and without male heirs, William decided to submit his claim to be MacMorrough Kavanagh to Gerard Slevin, Chief Herald of Ireland. He submitted his claim on September 4, 1958.

The Chief Herald registered William's pedigree and referred to him as MacMorrough Kavanagh, Chief of His Name, in the confirmation of his arms on January 2, 1959.[5] William attended the Chief Herald's office in person on June 19, 1959, to receive his recognition. A pedigree and armorial certificate were issued in March 1960.

William died in 1962 and was succeeded by his son, also William Butler Kavanagh. Writing to Madam MacMorrough Kavanagh on June 26, 1962, Gerard Slevin informed her that on the death of her husband, his eldest son "automatically becomes Chief of the Name according to our records." Slevin attached a note to the *Clar na dTaoiseach* recognizing both father and then his son William Butler Kavanagh as The MacMorrough Kavanagh.[6] William, the son, had been born on February 9, 1944, in Pembroke, and educated locally, attending Shenstone College before entering the oil industry. In July 1965, he married Margaret Phillips, and his sons are Simon (b. 1967) and William (b. 1974). Simon has been appointed his tanist. He was also a professional engineer following a career in the oil industry but in 2000 he moved to Ireland and started a degree course in management studies at Trinity College, Dublin. He married Alison Barnett on December 4, 1999.

William retired from the oil business and divides his time between Florida and Wales. With his sons, who are both learning Irish, he is working on a book about the family history.

Curiously, since the courtesy recognition by the Chief Herald in 1959, the Genealogical Office has given the impression that the line and title were dormant. This led to some embarrassing problems for the family, which we have discussed, namely the statement of "dormancy" made by *Debrett's* and authoritative reference works made apparently with the knowledge of the Genealogical Office. These statements have been used to the humiliation of the family. A clan association refused to admit that the MacMorrough Kavanagh was genuine and still insists on using his personal arms on the association letterheads.

At the beginning of May 2000, the current Chief Herald, Brendan O'Donoghue, summed up his view of the current situation:

> The factual position in relation to MacMorrough Kavanagh is that Mr. William Butler Kavanagh was referred to as "The MacMorrough Kavanagh" in a grant of arms in 1959. A search of the records of the Office for that period has failed, however, to turn up copies of any relevant documents or correspondence relating to this grant. We have asked the present Mr. William Butler Kavanagh to let us have copies of these documents, and we await a reply.
>
> No correspondence can be traced in this Office relating to the recognition of the current William Butler Kavanagh, or his father, as the MacMorrough Kavanagh. There is no entry in *Clár na dTaoiseach* relating to either gentlemen but only a small slip of paper, attached by means of a paperclip, with both names inscribed in what I am told is the hand of Mr. Slevin. We have asked Mr. William Butler Kavanagh to let us have copies of any correspondence or other documents he may have relating to his claim that his recognition as the MacMorrough Kavanagh was confirmed by Mr. Slevin.
>
> Mr. Butler Kavanagh has been seeking the preparation of a new document showing his pedigree and the insertion of this document into *Clár na dTaoiseach*. He has been advised that I am not prepared to make any further entries in *Clár na dTaoiseach* except on the basis of a fresh, rigorous and independent examination of the available evidence and records and, in particular, that I am not prepared to make such an entry on the basis of arms granted or pedigrees registered by one or other of my predecessors unless the documents and evidence on which those decisions were based is available to me for a review.[7]

Obviously, the Genealogical Office was feeling the "fallout" from the "MacCarthy Mór" affair, and perhaps one should applaud the new diligence within the Office. However, by May 22, 2000, the file with all the missing documentation and letters concerning MacMorrough Kavanagh was found and the Chief Herald admitted to Simon MacMorrough Kavanagh that "there can no longer be any doubt but that Mr. Gerard Slevin recongised your grandfather and, in turn, your father as The MacMorrough Kavanagh."

The new diligence does leave many Chiefs who received courtesy recognition from previous Chief Heralds in vulnerable positions. Perhaps the logical outcome of the new procedures is to review the pedigrees and recognitions of every family that has been given such recognition since the Office came into being in 1943.

What is of particular concern is the apparent "mislaying" of documents in the Genealogical Office, not simply those of the MacMorrough Kavanagh but also those of the O'Long of Garranelongy. How many other documentary records have gone missing at the Genealogical Office? The current author has been given access to the copies of these records as held by the families concerned.

That the Genealogical Office became nervous after the revelation of Terence McCarthy's bogus claims is demonstrated by the fact that the Deputy Chief Herald, Fergus Gillespie, had no problems addressing his correspondence to "MacMorrough Kavanagh" until July 1999. Thereafter, the form of address reverted to "*Mr.* William Butler Kavanagh."

The historian Nicholas Furlong, who has corresponded with the MacMorrough Kavanaghs since the 1970s, wrote to William Butler Kavanagh that, while he was researching his book between 1970 and 1976, he contacted Gerard Slevin on the matter of the succession of MacMorrough Kavanagh. He then believed that Andrew MacMorrough Kavanagh was head of the family. He was invited to the Genealogical Office by Slevin who told him that William Butler Kavanagh was the recognized head of the family and was shown the documentation of the Ballyhale line by Slevin. These documents, which the Genealogical Office now claimed were missing, were clearly in the Office in the early 1970s. In fact, in 1986, when Furlong published *Foster Son for a King*, he wrote: "It is of unusual interest that the descendant of Dermot and inheritor of the title 'The MacMurrough-Kavanagh' resides today in Pembroke."[8]

The MacMorrough Kavanagh admits that his family's claims to the title is based on being the senior surviving line of the royal house and is aware that Brehon law succession does not exclude such a claim. Yet he admits that his knowledge of the current legal situation in international law is insufficient to take any authoritative stand on the matter.

> It seems that the recognition of Chiefship accorded in Brehon Law may also be interpreted within European Law. Therefore this allows for a Chiefship to be recognized from the senior line of a family, by the senior member or members of that family. It is my present understanding that within my family, recognition of my own Chiefship, as successor to my father, gains recognition on this basis.

With his sons learning Irish, his plans to relocate his main residence to Ireland, and as an Irish citizen himself, MacMorrough Kavanagh is keen to play a full part as a member of the old Gaelic aristocracy:

Having been brought up in Wales, where the issue of language is an important facet in the cultural identity of the people, I can entirely sympathize with the problems encountered in Ireland today when trying to promote the use of the Gaelic language in daily life. Although English has become the international language used between nations to communicate, the identity of a nation may be more fully expressed within its own language. My sons are endeavoring to learn the Irish language, partly as an aid to their studies, but also the more they learn about their own history, the more determined they are to participate in its future. Language has its part to play in their endeavors, as they wish to spend an increasing amount of time in Ireland pursuing their studies.

It is only during the past few years that MacMorrough Kavanagh has started to become interested in gaining a higher profile for his dynasty and working with other surviving members of the Irish aristocracy. He says that he was previously disillusioned by the problems encountered at the Genealogical Office when no move had been made to correct the statements that his line had become dormant. Once the Genealogical Office finally confirmed the acceptance of his existence, he and his family became more involved in a more active form. "It is my hope, that with the recognition of the MacMorrough Kavanagh and the ancient Royal House of Leinster . . . we may then act as a catalyst for others with similar interests." Those interests, he stresses, are to take any opportunity that allows the promotion of the culture and heritage of Ireland. "I have always endeavored to promote the cultural and historical background through which the Chiefs hold their titles and will continue to do so."

THE O'MORCHOE OF OULARTLEIGH AND MONAMOLIN (Ó MORCHOE)

This cadet line of the princely house of the royal dynasty of the Uí Cheinnselaig takes its name from Murchadha, or Morrough, but in this instance, the Anglicized transmission of the name was in the form "Murphy." It is generally thought that the branch started out from the descendants of Morrough, the brother of King Dermot MacMorrough. Historian Alfred Smyth, in *Celtic Leinster*, believes that the split goes farther back to the Murchadha, a grandson of Fedlimid son of Énna Cennselach, whose branch became the Uí Felmeda that appears, in some annals, as the original designation of O'Morchoe chieftains in the sixteenth century.[9]

The ninth Earl of Kildare, when Lord Deputy in 1518, demanded taxes from "The M'Morrow country at Oulartleigh." (The name comes from the stem *abhallort*—an apple orchard.) On May 10, 1536, Donel Mór O'Morchoe of Oulartleigh entered into an agreement with the Lord Deputy, Leonard Grey, that he would agree to hold his country with feudal dues to Henry VIII if the English king maintained him in his "lordship."

In 1536, in keeping with the surrender agreements, Donal O'Morchoe had changed his name to the Anglicized form of Daniel Murphy and adopted the Anglican religion. This was even before the official policy for the surrender of Gaelic titles. He and his descendants lived quietly at Oulartleigh, but when the English administration during 1618 was sorting out what they called "defective titles," Brian Murphy (O'Morchoe) was made to agree to a deed of entail and the lands went to his son in trust. However, all the lands were forfeited because of the family's participation in the 1641 Irish uprising.

In more liberal times in the late nineteenth century, Arthur MacMorrough Murphy (1835–1918) decided to reassert the title abolished by English law over four hundred years previously and call himself O'Morchoe of Oulartleigh. Indeed, the family in 1892 commissioned H. Farnham Burke, Somerset Herald, to devise the pedigree for the family.

Arthur's eldest son, the Reverend Thomas Arthur MacMorrough Murphy (1864–1921), a graduate of Trinity College, went further than his father. He resumed the surname of O'Morchoe by Deed Poll on September 3, 1895. He was an Anglican minister and was rector of Kilternan, County Dublin (1894–1921). He was fascinated by historical issues and became a member of the Royal Society of Antiquaries of Ireland, a member of the Royal Dublin Society, served on the Dublin County Committee of Agriculture and Technical Instruction and was on the Board of Education as well as being a member of the General Synod of the Church of Ireland.

He seemed confused between his enthusiasm to reestablish the use of Gaelic titles, including his own, and his loyalty to the English Crown.

In 1904 he published a booklet "The Succession of the Chiefs of Ireland." In this he argued eloquently for the English Crown to recognize the old Gaelic titles. But he was not knowledgeable about Brehon law succession and thought tanistry was merely a transitional stage between election by the *derbhfine* to primogeniture descent. He also believed that the Tudor policy was not to *abolish* Gaelic titles, in spite of the evidence to the contrary. For entirely the wrong reasons, he argued:

> That the representatives of the former Chiefs at the present day are justified and within their rights in assuming the titles of their ancestors is supported by the numerous precedents quoted, in which the Crown (of England) recognizes the titles of native nobility in countries which have come under British rule.

The Reverend Arthur O'Morchoe referred to an official list of the Irish nobles and their titles made in 1515 as a list of the "Chief Captains of Ireland."[10] This roll, he felt, was a starting point for gathering evidence to judge claims. He believed a list of Chiefs should be drawn up and registered in the office of the Ulster King of Arms.

> Once the right to the use of titles shall have been determined by the official act of the Crown, it becomes only a question of the proof of the claimants pedigree that he is the lineal male representative of the last recognized Chief. To determine the right to the use of the titles rests with the Crown as the Fountain of Honour; and although the titles have been recognized by courtesy at the Royal and Viceregal Courts, yet the absence of any official act either to determine the right to their use or to accord them a definite precedent, as in the cause of the Maltese Nobles, leaves the matter in an unsatisfactory state, which only the Crown can settle.

When he died on November 18, 1921, he had seen that the English Crown was already becoming a matter of little importance in most of the country.

His eldest son, another Arthur Donel (b. 1892), educated at St. Andrew's College, Dublin, and Trinity College, Dublin, joined the Leinster Regiment in 1914, serving as aide-de-camp to Major General the Honorable Edward Montagu Stewart Wortley (1917–19). He held various military posts, ending his career as Commissioner of Police on the Gold Coast 1934. He served on the British General Staff at the War Office in 1940. He died in 1966 and was succeeded by his brother.

Nial Creagh O'Morchoe (1895–1970) was also educated in St. Andrews College and was commissioned into the Leinster Regiment in 1914. Mentioned in dispatches while serving in India, Colonel O'Morchoe commanded in the 4th Battalion of the 15th Punjab Regiment from 1939 to 1941. He served in Iraq, Persia and India until 1946 and retired in 1947. He had married Jesse Elizabeth Joly, the daughter of Charles Jasper Joly, the Astronomer Royal of Ireland. He died in 1970, leaving two sons.

The current O'Morchoe, David Niall Creagh O'Morchoe (b. May 17, 1928), Nial's eldest son, followed the military tradition of his immediate family. He is a former Major General of the British Army. Commissioned in the Royal Irish Fusiliers in 1948, having been educated in St. Columba's College, Dublin and the Royal Military Academy of Sandhurst, he commanded the 1st Battalion of the regiment in 1967/ 68 and saw service in the Middle East, northwest Europe, Kenya and Oman. He was Director of Staff at the Camberley Staff College in 1969 and the Royal College of Defence Studies in 1972. He commanded the Sultan of Oman's Land Forces, retiring in 1979 with an MBE (Member of the Order of the British Empire) and CB (Companion of the Bath). He is now a farmer in County Wexford, his ancestral territory.

Married to Margaret Jane Brewitt of Cork, he has two sons and two daughters. His heir is Dermot Arthur, born on August 11, 1956, who also was educated at St. Columba's College. Dermot's occupation is a horticulturist. The current O'Morchoe is also a Fellow of St. Columba's College. His hobby is sailing.

He sees the holding of an old Gaelic title

> as important solely as being of great historic interest. The rest of Ireland is so ignorant and ill-educated about the current chiefs that I think that the idea of representation in the Senate or other state bodies would be a non starter and not understood. Collectively we have no political role, particularly as there are so few of us who are able to trace our ancestry to the days when Chiefs had power.

He sees his role as a chief as being to create an interest in Gaelic heritage. He supports the teaching of Irish as a means of maintaining an important part of Irish heritage. He learned the Irish language at school and hopes that his grandchildren will continue to speak it. He supports various cultural activities.

As a member of the Church of Ireland, he does not agree with the state giving special recognition to one particular religious denomination.

He was chairman of the Standing Council of Chiefs and Chieftains, taking over from Maguire, Prince of Fermanagh, from 1994 to 1998.

THE FOX (AN SIONNACH)

Douglas John Fox runs a delicatessen shop in Mildura, Victoria, Australia. The surname has a very English appearance and, as such, excites little attention or interest among the majority of his customers. Very few of them realize that he is entitled to be called The Fox, Chief of the Name, or that he is given courtesy recognition by the Chief Herald of Ireland as heir male and direct descendant of a line of princes and petty kings whose genealogies claim to go back to Eremon, son of Míle Easpain, a thousand years before Christ. Even if one finds the pre-Christian genealogies unreliable, Douglas Fox is still a direct descendant of the famous Irish King Niall of the Nine Hostages (d. ca. A.D. 405).

It should be pointed out, of course, that not all Irish Fox's are descendants from the family that took the nickname *Sionnach* (Fox) as their surname in the eleventh century. Many who bear the surname Fox are of English settler families, so care has to be taken with lineage. When the name *Sionnach* was translated to its English equivalent Fox in the sixteenth century, it may be said that the princely family, in spite of their ancient Gaelic lineage, quickly accepted the conquest and changed their religion, language and name to become part of the new English order in Ireland. The Fox's have the unenviable place in Irish history as the first Gaelic nobles that we know of to completely Anglicize themselves.

Yet there is no questioning the ancient Gaelic pedigree of The Fox.

Niall Naoi-Ghiallach was the eponymous ancestor of the Uí Néill, the family that was to dominate in many of the kingdoms of Ireland except in Munster. Ancient Irish literature gives a detailed, although accepted as mythological, account of his career.

Of Niall's sons, Maine established one of the southern Uí Néill dynasties. Maine was a fairly popularly name at the time. Maine is recorded as dying in A.D. 440, having founded the kingship of Tethbae (sometimes Anglicized as Teffia), a territory covering modern Counties Longford and Westmeath.

The descendants of Maine are referred to until after the Norman invasion as "Kings of Tethbae." Sometime before the eleventh century, the dynasty took as their surname Ó Catharnaigh (O'Kearney or Carney) from one of the Kings of Tethbae named Catharnaigh. In 1084 the annals record that Tadhg Ó Catharnaigh was nicknamed *An Sionnach* (The Fox) because of his wily ways. He was killed with one of his sons that year in a battle by High King Maelseachlin O'Melaghlin. It was from Tadhg Ó Catharnaigh that his descendants added the nickname as a patronymic. An Sionnach became Chief of the Clann Catharnaigh.

The influence of the family as providing Kings of Tethbae eventually waned. It was Tairrdelbach Ua Conchobair, the High King (d. 1156), who partitioned the kingdom in 1140, giving Westmeath to Donogh MacMorrough O'Melaghlin and East Meath to Tigernan Ó Ruairc of Breifne. Nevertheless, we still find the annalists and chroniclers referring to An Sionnach as "kings of Tethbae" as late as 1234, when Néill An Sionnach is reported killed in a skirmish. In 1400 we find Donogh An Sionnach referred to as "lord of the country of Moyntir, and by right prince of the country of Tethbae."

By 1526 there was another change. An Sionnach, who had been fairly independent princes, were now referred to as merely Chiefs. They and their followers were seen as vassals to The Mac Eochagáin (MacEgan). From rulers of a petty kingdom they had been reduced to princes and then lords of a small clan territory, known as "the country of An Sionnach," which was centered in the barony of Kilcoursey.

In 1541 it appears that An Sionnach and his clan initially resisted the conquest. On June 13, 1558, Sir Henry Radcliffe was given a commission to enter into negotiation with The Fox, as the English now called An Sionnach, translating the name rather than merely Anglicizing it as happened elsewhere. The commission also gave Sir Henry permission to accept The Fox's surrender and, if he did not do so, to "punish with fire and sword."

On April 1, 1559, the Tudor administration in Ireland granted a pardon to Brassell (Breasail) Shennaghe (An Sionnach), "alias The Fox," "Chief of his Nation" and his wife, sons and members of his clan. On November 8, 1565, they were granted "English liberties." Breasal's pardon was further confirmed on October 8, 1567. From then on, the title An Sionnach was dropped and the English translation "The Fox" was always used. The original name still appears, however, in the motto of the arms of the family—"Sionnach Aboo!" (The Fox Forever!).

On June 26, 1591, with the English conquests continuing, we find the administration issuing a grant to Hubert Fox *Gentleman* as seneschal of Fox's County called "Mointerragan" in King's County (County Offaly) "to hold during good behaviour." On March 1, 1599, Hubert Fox, of Lehinch, in the barony of Kilcoursey, King's County, surrendered all manors and baronies to the Tudor administration. On April 4, 1600, under a Letter Patent of January 29, a portion of lands were regranted back to Hubert as "seneschal" and he was allowed to hold a monthly court baron and a court leet twice a year. By the same letter, Hubert was granted a pension of five shillings sterling a day for life. This was an extraordinary sum for the period and one wonders what exactly Hubert had done to earn it from the conquerors.

Hubert, The Fox, was succeed by his nephew, who died within a few months. Against the background of the wars, there is, alas, no record of where and how these members of the Fox family met their deaths. The succession went to Brassil (d. 1629), and he was succeeded by Hubert of Kilcoursey. This Hubert appears as a supporter of the Irish uprising in 1641 and the establishment of the Irish Confederate Parliament in Kilkenny. With the reconquest by England, the great part of his estates granted during the Tudor conquests were confiscated and given to the Earl of Cavan.

From now on The Fox became a title secretly passed down within the family. The family had become Irish Protestant petty gentry who produced doctors, army officers, even an inspector of the Royal Irish Constabulary and whose daughters tended to marry regularly into the Anglican clergy.

The Reverend Matthew Maine Fox, the rector of Galtrim, County Meath (1804), was the eldest son of James Fox, The Fox of Foxbrooke and Galtrim House, County Meath (1773–1850). He was succeeded by his grandson James George Hubert as The Fox (1842–1919). James George Hubert began his career as an officer in the 5th Royal Irish Lancers. He became a Justice of the Peace for County Tipperary and his first marriage was to the daughter of the Anglican rector of Rathconrath, County Westmeath. He married a second time to a daughter of George Ogle Moore, Member of Parliament for the City of Dublin. His eldest son, Brabazon Hubert Maine (b. 1868), succeeded to the title in 1930 on his father's death. Brabazon was a major in the Royal Irish Rifles. He married the daughter of Colonel William Le Mottée of Fermoy, County Cork. His son Nial Arthur Hubert Fox (b. 1897) succeeded to the title. He died in 1959 in Cork without issue.

In tracing the next in line to the title, the family went back to James Fox, The Fox of Foxbrooke and Galtrim House (1773–1850). His third son, James D'Arcy, had married Sara Tarrant of Mallow, County Cork, in 1835 and emigrated to New Zealand in 1863. When he died in 1876, he left a son named Brassil (1844–1913), who then settled in New South Wales, Australia. His son James George (1873–1957) also married, and it was his third son who now aspires to the title The Fox.

With the death of Nial Arthur Hubert Fox, The Fox, in Ireland in 1959, the seat of The Fox changed to Koorlong, Victoria, Australia, when John William Fox succeeded to the title. John was a poultry farmer, born in Tempy and educated at Gipson State School. He had been born on August 22, 1916. He married Margaret Frances Wilson in 1939 and had five children, a daughter and four sons.

Today, John, of course, is elderly, and, since the death of his wife in 1997, takes no interest in his ancestral heritage. It was, therefore, decided in early 1998 that the family would resort to the Brehon way of doing things. With the approval of the family (*derbhfine*), John's eldest son and tanist, Douglas John, born on August 23, 1942, assumed the title and duties of The Fox. Douglas was born in Mildura and went to St. Joseph's College there. The family is Catholic, which is a strange twist, as the Irish branch, which was Anglicized in Tudor times, had now changed back to Catholics through the influence of their distaff side. He is married to Marjorie Adeline and has four children, three sons, of which Garry John (b. 1964) has now become his tanist.

Douglas John is a small businessman, running his delicatessen shop in Mildura, and does not seem overly enthusiastic about his role as a lineal heir to the Gaelic title he holds. The new Fox, however, freely admits that he has little knowledge of matters Irish although "would like to see the preservation of the Irish language." The Fox and his family are decidedly Australian and are happy to be so. Neither his father John William nor Douglas John has ever attempted to take their seat on the Standing Council of Irish Chiefs and Chieftains.

In fact, Douglas John admits, they have never visited Ireland nor is he involved in any Irish cultural endeavors in Australia. However, he does feel that,
as the bearer of an Irish title, he would like to hold an Irish passport if the law
allowed it; and, business concerns willing, he would like to make a trip to the
land of his origins. At the same time, he seems undaunted by the courtesy
recognition of his title by the Chief Herald of Ireland, and by the facts that his
banner hangs in the Heraldic Museum in Dublin and the ancient genealogies
of Ireland give him a generation by generation lineage back to Adam. Nor is he
unduly impressed by the fact that he is the male heir in an unbroken descent
from some of the famous Uí Néill kings of Ireland. The concern of the current
holder of the title The Fox, of a family who were sometime kings and princes
of Tethbae, is running his deli in Mildura and the welfare of his immediate
Australian family rather than the wider concerns of his Irish clan.

PART THREE

RANK AND MERIT

CHAPTER TWELVE

"THE MACCARTHY MÓR AFFAIR"

THE MOST DEVASTATING BLOW TO THE CREDIBILITY of the Irish Gaelic Chiefs in modern times was the revelation that their most outspoken and highest profile representative was a fraud. The foreword of this volume has enumerated the honors and patronage that Terence McCarthy, as The MacCarthy Mór, Prince of Desmond and Lord of Kerslawny, received not just in Ireland but throughout the world. He contributed the original foreword to the first edition of this book, which was in print when the news of his fraud was announced.

On July 13, 1999, after an exhaustive two-year investigation, Brendan O'Donoghue, Chief Herald of Ireland, wrote to John G. O'Donnell of Tipperary, the solicitor acting for Terence McCarthy, to state that the portion of the pedigree of the MacCarthys of Srugrena, County Kerry, relating to Terence McCarthy's alleged descent from that family via his great-great-grandfather, registered by the Office in 1980, was "without genealogical integrity." Therefore, the confirmation of arms made by the Office in 1979 was declared invalid and the "courtesy recognition" of Terence McCarthy as MacCarthy Mór, Chief of the Name, made in 1992, was null and void.

On July 21, 1999, the Chief Herald made his decision public.

Even before the Chief Herald's announcement, the *Sunday Times* (Irish edition) of June 20, 1999, had carried a report that Terence McCarthy was bogus. However, Terence had been subtly building up a group of supporters by implying that his outspoken advocacy of Brehon law succession of Gaelic titles was the key reason why he was being attacked by "vested interests" that supported the state's line on primogeniture succession only. Even after the Chief

Herald's statement, Terence McCarthy had so confused the issues at stake that many who had closely followed the affair, including the current author, continued to believe his persuasive argument that support of Brehon law was the crux of the conflict. Because of this confusion, the Chief Herald had to issue a further statement in mid-August 1999, explaining that his withdrawal of the courtesy recognition had nothing to do with any conflict of the principles of legal succession but was based solely and exclusively on the integrity of Terence McCarthy's pedigree.

The implications of this were staggering. How could such an imposture, with its worldwide consequences, have been allowed to come about? This chapter will attempt to explain the story.[1]

Terence McCarthy was the second son of Thomas McCarthy, a Belfast dance teacher, and Harriet Maguire, a typist, who were married in the city on July 20, 1955. Terence was born on January 21, 1957, at the Antrim House Nursing Home, 60 Cliftonville Road, in north Belfast. His parents were then living nearby at 59 Harcourt Drive. Terence would later boast of being born at Antrim House, giving the impression that it was a stately country house. He had an elder brother, three younger brothers and a sister. His registered name was simply Terence, although he later affected the name Terence Francis and, from October 1999 he writes from Tangier as "Dr. Terence Francis Justin McCarthy."

In his entry in *Debrett's*, Terence claims to have been privately educated. In fact, he attended The Holy Child Primary School in Andersonstown. His family was then living in Waterford Street, off the Falls Road. In 1968, on reaching secondary school age, he went to La Salle Boys' School at Edenmore Drive, Ladybrook, Belfast 11. This was an intermediate school, and, at the time, it usually took children who had failed their entrance examination into a grammar school.

Terence left this school in 1973, a week after he reached his sixteenth birthday, the legal minimum age for leaving school. He started work but also enrolled as a part-time student at Brunswick Street College, central Belfast, which is now part of the Belfast Institute of Further and Higher Education. He was there between 1973 and 1976 and managed to obtain his school leaving certificates. He was thus able to apply for a place at university, and he succeeded in entering the Department of Modern History at Queen's University, Belfast. One of his tutors was Professor A. T. Q. Stewart. He took his BA (Hons.) in 1980 and followed this in 1983 with his master's degree. His master's thesis was, significantly, on the history of the former main Irish heraldic office, the Office of the Ulster King of Arms. He later expanded his dissertation into a book entitled *Ulster's Office 1552–1800* (1996), which contained some forceful criticism of the Irish Genealogical Office, which had replaced Ulster's Office in Dublin in 1943.

In other circumstances, his educational achievement would be very laudable, except for the false claims with which he later surrounded himself.

Far from being a descendant of the royal MacCarthy family of Munster, and far from his father and grandfather being befriended by the monarchs and ex-monarchs and nobility of Europe who showered them with knighthoods and honors, Terence's family was a poor, Belfast working-class family who were mainly laborers and of whom several were illiterate, as demonstrated by the X's with which they witnessed their signatures on official documents. Even Terence's grandmother, a former mill worker who died in 1962, was illiterate. The addresses given on the birth, death and marriage certificates for those generations of the family that have been identified demonstrate that they lived in extremely poor quarters of Belfast in what can be termed as "slum tenements." This is no reflection on them, but it does reflect on the grandiose claims that Terence subsequently made for them.

Terence claimed that his grandfather, Thomas, was recognized by the kings and princes of Europe as "The MacCarthy Mór, Prince of Desmond, Lord of Kerslawny," and "privately educated at home." In fact, he had been raised in a tenement building in Stream Mill Lane, a tiny dockside slum area that, it may be said, many Belfast men hesitated to visit after dark. And in this tenement slum, Terence assures us, the McCarthy family of laborers managed to keep some forty-two ancestral portraits, not to mention the royal regalia of the Kings of Munster, treasures unknown prior to 1990, which Terence later gave on permanent loan to the Cashel Heritage Museum, an exhibition that has since been removed.

It was on May 6, 1977, that Terence McCarthy, then living with his parents at 12 Gardenmore Drive, on the council housing estate of Twinbrook, Dunmurray, first wrote to the Genealogical Office in Dublin asking for help in researching his family history. He enclosed a check for £4 for two hours' research. He was then approaching the end of his first year at Queen's University. A fellow student, Charles McKerrell, a Scottish Chief styled McKerrell of Hillhouse, says that around this time Terence joined the university's Monarchist and Heraldic Club. His correspondence with the Genealogical Office indicates that he was developing social pretensions; perhaps this is understandable in view of his background. It was obvious from his first letter that he had already read Samuel Trant McCarthy's book *The MacCarthys of Munster,* and he suggests that one of his Belfast ancestors might have arrived from "Cork," as if implying that the Genealogical Office should make a connection.

His knowledge of heraldry was obviously poor at this time for, on December 1, 1977, he wrote to the Chief Herald, Gerard Slevin, asking if he could inherit a coat of arms from a maternal line; the arms in question, he says, were those of the family of his great-grandmother, Bridgit McKeown, his mother's paternal grandmother. There is little need to point out that had his father and his grandfather been MacCarthy Mórs, Terence would not have felt the necessity to derive a coat of arms from his great-grandmother, even if such a thing had been possible. He would have been well aware of his own right of arms. Yet, in his letter he explains that he has no proof of the existence of this coat of arms, as it had been on a tomb that was destroyed when "the family vault was levelled by the Belfast Corporation." Other records, he alleged, had been destroyed during a fire in the family home. This would not be the last time such "crucial evidence" would be claimed to have been destroyed in such a fashion, although later the alleged destruction would occur on his father's business premises. Terence suggests that family and friends might simply supply "affidavits" saying the arms had existed. In response the Chief Herald had to explain the principles of heraldry.

On January 29, 1979, two years later, Terence made a formal application for a grant of arms based on the arms of the MacCarthys of Munster. At this stage, had Terence's father and grandfather been MacCarthy Mórs, then they would have already been armigerous and a grant of arms would have been unnecessary. However, Terence filled in the official form with a covering letter on February 6, 1979. On August 27 of that year, he even went so far to ask for the grant of arms to be backdated to include his grandfather.

Terence's submission was that his family descended from the MacCarthys of Srugrena Abbey, Cahersiveen, County Kerry, and that his great-great-grandfather was Daniel, the third son of Jeremiah McCarthy of Srugrena, who had married in 1788. Jeremiah, in turn, was the second son of Andrew McCarthy of Srugrena, of the direct line of Teig na Mainistreach, MacCarthy Mór, King of Desmond, (d. ca. 1410).

This was the start of the gradual transformation of Terence McCarthy into a European prince.

In presenting his submissions to the Genealogical Office, Terence claimed that his family documents and papers had been variously destroyed by flood, fire or bomb explosions in 1971, 1973 or 1976. He does not appear to have maintained any consistency on this point. Terence claimed to have managed to make written copies of several letters, which before the originals were destroyed were essential to proving his claims. He sent these handwritten copies to the Genealogical Office with no independent evidence of the existence of the originals.

In retrospect, the inconsistencies of the dates and methods of destruction were glaring. In the submission made on his behalf by his solicitor, John G.

O'Donnell of Tipperary, on October 20, 1998, an attempt was made to tidy them up. It was claimed "almost all his family's papers . . . had been destroyed by an IRA bomb attack in 1971 on his father's principal business premises (the Club Cordova, Upper North Street, Belfast. . . .)" In the same submission, however, the address is stated at North Street and the year as 1971/2. The same submission claimed that the Club Cordova was a "nightclub" and that his father owned another nightclub called Tudor Hall, in Royal Avenue, Belfast.

Terence's solicitor suggested that this information could be easily checked. This author took up that challenge. Research attempting to find a Club Cordova in Upper North Street or a Tudor Hall nightclub in Royal Avenue at that time produced no sign of their existence; nor was there any evidence of the destruction of the Club Cordova by a bomb attack. What emerged is that between 1950 and 1952 there was a Tudor Hall Restaurant at 55 Royal Avenue, above a laundry shop called the 60 Minute Cleaners. From 1953/54 the restaurant was replaced by the Strain School of Ballroom Dancing. In 1955 the premises were vacant and then, in 1956, Thomas McCarthy, the dance teacher and father of Terence, opened his McCarthy Dance Studio there. In 1967 the McCarthy Dance Studios (a plural form is now used) removed to 170 Upper North Street, sharing the premises with clothiers and a wholesale bookseller. *The Belfast and Northern Ireland Directory*'s professional and trades section locates Thomas McCarthy's dance studio at the same address until 1983, when the Manor Snooker Club moved into the premises. Thomas McCarthy would have been seventy years old in 1983, and he probably retired at this time. On his wife's death certificate in October 1987, he is described as "a dance teacher (retired)."

In Terence's story this second-floor dance studio was a nightclub and ballroom and one of two that his father was supposed to have owned in 1971, where he "taught European princes and international celebrities."[2] The premises certainly seemed to have survived the floods, fire and explosion that Terence visited upon it at various times.

The most pivotal of the copies of the alleged documents sent to the Chief Herald on April 14, 1980, was that of a letter purportedly written by Samuel Trant McCarthy, who was acknowledged by the Ulster King of Arms, Sir Arthur Vicars, as the senior surviving head of the MacCarthy family and whose pedigree was listed in *Burke's Landed Gentry of Ireland* and then in *Thom's Directories* as The MacCarthy Mór. The rule of the Genealogical Office was that courtesy recognition would be given to the senior male heir descendant from the last acknowledged Chief of the Name.

Terence's intention was initially to prove that he had such credentials, that he was Samuel's heir. The copy of the letter Terence presented is dated February

23, 1923, at Srugrena Abbey, Cahersiveen, County Kerry. It purports to show that Samuel Trant is acknowledging a letter from Terence's grandfather, Thomas, recognizing his family as being a cadet branch of his own Srugrena line and apologizing for leaving this Belfast branch out of his book, *The Mac-Carthys of Munster* (1922). Furthermore, the letter assures Thomas that the "Belfast line" would be included in any future editions. Terence told the Chief Herald that Samuel Trant later nominated his grandfather as his successor and Thomas became The MacCarthy Mór on Samuel Trant's death in 1927.

There were several things wrong about this letter that, surprisingly, were not picked up by the Chief Herald at the time. The most glaring error was that Samuel Trant did not live at Srugrena Abbey in 1923. He had sold it in 1920 and was then living at Highcliffe Hotel, Folkestone, Kent, in England. It was from here that Samuel Trant wrote several letters to Trinity College, Dublin, about his 1922 book, which he had sent as a gift to Trinity College library. The sale of Srugrena Abbey is well documented.[3] Next, Samuel Trant generally signed his letters as "S. T. McCarthy," not "Samuel Trant McCarthy," as given on the letter. However, the final flaw was that while *The MacCarthys of Munster* was never republished until Terence produced his annotated version in 1997, Samuel Trant did write a second book on the MacCarthys of Munster, entitled *A MacCarthy Miscellany*, published just after his death in 1928.[4] That book is conspicuously silent on the McCarthys of Belfast.

However, Terence's claim to be a member of the Srugrena line was funda-mental to the Genealogical Office's recognition of his family pedigree in 1979 and 1980 and to the final courtesy recognition of his title in 1992. In fact, it was in answer to "this evidence" that Gerard Slevin, the Chief Herald, wrote on May 9, 1980, to Terence:

> Taking the evidence and the circumstances into account I think the pedigree from Daniel McCarthy of Belfast to the present day is acceptable. An obvious difficulty arises out of the identification of this Daniel with Daniel son of Jere-miah McCarthy and Ellinor Segerson. How do we know they are one and the same? The identification would appear to depend solely on the copy made by you of Samuel Trant McCarthy's letter of 1923.

Seeking to reassure the Chief Herald, Terence replied on May 12, enclosing some further handwritten copies made before the originals were allegedly de-stroyed. These purported to show that Daniel had moved from Kerry to Belfast. One, said to have been a fragment of a letter written in 1826, is sup-posed to be from Andrew McCarthy of Lative to his brother Daniel in Belfast, asking when Daniel will bring his new bride to visit them and giving details of the expectation of a good crop that year on his farm.

Unfortunately for the composer of this letter, the real Daniel had inherited a farm at Lative next door to his brother Andrew. Consequently, Daniel was neither in Belfast nor in need of a report on crop expectations in the area. The details of Jeremiah McCarthy's will and the location of Daniel of Lative were actually printed in *A MacCarthy Miscellany*.

It is worth pointing out that even had Daniel of the Srugrena line been the progenitor of Terence's family, which he was decidedly not, he represented only a cadet branch to the main Srugrena branch of which Samuel Trant Mc-Carthy, descending from Andrew's first son, was the senior head. Under the Genealogical Office's rules, any primogenitive male heir of Samuel Trant Mc-Carthy would be senior to a cadet branch. This was undoubtedly why Terence was later to swing to Brehon law succession.

At this time, however, Terence's claim was that Daniel (b. ca. 1790) had moved from Kerry to Belfast and married a Bella Collins in 1825. A son John was claimed as Terence's great-great-grandfather. No documentary evidence was found that Daniel of Lative ever went to Belfast, that he married a Bella Collins, or that he had a son John who married a Mary Corrigan. In other words, as pronounced by the Chief Herald, Brendan O'Donoghue, Terence's entire claim was without genealogical integrity.

Terence's genuine pedigree could be traced back, with any degree of relia-bility, only to his great-grandfather, James McCarthy, whose earliest appear-ance is on his son Hugh's birth certificate in August 1870, when he was a dock laborer working in London's East End. James had married a Maria Mont-gomery. After returning to Belfast, with Maria presumably dead, he married Mary Anne Early. It is on this record of his second marriage that we find James's parents given as Bernard and Mary McCarthy.

Another problem now was obvious and one that should have been insur-mountable according to the rules that the Genealogical Office was supposed to have adopted. The Genealogical Office used a system of primogeniture, recog-nizing the eldest male heir descendant from the last recognized title holder. The tenuous claims of descent from the McCarthys of Srugrena aside, in the generations of Terence's provable family tree, Terence does not represent the senior line of even his own family. Terence himself had an older brother, who had four sons. Terence's father, Thomas, was still alive in January 2000, and he himself had two older brothers. Terence's grandfather had three older brothers, and even his great-grandfather is recorded as having three older brothers. All these senior male lines had male offspring.

It becomes clear that the Genealogical Office did not follow its own rules concerning Terence's eventual recognition. Perhaps it is not uncharitable to suggest that it was at this point that Terence became firmly committed to the old Gaelic law of succession, as enshrined in the Brehon laws, the ancient laws of Ireland, which we have already discussed.

Having mentioned Terence's elder brother, Anthony, normal ethics might cause one to observe that his career and death have no bearing on Terence's claims and are best forgotten for the sake of his widow and children. It was inevitable that the press and media would seize upon the case of Anthony McCarthy in any discussion of Terence's "princely career." As many of the accounts were distorted, it is right that some corrections should be made.

Anthony McCarthy was born on December 30, 1955. He married a local Belfast girl in April 1979, when he was working as a storeman. On his four sons' birth certificates, his occupation is given variously as a dispatch clerk, security officer, security guard, a laborer (on his death certificate) and then an "electrical engineer" when Terence supplied details for the birth certificate of his brother's fourth son, born after Anthony's death.

The manner of Anthony's death in 1987 was highly dramatic. He was shot in an internal Irish National Liberation Army (INLA) feud in West Belfast on March 15 of that year. He was acknowledged as a republican and far left socialist—an unlikely person to sign himself "Prince" Andrew McCarthy, despite a paper subsequently produced by Terence, said to have been signed in 1980.

In their book on the INLA, two respected journalists, Jack Holland and Henry McDonald, recorded that Anthony was nicknamed "Boot" McCarthy for obvious reasons.[5] He had been a member of the INLA but resigned in 1977. He had been a school friend of Gerard Steenson, the former INLA leader known as "Doctor Death" to the Royal Ulster Constabulary, even though Steenson was two years his junior. Anthony remained his close friend during the period that Steenson led a breakaway group from the INLA known as the Irish People's Liberation Organization (IPLO). This split had led to a feud. Steenson had been jailed for life but released on appeal based on the fact that the principal witness was a police informer. On Steenson's release the feud between the INLA and IPLO escalated and resulted in ten deaths and eleven woundings.

On the night of March 14/15, 1987, Steenson and Anthony McCarthy were reported to have been drinking in the Washington Bar in Belfast. Just before midnight they climbed into Steenson's red Volkswagen with the intention of going to Ballymurphy. It was subsequently revealed that a Browning pistol and a Scorpion machine pistol were found in the vehicle. It was reported that Steenson had gone to the area to kill Hugh Torney of the INLA. The car was ambushed in Springhill Avenue shortly after midnight by INLA men, and twenty shots were fired. Both occupants were killed. An inquest was held in October 1987. At the McCarthy family's insistence, an RUC spokesman stated that Anthony McCarthy had no known criminal record and was not known to be associated with any terrorist group.[6] However, Holland and McDonald, authors of *INLA: Deadly Divisions*, quote a source within the INLA claiming that Anthony had not only been a member of the INLA, from which he had resigned, but implying that he had followed Steenson into the ILPO. The same source stated that Anthony was suspected of working as an informer for the British security forces. The author of *Ballymurphy and the Irish War* states:

> Tony McCarthy was buried under a massive RUC presence at the City Cemetery, within a stone's throw of Ballymurphy. Although his wife, Anne-Marie, was a native of the area, few people attended, such was the community's revulsion at the feud and people's wish not to be identified in any way with either faction.[7]

This sad background must have had an effect on Terence. It should be considered in any speculation on Terence's motivations for transforming into a "Prince" who, although strongly nationalist, would utter tirades against republicans as "murderers."[8]

It is wise in retrospect to suggest that the Genealogical Office should have been alert to all the inconsistencies appearing in Terence's claims and to the obvious discrepancies.[9] It has been suggested, in defense of the Office, that Terence's correspondence with the Office was already substantial by 1980, and it was easy to miss the inconsistencies that were occurring.

Terence was at least consistent on one fact until he received his recognitions and even for a while after that. He adhered to the claim that his family had descended from a cadet branch of the Srugrena line and that his grandfather, Thomas, had "succeeded his cousin Samuel Trant McCarthy, The MacCarthy Mór of Srugrena, County Kerry in 1927 and died in 1947."[10]

Yet Terence could not even be trusted on the accuracy of the details concerning his grandfather's death. He did not die in 1947 but on December 26, 1943, in the Victoria Hospital, Belfast. He was described as an "army pensioner," although not with the colorful career that Terence had given him, which included being "mentioned in dispatches" while serving in the second Boer War. The Ministry of Defence's records were only able to show that No. 5202 Thomas McCarthy had enlisted in the regular army in July 1898 and served in the 8th Hussars and then 11th Hussars. He served in South Africa from 1900 to 1903 and was discharged from the army in June 1904 on the completion of his service. He did not rise to noncommissioned rank. He was given the campaign medal, Queen's South Africa Medal, with clasps for service in Cape Colony, Orange Free State and Transvaal.

It was sometime in the late 1980s that Terence was unwittingly alerted by Gerard Crotty to the existence of the T. G. Grey Manuscripts, dated October 1944, lodged in the Genealogical Office. Perhaps he realized for the first time that there existed a genuine male heir descendant of Samuel Trant's family. Was this the point when he began to change the basis of his claim to be Mac-Carthy Mór? He was certainly now firmly attached to the concept of Brehon law succession, tanistry, being a member of the blood line elected by the *derbh-fine*. To secure his position, he could not rest on an acceptance of the Genealogical Office criterion of eldest male heir descendant from the last recognized Chief. Sometime soon the genuine heir male of Samuel Trant might emerge, and of course did.

From 1992, after Terence's recognition, he began to denounce Samuel Trant as a fraud and stated that his own grandfather had become MacCarthy Mór as early as 1905 by a "Pacte de Famille" in Nantes, where the heads of the French MacCarthy families had met and elected him in Brehon law tradition. This was when it was claimed that his grandfather had been presented with the MacCarthy royal regalia and other heirlooms.

His father had thereafter succeeded his grandfather he claimed; then, on August 5, 1980, Terence's father is supposed to have abdicated at which time Terence became MacCarthy Mór. An "abdication document" to this effect, bearing signatures and seals of Thomas and all his sons, was suddenly produced; a copy of that document, not the original, was presented to the Chief Herald in October 1998. It was the first time the Genealogical Office had seen the document. Terence was now claiming that he had been MacCarthy Mór for twelve years before he was recognized by the state. Indeed, he was certainly signing himself as such in anticipation in the mid-1980s.

These new claims were accepted by other heraldic jurisdictions, the Italian Court of Arbitration and learned bodies as well as individual scholars. But the reason for their ready acceptance was that it was presumed that two Chief Heralds of Ireland, Gerard Slevin and Donal Begley, between 1979 and 1992, had investigated and authenticated these claims. The court did not realize that the criteria on which authentication had been made was completely different from the claims now being put forward.

The Genealogical Office became suspicious only when notified of the change in Terence's claims. The Chief Herald, in his public statement of August 1999, pointed out:

In making application for courtesy recognition in 1985, and in subsequent correspondence with the Genealogical Office, Mr McCarthy advanced a particular set of facts and statements on the basis of which recognition was formally granted in 1992. Central to this case was the assertion that Samuel Trant McCarthy revived the style and title of MacCarthy Mór in 1921, and that Terence McCarthy's grandfather succeeded, by tanistry, on the death of Samuel Trant McCarthy in 1927. An entirely different set of facts has been relied on by Terence McCarthy in more recent times as the basis of his claim to be known as MacCarthy Mór.

It is now worthwhile reiterating Terence's new claims:

1. That Samuel Trant McCarthy had appointed himself MacCarthy Mór by changing his name by deed poll and was fraudulent.
2. That his grandfather, Thomas, had been elected at a *Pacte de Famille* in Nantes, France, in 1905, by the senior heads of the French McCarthy households, including a gentleman called "Pol, 7th Duc de Clancarhy-Blarney," Comte McCarthy de Marliere and Comte McCarthy Reagh de Toulouse.
3. That his grandfather, Thomas, had his pedigree compiled and endorsed by the Ulster King of Arms, Sir Arthur Vicars, on October 30. (No such documentation exists to this effect except a photocopy of a letter apparently in Sir Arthur's handwriting but not addressed to anyone specifically stating that he thought the person he was addressing was descended from a MacCarthy Mór.) Attached to this, written in a different hand, was a sketch of Terence's Belfast pedigree linked to Srugrena. (Obviously, in the circumstances, this could not be accepted as evidence, and no such pedigree had ever been registered with Ulster's Office. The Chief Herald said: "No reliable evidence has been adduced to support the claim by Mr. McCarthy that his grandfather was invested as MacCarthy Mór in 1905, and no independent evidence has been submitted to show that an *alleged Pacte de Famille* ever existed, or as to the personalities who took part in the alleged pact.")
4. That his grandfather died in 1947 (the truth being he died in 1943) and his father, Thomas, became The MacCarthy Mór at that date.
5. That his father had abdicated on August 5, 1980, at which time he, Terence, became MacCarthy Mór.
6. That the title always passed through his family in accordance with Brehon law, that is, tanistry, and not by primogeniture.

In addition to the new claims, it was noted by the Chief Herald, with some surprise, that the arms being used by Terence were no longer the arms that the Chief Herald had confirmed to him in 1979 but were a more elaborate affair with a surmounted crown.

Terence's high profile, his vast range of public activities, was to prove his undoing. It was when Barry Trant McCarthy, the great-nephew of Samuel Trant, wrote to the Chief Herald on June 6, 1997, supported by other members of his family, pointing out that they had no knowledge of any Belfast branch, that the new Chief Herald, Brendan O'Donoghue, decided to act.

The Genealogical Office had to examine two contradictory sets of claims by Terence covering two periods. The first was *before* he received courtesy recognition and the second *after* he had received that recognition. An independent genealogist, Gorry Research of Dublin, was employed and was to produce an initial report by March 1999.

Meanwhile, in February 1998, the Chief Herald advised Terence that a rival claimant to the title had emerged. He was invited to make a submission with substantiating documents. Terence's solicitor eventually submitted a sixty-one-page argument with photocopies of fifty-one documents. These were in favor of Terence's second series of claims rather than those he had made prior to 1992 and on which his recognition had been received. During this thorough investigation, it was observed that the documentation submitted by Terence contained hardly any original documents; his arguments rested solely on his assertions and affidavits produced by his friends. Indeed, no original documents of historical integrity or independent sources were adduced in evidence. No independent sources were produced to confirm the destruction of the original documents, which Terence had said he had managed to copy before they had been destroyed in his father's "nightclub." He still held on to his claim of descent from a cadet branch of the Srugrena line but argued that primogeniture did not apply and that he was the successor by Brehon law.

Given the evidence, the Genealogical Office came to the conclusion that they were witness to an amazing imposture.

One of the sadly amusing aspects to the new claims was the conjuring of "Pol, 7th Duc de Clancarthy-Blarney" as the French MacCarthy Mór who had passed on the title and royal regalia to Terence's grandfather in 1905. There is no reference to such a title in France from the seventeenth through to the twentieth centuries. The title was mentioned in a French magazine *La France Litteraire* in 1905 when a man claiming this title wrote about his "family." One source says that the "Duc" wound up in a French jail for fraud. But the article that the "Duc" wrote was picked up and translated in the *Cork Archaeological and Historical Journal* in 1907. The "Duc" was accepted as genuine at the time even by Samuel Trant McCarthy and T. Grey.

Pol's ducal ancestors simply did not exist. But his fraudulent claims were then added to, by misquotation, by Terence in support of his attempts to prove that his reinvented dynastic order, the Niadh Nask, had continued to exist from the time of the last Kings of Desmond through three centuries of exile in France. Terence now added the claim that this mythical Duc de Clancarthy-Blarney had styled himself as The MacCarthy Mór. There is no evidence of that claim in either *La France Litteraire* or the *Cork History and Archaeological Journal.* Terence himself appears to have been fooled by an earlier McCarthy impostor and built on his imposture.

The inevitable question arises as to whether Terence created his "princely" life single-handedly or whether he had assistance in this amazing fabrication. It was noticed that at no time between 1990 and 1999 did Terence's father or his brothers play any part in his "court" or in attending any MacCarthy Clan gatherings. He was, however, assisted by a Belfast man whom Terence always introduced as his "cousin."

"The Count of Clandermond" emerged into public life between 1991 and 1999 as the "Hereditary Chamberlain to The MacCarthy Mór" and as "Secretary-General of the Niadh Nask," "Administrator of the Royal Eóghanacht Society" and author of several volumes on matters pertaining to the dynasty. According to *Debrett's People of Today* (1995), "The Count of Clandermond" was a title that originated in 1250 in the kingdom of Munster and was confirmed in 1756 by Louis XV of France. According to "The Count" himself, it was granted by Daniel McCarthy, Lord of Cappagh, to his son-in-law, Daniel Davison, a Belfast laborer in real life, in 1843. Finally, Terence McCarthy claimed, in a letter he wrote to the Genealogical Office in 1991, that he had created the title for his "cousin."

"The Count of Clandermond" was, in reality, John Andrew Brodie Davison, born on July 6, 1954, at Wandsworth Nursing Home, Wandsworth Parade, Belfast. His father, John Spence Gibson Davison, and his mother, Iris Elizabeth (née Brodie), lived at 104 Barretts Road. His father was a joiner but had previously been a constable in the Royal Ulster Constabulary. He died in 1971.

Not much is known of Davison's early career or of when he and Terence first met and became partners. One has to bear in mind the political and social life of working-class Belfast and its prejudices to appreciate the intriguing aspect of their relationship. Terence was from a poor Catholic background and his brother had republican and socialist connections. Davison was from a Protestant family whose father, and perhaps he himself, had been in the Royal

Ulster Constabulary. The two cultures were inimical to one another, and at the same time both had the same hostility toward homosexuality. Both men claimed to be converts to the Eastern Orthodox Church. As previously mentioned, Terence was to be granted "the style of Orthodxissumus Princeps or Most Orthodox Prince" by Evloghios I, Archbishop of Milan and Aquileia, Metropolitan of the Autonomous Metropolitanate of Western Europe of the Holy Ukranian Orthodox Church, in March 1998. It seems, from the wording of the grant, that Terence was now claiming descent from "the Holy Saints, Vladimir, Enlightener of Russia, and Olga."

Terence's story about his early years with Davison was that they had traveled the world as youths. The earliest provable connection was in the mid-1980s when they were running a genealogical research business in partnership from Comber, County Down. Certainly by September 1985 Terence was writing as "Hereditary Commander of the Military and Hospitaller Order of Saint Lazarus of Jerusalem: Hereditary Commandery of Saint Stephen" and on the notepaper the name of J.A.B. Davison OLJ appears as secretary.

On June 16, 1986, Davison was charged at Downpatrick Crown Court with six counts of demanding money with menaces "with a view to gain for him or another." He pleaded guilty and on June 20 he received a sentence of imprisonment for two years on each count, to run concurrently, and was ordered to pay restitution of £10,000. One account of the trial, with photographs, appeared in a Sunday newspaper under the headline "Fergie's Gay Roots Tracer Jailed for Blackmail."[11] The story pointed out that Terence McCarthy and Davison had been commissioned by Sarah Ferguson, the Duchess of York, to trace her Irish pedigree. She flew into Belfast, presumably to pick up the pedigree; three days after Davison was sent to jail. The newspaper report said that Davison, at this time, styled himself as "Chevalier." On his release from jail, Davison and Terence compiled a family history claiming that he was linked to the Davisons who bore the title Baron Broughshane, a genuine United Kingdom title created in 1945 taken from Broughshane in County Antrim. This claim was put forward in 1988, and there is, significantly, no mention at the time of the "Counts of Clandermond."

However, in 1991, the "5th Count of Clandermond' appeared and, a few years later, a book was published entitled *The Davisons of Knockboy, Broughshane, County Antrim*, written by Alexander Davison with an introduction by "The Count of Clandermond." There is some mystery about who the author of the book was. Alexander Davison, who was then the heir to the second Baron Broughshane, has denied that he was the author. Speculation has it that it was none other than "The Count" himself, tracing his fabricated pedigree. One commentator has found it amusing to observe that the Shankill, in north Belfast, the Protestant enclave that the Davisons had connections with, was attached, after the Reformation, to the "Deanery of Clandermont"![12] However, a map of the "Lordship of Mac Carthy Mór" used by Sir Aubrey Metcalfe regarding the MacGillycuddys shows that Clandermond is an area on the Beara Peninsula behind Castletown. However, the claims by Davison that his arms were confirmed by the Chief Herald in 1985 and that "new arms were granted for services to the Dublin Office of Arms" is incorrect. Arms were granted to Davison because of a normal petition and not for "services."

A sad aspect of this matter is that *Debrett's* also gave an entry for the Countess of Clandermond, Iris Elizabeth, Davison's mother, whose career is given as "Hon. Lady in Waiting to HM Queen Susan of the Albanians." This lady had appeared at many functions bedecked with various orders and honors. *Debrett's* claimed that in 1952 she married John Spence Gibson Davison, Baron of Kilcoe, son and heir of Walter Scott Davison, Count of Clandermond, and that her husband succeeded as the fourth Count of Clandermond in 1953, and her son as fifth count in 1979. As she was fully aware that her father-in-law was a laborer, her mother-in-law was illiterate and her husband, a joiner, was certainly not a count or baron, one must speculate on her role in the affair. Documents lodged in the Genealogical Office show that Davison's claims to an aristocratic genealogy were totally without foundation.

Terence and his partner, Davison, had lived in Tangier, Morocco, for the major part of each year since Terence's recognition and possibly for a few years before that. They were also able to buy a Georgian house in the fashionable Anne Street, Clonmel, County Tipperary. Following the announcement by the Chief Herald in July 1999, they seem to have removed to Tangier on a permanent basis.

What was the purpose of Terence's claim to a title? Was it merely to escape his Belfast background? Or did he see the possibility of a lucrative income from being the "Prince of Desmond"? His main source of revenue since his recognition by the Genealogical Office appears to have been the sale of "lordships" and the fees charged for joining his dynastic order—the Niadh Nask. The Niadh Nask, while based on a genuine ancient Gaelic military elite concept, was reinvented by Terence in the 1980s and given substance by some questionable historical quotations that were then doctored to prove historical continuity. These were put together in a volume *Links in a Golden Chain*, edited by Davison, using his soi-disant "Count of Clandermond" title.

As the bestowal or selling of feudal titles was never part of the original Gaelic system, it is questionable whether these were valid even had Terence been a genuine MacCarthy Mór. Terence's main support was, of course, the St. Ledger report of the lordships of Donal IX. Terence sought to justify his position in an "Open Letter," responding to an article in the June 20, 1999 *Sunday Times:*

> I was first approached by *Burke's Peerage* in 1988, at the suggestion of the then Chief Herald (being Donal F. Begley) with a request to sell them feudal titles. To ensure the propriety of my actions I sought and obtained the written permission of the then Chief Herald before making any decision to grant any titles (letter dated June 16, 1988). Furthermore, the Chief Herald confirmed again in writing, that I enjoyed such a right, under the Irish Constitution to Mr Harold Brooks-Baker, the publishing editor of *Burke's Peerage* (Letter dated November 3, 1988).[13]

This is curious, as the dates given are nearly four years before the Chief Herald recognized Terence as MacCarthy Mór. While the Chief Herald of the time said his Office would raise no objection to such sales, in fact, even if the historical argument was favorable for the bestowal of feudal titles in a Gaelic context, only a genuine and recognized MacCarthy Mór could dispose of such titles. In 1988 Terence was not recognized, nor, as it turned out, was he genuine. The Italian Arbitration Court, however, believed that the "Prince of Desmond" was entitled to bestow and dispose of such titles.

It is hard to estimate the income from such sales. Terence did admit to the *Sunday Times* correspondent, John Burns, that he charged an initial fee of $800 plus an annual subscription of $100 per year for membership to his Niadh Nask dynastic order.[14] However, distinguished members were not charged. These included the former Irish Prime Ministers Charles Haughey and Albert Reynolds; fellow Gaelic Chiefs such as Lord Inchiquin (The O'Brien); the former U. S. Army Chief of Staff (1968–71) General William C. Westmoreland, who commanded the U. S. troops in Vietnam from 1964 to 1968; and leading Irish historians such as Dr. Katharine Simms and the current author. By 1998 the confraternity of the Niadh Nask numbered well over 400 worldwide. If only 50 percent had paid the full fees, we are still speaking of a potential initial income of $160,000 and an annual income of $20,000 a year. Subscriptions to the *International Journal of the Niadh Nask*, a biannual publication, was extra. There was also a small business in Niadh Nask insignia, lapel pins, cuff links, pendants and other ephemera. Each Christmas members of the Niadh Nask were invited to send donations to Davison, as administrator of the Niadh Nask, which would be paid to a charity nominated by Terence. In addition, Terence and Davison kept up a prodigious outpouring of books under their respective titles and a Clan Society journal, *The Stag Trippant.*

Of course, the Niadh Nask fees were not the only source of income. The sale of "lordships," especially to Americans, was a major money maker. One of the first Americans to purchase a lordship from Terence also become involved in helping him run this business in the belief that he was genuine. William F. K. Marmion signed a statement that "early in 1992 I had become probably the source of well over a million dollars directly or indirectly into Terence McCarthy's pockets."[15] On that basis, one is left to contemplate how much money was paid by those believing they were buying genuine old Irish lordships between 1992 and 1999. Some thirty-five "lordships" had been sold to Americans by the mid-1990s.

In spite of such evidence, Terence told the *Sunday Times:* "To suggest that I am making a good living out of all this is untrue. I have not made my livelihood out of it."[16] It is difficult to see what other sources of income were available to him, as a full-time "prince" from a poor background, to not only maintain his residences in Clonmel and Tangier but to indulge his taste for antiques and provide him and his partner with their world-traveling lifestyles. He also needed money to acquire antiques not only to adorn his home but to use as the "royal regalia" that he was supposed to have inherited.

Unless one has actually met Terence, it is difficult to appreciate his persuasiveness, his obsessiveness, his utter involvement and apparent belief in his role of "Prince of Desmond." That he was able to convince serious heraldic authorities, and law courts, as well as scholars and his fellow chiefs, is a tribute to a flawed talent. He had a good grasp of the historical reality of the Gaelic aristocracy of Ireland, enough to convince many scholars that he had lived his entire life steeped in such lore. Once he caught on to the Brehon laws of succession, he studied them assiduously. He was an articulate and convincing, albeit flamboyant, debater and polemicist. Had he kept his talents to mere historical research, instead of "living" Gaelic aristocracy, then he may well have achieved some scholastic reputation.

As it was, personal ambition overrode not only any academic objectivity he possessed, but in his determination to recreate his own world of Gaelic aristocracy he demonstrated that he was capable of distortion and invention to prove his arguments. No reliance can now be placed on his books, especially in relation to his re-creation of the Niadh Nask. No one can accept the quotations as given by Terence from historical documents, sources and even reputable historians without a close double-checking to ensure that they are accurate.

Following the Chief Herald's announcement, Terence, keeping his aplomb to the last, claimed that he was the innocent victim of plot. Due to the ill health brought on by the machinations of his "enemies," he announced his "abdication" on October 6, 1999.

One of his younger brothers, Eoin, who had been named "His Excellency, An Tánaiste Eoghan MacCarthy, Lord of Valentia, Tanist of Munster," but who had never played a part in Terence's world, did not do so now. Although "heir apparent," he did not make any public statement and now appears to be living in Germany.

However, soon after the "abdication," Terence's youngest brother, Conor Michael McCarthy (b. March 19, 1969), began writing to members of the various organizations formed by his brother, claiming that the *derbhfine* of his family had met and elected him as the new MacCarthy Mór. Needless to say, no authority is taking the claim seriously. However, a small number of supporters appear to have gathered around Conor, proving that it is a human condition to prefer myth to reality.

In July 2000 The Clan MacCarthy Society Inc. of New York received a thirteen-page letter from Conor, written in the verbose style of Terence, making the claim that "not a single voice has been raised against my Chiefship." The press and media continue to write the occasional amusing article on Terence's claims. The *Irish Times Magazine* of December 2, 2000, devoted four pages with color photographs to Frank Donald's trip to Tangier to seek out Terence and Davidson. The reporter noted: "This pair may be seen almost daily making a regal progress through the Grand Socco, Tangier's bustling marketplace. Protocol required that Davidson walks a deferential three paces behind the man who ennobled him, usually carrying their 'royal cat' in a wicket basket."[17]

Terence's rise and fall as The MacCarthy Mór has been highly damaging to the state's Genealogical Office and the reputation of the office of Chief Herald of Ireland. It was initially thought that the affair might have been a catalyst which would cause the Irish state to give more serious consideration to the ramifications of what it is, in fact, doing when recognizing old Gaelic titles under a law system that vanquished them forever.

Great hope was placed in the announcement by Arts and Heritage Minister Síle de Valéra that an inquiry would be set up into how Gaelic titles should be recognized. But now the Irish Government has decided against that course of action. It will be left, once again, to the Genealogical Office to draw up rules.

Financially, many people have lost money. These were mainly the people throughout the world who confidently gave money to receive the titles and honors from the soi-disant "Prince of Desmond" and his "Hereditary Chamberlain." There has been some discussion of a possible police investigation in the United States following a complaint to the authorities concerning the sale of bogus feudal titles, one of which may have involved the inclusion of real estate.

Others seem to have had their reputations tarnished, like the heraldic offices who initially accepted Terence's claims. There is also the fallout of the fraud felt by the other Gaelic Chiefs of Ireland, some now having their own pedigrees claimed as bogus.

The worst aspect of the affair, in my view as a historian, is that because Terence embraced the argument, long held by many scholars and lawyers, that Gaelic titles can exist only within the Brehon system of succession, the song may vanish with the singer. Terence may well have destroyed any credibility for the genuine academic debate and allowed a Disneyland world of "primogeniture Chiefs" to be given final imprimaturs from the Irish State.

CHAPTER THIRTEEN

GAELIC KNIGHTS

"THERE IS MERIT WITHOUT RANK BUT THERE IS NO RANK without some merit," wrote the Duc François de la Rochefoucaud (1613–80) in his *Maximes* (1665). It is an observation that most of the kings of Ireland would have agreed with. The Brehon law of succession clearly places merit before heredity. A king, even a minor chief, had to merit his position by his ability and did not take office purely because he was the eldest son of his father. Similarly, the king and his nobles were the patrons of the arts and learning. An *ollamh* was treated as of princely rank. An *ollamh* of law and poetry was even considered the equal of a king at the court; he, or she, for both were equal under the law, could speak even before the king at a council and give advice. She could cross boundaries from one kingdom to another and command respect wherever she was. This high status reflects the preoccupation of Gaelic society with merit and the honor that must be accorded to it. If a king even dared contemplate the assassination of an *ollamh* or a bard out of dislike or disagreement with what had been said, he had to beware, for an *ollamh* could bring about even a king's death if such offense was committed. The concept that a satire could raise a blemish on a king or noble was symbolic; it merely meant that the "word" could destroy a king's reputation and dishonor him before the people.

In ancient Irish society, in which each person had an honor price, the honor price of a king was the same as that of his chief bishop or his chief *brehon* or *ollamh*, professor of law. A petty king was on the same level as bishops, lawyers and poets. The honor price of a tanist, the heir-apparent to the kingship, was just marginally higher than other classes of poets, chief architects, doctors, smiths and musicians. When we compare the social values of such professions in other European cultures even in medieval times, we can see the essential meritocracy of Gaelic Ireland.

It is often claimed that the system of knighthood, chivalric orders and honors was not introduced to Ireland until after the Anglo-Norman invasion of the twelfth century. This is incorrect. Such a system was already in place, having arisen out of the practice of admitting those most worthy into elite warrior groups, as was done in most other Indo-European societies.

There are several orders of elite warrior corps mentioned in the sagas and chronicles of ancient Ireland. Perhaps the best known were the Ulster Red Branch Knights, or the *Craobh Ruadh*. They emerge in the Ulster Cycle of myths, especially in the famous epic *Táin Bó Cualigne* (Cattle Raid of Cooley), which has been compared with the Greek *Iliad*. Its date of origin is uncertain. Scholars have identified it as having been handed down in oral form probably from the La Tène period, from about 500 B.C. The first reference to it in a written form occurs in the seventh century A.D. The earliest complete surviving texts are found in the eleventh-century *Leabhair na hUidhre* (Book of the Dun Cow) and the twelfth-century *Leabhar na Nuaconghbhála Laighnech* (Book of Leinster).

The Red Branch Knights were represented only in the service of the Kings of Ulster. Few scholars have been able to come up with a satisfactory reason why they were so called, but Thomas O'Rahilly, one of the leading experts in this field, believed, from the epigraphic evidence, that instead of being *Craobh Ruadh* (Red Branch) they were actually called *Craobh Rígh* (Royal Branch), and the transformation took place through the mistranscription of a lazy scribe.[1]

There was a curious irony in 1993 when it was announced that the O'Conor Don had instigated Chompanach na Craoibhe Ríoga (Companions of the Red Branch) as a chivalric confraternity. It was subsequently pointed out that the Red Branch was an Ulster military elite and that the stories concerning them clearly depict them fighting *against* the monarchy of Connacht, not *for* it! It would have been as illogical for the Roman emperors to have established an order of "Gaesatae," the Celtic military elite who fought Rome in 225 A.D. at Telemon and elsewhere. The O'Conor Don was persuaded to cancel the plan, although in 1995 he considered the establishment of "The Noble and Equestrian Order of the Collar of Ériu" to reward outstanding contributions in Irish culture, the arts, literature, science, medicine and philanthropy. This was also cancelled after some consideration. But in its September 8, 2000 edition, the Dublin magazine *The Phoenix* revealed that The O'Conor Don had established the Companionate of the Royal House of O'Conor and invested some sixty people with the order before his death, including the Duke of Saxe-Coburg Breganze, the Prince of Lippe and Abbot Cassati of Palermo in Sicily.

Contemporary with the Ulster knights were the Degad, or Clanna Deagha, who appeared in Munster; the Clanna Baoiscne of Leinster; and Gamanrad or Gamhanrhide of Connacht. The Degad, however, were revealed by Eugene O'Curry not to be native to Munster but a group of Ulster warriors who had been banished to Munster to serve their exiled prince Cú Roi Mac Daire. There were also the Fianna, famous in the Fenian Cycle of tales of Fionn Mac Cumhail, sometimes Anglicized as Finn MacCool. The Fianna were bodyguards of the High Kings, recruited from the Clan Baoiscne of Leinster and the Clan Morna, and their headquarters were on the Hill of Allen in Kildare. When the Irish Republican Brotherhood was formed in 1858, they adopted the sobriquet "Fenians." The word *fianna* has become the modern Irish term for soldiers, as in the political party Fianna Fáil (Soldiers of Destiny). The Fenian Cycle consists of one of the largest body of stories in early Irish literature, and the stories are basically set during the reign of Cormac Mac Airt in the third century.

The concept of elite bands of warriors is certainly traceable in ancient Celtic culture and shows parallels to its sister Hindu Indo-European culture in its warrior caste (*kshatriya*).

There is another fascinating trace of an elite Irish warrior group called the *Ríglach*. In the *Metrical Dindsenchus*, the *Betha Colmáin maic Lúachain* and the text of the *Táin Bó Cuailgne*, as given in the Book of Leinster, the word *Ríglach* is used to denote a high-ranking warrior elite. With the root *ríg*, meaning "royal," in it, it is clearly a royal bodyguard. The Middle Irish glossators had difficulty understanding the concept behind the word. They glossed it as "veterans" (veteran warriors), and from "veterans" it degenerated in use over the centuries to now mean "old people."

The clue to the ancient *Ríglach* seems to lie in the warrior caste of northern India, the Rajputs. The name derives from *Raj*, meaning "king," and *putra*, meaning "sons." This group became a tribe—"the sons of kings"—claiming all to be descended from the original *kshatriya*, the elite bodyguards to the kings presumably recruited from the king's family to ensure personal loyalty. The Rajputs formed the principality of Rajputana in northwest India as a powerful state in the seventh century A.D., but had to submit to the Mughals in the seventeenth century and finally agreed a treaty with the English Crown in the nineteenth century.

There are several ancient Continental and British Celtic tribes noticed by Classical writers as being "king" or descendants of kings with names ending in the element "*riges*." Might it be that the Ríglach of ancient Ireland, clearly an important and distinctive group in the early references, were the equivalent of their fellow Indo-Europeans, the Rajputs of India? Were they also the "sons of kings," and did some awareness of this survive in folk tradition, which would explain the popular Irish notion that "we are all kings' sons"?

It is clear, then, that there was a concept of elite warriors, honored by the kings. But did this practice develop as it did in other parts of Europe?

An English jurist and legal antiquarian, John Sladen (1584–1654), was in no doubt when he stated that the Irish had an "ancient custom of knighthood before they received manners of English civility."[2] When Richard II was in Ireland in 1395, one of his advisors asked the Leinster King Art and his nobles:

> if they would not gladly receive the order of knighthood and that the King of England should make them knights according to the usage of France and England and other countries. They answered him how they were knights already and that sufficed for them. I asked where they were made knights, and how, and when? They answered that at the age of seven years they were made knights in Ireland, and that a King maketh his son a Knight. . . .

The person recounting this conversation was Enrique de Castile; he might have misheard the number, for seven was when a boy went to be educated and *seventeen* was the age of maturity, when he was entitled to take his role in society.[3]

All these bodies of Gaelic elite warriors and knights have now passed into oblivion. However, in the early 1980s, Terence McCarthy began to reinvent a Munster warrior elite called the Nasc Niadh as part of his scheme to make himself "Prince of Desmond." He claimed that the "Niadh Nask," as he called it, had survived since ancient times and was the dynastic honor of the Munster and Desmond kings.

The Nasc Niadh actually indicated a gold necklet and would have originated from the famous gold torcs that ancient Celtic warriors wore around their necks. *Nasc* means a chain or collar worn around the neck and *Nia(dh)* was a champion. Terence designated his order as the Military Order of the Golden Chain.

By 1999 Terence's reinvention had been so successful that it was internationally recognized as a genuine nobiliary fraternity, but it is not an order of chivalry or knighthood and admission was not restricted to persons of Irish descent. It undertook charitable work and, so its literature claimed, the relief of suffering among the very young and elderly.

In July 1984 it was recognized as a valid dynastic and nobiliary association by a body called the International Commission for Orders of Chivalry. It was recognized by other European royal dynasties and by many heraldic authorities, such as the Heralds of South Africa (1983), Canada (1984), the United

States (1986), Spain (1998) and so on. An *International Niadh Nask Journal* was published twice yearly. Members included two former prime ministers of the Irish Republic and many other distinguished personalities. A detailed "history" of the order was published as *Links in a Golden Chain*, edited by Andrew Davison, as "The Count of Clandermond," in 1998.

Terence had based his Niadh Nask on references to the Nasc Niadh found in many ancient Irish texts. In the *Annals of Clonmacnoise* it was said that King Muinmhamhóin, in 681 B.C., "was the first king that ever devised a golden chain fit to be worn about men's necks and rings to be put on their fingers, which was then in great use, he reigned five years and then died. He was of the sept of Munster."[4] The reference does not, in fact, say that he instituted a dynastic order, but this was the interpretation Terence McCarthy gave to the reference.

The Irish historian Séthrún Céitinn (ca. 1580-ca. 1644), in his famous *Foras Feasa ar Éireann* (History of Ireland), relates how an unlawful claimant to the High Kingship forced his way into the palace at Tara:

> a learned druid came into his presence and said to him that it was not lawful for him to violate the *geasa* (prohibition laws) of Tara, "for it is one of its *geasa*," he said, "that no king should settle down in Tara with a view to assuming the sovereignty of Ireland till he should first wear the nasc niadh round his neck." This was the same as to say that he should have received the degree of Knight of Chivalry. For as the Knight of Chivalry is called Miles Torquatus, so also *Nia Naisc* is applied in Irish to the champion who wore a *nasc* or chain round his neck. For *nia* means "champion" or "valiant" man and *nasc* means "a chain."[5]

Comte O'Kelly d'Aughrim, writing on Irish history in the nineteenth century, was claimed by Terence to be "a Niadh Nask of the French succession." There is no evidence for this. However, the Comte does echo references to the existence in "*anciens Irlandais*" of "*chevaliers*" called "Niadh-Nask."[6] This reference was eagerly seized upon by Terence, but there was no proof, apart from his word, that such "chevaliers" continued to exist in France.

Anthony Marmion also points out:

> There were five Equestrian orders: the first of these was the Neagh Nase [*sic*], or Knights of the Golden Collar, instituted by King Muinhamhoin, one of the ancient Milesian Kings, which derived from the golden chain worn about the neck like the golden collar of the Roman knights. This order was peculiar to the blood royal, and none could be a candidate for the monarchy without being admitted to it. . . .[7]

Patrick Weston Joyce agrees:

> There was an order of chivalry the distinguishing mark of which was what was called *nasc-niad* ("champion's ring or collar"; *nia* gen. *niad*, a *trenfer* or champion). Neither the order—nor of course the decoration—was conferred except it was won on the field of battle; and the person who won the *nasc niad* was called *Nia Naisc* "champion of the collar" (like the English "Knight of the Garter"), and also *ridire gaisge*, or "knight of valour." This collar, according to Keating (Céitinn), was worn around the neck.[8]

While it has been argued that these scholars were drawing conclusions from material considered to be part of the "mythical history" of Ireland, mention of *Nasc Niadh* does occur in several ancient references, especially those emanating from Munster. Terence's task was to prove the existence of the Nasc Niadh through to Tudor times, and then, after the conquests, to demonstrate that it was a dynastic order kept by the MacCarthy family during their exile in France.

The poet Aodhagan Ó Rathaille (Anglicized as Egan Rahilly; 1670–1728), of a family long in the service of the MacCarthy Mór, referred to the Nasc Niadh in one of his elegies. Referring to Gerard Fitzgerald, son of the Knight of Glin, he hails him thus:

> Nasc Nia of all Connello, without fault
> Nasc Nia of Glina
> sore wound to his friends;
> Nasc Nia of Dingle, I utter not lies;
> Nasc Nia of defence with his flock.

One authority points out that the meaning of Nasc Niadh had, by this time, come to mean not only a collar of gold but "a rallying chief."[9] Therefore, the poet could simply have been hailing the Knight of Glin as a "rallying chief" and not someone holding a dynastic order. This is how the poem is translated by Patrick Dineen.[10] However, in fairness, it should be pointed that the *RIA Dictionary of the Irish Language*, regarded as the authority, also states: "*nasc niadh* (equivalent of knighthood in chivalry)."

Terence was determined to present evidence that the Nasc Niadh had continued to be bestowed by the MacCarthy Mórs of the Muskerry branch of the MacCarthys after they had been driven into exile in France. He found a reference in a 1768 edition of an Irish-English dictionary published in Paris.[11]

His greatest coup came in the form of an article in the *La France Litteraire* in 1905/07 in which a Pol McCarthy claimed to be the seventh Duc de Clancarty-

Blarney and descendant of Justin MacCarthy, Lord Mountcashel, whom he claimed had been made a duke by James II and was able to pass on the title to his heirs. The material was accepted by a contributor to the *Journal of the Cork Historical and Archaeological Society* in 1907, writing on "Justin MacCarthy, Lord Mountcashel."

The author claims that Pol MacCarthy, born in 1844, became seventh Duc de Clancarthy-Blarney in 1903: "he is, therefore, lineally represent[ed] as the MacCarthys More [*sic*], the former Sovereign Princes of Desmond and Cork." The author says that Pol resided at Nantes, fought in the Franco-Prussian War in 1870 as an artillery officer and was made a chevalier by the King of Portugal. Not only did the journal's author accept Pol MacCarthy as genuine, but Samuel Trant McCarthy was also fooled and included Pol's "pedigree" in his book.[12]

The fact was that no "Duc de Clancarthy-Blarney" existed in France. No Duc de Clancarthy received the Légion d'Honneur, nor did these nonexistent "dukes" style themselves MacCarthy Mór and hand out a dynastic honor called the Niadh Nask. These last two claims were added by Terence to the story by misquoting the article from the journal.

The reinvention of the Niadh Nask received a boost in the person of Lieutenant Colonel Baron O'Kelly de Conejera. He had been serving on the International Commission for Orders of Chivalry since 1981 and was also interested in references to the Niadh Nask. He stated that he approached the Chief Herald of Ireland, Gerard Slevin, who informed him of the existence of Terence McCarthy. Having contacted Terence, Baron O'Kelly said he was astonished to be presented with Terence's arguments for the continued existence of the Nasc Niadh, now firmly called Niadh Nask. He invited Terence to submit his evidence to the International Commission for Orders of Chivalry.[13]

In the summer of 1984, eight years before the Irish state recognized Terence as "MacCarthy Mór," the Niadh Nask was recognized and duly placed on the register of the Commission. However, because of the uniqueness of the order, a new category had to be created and it was categorized as a "Nobiliary Association." The president of the International Commission, His Serene Highness The Prince Ernst August zur Lippe, ordered the publication of the Commission's recognition of the order on October 10, 1984.[14]

The late Right Honorable Lord Borthwick of that Ilk (d. 1996), a president of the International Commission, wrote:

> The Niadh Nask is without doubt one of the most ancient nobiliary honours in the world, if not the most ancient! Its origins are shrouded in the mists of

time. According to Gaelic historians writing in the fifteenth century, it was founded almost a thousand years before the birth of Christ! Whether this is true or not we cannot say, but it is evident that the order is at least pre-Chivalric in origin if not pre-Christian.[15]

Lord Borthwick reflected:

> When, in 1984, after several years of scrutiny, the International Commission for Orders of Chivalry recognized the Niadh Nask, or Military Order of the Golden Chain, as a perfectly valid and legal Dynastic Honour of the ancient Irish Royal House of Munster, under the Chiefship of The MacCarthy Mór, Prince of Desmond, it had to devise the entirely new category of "Other Nobiliary Bodies" to list it under, not because it was "less important" than the great and ancient Dynastic Orders of Chivalry, but because it was even more ancient in its origins![16]

In writing a preface to the 1996 membership roll of the Niadh Nask, Lord Borthwick pointed out:

> The Roll itself is a testimony to the validity of the Niadh Nask and the Order's fidelity to its Gaelic origins, for whilst it is a nobiliary Order it does not define "nobility" in the narrow genealogical sense but adheres to the Celtic definition whereby military officers, doctors, religious and Ollamhs (professors and other graduates) are considered of "equal" rank. Similarly as a pre-Christian Order The Niadh Nask has no "sectarian" qualification. This is perhaps most eloquently illustrated by reference to the membership of the First Division which lists simultaneously as members His Holiness Patriarch Diodorus I, Greek Orthodox Patriarch of Jerusalem, and His Majesty King Leka I of the Albanians, the only Muslim Sovereign in Europe![17]

As suspicions began to grow in the 1990s about Terence, Professor Marco Horak made four claims in public:

1. There was no historical evidence for knighthood existing in Gaelic Ireland;
2. There were no historical references to the Niadh Nask;
3. In Consequence, the conferal of the order by Terence McCarthy was illicit and unjustified;
4. Even had such an order existed in the past, it had been abolished by the constitution of the Irish Republic.

Terence, with his usual confidence, began a legal action. The action, which took place in an Italian arbitration court, has already been covered. The judgment on this matter formed the second of the two judgments and was issued in June 1998. The court at Casale Monferrato, having heard all the evidence, found:

> It is proven that knighthood existed as a rank in Gaelic Ireland before the advent of the Anglo-Normans in 1169 and accordingly that The Niadh Nask, or Military Order of the Golden Chain, existed and, according to documentary evidence, was established by King Muinheamhoin who has been proven to be the direct ancestor of the Eóghanacht Kings of Munster and specifically of the Royal House of MacCarthy Mór; that the Office of Grand Master or Hereditary Head of the Niadh Nask (in Italian: "*Ufficio di Gran Maestro e Capo Ereditario del Niadh Nask*") is inalienably vested in the Chieftainship of the Royal House of MacCarthy Mór as a Dynastic honour of non Chivalric knighthood (in Italian: *Ordine Dinastico di natura non Cavalleresca'*), so that The Niadh Nask must be considered in International Law as a Dynastic honor of the Royal House Munster, which lawfully exists as a nobiliary body corporate and politic being so recognized by various States and by the International Commission for Orders of Chivalry.[18]

The existence of the Niadh Nask now seemed unassailable. By 1999 there were over four hundred members of the order worldwide, which, as we have discussed, was making a minimum income for Terence of an initial $160,000 plus $20,000 a year. Only a distinguished minority received the "order" free. These included the heads of several ex-royal houses, the Ukranian Orthodox Patriach of Kiev, former prime ministers of Ireland, distinguished historians, prominent writers such as Count Nikolai Tolstoy, American generals, admirals and ambassadors.

Once the full implications of Terence's intrigue were made known, the Niadh Nask quickly began to dissolve, although not without some reluctance on the part of many people who had firmly believed in the authenticity of the claims he had made for the order, even though they had also reluctantly come to the realization that he was not who he claimed to be. Conor McCarthy still tries to carry on his brother's reinvented order, while others have tried to form independent Niadh Nask groups.

CHAPTER FOURTEEN

A FUTURE FOR GAELIC ARISTOCRACY?

TO REITERATE THE INTRODUCTION OF THIS BOOK, this has been a study of a much-neglected area of Irish history. No assessment of Irish history can ever be complete without a consideration of the history of the families who ruled in Ireland for at least two thousand years prior to the English Tudor Conquests.

The pedigrees of those Gaelic aristocrats are as old as the written word in Ireland, if not older, and stem from a number of genealogies dating back as early as the seventh century A.D., but most survive from twelfth-century books and annals.

What seems to be a matter of contention is whether the current Chiefs have any right to hold their Gaelic titles and under what legal criteria they may do so. This problem is discussed in detail in the early chapters of this work, and I share the opinion of most international scholars and jurists that any recognition by the modern Irish state of such titles can only follow the precedents and rulings of accepted international practices.

Whether these survivors of the ancient kings and nobles of Ireland, the oldest traceable aristocracy in Europe, now have any role to play in the modern Irish state is a matter for debate and, in the end, depends on the members of that aristocracy and the decisions of the Irish state. It was Napoleon Bonaparte who observed: "The practical policy of a [republican] government is to make use of aristocracy, but under the forms and in the spirit of democracy." Admittedly, Napoleon had his own agenda to pursue, although he did make this point in his *Maximes* (1804–15), having already abolished the teetering French Republic and made himself emperor.

Eversheds professor of International Law Anthony Carty not only believes that the Irish state should give "courtesy recognition" to the holders of Gaelic titles under the Brehon law of succession, as clearly supported by international law, but he feels that the Irish Constitution should be amended to give recognition to the heads of these families. He writes:

> I believe there should be some formal recognition in the Irish Constitution of the world which was lost by the violence of Irish history, i.e. the violence done to Ireland, particularly in the sixteenth and seventeenth centuries. That should find reflection in the present Constitution, for instance in a place for at least some of the old Irish Houses in the Irish Senate through election from among themselves.[1]

Some individual members agree with Professor Carty and consider the opportunity for a political role within the modern state. Whether an allocation of seats in the Seanad Éireann (Irish Senate) needs a Constitutional change is arguable. The Irish Prime Minister can, constitutionally, appoint members of the Senate by nomination. In 1998 there were eleven Prime Minister's nominees sitting in the Senate. It has been pointed out there is no reason why the heads of the royal dynasties might not be appointed in such a manner, sitting as independents, and using their expertise under Article 18 in the areas of the national language, culture, literature, art and education.

The Standing Council of Irish Chiefs and Chieftains, reflecting the individual concerns of its members, does envisage its primary functions as promoting Gaelic culture, an awareness of history, and tourism, especially through the Irish diaspora, with an interest in clan gatherings. It already presents, through University College Cork, an annual prize for writing in the Irish language.

However, to sit in the Senate one is required to be a citizen. Not all the members of these Gaelic noble families are Irish citizens, for they have been in exile too long. The O'Neill of Clanaboy, for example, is a Portuguese citizen, his family exiled since the seventeenth century. Like others, he does not automatically qualify for an Irish passport or citizenship rights. However, the Minister of Justice has explained that he has the power to dispense with the standard conditions of granting citizenship, under the Irish Nationality and Citizenship Acts of 1956 and 1986, in certain circumstances, "including where the applicant is of Irish descent or Irish association."[2]

> It is therefore open to anyone who feels that they have sufficiently strong Irish associations to make a case to the Minister that he exercise this exception on

their behalf and, from time to time, individuals are successful in this regard. You will appreciate, however, that the association would have to be exceptional to warrant the Minister waiving the specified statutory requirements. Having regard to the very significant numbers of people who might be able to claim Irish origins, the Minister is unlikely to consider ancestry alone as being sufficient and it would certainly not be equitable to discriminate in favor of those who are descended from particular families.

In other words, being a direct descendant of Irish kings and High Kings who reigned in Ireland for two thousand years or more, families who were forced into exile due to the English conquests, is not regarded as being an "exceptional" circumstance to claim an "Irish association" by the office of the current Irish Minister for Justice. One also has to bear in mind that the Ministry was sensitive at this time, due to press and media revelations of passports being supplied to foreign citizens for cash payments when there were patently no "Irish associations" at all to justify the granting of them, nor even the qualification of residency.

Another idea has been proposed to the modern Irish state. Many of the old castles, manors and estates owned by the Gaelic aristocracy and confiscated during the conquests of the sixteenth and seventeenth centuries are now the property of the Irish state. Most of the properties are owned by departments that eventually come under the direction of the Ministry of Arts, Heritage, Gaeltacht and Islands. Only The O'Brien, due to the accidents of the history, still lives on his family's original Dromoland estate, although his family sold Dromoland Castle in the 1980s.

The idea that has been suggested by some of the descendants of the royal dynasties, and passed on to the Ministry of Heritage, is that many of the state-owned castles and manors were once the seats of these royal dynasties and could be used to promote tourism. An apartment in a castle or manor could be given rent- and expense-free to the holder of the title, either in perpetuity or for reversion after a reasonable time, in return for a degree of involvement in promoting the ancient site for tourist purposes. In Britain, the visitors to "stately homes" have brought in considerable revenues because of the many "ancient families" still in residence in these castles and manors. What better, some have argued, for Bord Fáilte to promote visits to castles and manors that are not empty shells, in which people are told kings or high kings once lived centuries ago, than to actually have the modern-day heir of that king or high king in residence and willing to give some input into the process? The increase in tourism and the resulting interest in Irish history and culture would make any outlay on such apartments pay for themselves if, in fact, extra financial outlay was even needed. The state already has to maintain these properties. The Irish state, in fact, already gives grants to Anglo-Irish peers for the upkeep of their stately homes.

In many of the former communist states of Europe, as a gesture of restitution for confiscated property, governments have returned property or paid compensation.

However, this idea also received scant enthusiasm at the Ministry of Heritage when asked to comment on the suggestion that had been put forward. The Ministry asked the Chief Herald, Brendan O'Donoghue, to state its policy in this area.

> Property rights are fully protected and guaranteed by the Constitution, and the Courts are there to vindicate those rights. There are no proposals, and unlikely ever to be any proposals, to vest additional property rights on particular classes of citizens or other persons by references to circumstances that may have prevailed in the past. It should also be borne in mind, of course, that the ownership of the castles and estates to which you refer may have been passed, in full accordance with law, over the centuries, to persons other to whom titles passed.[3]

This, again, was not addressing the actual question. It is not surprising that such suggestions would meet with some incomprehension when the Irish state has not even been able to agree to give courtesy recognition to Gaelic titles as *titles* in accordance with international precedence and usages, but has sought to prevaricate on whether they are, in reality, titles or, semantically, "designations."

As we have seen, during the period of 1541 to 1610, all Gaelic titles, as well as the native Irish legal system, were abolished and made "utterly extinct" under English common law and statute law. Those laws, the language and customs were forced on the Irish people by military conquest. The policy was to recreate the country in the English image. The Irish aristocracy, from kings on downward, were forced to surrender their titles and their territories and to accept from the English kings English titles. The clan territories they had controlled under the restrictions of Brehon law were regranted to them in part, making them tenants under English feudal law. As kingship was an electoral as well as a hereditary office, and as the king was not a feudal monarch with complete ownership of the land, it was impossible for a king to agree to this change of social system against the will of both his family and people. He simply did not have such rights under the Irish law. Some Irish aristocrats did surrender, and internal dynastic wars immediately commenced, weakening the Irish defense against England and allowing the English forces to move in and seize territories during the internecine struggles that had been created. Where the Irish held out with a degree of unity, a vicious campaign of military conquest was pursued, creating near deserts in the once-affluent kingdoms.

When an Irish state reemerged in 1922, the state had, for convenience sake, adopted the English legal system, the most important aspect of which—for the surviving Gaelic aristocracy—was the concept of primogeniture, inheritance by the eldest male heir. This was not a concept of inheritance under Irish law.

When in 1944 the Irish state started to give courtesy recognition to those surviving chiefly houses, the state announced that recognition of their legitimacy could be made only by a civil service office procedure based on the inherited state laws of English primogeniture. This caused immediate criticism from historians and Gaelic scholars and even from some of the chiefly houses themselves. Having been abolished in both statute and common law, no Gaelic titles can exist in modern times under those laws that were adopted by the emerging Irish state.

Gaelic titles, it was also pointed out, could exist only by an acknowledgment that the laws of the conquerors, enacted by force majeure and not by the will of the people, were invalid as legal authority. It did not, therefore, abolish those titles or the dynastic laws of succession in the perception of the people. Indeed, the parallel to this is the very assertion by the Irish people, by force of arms, generation after generation since the Tudor Conquests, that England's presence in Ireland and its conquests and laws imposed through force majeure were illegal and not binding on the Irish people. This concept has always been the raison d'être and the justification of Irish military uprisings against English rule, which is clearly demonstrated in the various insurgent proclamations, culminating in the Irish Declaration of Independence of January 21, 1919.

The first great problem to be resolved for the chiefly houses, therefore, is the one arising from the initial policy mistake of 1944, which we have previously discussed. The Standing Council of Irish Chiefs and Chieftains has declared that its titles stem from the Brehon law system and that the dynastic laws of succession cannot be altered retrospectively. In seeking to force a retrospective change of those successional laws, the modern Irish state can only be seen as acting in an illegal fashion. It also places itself in a ridiculous position by declaring that it will only give courtesy recognition to Gaelic titles if they are claimed within the parameters of the law system that has "utterly abolished" the same titles.

As has been pointed out earlier, this is as nonsensical as if the Irish state were demanding that the Anglo-Irish peers could be given courtesy recognition in Ireland only if they changed their primogeniture successional method to that of elected tanistry. Successional laws cannot be changed retrospectively.

International law, applied to these matters, argues that such titles can exist only through the maintenance of the native dynastic laws of inheritance before the conquest of the state. It further argues that no "successor state" can arbitrarily and retrospectively change the laws of inheritance of the aristocratic dynasties of the former state that succumbed by alien conquest.

Therefore, international law is quite clear that without a recognition of the Brehon law of succession, any claimant to a Gaelic title has no authority to use such a title. Even if their genealogies prove their direct ancestry to the last established holder of that title, before the title was abolished by statute and Common Law during the conquests, they can only be "recognized" as lineal descendants and not holders of any title. The title is not transmitted by primogeniture and therefore cannot be claimed by primogeniture. A Gaelic title is the "ideal property" of the family, and remains at the disposal and bestowal of those members of the family who constitute the *derbhfine* as prescribed by dynastic law, and cannot be devised, bestowed or conferred by any authority outside of the *derbhfine* of the family, even if exercising heraldic or state jurisdiction. Even if the Irish State subsequently refused to allow courtesy recognition to the Gaelic aristocracy, it would not invalidate their titles so long as they were handed down in the recognized chiefly branch of the family in accordance with the wishes of the *derbhfine*.

However, all these arguments may now be negated simply because their principal advocate of Brehon law succession among the modern Chiefs, from 1992 to 1999, was the bogus MacCarthy Mór, Terence McCarthy. The damage caused to the validity of the Irish Chiefs cannot, as yet, be calculated. In reaction against him as a personality, it may well be that the Brehon principals he espoused will be dismissed as well. Now the promised Irish Government inquiry into the method of recognizing Gaelic titles, announced in the Dáil on September 29, 1999, has been rescinded and the matter placed back in the hands of the Genealogical Office. It is known that the Office still favors primogeniture as a method of recognition, as, indeed, do several of the holders of these titles.

In view of the length of time that has elapsed between the last holders of Gaelic titles attaining their titles by Brehon law succession, perhaps the wisest course is not to recognize Gaelic titles at all. The current Chief Herald is of the opinion that his office merely recognizes the head of the senior branch of the family descending from the old kings and princes and it is up to the head of that family how he designates himself. This is not entirely accurate, for the state clearly, in its patent, specifies the titles as a cognitive act. Perhaps a compromise solution, and the most practical, might be for the state to identify the head of the senior branch of the family descending from the last acknowledged holder of a title at the time such titles were proscribed by English law. Then the state could allow the family to reconstitute its *derbhfine* to pass on the title under the old tanistry forms of succession. This would provide some continuity of the Gaelic reality.

Whatever course the Chief Herald decides upon, the path will not be easy. In the period that I have been working on this project, I have come to a closer understanding of the old Irish proverb: "*Is sleamhuin leac dorus tigh móir*"—the door-step of a great house is slippery. But, as a republican, I have also been re-minded of some lines from Thomas Paine (1737–1809): "But such is the irre-sistible nature of truth, that all it asks, and all it wants, is the liberty of appearing."

Certainly the argument that primogeniture, had it been historically and legally valid, might be a better method of recognition than tanistry, and would prevent fraudulent claims, is a *non sequitur*. Terence McCarthy was recognized under a claim of primogeniture and he was not the first to make such fraudu-lent claims.

The question of whether or not the Gaelic aristocracy have any relevancy in the modern world and the modern Irish Republic is yet another matter. Could the Standing Council of Irish Chiefs and Chieftains have a similar role in Ireland to that of the Standing Council of Scottish Chiefs in Scotland? Was Irish Prime Minister Eamon De Valéra really serious when, in 1937, he exam-ined the idea of installing the direct descent of the High King Brían Boroimhe as "Prince President" under the new Irish Constitution?

There are now some twenty heads of Gaelic aristocratic houses given courtesy recognition. This does not mean that there are only twenty families descended from the Gaelic aristocrats who have survived the centuries of re-pression, maintaining the right to their ancient titles. It would be curious, in-deed, if descendants from every old Gaelic noble house had not survived in some part of the world. Perhaps they can even prove a direct descent from the ancestor who held the title. But does a primogeniture claim really have any meaning, historically, legally or morally?

Several new claims have been submitted to the Chief Herald of Ireland and to the Standing Council, which, under its constitution, has its own Committee of Privileges, and therefore can give recognition to such claimants irrespective of the Irish Genealogical Office. Yet the Standing Council will probably admit that it does not have the qualified personnel to adjudicate any such claims. Claims for recognition of the titles The MacSweeney Doe, The O'Dignan, The O'Dowd and The O'Gara have been made. Other claimants do not even bother to seek recognition but merely adopt their styles arbitrarily, and many appear accepted by the general public.

Pierce Charles Mahony (1850–1930) changed his name in 1912 by Deed Poll to The O'Mahoney of Kerry and was acknowledged by the *Irish Times*, February 7, 1998, as holding a chiefly title. When Gerald O'Brennan of Ballyragget (1912–99) styled himself The O'Brennan, Prince of Idough, his title was accepted and the December 10, 1999 edition of the *Kilkenny People* wrote his obituary acknowledging the title and claiming that he was the last of the old princely family.

The promised Government review of the situation might have clarified matters by calling on scholars in all related fields. Now it is left to the very Office from which the current problems emanated in 1944. In an editorial in the Spring 2000 issue of *Gaelic Heritage*, Dr. Patrick O'Shea said:

> there is tremendous interest, particularly among descendants of the Irish Diaspora, in the history and genealogy of the great Gaelic and Anglo-Norman Irish families. Unfortunately, some have capitalised on this well-meaning enthusiasm by publishing poorly researched or deliberately misleading books, establishing organisations of dubious validity, or selling merchandise which inaccurately and improperly explains or displays historical, genealogical, or heraldic material.

This book mainly has confined itself to those who have been acknowledged by both the Standing Council and Chief Herald. There are, in the opinion of the author, some necessary exceptions to this rule. One is MacDonnell of The Glens, recognized by the Chief Herald but, at the time of writing, still excluded from the Standing Council, having previously been "blackballed" by Terence McCarthy. Another is MacMorrough Kavanagh; although his father was recognized in 1959 and accepted as the successor in 1962, MacMorrough Kavanagh was questioned by subsequent Chief Heralds and not fully acknowledged until July 2000, and is still not a member of the Standing Council. Additionally, the book deals with The O'Neill of Tyrone, who styles himself as The O'Neill Mór. While he has not felt the necessity to seek recognition from Ireland, he is a grandee of Spain, and widely acknowledged as the lineal descendant of the Tyrone house.

The book has also dealt with MacSweeney Doe, who has long been acknowledged by many genealogists and historians as an authentic scion of the Chiefs of Doe, despite other claimants. His recognition by the Chief Herald was held up because of the "McCarthy Affair" and the subsequent "hold" put on all further recognitions.

The Heraldic Adviser to the Standing Council, Gerard Crotty, explains the basis for those claiming Gaelic titles.

When the Office registers a Chief or Chieftain the act is one of recognition only, not of creation. This recognition is by courtesy only, and therefore a recognized Chief is in a position hardly differing from the holder of a foreign title, though the courtesy has been formally accorded to him. This is an important point in connection with those Chiefs whose families have allowed the use of the title to lapse. In such cases, the newly resumed title is not a new creation. The underlying concept must be one of continuity. There are no new chiefs. The title must be deemed to have been vested *de jure* in all their intervening predecessors from the time of the last acknowledged holder before the period of dormancy began.[4]

This volume, then, has not been simply a study of several extraordinary family histories; nor merely the story of their loss of power as the ruling Gaelic elite of Ireland and their subsequent struggle for survival; likewise it is not a voyeuristic examination of the current lifestyles of families who had their origin in the primeval beginnings of an archaic Celtic society, whose lineages were claimed as ancient even at the time of the birth of Christ.

It may be all those things . . . but more.

It is the story of the attempted destruction of an venerable civilization and culture; the near eradication of a language, social concepts and an ancient law system. In many respects, the current conflicts of the Chiefly Houses over the manner of their recognition by the modern Irish state may, sadly perhaps, be seen as the last dying kicks of a cultural incompatibility; the final destruction of what was one of the most vibrant, artistic and philosophical of European cultures; the final twilight of three thousand years of cultural continuum. Or is it, one might wonder, the initial pangs of a rebirth?

Acknowledgments

I would like to express my gratitude to the people without whose cooperation, warm hospitality and assistance this book would not have been possible—to the members of the *Buanchomhairle Thaoisigh Éireann*, the Standing Council of Irish Chiefs and Chieftains and their representatives, both collectively and individually, whom I list herewith alphabetically:

The Fox; MacDermot, Prince of Coolavin; MacGillycuddy of The Reeks; Maguire, Prince of Fermanagh; O'Brien, Prince of Thomond; O'Callaghan; O'Carroll of Ely; O'Conor Don, Prince of Connacht and his late father; O'Doghartaigh of Inis Eoghan and his representative and brother Rear Admiral Pascual O'Dogherty; The O'Donoghue of the Glens; the Tanist of The O'Donel of Tirconnell, Don Leopoldo O'Donnell, Duque de Tetuan; O'Donovan; the late Philip, The O'Grady and his successor, the current O'Grady; O'Kelly of Gallagh and Tycooly; O'Long of Garranelongy; O'Morchoe; O'Néill, Prince of Clanaboy; and The O'Ruairc, Prince of Breifne.

Thanks also go to those holders of Gaelic titles who are not members of the Council yet have the recognition of the Chief Herald at the time of writing: The MacMorrough Kavanagh, Prince of Leinster, and his Tanist, Simon Mac-Morrough Kavanagh, and Count Randal, The MacDonnell of The Glens, to whom is due a special word of thanks for his advice and tenacity in research, without which this new edition could not have been written.

I am also appreciative of the replies given by The O'Néill of Tyrone, Don Carlos O'Neill y Castrillo, Marqués de la Granja e del Norte y de Villaverde de San Isidro, Conde de Benagiar, and to Tom Sweeney, The MacSweeney Doe, for all his kindness and assistance.

Thanks must go to Barry Trant McCarthy and to Liam Trant McCarthy for meeting with me and showing me their family papers.

I should express my thanks and appreciation to the Chevalier Gerard Crotty, formerly Honorable Secretary to, and now Heraldic Adviser of, the Standing Council of Irish Chiefs and Chieftains for his support, cooperation and advice.

I would particularly like to record my additional appreciation to O'Brien of Thomond, O'Donoghue of the Glens, O'Long of Garranelongy and O'Ruairc of Breifne, who went out of their way to express their support for me when the first edition of this book was published coinciding with the revelations about Terence McCarthy. In that expression of thanks, I would like to include Ben Glazebrook, chairman of my London publishers, Constable, and my editors Carol O'Brien (Constable) and Michael Flamini (Palgrave, New York), and my colleagues and friends for their support during a very arduous time.

Special thanks have to be accorded my indefatigable researcher, Mrs. Elizabeth Murray.

Further appreciation must be tended to Mary Aylward for her linguistic assistance; to Anthony Carty, Eversheds Professor of International Law, University of Derby; to Collette Ellison, Executive Secretary of the Royal Society of Antiquaries of Ireland; to Dr. Tommy Graham, Trinity College, Dublin; to Terry McBride (Irish and Reference Department) of The Linen Hall Library, Belfast; to Hubert Cheeshyre, former Norroy and Ulster King of Arms and now Clarenceux King of Arms; to Rosemary MacGillycuddy of Baltimore, County Cork; to Maurice McCann; to the late Professor Brían Ó Cuív who, although he had retired from the Dublin Institute for Advanced Studies at the time, was still willing to deal with my obscure questions; to his son Eamon Ó Cuív, Minister of State Department of Arts, Heritage, Gaeltacht and Islands, and his cousin and departmental head, Minister Síle De Valéra, for consideration of my questions; to Brendan O'Donoghue, Chief Herald of Ireland, for his courtesy and assistance in a difficult time; to John O'Donoghue TD, Minister of Justice; to Seán Ó Ceallaigh BA, LLB, of Phibsboro, Dublin; to Colonel Philip O'Grady of Askeaton, County Limerick; to Donall Ó Luanaigh, Keeper (Collections), National Library of Ireland; to Dr. Patrick M. O'Shea of Minnesota; to Kevin O'Toole, secretary of Clann Ua Tuathail; to Colonel Stewart Boone McCarty USMC; to my Spanish interpreter, Francis H. Westwood; to Thomas Woodcock, Norroy and Ulster King of Arms; to Dr. Margaret Tierney, chairperson of Clans of Ireland Ltd; to David R. Wooten of The Gaelic Heritage Society; to M. Jean-Louis Courtois de Viçose, whose family inherited the L'Hotel MacCarthy, Toulouse, in 1868.

Finally, last but by no means least, warmest thanks and appreciation to my wife, Dorothy, for her encouragement and advice, as well as some practical and tenacious research assistance in a couple of difficult areas, and for her support and counsel in the dark days following the revelation of the bogus MacCarthy Mór. Above all, Dorothy, thanks for just for being there!

NOTES

CHAPTER ONE

1. Thomas F. O'Rahilly, *Early Irish History and Mythology* (Dublin: Dublin Institute for Advance Studies, 1946).
2. Eoin MacNeil, *Phases of Irish History* (reprint; Dublin: M. H. Gill, 1968).
3. Kuno Meyer, "Über die Aeltiste irische Dictung," in *Abhandlungender koniglich Preussichen Akademie de Wissenschaften* (Berlin, 6, 1913/14).
4. Myles Dillon, *Celts and Aryans: Survivals of Indo-European Speech and Society* (Simla: Indian Institute of Advanced Study, 1975).
5. Gerard Crotty, "Chiefs of the Name," *Aspects of Irish Genealogy*, ed. by M. D. Evans (Dublin, 1999).
6. See bibliography (unpublished manuscripts). This document was last in the keeping of Terence McCarthy. The author has a photocopy given to him in 1997 by Mr. McCarthy.
7. Mary Hayden and George Moonan, *A Short History of the Irish People* (Dublin: Talbot Press, 1921).
8. Katharine Simms, "The O'Hanlons, the O'Neills and the Anglo-Normans in Thirteenth Century Armagh" (Armagh: *Seanchas Ard Mhaca* 9, 1978/79): 70–94.
9. William E. Montgomery, *Land Tenure in Ireland* (Cambridge: Cambridge University Press, 1989).
10. Laurence Ginnell, *The Brehon Laws: A Legal Handbook* (London: T. Fisher Unwin, 1894).
11. Montgomery, *Land Tenure in Ireland,* op. cit.
12. G. Webb and A. Walker (trans.), *St. Bernard of Clairveaux: The First Life* (London, 1960).
13. Edmund Curtis and R. B. McDowell, *Irish Historical Documents 1172–1922* (reprint; London: Methuen, 1968), pp. 19–24.
14. Edmund Curtis, *A History of Medieval Ireland from 1086 to 1532* (Dublin: Maunsel and Roberts, 1923).
15. Curtis and McDowell, *Irish Historical Documents,* op cit. pp. 18–19.
16. Mike Ashley, *British Monarchs* (London: Robinson, 1999).
17. Curtis and McDowell, *Irish Historical Documents,* op. cit. pp. 38–46.
18. Patrick C. Power, *A Literary History of Ireland* (Cork: Mercier Press, 1969).
19. *State Papers Henry VIII,* vol. 2, 1–31 (London, 11 vols., 1830–1852); also quoted in Constantia Maxwell, *Irish History from Contemporary Sources, 1509–1610* (London: George Allen & Unwin, 1923).
20. Ibid., vol. 2, pp. 162–63.
21. *State Papers, Henry VIII,* vol. 3, p. 48.
22. *State Papers, Henry VIII,* vol. 2, p. 480.
23. The text of this translation is in Sir James Ware's Papers, Oxford MS Rawlinson B 488, reprinted in *Analecta Hibernica,* vol. 1, p. 140.
24. *State Papers, Henry VIII* vol. 3 (Ireland II, 140).

25. *Letters & Papers, Henry VIII*, 16, no 755 and *Calendar of Carew MSS*, III, 523, ed. J. S. Brewer and W. Bullen, (London, 6 vols., 1867–73).
26. *State Papers of Henry VIII*, vol. 3, 304–305.
27. James Lydon, ed., "The Interaction of Laws," *The English in Medieval Ireland* (Dublin: Royal Irish Academy, 1984).

CHAPTER TWO

1. Calvert Watkins, "Indo-European Metrics and Archaic Irish Verse," *Celtica* 6 (1963).
2. D. A. Bincy, "The Linguistic and Historical Value of the Old Irish Law Tracts," *Proceedings of the British Academy* 29 (1943).
3. See Myles Dillon, "Celt and Hindu" (University College, Dublin, 1973); and Myles Dillon, *Celts and Aryans: Survivals of Indo-European Speech and Society* (Simla: Indian Institute of Advanced Study, 1975).
4. *Ancient Laws of Ireland*, vol. 4 (Dublin: Stationery Office, 1865–1901), p. 373 et. seq.
5. Eoin MacNeill, *Early Irish Laws and Institutions* (Dublin: Burnes, Oates and Washington, 1935), p. 97.
6. T. M. Charles-Edwards, "The Heir-Apparent in Irish and Welsh Law," *Celtica* 9 (1971).
7. Donnchadh Ó Corráin, "Irish Regnal Succession: A Reappriasal," *Studia Hibernia*, no. 11 (1971).
8. James Hogan, "The Irish Law of Kingship: With Special Reference to Aileach and Cenél Eoghain," *Proceedings of the Royal Irish Academy* 40 (1931–32).
9. Green's interpretation is discussed in Charles-Edwards, "The Heir-Apparent," op. cit. See also David Greene, "The Making of Insular Celtic," in *Proceedings of the Second International Congress of Celtic Studies*, 1963 (Cardiff, 1966): 9–21.
10. Laurence Ginnell, *The Brehon Laws: A Legal Handbook* (London: T. Fisher Unwin, 1894).
11. Kenneth Nicholls, K. Lydon and M. MacCurtain, *Gaelic and Gaelicised Ireland in the Middle Ages* (Dublin: Gill and Macmillan, 1972), p. 27.
12. See Hogan, "Irish Law of Kingship," and Ó Corráin, "Irish Regnal Succession."
13. James Lydon, ed. "The Interaction of Laws," in *The English in Medieval Ireland* (Dublin: Royal Irish Academy, 1984).
14. Hogan, "Irish Law of Kingship," op cit.
15. *Analecta Hibernia* 3, pp. 73–74.
16. *Ancient Laws of Ireland*, vol 1, pp. 45–49.
17. R. Thurneysen et al, *Studies in Early Irish Law* (Dublin: Royal Irish Academy, 1936).
18. *Zeitschrift für Celtische Philologie* 14 (1911): 365. One of the clearest studies on the subject if Dr. Sophie Bryant, "The Right of Women as Owners of Property," in *Liberty, Order and Law Under Native Irish Rule* (London: Harding and More Ltd., 1923).

CHAPTER THREE

1. Morrin,ed., *Cal. Pat. Rolls*, I, 81.
2. *States Papers*, Henry VIII, vol. 3, pp. 332–34.
3. *Calendar Carew Mss* I, pp. 245–46.
4. John Daview, *A Discovery of the True Causes Why Ireland Was Never Entirely Subdued* (London, 1912).
5. Act of Attainder II Elizabeth c. I, see Maxwell, op cit.
6. Maxwell op cit.

7. *The Irish Fiants of the Tudor Sovereigns*, 4 vols., introduced by Kenneth Nicholls and preface by Tomás G. O'Canann (Dublin: Edmund Burke, 1994). These volumes are the essential records of the surrender and regrant period and have an extensive index.
8. Ibid.
9. See chapter 1, note 6.
10. *The Fiants.*
11. Ibid.
12. Hogan, op cit.
13. Davies, op cit.
14. Ibid.
15. Ibid.
16. O'Donovan Mss: "Letters of Dr. John O'Donovan to Morgan William O'Donovan" (see bibliography) privately held by The O'Donovan.
17. Ibid.
18. *The Fiants* op cit.
19. *The Fiants* op cit.

CHAPTER FOUR

1. Anthony Carty, *Was Ireland Conquered?: International Law and the Irish Question* (London: Pluto Press, 1996).
2. Marilyn Gerriets, "The King as Judge in Early Ireland," *Celtica*, vol. XX, (1988).
3. Standish Hayes O'Grady, ed. *Catalogue of Irish Mss in the British Museum*, London, p. 473.
4. *Brían Ó Cuív, "A Sixteenth Century Political Poem,"* Éigse 15 (1973074).
5. R. Brodie, ed., *Letters and Papers, Henry VIII* (London, vols. 14–21); see specifically 19, no 78.
6. H. C. Hamilton, E. G. Atkinson, and R. P. Mahaffy, ed., *Calendar of State Papers, Ireland 1509–73* (London, 24 vols., 1860–1969), pp. 289–312.
7. Raphael Holinshed, *Chronicles of England, Scotland and Ireland* (London, 1578), vol. 6, p. 331.
8. *State Papers Henry VIII* (Ireland) vol. 2, p. 288.
9. Ivar O'Brien, *O'Brien of Thomond: The O'Briens in Irish History 1500–1865* (Chichester: Phillimore, 1986), p. 19.
10. *The Fiants*, op cit., see 4761; see Rolls Office (Miscellaneous), no. 23.
11. Ibid.
12. Ibid.
13. Ibid.
14. Maxwell, op cit.
15. Ibid.
16. *Calendar of State Papers 1509–73*, pp. 509–511, 515.
17. Richard Bagwell, *Ireland Under the Tudors* (London, 3 vols. 1885–1890, reprint; London: Holland Press, 1963); see vol. 3, p. 105.
18. Maxwell op cit., see p. 48.
19. Ibid.
20. John Murphy, *Ireland, Industrial, Political and Social* (London: Longmans, Green and Co., 1870), p. 255.
21. *The Fiants.*
22. *The Fiants.*
23. SirCharles Petrie, "Ireland in Spanish and French Strategy 1558–1815," *Irish Sword*, vol. VI (24):154–65.
24. Davies op cit.
25. Ibid.

26. Ibid.
27. Hogan op cit.; see p. 252.

CHAPTER FIVE

1. *The Fiants*, op cit.
2. See Davis op cit., enacted in Hilary (term) 3rd Year of King James I.
3. John Murphy, *Ireland, Industrial, Political and Social* (London: Longmans, Green and Co., 1870), p. 261.
4. Text is given in M. J. Bonn, *Die englishe kolonisation in Irland* (Berlin, n.d.), vol. 1, pp. 394–397.
5. Mathew O'Conor, *The History of Irish Catholics* (Dublin: Hodges, 1813).
6. Hohn P. Prendergast, *The Cromwellian Settlement of Ireland* (London: Longmans, Green and Co., 1865), p. xxii.
7. *Irish Statutes*, vol. 2, p. 169, 10, and 11 Charles I c. 16, (Dublin, 20 vols., 1786–1801).
8. Prendergast, *Cromwellian Settlement* op cit.
9. Sir Henry Ellis Original Letters, 3rd series, Public Record Office of Northern Ireland, Ellis Papers D 686.
10. Father Patrick O'Curneen, "A Tract on the O'Rourkes," 1714, Royal Irish Academy, Ms C iv I, translated by Professor James Carney, *Celtica I* (1950). Also see Betty MacDermot, *Ó Ruairc of Breifne* (Manorhamilton, Leitrim: Drumlin Publications, 1990), pp. 207–215.
11. Micheline Walsh, *Spanish Knights of Irish Origins*, 4 vols. (Dublin: Stationery Office, 1960, 1965, 1970, 1978).
12. Calendar of State Papers, Ireland, op cit. p 13; see also the full text in Fynes Moprrison, *An Itinerary*, vol. 3 (Glasgow: James MacLehse, 1907–1908), pp. 299–301.
13. Charles O'Kelly, *Macariae Excidium, or the Destruction of Cyprus* (London: Camden Society, 1841).
14. Michael Kelly, *Reminiscences* (London, 1826).
15. Arthur Yound, *A Tour of Ireland 1776–1779* (London: 3 vols., 1779).
16. Daniel Corkery, *The Hidden Ireland* (Dublin: M. H. Gill, 1924).
17. Denish Gwynn, *Daniel O'Connell* (reprint; Cork: Cork University Press, 1947), pp. 16–17.
18. Corkery, *Hidden Ireland*.
19. Eugene O'Curry, *On the Manners and Customs of Ancient Ireland* (London, 1873; facsimile: Edmund Burke, 1996); see introduction by Dr. W. K. O'Sullivan.
20. Article by H. M. J. O'Hanlon in *Dublin Penny Journal* (1904), reprinted in Thomas Mathews, *The O'Neills of Ulster: Their History and Genealogy*, 3 vols. (Dublin: Sealy, Bryers & Walker, 1903), vol. 3, p. 348.
21. *Illustrated London News*, April 14, 1902.
22. Marcus Bourke, *The O'Rahilly* (Kerry: Anvil Books, 1967).
23. Richard Davis, *Arthur Griffith and Non Violent Sinn Féin* (Dublin: Anvil Books, 1974).
24. Bourke, *The O'Rahilly*, op cit.
25. Dorothy Macardle, *The Irish Republic* (London: Victor Gollancz, 1937).

CHAPTER SIX

1. Charles Lysaght, *Edward MacLysaght 1887–1986* (Dublin: National Library of Ireland, 1988), p. 20.
2. R. B. McDowell, *The Irish Convention 1917–18* (London: Routledge and Kegan Paul, 1970), p. 113.

3. Grania O'Brien, *These My Friends and Forbears: The O'Briens of Dromoland* (County Clare: Ballinakella Press, n.d.).
4. C. J. O'Donnell, *The Irish Future with the Lordship of the World* (London: Cecil Palmer, 1929), p. 247.
5. Edward MacLysaght, "The Irish Chieftainries," in Hugh Montgomery-Massingberd, ed., *Burke's Introduction to Irish Ancestry* (London: Burke's Peerage, 1976), pp. 454–56.
6. Gerard Crotty, "Chiefs of the Name," in M. D. Evans, ed., *Aspects of Irish Genealogy II* (Dublin, 1996), p. 203.
7. MacLysaght, "Irish Chieftainries."
8. Italian texts of both verdicts are registered at the District Magistrate Court of Casale Monferrato, Republic of Italy, January 20 and June 19, 1998. English translations of the two verdicts were registered by the Administrative Office of the U.S. Courts, Federal Certified Interpreter, State of California, Identification No 439067, for Luce, Forward, Hamilton and Scripps, Attorneys-at-Law (founded 1873). These texts were used in the Count of Clandermand, ed., *New Book of Rights* (Royal Eóghanacht Society, 1998).
9. Crotty, "Chiefs of the Name."
10. Ibid.
11. Letter to author, May 2, 2000.
12. Letter to author, April 15, 1998.
13. Letter to author, June 22, 2000.
14. *The Royal O'Briens: A Tribute* (published by Clan O'Brien Association, 1992).
15. Ibid.
16. Letter to author, March 6, 1998.
17. Letter to Dr. Jean MacCarthy from Rory O'Connor of Clans of Ireland Ltd., June 1, 1993. Copy with author.
18. Terence McCarthy wrote a fan letter to me dated December 30, 1992. I replied to him on January 7, 1993. Copies with author.
19. Italian judgements, certified copies with author in Italian and English, reprinted in *New Book of Rights* (see bibliography).
20. Ibid.
21. Ibid.
22. "Kaiser's Rule on Marriage still Applies to Heirs," *Daily Telegraph* (December 18, 1999). Dr. Rainer Kramer's helpful comments in letter to author of September 8, 2000.
23. Letter to author, April 10, 1998.
24. Letter to author, March 6, 1998.
25. Letter to author, April 15, 1998.
26. Letter to author, January 28, 2000.
27. Letter to author, July 21, 1998.
28. Crotty, "Chiefs of the Name," op cit.

CHAPTER SEVEN

1. Mairtín Ó Murchú, *The Irish Language* (Dublin: Department of Foreign Affairs and Bord na Gaeilge, 1985).
2. *Ériu 2*, p. 49.
3. Kuno Meyer, "Über die Alteste irische Dichtung," *Abhandlungender Königlich Preussischen Akademie der Wissenschaften* (Berlin: 1913 and 1914).
4. Myles Dillon, "The Story of the Finding of Cashel," *Ériu* 16 (1952): 61–73.
5. Séamus Ó hInnse, ed. and trans., *Miscellaneous Irish Annals: A.D. 1114–1437* (Dublin, 1947).
6. Dillon, "Story of the Finding of Cashel," op cit.

7. A. Bugge, ed., *Caithreim Cheallacháin Chaisil* (Denmark: University of Christiana, 1905).

8. *The Vision of Tnugdal*, trans. Jean-Michel Picard (Dublin: Four Courts Press, 1989).

9. Patrick M. O'Shea, "Liturgy and Music at Cashel During the Reign of Cormac III MacCarthy," *Journal of the Gaelic Heritage Society* (Arkansas, 2000): 14–19.

10. *Cork Archaeological Journal*, no. 247 (1983).

11. Edmund Curtis, *A History of Medieval Ireland from 1086–1532* (Dublin: Maunsel and Roberts, 1923), p. 143.

12. John A. Murphy, *Justin MacCarthy, Lord Mountcashe, Commander of the First Irish Brigade in France* (Cork: Cork University Press, 1958; new edition, Clonmel: Royal Eóghanacht Society, 1999).

13. Valerie Bary, *Houses of Kerry* (County Clare: Ballinakilla Press, n.d.).

14. Interview with author, April 18, 2000.

15. Letter to author, May 17, 2000.

16. *Burke's Irish Family Records* (London: Burke's Peerage, 1976), p. 890.

17. "History of the Descendants of Richard, The MacGillycuddy of the Reeks (1826–1866)," by his grandson Sir Aubrey Metcalfe (up to 1957), mss., duplicated and distributed by the McGillycuddy Clan Society.

18. Enno Stephan, *Geheimauftrag Irland* (Hamburg: Gerhard Stalling Verlag, 1961); English translation, *Spies in Ireland* (London: Macdonald & Company, 1963).

19. Richard Doherty, *Clear the Way! A History of the 38th (Irish) Brigade, 1941–47* (Dublin: 1993).

20. Public Record Office, London, ref. CAB 68, 8.

21. Joseph T. Carroll, *Ireland in the War Years, 1939–1945* (Newton Abbot: David & Charles, 1975).

CHAPTER EIGHT

1. Francis John Byrne, *Irish Kings and High Kings* (London: Batsford, 1973), pp. 11, 181, 212, 228, and 291 on the spurious pedigree of the Dál gCais.

2. Ibid.

3. A. Bugge, ed. *Caithreim Cheallacháin Chaisil*, op cit.

4. Brían Ó Cuív, "A Sixteenth Century Political Poem," *Éigse* 1 (1973–74).

5. Byrne, *Irish Kings and High Kings*.

6. *State Papers, Henry VIII*, vol. 3, pp. 304–5, op cit.

7. Ivar O'Brien, *O'Brien of Thomond: The O'Briens in Irish History 1500–1865* (Chichester: Phillimore, 1986).

8. One cannot help being reminded of Terence McCarthy's case against Professor Horak, in which the bogus MacCarthy Mór took out an action to prove he was the rightful claimant in the Italian Courts. See chapter 12.

9. Kit and Cyril Ó Céirín. *Women of Ireland: A Biographical Dictionary* (Newtownlynch, County Galway: Tír Eolas, 1996), pp. 178–79.

10. Alfred Perceval Graves, *To Return to All That* (London: Jonathan Cape, 1930.)

11. Grania O'Brien, *These My Friends and Forbears: The O'Briens of Dromoland* (County Clare: Ballinakella Press, n.d.)

12. Ibid.

CHAPTER NINE

1. Charles MacNeill, in *Analecta Hibernia* (1934), vol. VI.

2. Patrick O'Connor, *The Royal O'Connors of Connaught* (Swinford, County Mayo: Old House Press, 1997).

3. Ibid.

4. Pyers O'Conor Nash, *The History and Heritage of the Royal O'Conors* (Boyle: Purcelle Print, 1990).

5. *Anthologia Hibernica*, vol. 2, Dublin, 1793.

6. Right Honorable Charles Owen O'Conor Don, *The O'Conors of Connaught* (Dublin, Figgis: 1891).

7. *The Fiants*, op cit.

8. Dermot MacDermot, *MacDermot of Moylurg: The Story of a Connacht Family* (Manorhamilton, Leitrim: Drumlin Publications, 1996).

9. T. P. Kilfeather, *Graveyard of the Spanish Armada* (Tralee, Anvil Books. 1967).

10. Ibid.

11. Hist. Mss. Comm. Ceciil. Mss. 3–4, no. 32, p. 509, National Library of Ireland. See also Betty MacDermot, *Ó Ruairc of Breifne* (Manorhamilton, Leitrim: Drumlin Publications, 1990).

12. Ibid.

CHAPTER TEN

1. Francis John Byrne, *Irish Kings and High Kings* (London: Batsford, 1973), pp. 64, 78–81, 93.

2. Dáithí Ó hÓgáin, *Myth, Legend and Romance* (London: Ryan, 1990), pp. 322–32.

3. Renagh Holohan, *The Irish Chateaux* (Dublin: Lilliput, 1989), pp. 130–21.

4. Ian Moncrieffe contributed the genealogical section of the *O'Neill Commemorative Journal* (Belfast: 1982). He divides the family clearly into "The O'Neill Mór of Tyrone," tracing the line to the Marques de la Granja (pp. 22–27) and "The O'Neill Buidhe of Clanaboy," tracing it to the Portuguese O'Neills (pp. 28–33).

4. Ibid., pp. 22–23.

5. Cyril Fall, *The Birth of Ulster* (London: Methuen, 1936), p.62ff.

6. Ibid.

7. Moncrieffe, in *O'Neill Commemorative Journal*, p. 27.

8. Hugo O'Neill's letter to author, February 17, 1999.

9. Moncrieffe, in *O'Neill Commemorative Journal*, op cit.

10. Tadhg Ó Donnchadha, *Leabhar Cloinne Aodha Bhuide* (Dublin: Stationery Office, 1931).

11. Hugo O'Neill's letter to author, February 17, 1999

12. John Bannerman, *Studies in the History of Dal Riata* (Edinburgh: Scottish Academic Press, 1974).

13. Eoin MacNeill, *Phrases of Irish History* (reprint; Dublin: M. H. Gill, [1919]1968).

14. These have been illustrated and discussed in *The Ulster Journal of Archaeology 5* (1899) and in *The Glynnes*, Journal of The Glens of Antrim Historical Society: 22–23. The family has also appeared in *Burke's Landed Gentry* from its first edition. Literature on the MacDonnells is vast. One of the best accounts is still Reverend George Hill's *An Historical Account of the MacDonnells of Antrim,*. (Belfast: Archer & Son, 1873).

15. See Marx and Engels: *Marx and Engels on Ireland* (London: Lawrence & Wishard, 1971), pp. 154, 167–69, 390–91.

16. *The Irish Times* makes his recognition clear in his obituary, headed "Count Robert MacDonnell of The Glens. March 15, 1984.

17. Ibid.

18. Thomas F. O'Rahilly, *Dánta Grádha* (Cork: Cork University Press, 1926).

19. Maghnus Ó Domhnaill, *Betha Colaim Chille*, trans. A. O. Keller and Gertrude Schoepperle (Chicago: University of Chicago Press, 1918).

20. Anne M. Brady and Brian Cleeve, eds., *Biographical Dictionary of Irish Writers* (Dublin: Gill and Macmillan, 1985).

21. *Archivium Hibernicum*, vol. 7 (Dublin, 1922).

22. *Éire Iris Oifigiúil* (Official Government Gazette [Ireland]), December 22, 1944.
23. Statement issued by Chief Herald of Ireland, May, 2000.
24. Terence McCarthy, "A Brief Genealogical Account of the Maguires, Princes of Fermanagh and Barons of Enniskillen," *Familia* (Journal of the Ulster Historical Foundation) 2, no. 6, 1990.
25. Earl of Belmore, "Gleanings for Former Fermanagh Articles," *Ulster Journal of Archaeology*, series 2, 3 (1897).
26. Letter to author, May 2, 2000.
27. See "From Doe to Derryveigh," Clan Sweeny publication.
28. Ibid.
29. See John O'Donovan's letters in Michael O'Flanagan, ed., *Letters containing Information Relating to Antiquities in the County of Donegal Collected during the Progress of the Ordnance Survey in 1835* (Bray: privately issued, 1927), pp. 26–32.
30. For a full account of the evictions, see Liam Dolan, *Land War and Evictions in Derryveagh* (Dunland: Annaverna Press, 1980); and W. E. Vaughan, *Sin, Sheep and Scotsmen: John George Adair and the Derryveigh Evictions 1861* (Dublin: Appletree Press and Ulster Society for Historical Studies, 1983).
31. "Tarlach Mac Suibhne: An Píobaire Mór," Clan Sweeny publication.
32. Copies with author.
33. Ibid.
34. Ibid.

CHAPTER ELEVEN

1. Nicholas Furlong, *Dermot, King of Leinster and the Foreigners* (Kerry: Anvil Books, 1973).
2. Jean Creton, "Histoire de Roi d'Angleterre Richard," ed. by J. Webb, *Archaeologia* 20.
3. Edmund Curtis, *A History of Medieval Ireland from 1086 to 1532*, op cit. See also Robin Frame, "Two Kings in Leinster: The Crown and the MicMhurchadha in the Fourteenth Century," in T. B. Barry, R. Frame, and K. Simms, *Colony and Frontier in Medieval Ireland: Essays Presented to J. F. Lydon* (Dublin: Royal Irish, 1995).
4. Letter to author, May 2, 2000.
5. Genealogical Office, Mss. 171, pp. 49–54; see p. 53 for Ballyhale pedigree; also Mss. 182 a.
6. Genealogical Office, Mss. 627, p. 40. Copies of the correspondence among the Chief Herald, Genealogical Office, and MacMorrough Kavanagh are with the author.
7. Letter to author, May 2, 2000. This letter was superceded by a letter to the author of May 22, 2000, copying the Chief Herald's letter to Simon MacMorrough-Kavanagh of the same date.
8. Nicholas Furlong, *A Foster Son for a King* (Dublin: Hawthorne Books, 1986), p. 11. Furlong recounts his story of seeing the now-missing papers in the Genealogical Office in a letter to Simon MacMorrough-Kavanagh dated August 4, 1999; copy with the author.
9. *Calendar of Carew Mss.*, vol. 5, p. 255.
10. Alfred Smyth, *Celtic Leinster* (Dublin: Four Courts. 1982).

CHAPTER TWELVE

1. This chapter is based upon very extensive documentation. The correspondence, official applications and copies of documents from Terence McCarthy and copies of replies from the Genealogical Office, Dublin, between 1977 and 1999 are held as records by that office. These are available for public inspection on application

under Ireland's Freedom of Information Act (1997). These documents also contain the official report to the Office from Gorry Research of Dublin "On the Pedigree of Mr. Terence McCarthy of Belfast," dated March, 1999.

2. The author also holds an extensive file of letters and copies of letters from Terence McCarthy, as well as a copy of the sixty-one page submission of October 20, 1998, and a file of fifty-one copies of documents, prepared by Terence McCarthy's solicitor, John G. O'Donnell of Tipperary, sent to him without solicitation at the request of Terence McCarthy. The author also holds files of additional research material and records collected from September, 1999 to date clarifying aspects of the life and careers of Terence McCarthy and Andrew Davison, which were not covered by the Genealogical Office. A list of publications by McCarthy (as MacCarthy Mór, Prince of Desmond) and Davison (as Count of Clandermond) is found at the end of the bibliography.

3. Mentioned in the *Cork Archaeological and Historical Journal* of 1921.

4. Samuel Trant MacCarthy Mór, *A MacCarthy Miscellany* (Dundalk: Dundalgen Press, 1928).

5. Jack Holland and Henry McDonald, *INLA: Deadly Divisions* (Dublin: Poolbeg Press, 1994), pp. 296–97.

6. *Belfast Telegraph*, October 10, 1987.

7. Ciarán de Baróid, *Ballymurphy and the Irish War* (revised; London: Pluto Press, 2000), pp. 294–95.

8. Samuel Trant MacCarthy Mór, *The MacCarthys of Munster*, facsimile edition with introduction and commentary by the MacCarthy Mór, Prince of Desmond, 1997 (see introduction, p. I).

9. *Pointe de Vue*, July 21, 1992 and material posted on the Niadh Nask website on August 19, 1999, copy with author, November, 1999.

10. Conversation with author, November, 1999.

11. *Sunday World*, June 29, 1986. A file on Andrew Davison and his claims to be a Davison of Broughshane is also held by the Genealogical Office.

12. *A History of the Town of Belfast* (Belfast: A. MacKay, June, 1823).

13. This letter was never published by the *Sunday Times* but was posted on McCarthy's website. A copy of it was sent to the author among others by Terence McCarthy.

14. *Sunday Times* (Irish edition) June 20, 1999. (See "Irish Clan Chief's Reign May Be Over").

15. Statement by William F. K. Marmion, dated October 4, 1999, copy sent to author.

16. *Sunday Times* (as above).

17. Press and media stories relating to Terence McCarthy and Andrew Davison have appeared from time to time since July 1999. *Irish Roots*, the Cork-based genealogical magazine, of Autumn 1999 (no. 3) carried an editorial and two-page article "The MacCarthy Mór Controversy." Many other stories have appeared in the Dublin weekly satirical magazine the *Phoenix*, which has delighted in "exposing" bogus Chiefs (May 11, 2001) but, sadly, linking McCarthy to more genuine claimants (September 8, 2000).

CHAPTER THIRTEEN

1. Thomas O'Rahill, *Early Irish History and Mythology* (Dublin: Dublin Institute for Advanced Studies, 1946).

2. John Sladen, *Titles of Honour* (London, 1614), chap. 6, pt. 2, p. 842.

3. *Froissart's Chronicle*, ed. G. C. MacCauley (London, 1904), chap. 197, p. 433.

4. *The Annals of Clonmacnoise*, trans. 1627 by Connell Mageoghagan, ed. Denis Murphy, (Dublin, 1896), p. 34.

5. Irish Text Society, London, 1914 ed., vol. 1, p. 405.

6. Comte O'Kelly d'Aughrim, *Essai Historiques sur Irland* (Brussels: 1837), p. 8.
7. Anthony Marmion, *The Ancient and Modern History of the Maritime Ports of Ireland*, (London, 1858), pp. 45–47.
8. Patrick Weston Joyce, *A Social History of Ancient Ireland*, (London: Longmans, 1903), vol. 1, pp. 99–100.
9. *Dictionary of the Irish Language Based Mainly on Old and Middle Irish Materials* (Dublin: Royal Irish Academy, 1983).
10. Patrick S. Dineen, *Dánta Aodhagáin Uí Rathaile* (Poems of Egan O'Rahilly) (London: Irish Text Society, 1900, rev. 1911).
11. John O'Bishop of Cloyne, comp., *Focalóir Gaoidhilge Saxs-Bhearla* (Paris: Nicholas-Francis Valleyre, 1768).
12. Samuel Trant McCarthy, *The MacCarthys of Munster*, pp. 226–27, op cit.
13. O'Kelly de Conejera, "The Recognition of the Niadh Nask by the International Commission for Order so of Chivalry," in *Links in a Golden Chain: A Collection of Essays on the History of the Niadh Nask or the Military Order of the Golden Chain*, ed. by Count of Clandermond (AR: Gryfons Publishers, for the Royal Eóghanacht Society, 1998).
14. Ibid.
15. Lord Borhtwick, "Preface to Niadh Nask History and International Roll 1996," reprinted in Ibid., pp. 165–166.
16. Ibid.
17. Ibid.
18. Text of Italian judgements. Op cit.

CHAPTER FOURTEEN

1. Letter to Terence McCarthy, February 9, 1999.
2. Letter to author, May 28, 1998.
3. Letter to author, April 15, 1998.
4. Gerard Crotty, "Chiefs of the Name," in M. D. Evans, ed., *Aspects of Irish Genealogy*, op cit.

BIBLIOGRAPHY

SPECIALIZED BIBLIOGRAPHY ON BREHON LAW

ANCIENT LAWS OF IRELAND, 6 vols. Stationery Office, Dublin. 1865–1901.
BINCHY, D. A. "The Linguistic and Historical Value of the Old Irish Law Tracts." *Proceedings of the British Academy*. Vol. 29. 1943.
———. *Celtic and Anglo-Saxon Kingship* (O'Donnell Lecture for 1967–68). Oxford: Clarendon Press. 1970.
———. "Irish History and Law II." *Studia Hibernetica* 16. 1976.
———. "Ancient Irish Law." *The Irish Jurist*. Dublin. 1966.
———. *Corpus Iuris Hibernici*, 6 vols. Dublin. 1966.
———, ed. *Crith Gablach* (Medieval and Modern Irish Series, vol. xi). Stationery Office, Dublin. 1941.
BRYANT, Sophie. *Liberty, Order and Law under Native Irish Rule*. London: Harding and More Ltd. 1923.
CHARLES-EDWARDS, T. M. *Early Irish and Welsh Kinship*. Oxford: Clarendon Press. 1993.
CHARLES-EDWARDS, T. M. "The Heir-Apparent in Irish and Welsh Law." *Celtica*. Dublin Institute for Advance Studies. 1971.
GERRIETS, Marilyn. "The King as Judge in Early Ireland." *Celtica*. Dublin Institute of Advanced Studies. 1988.
GINNEL, Laurence. *The Brehon Laws: A Legal Handbook*. London: T. Fisher Unwin. 1894.
HOGAN, James. "The Irish Law of Kingship: With Special Reference to Aileach and Cenél Eoghain." *Proceedings of the Royal Irish Academy*. Vol. 40. Dublin: Hodges, Figgis & Co. 1931–32.
JASKI, Burt. *Early Irish Kingship and Succession*. Dublin: Four Courts Press. 2000.
KELLY, Fergus. *A Guide to Early Irish Law* (Early Irish Law Series, vol. 3). Dublin: Dublin Institute for Advanced Studies. 1988.
MACNEILL, Eoin. *Early Irish Laws and Institutions*. Dublin: Burns, Oates and Washington. 1935.
———. "The Irish Law of Dynastic Succession." *Irish Historical Studies* 8. 1919.
MAC NIOCAILL, Gearóid. "The Interaction of Laws," pp. 105–117. In *The English in Medieval Ireland*. Ed. by James Lydon. Dublin: Royal Irish Academy. 1984.
———. "The Heir-Designate in Early Medieval Law." *The Irish Jurist*, 3. Dublin. 1964.
NICHOLLS, Kenneth W. "Land, Law and Society in Sixteenth Century Ireland,"(O'-Donnell Lecture). Cork: University College (pamphlet). May 1976.
Ó CORRÁIN, Donchadh. "Irish Regnal Succession: A Reappraisal." *Studia Hibernica*, no. 11. Dublin: Coláiste Phádraig. 1971.
THURNEYSEN, R.; Power, Nancy; Dillon, Myles; Mulchrone, Kathleen; Binchy, D. A.; Knock, August; Ryan, John. *Studies in Early Irish Law*. Dublin: Royal Irish Academy. 1936.

SELECTED GENERAL BIBLIOGRAPHY

AITICHSON, N. B. *Armagh and the Royal Centres in Early Medieval Ireland.* Suffolk: Boydell & Brewer. 1994.

ASHLEY, Mike. *British Monarchs: The Complete Genealogy Gazetteer and Biographical Encyclopedia of the Kings and Queens of Britain.* London: Robinson. 1998.

BLAKE-FOSTER, Charles French. *The Irish Chieftains: or A Struggle for the Crown.* Dublin: McGlashen. 1871.

BOURKE (De Búrca), Eammon. *Burke, Bourke & De Burgh People and Places.* Clare: Edmund Bourke and Ballinakella Press. 1995.

BOURKE, Marcus. *The O'Rahilly.* Kerry: Anvil Books. 1967.

BRALY, David. *Uí Neill: A History of Western Civilisation's Oldest Family.* America Media Company. 1976.

BREIFNE, *Journal of the Breifne Historical Society.* 12 vols. Cavan. 1966–84.

BURKE'S Irish Family Records. Preface by Hugh Montgomery Massingberd. London: Burke's Peerage. 1976.

BURKE'S INTRODUCTION TO IRISH ANCESTRY. Hugh Montgomery, ed. London: Massingberd, Burke's Press. 1976.

BURKE, Sir Bernard. *A Genealogical and Heraldic History of the Land Gentry of Ireland.* Revised by A. C. Fox-Davies. London: Harrison. 1912.

BUTLER, William F. T. *Gleanings from Irish History.* London: Longmans. 1925.

BYRNE, John Francis. *Irish Kings and High Kings.* London: Batsford. 1973.

CALLANAN, Martin. *Records of Four Tipperary Septs, The O'Kennedys, O'Dwyers, O'Mulryans and O'Meaghers.* Shannon: JAG Publishing. 1995.

CANNY, Nicholas. *The Elizabethan Conquest of Ireland, A Pattern Established 1565–76.* Hassocks: Harvester Press. 1976.

CARNEY, James, ed. *A Genealogical History of the O'Reillys* (written in the eighteenth century by Eoghan Ó Raghallaigh). Dublin: Institute for Advanced Studies. 1959.

CARTY, Anthony. *Was Ireland Conquered? International Law and the Irish Question.* London: Pluto Press. 1996.

CASTANET, J. *Mémorial Historique et généalogique de la maison O'Neill de Tyrone et de Claneboy.* France: Bergerac. 1899.

CLIFFORD O'DONOVAN, P. *The Irish in France.* London: DeBeauvoir. 1990.

COLLINS, John T. "The Longs of Muskerry & Kinalea." *Journal of Cork Historical and Archaeological Society*, vol. 51, no. 173. January-June 1946.

CONE, Polly, ed. *Treasures of Early Irish Art 1500 BC to 1500 AD (from the collections of the National Museum of Ireland).* New York: The Metropolitan Museum of Art; Dublin: Royal Irish Academy and Trinity College. 1977.

CONNELLY, Richard F. *Irish Family History: An Historical and Genealogical Account of the Gaedhals, from the Earliest Period to the Present Time & etc.,* 2 vols. Dublin: Tallon. 1864–65.

CORKERY, Daniel. *The Hidden Ireland.* Dublin: M. H. Gill. 1924.

CROTTY, Gerard. "Chiefs of the Name." In *Aspects of Irish Genealogy.* Ed. by M. D. Evans. Dublin. 1996.

CUNNINGHAM, Bernadette. "The Composition of Connacht in the Lordships of Clanricade and Thomond 1577–1641." *Irish Historical Studies*, vol. 24, no. 93. May 1984.

CURTIS, Edmund. *A History of Medieval Ireland from 1086–1532.* Dublin: Maunsel and Roberts. 1923.

———. *Richard II in Ireland 1394–95 and the Submission of the Irish Chiefs.* Oxford: Oxford University Press. 1927.

——— and McDOWELL, R. B. *Irish Historical Documents 1172–1922.* London: Methuen. 1943.

D'ANGERVILLE, Count, ed. *The Royal, Peerage and Nobility of Europe* (Annuaire de la Noblesse de France), International edition in English. Monte Carlo, Monaco. 1997.

DE BLACAM, Aodh. *Gaelic Literature Surveyed.* Dublin: Talbot Press. 1929.

———. "The Hindu Act of Truth in Celtic Tradition." *Modern Philology*, vol. 44, no. 3. February 1947.

———. "Celt and Hindu" (pamphlet). Dublin: University College. 1973.

———. *Celts and Aryans: Survivals of Indo-European Speech and Society.* Simla: Indian Institute of Advanced Study. 1975.

———, ed. *Lebor na Cert* (The Book of Rights). London: Irish Text Society. 1962.

DOBBS, Margaret C. "The Ben Shenchus." *Revue Celtique.* Paris. Vols. 47 (1930), 48 (1931), and 49 (1932). A translation and commentary on *The Banshenchus* (History of Irishwomen).

DOHERTY, Murray. *The O'Doherty Historic Trail.* Derry: Guildhall Press. 1985.

DOLAN, Liam. *Land War and Evictions in Derryveagh.* Dunald: Annaverna Press. 1980.

DONEGAL ANNUAL 1978. See "Tarlach Mac Suibhne: An Píobaire Mór," Seán Ó Gallchóir.

DUHALLOW, The Lord of (William Marmion). *Gaelic Titles and Forms of Address*, 2nd ed. Kansas: Irish Genealogical Foundation. [1990]1997.

ELENCO DE GRANDEZAS Y TITULOS NOBILIAROS ESPAÑOLES. Revised edition. Madrid: Hilalguia. 1997.

ELLIS, Peter Berresford. *Hell or Connaught! The Cromwellian Colonisation of Ireland, 1652–1660.* London: Hamish Hamilton. 1975.

FIANTS: The Irish Fiants of the Tudor Sovereigns. With new introduction by Kenneth Nicholls, preface by Thomás G. Ó Cannann. 4 vols. 1521–1603. Dublin: Éamonn de Burca for Edmond Burke Publisher. 1994 (limited edition).

FLANAGHAN, M. T. *Irish Society, Anglo-Norman Settlers, Angevin Kingship.* Oxford: Oxford University Press. 1989.

FURLONG, Nicholas. *Dermot, King of Leinster and the Foreigners.* Kerry: Anvil Books. 1973.

GENEALOGICAL ATLAS OF IRELAND. Ed. by David E. Gardner, Derek Harland, and Frank Smith. Utah: Salt Lake City. Stevenon's Genealogical Centre. 1972.

GENEALOGICAL HISTORY OF THE MILESIAN FAMILIES OF IRELAND, 3 parts. Dublin: Herald Artists Ltd. 1968.

GLEESON, Rev. John. *History of the Ely O'Carroll: Territory of Ancient Ormond.* Dublin: M. H. Gill. 1915.

GREHAN, Ida. *Irish Family Names.* London: Johnston. 1973.

GRENHAM, John. *Clans and Families of Ireland: The Heritage and Heraldry of Irish Clans and Families.* Dublin: Gill and Macmillan. 1993.

GWYNN, Denis. *The O'Gorman Mahon: Duelist, Adventurer, and Politician.* London: Jarrolds. 1934.

HAMILTON, Hans Claude. *Calendar of the State Papers Relating to Ireland of the Reign of Elizabeth 1574–1585.* London: Longmans for HMSO. 1867.

HAYDEN, M and MOONAN, G. *A Short History of the Irish People.* Dublin: Talbot Press. 1921.

HAYES, Richard. *Ireland and Irishmen in the French Revolution.* Preface by Hilaire Belloc. London: Benn. 1932.

———. *Irish Swordsmen of France.* Dublin: M. H. Gill. 1934.

HENNESSY, Maurice. *The Wild Geese: The Irish Soldier in Exile.* London: Sidgwick and Jackson. 1973.

HILL, George. *An Historical Account of the MacDonnells of Antrim.* Belfast: Archer & Sons. 1873.

JENNINGS, Brendan, ed. *Wild Geese in Spanish Flanders 1582–1700.* Dublin: Dublin Stationery Office. 1964.

JEFFRIES, Henry Alan. "Desmond: The Early Years & the Career of Cormac Mac Carthy." *Journal of the Cork Historical and Archaeological Society.* Vol. 88, no. 247. January-December 1983.

————. "Desmond Before the Norman Invasion: A Political Study." *Journal of the Cork Historical and Archaeological Society.* Vol. 89, no. 248. January-December 1984.

JOYCE, Patrick Weston. *A Social History of Ancient Ireland,* 2 vols. London: Longmans. 1903.

KAVANAGH, Art, and MURPHY, Rory. *The Wexford Gentry: Irish Family Names.* Bunclody. 1994.

KEATING, Geoffrey (Séthrún Céitinn ca. 1580-ca.1644). *Foras Feasa ar Éirinn* (The History of Ireland). 4 vols. London: Irish Text Society. 1902, 1907, 1908, 1914 Reprinted in 1987 with separate foreword by Dr. Breandán Ó Buachalla.

KILFEATHER, T. P. *Graveyard of the Spanish Armada.* Kerry: Anvil Books. 1967.

LUCAS, W. Leslie. *Mevagh Down the Years,* 3rd ed. Dublin: Appletree Press. 1983.

LYDON, James. *The English in Medieval Ireland.* Dublin: Royal Irish Academy. 1984.

————, ed. *Law and Disorder in Thirteenth Century Ireland: The Dublin Parliament of 1297.* Four Courts Press. 1997.

MACALISTER R. A. S., ed. *Book of MacCarthaigh Riabhach, otherwise the Book of Lismore.* Collotype facsimile. Dublin: Dublin Stationery Office. 1941.

MACARDLE, Dorothy. *The Irish Republic.* London: Victor Gollancz. 1937.

MACCARTHY CLAN SOCIETY. *The Last King: Donal IX MacCarthy Mór, King of Desmond and the Two Munsters, 1558–1596.* Kanturk, County Cork: The MacCarthy Clan Society. 1996.

MacCARTHY, Dan and BREEN Aideen. "Astronomical Observations in the Irish Annals and their Motivation." *Peritia.* Journal of the Medieval Academy of Ireland. Vol. 2. 1997.

MacCARTHY, MÓR, Samuel Trant McCarthy. *The MacCarthys of Munster: The Story of A Great Irish Sept.* The Dundalgan Press. 1922. (See also under The MacCarthy Mór, Prince of Desmond).

MacDERMOT, Betty. *Ó Ruairc of Breifne,* Manorhamilton, Leitrim: Drumlin Publications. 1990.

MacDERMOT, Dermot. *MacDermot of Moylurg: The Story of a Connacht Family.* Manorhamilton, Leitrim: Drumlin Publications. 1996.

MacGEOGHEGAN, Abbé James. *Histoire de l'Irlande Ancienne et Moderne.* 3 vols. Paris and Amsterdam: Chez Antoine Boudet. 1758-63. (Trans. by P. O'Kelly. New York and Dublin: Duffy & Sadleir. [1844]1868.

MacGILLYCUDDY, Rosemary Brownlow. *A Short History of the Clan MacGillycuddy.* Blackrock, Dublin: MacGillycuddy Press. 1901.

MacHALE, Conor. *Annals of the Clan Egan.* Enniscrone: MacHale. 1990.

————. *The O'Dubhda Family History.* Enniscrone: MacHale. 1990.

McKENNA, Lambert, ed. *The Book of Magauran, Leabhar, Méig Shamradháin (with Genealogical Chart).* Dublin: Institute for Advanced Studies. 1947.

————. *The Book of O'Hara, Leabhar Ó hEaghra (written by Cormac Ó hEadhra, d. 1612).* Dublin: Institute for Advanced Studies. 1951.

MacKENZIE, Alexander. *History of the MacDonalds and Lords of the Isles.* Edinburgh: A. & W. MacKenzie. 1881.

MacLYSAGHT, Edward. *Irish Families, Their Names, Arms, and Origins.* Dublin: Allen Figgis. 1971.

————. *More Irish Families (with essay on Irish "chieftainries").* Dublin: Irish Academic Press. 1982.

MacMAHON, Noel, ed. *Here I Am, Here I Stay! Marshal MacMahon 1808–1893.* Clare: Ballinakella Press. 1993.

MacNEILL, Eoin. *Phrases of Irish History.* Dublin: M. H. Gill. [1919]1968.

MacNEILL, Máire. *Máire Rua, Lady of Leamaneh.* Clare: Ballinakella Press. 1990.

MADDEN, Thomas More. *Genealogical, Historical and Family Records of the O'Maddens of Hy-Many and Their Descendants.* Dublin: Powell. 1894.

MAGAN, William Umma-More. *The Story of an Irish Family (the Magans).* Wiltshire: Element Books. 1983.

MAGUIRE of Fermanagh, The. *Historic Maguire Chalices.* Fermanagh District Council. 1996.

MARMION, Anthony. *The Ancient and Modern History of the Maritime Ports of Ireland.* London : J. H. Banks. 1855.

MATHEWS, Anthony. *Origins of the O'Kellys and a History of the Sept.* Dublin: Printed for Mathews. 1970.

———. *Origin of the O'Rourkes and a History of the Sept.* Dublin: Printed for Mathews. 1970.

MATHEWS, Thomas. *The O'Neills of Ulster: Their History and Genealogy.* Introduction by Francis Joseph Biggar. 3 vols. Dublin: Sealy, Bryers & Walker. 1903.

MAXWELL, Constantia. *Irish History from Contemporary Sources (1509–1610).* London: George Allen and Unwin. 1923.

MITCHELL HILL, J. *Fire and Sword: Sorley Boy MacDonnell and the Rise of Clan Ian Mor 1538–1590.* London. The Athlone Press 1927.

MONTGOMERY-MASSINGBERD, Hugh, ed. *Burke's Introduction to Irish Ancestry.* London: Burke's Peerage. 1976.

MOODY, T. W., MARTIN, F. X., and BYRNE, F. J. *A New History of Ireland.* Vol. 9. *Maps, Genealogies, and Lists, A Companion to Irish History.* Part II (Royal Irish Academy, 10 vols.). Oxford: Oxford University Press. 1984.

MORGAN, Hiram. *Tyrone's Rebellion.* The Royal Historical Society. Suffolk: Boydell Press. 1993.

MORLEY, Henry. *Ireland Under Elizabeth and James the First.* London: George Routledge. 1890. (Containing the works of Edmund Spenser, Sir John Davies and Fynes Moryson on Ireland.)

MULLEN, Rev. T. H. and MULLEN, Rev. J. E. *The Ulster Clans O' Mullen, O'Kane and O'Mellan.* Belfast: B.N.L. 1966.

MURPHY, Rev. Denis. *The Life of Hugh Roe O'Donnell, Prince of Tirconnell (1586–1602) by Lughaidh O'Clery.* Trans. and notes from Cugory O'Clery's Irish Mss in Fallon, Dublin, the Royal Irish Academy. 1895.

MURPHY, John. *Ireland, Industrial, Political and Social.* London: Longmans, Green and Company. 1870.

MURPHY, John A. *Justin MacCarthy, Lord Mountcashel, Commander of the first Irish Brigade in France.* Cork: Cork University Press. 1958. New edition published by the Royal Eóghanacht Society, Clonmel. With a foreword by MacCarthy Mór, Prince of Desmond, 1999.

NASH, Pyers O'Conor. *The History and Heritage of the Royal O'Conors.* Boyle: Purcell Print. 1990.

NEWMAN, Roger Challeston. *Brian Boru, King of Ireland.* Dublin: Anvil Books. 1983.

NEILL, Kathleen. *O'Neill Commemorative Journal of the First International Gathering of the Clan, June 20–27, 1982* (containing three essays on the O'Neill family history by Sir Iain Moncrieffe of that Ilk). Dunmurry, Belfast: Irish Genealogical Association. 1982.

NICHOLLS, Kenneth. *Gaelic and Gaelicised Ireland in the Middle Ages.* Dublin: Gill and Macmillan. 1972.

NOLAN, William, RONAYNE, Liam, and DUNLEAVY, Mairead, eds. *Donegal History and Society: Interdisciplinary Essays on the History of an Irish County.* Templeogue, Dublin: Geography Publications. 1995.

O'BRIEN CLAN ASSOCIATION. *The Royal O'Briens—A Tribute.* Dromoland, Clare. 1992.

O'BRIEN, Hon. Donough. *History of the O'Briens from Brian Bóroimhe AD 1000 to AD 1945*. London: B. T. Batsford. 1949.

O'BRIEN, Grania. *These My Friends and Forebears: The O'Briens of Dromoland*. Clare: Ballinkella Press.

O'BRIEN, Ivar. *O'Brien of Thomond: The O'Briens in Irish History 1500–1865*. Phillimore, Chichester. 1986.

O'BRIEN, Lucius. *Case of the Rt. Hon. Lucius, Lord Inchinquin in the Peerage of Ireland on His Claiming the Right to Vote at the Election of the Representative Peers for Ireland, 1861*. Walmsley, London. 1861.

O'BRIEN, Maureen Concannon. *The Story of the Concannons*. Dublin: Clan Publications. 1990.

O'BRIEN, M. A. *Corpus Genealogarium Hiberniae*, Dublin, 1962. (vol. 1.) rev. imp. By J. P. Kelleher, 1976.

O'CARROLL ROBERTSON, June. *A Long Way from Tipperary: The Carrolls of Lissenhall and Tulla*. Upton-Upon-Severn, England. Images Publishing. 1994.

Ó CIANÁIN, Tadhg. *The Flight of the Earls*. Dublin: M. H. Gill. 1916.

O'CONNOR, Patrick. *The Royal O'Connors of Connaught*. Swindford, Co. Mayo: Old House Press. 1997.

O'CONOR DON, Rt Hon Charles Owen. *The O'Conors of Connaught*, Figgis, Dublin. 1891.

O'CONOR, Matthew. *The History of Irish Catholics*. Dublin: J. Stockdale. 1813.

O'CONOR, Roderic. *An Historical & Genealogical Memoir of the O'Conors, Kings of Connaught and Their Descendants*. Dublin: McGlashan and Gill. 1861.

Ó CRÓNÍN, Dáibhí. *Early Medieval Ireland AD 400–1200* (Long History of Ireland). London: Longmans. 1995.

Ó CUÍV, Brían, ed. *Seven Centuries of Irish Learning AD 1000–1700*. Dublin: Stationery Office. 1961.

———. "A Sixteenth Century Political Poem." *Éigse* 15. 1973–74.

Ó'DÁLAIGH, Aonghus Ruadh. *The Tribes of Ireland: A Satire*. Ed. John O'Donovan. Trans. Dublin: James Mangan. 1852. New ed. (facsimile) Cork: Tower Books. 1976.

Ó DONNCHADHA, Tadhg. *Leabhair Cloinne Aodha Buidhe* (Book of Clanaboy). Baile Atha Cliatha. Oifig Díolta Foillseachan Riatais. 1931.

O'DONOGHUE, John. *Historical Memoir of the O'Briens*. Dublin: Hodges, Smith & Company. 1860.

O'DONOGHUE, Rod. *O'Donoghue People and Places*. Clare: Ballinakella Press. 1999.

O'DONOVAN, John. "The O'Donnells in Exile" series. In *O'Duffy's Hibernian Magazine*, no. 1 to no. 7. Dublin. (June-December 1860.)

———. *The O'Conors of Connaught: An Historical Memoir with Additions from the State Papers and Public Records by Charles Owen O'Conor Don*. Dublin: Hodges, Figgis. 1891.

———, ed. *Tribes and Customs of Hy-Many (published from The Book of Lecan)*. Cork Tower Books. 1976.

O'DUGAN, John (Seán Ó Dubhagáin). *The Kings of the Race of Eibhear: A Chronological Poem*. Translation by Michael Kearney, A.D.1635. Edited by John Daly. Dublin. 1847. (See also under soi-disant MacCarthy Mór.)

O'DWYER, Sir Michael. *The O'Dwyers of Kilnamangh: The History of an Irish Sept*. London: John Murray. 1933.

O'FLANAGAN, Rev. Michael. *Letters Containing Information Relating to Antiquities in the County of Donegal Collected During the Progress of the Ordnance Survey in 1835*, private issued. Bray. 1927.

"O'H. E." *The O'Reillys of Templemills, Celbridge and a pedigree from the old Irish mss & etc.* Moorfield, Dundrum, County Dublin: M. W. O'Reilly. 1941.

O'HART, John. *Irish Pedigrees: or the Origin and Stem of the Irish Nation*. 2 vols. Dublin: Duffy. 1887–88.

O'HART, John. *The Irish and Anglo-Irish Gentry*. Introduced by Edward MacLysaght. Shannon: Irish University Press. 1969.

Ó' hINNSE, Séamus, ed. and trans. *Miscellaneous Irish Annals: A.D. 1114–1437*. Dublin: Dublin Institute for Advanced Studies. 1947. (Including The MacCarthy's Book.)

O'KEEFE, J. C., H., and A. J. *Record of the O'Keefe Family of Co. Cork*. Cork: privately printed. 1927.

O'KELLY d'AUGHRIM, Comte P. *Essai Historique sue l'Irlande contenant l'origine des toutes les familles nobles de ce pays*. Brussels: Wiarts. 1837.

O'LONG, The (Denis C. Long). *A History of the Longs*, pamphlet no. 1. Canovee Historical and Archaeological Society. N.d.

O'MAHONY, Rev. Canon John. *A History of the O'Mahony Septs of Kinelmeky and Ivagha*. County Cork: Crookstown. N.d.

O'MEAGHER, Joseph Casimir. *Some Historical Notices of the O'Meaghers of Ikerrin*. London and New York: Elliott Stock. 1890.

O'MORCHOE, Rev. Thomas. *The Succession of the Chiefs of Ireland*. Dublin: Ormond Printing. 1904.

O'NEILL, Seán. *O'Neill People and Places*. Clare: Ballinakella Press. 1991.

"OLLAMH." *The Story of Shane O'Neill: Hereditary Prince of Ulster Surnamed "An Díomais" or the Proud*. Sealy Dublin. N.d.

O'RAHILLY, Thomas F. *Early Irish History and Mythology*. Dublin: Dublin Institute for Advanced Studies. 1946.

O'REILLY, I. J. *The History of the Breifne O'Reilly*. New York: Vantage Press. 1976.

ORPEN, Goddard Henry. *The Song of Dermot and the Earl*. (From Carew Mss No. 596 Archiepiscopal Library, Lambeth Palace, ed., trans. and notes). Oxford: Clarendon Press. 1892.

O'TOOLE, John. *The O'Tooles, Ancient Lords of Powerscourt*. (*Feracualan, Fertie and Imale, with some notice of Feagh Mac Hugh O'Byrne, Chief of Clan Ranelagh*.) Dublin: Sullivan. N.d.

POINT DE VUE (Paris) series of articles: July 14, 1992 to August 8, 1992. The Maguire (July 14, 1992) and O'Conor Don (August 8, 1992).

POWER, Patrick C. *A Literary History of Ireland*. Cork: Mercier Press. 1969.

PRENDERGAST, John P. *The Cromwellian Settlement of Ireland*. London: Longmans, Green & Co. 1865.

QUIEN ES QUIEN EN ESPANA. Editorial Campillo S.L. Madrid: Edicion. 1996.

ROCHE, Richard. *The Norman Invasion of Ireland*. Kerry: Anvil Books. 1970.

ROYAL EOGHANACHT SOCIETY. *Cashel '96: The Quartercentenary of the Death of King Donal IX, MacCarthy Móe, 1596–1996*. Clonmel: Royal Eóghanacht Society. 1996. (Commemoration book with pictures of the quartercentary commemoration ceremonies.)

RUSSELL, C. W. and PRENDERGAST, John P. *Calendar of the State Papers Relating to Ireland of the Reign of James I, 1606–1608*. London: Longman & Co. 1874.

SIMMS, Katharine. "The O'Hanlon, O'Neill and Anglo-Normans in 13th Century Armagli." *Seanchas Ard Macha*, vol. 9 (1978): 70–90.

———. *From Kings to Warlords: The Changing Political Structure of Gaelic Ireland in the Later Middle Ages*. Suffolk: The Boydell Press. 1987.

SOMERVILLE-LARGE, Peter. *From Bantry Bay to Leitrim: A Journey in Search of O'-Sullivan Beare*. London: Victor Gollancz. 1974.

SULLIVAN, T. D. *Bantry, Berehaven and the O'Sullivan Sept*. Cork: Tower Books. 1978.

SWEENY CLAN PUBLICATION. *The Sweenys: Fanad, Doe, Banagh, International*. Edited by J. P. Sweeny, Clann tSuibhne, Gaoth Dobhair, Leitir Ceannain, Tir Chonaill. 1997. (See especially "From Doe to Derrybeigh," by Tom Sweeny, the MacSweeny Doe.)

TAYLOR, J. F. *Owen Roe O'Neill*. London: Fisher and Unwin. 1906.

UA CRONÍN, Risteard O'Dea. *Ua Déaghaidh: The Story of A Rebel Clan.* Clare: Balli-nakella Press. 1992.

UA DUINNÍN, An Athar Pádraig. *The Maguires of Fermanagh.* Dublin: M. H. Gill. 1917.

VAUGHAN, W. E. *Sin, Sheep and Scotsmen: John George Adair and the Derryveigh Evic-tions 1861.* Dublin: Appletree Press & Ulster Society for Historical Studies. 1983.

VON DASSANOWSKY, Dr. Robert. "The Gaelic Royal Houses of Ireland." *Monarchy* (December 1988).

WALPOLE, Charles George. *A Short History of the Kingdom of Ireland.* London: Kegan Paul. 1885.

WALSH, Micheline Kerney. *Destruction by Peace: Hugh O'Neill After Kinsdale.* Cumann Seanchis Ard Mhaca. 1986.

———. *Hugh O'Neill, Prince Of Ulster, An Exile Of Ireland.* Dublin: Four Courts Press. 1996.

———. *The MacDonnels of Antrim and on the Continent.* Dublin: privately published. 1960.

WALSH, Father Paul. *The Will and Family of Hugh O'Neill, Earl of Tyrone* (with an ap-pendix of genealogies). Dublin: Sign of the Three Candles. 1930.

———. *Irish Chiefs and Leaders (Maguires, O'Reillys, MacSweeenys, MacDonnells, Bissets, Gallagher, MacGeoghegan, O'Molloys and Kirbys of Munster).* Ed. Colm Ó Lochlainn. Dublin: Sign of the Three Candles. 1960.

———. *Irish Men of Learning (O'Duigenan, O'Maolconaire, O'Curnin, Mac an Baird, Mac Firbisigh).* Ed. Colm Ó Lochlainn. Dublin: Sign of the Three Candles. 1947.

WARE, Sir James. *De Hibernia & Antiquitatibus eius Disquisitiones.* London: J. Crook and Thomas Heath. 1653. (English trans. *The Antiquities and History of Ireland.* Dublin: A. Crook. 1705.)

WATKINS, Calvert. "Indo European Metrics in Archaic Irish Verse." *Celtica,* vol. 6 (1963).

WEIR, Hugh W. L. *O'Connor People and Places.* Clare: Ballinakella Press. 1994.

———. *O'Brien People and Places.* Clare: Ballinakella Press. 1994.

WEIR, H. W. L., ed. *Ireland: A Thousand Kings.,* Clare: Ballinakella Press. 1998.

WHITE, Rev. P. *History of Clare and the Dalcassian Clans of Tipperary, Limerick and Gal-way.* M. H. Gill, Dublin. 1893.

WILLIAMS, J. D. *History of the Name O'Neill.* Dublin: Mercier Press. 1978.

———. *History of the Name MacCarthy.* Dublin: Mercier Press. 1978.

———. *History of the Name O'Brien,* Dublin: Mercier Press. 1977.

———. *History of the Name O'Kelly,* Dublin: Mercier Press. 1977.

YOUNGS, Susan, ed. *The Work of Angels; Masterpieces of Celtic Metalwork, 6th–9th Cen-turies A.D.* London and Ireland: British Museums Publications, in association with National Museum of Ireland. 1989.

SOME UNPUBLISHED MANUSCRIPTS

I was particularly grateful to be allowed access to many unpublished sources, manu-scripts, and letters too numerous to be accounted here. I would, however, like particu-larly to acknowledge the following:

MacCARTHY. "Généalogie de la Royale et Sérénissime Maison de MacCarthy." Com-piled by Sir Isaac Heard, Norroy King of Arms, and Ralph Bigland, Clarenceux King of Arms for England for Justin MacCarthy, ca. 1760.

This manuscript is said to be a single-volume copy of the original two volumes. It was last known to be in the hands of Terence McCarthy, who had lent it to the Cashel Heritage Museum for display. In the wake of the McCarthy scandal, there was some question as to its authenticity. According to Jean-Louis Courtois de Viçose of the former Hôtel du MacCarthy, Toulouse, it was sold on December 11, 1811, by the Hôtel. Of the original two volumes, the following reference appears in *Généalogie de la Maison de MacCarthy*, published in Paris, in 1834, p. 15:

> Ces nombreux témoinages, recueillis par les rois d'armes Ralph Bigland (Clarenceux) et Isaac Heard (Norroy) et complétés par tout ce que le collège héaldique á Londres renferme de chartes et de monuments authentiques sur les Mac-Carthy, ont été transcrits dans un registre de famille, intitulé *Généalogie de la Royale et Sérénissime Maison de MacCarthy*, en deux volumes in folio, parchemin-vélin; le premier volume consacré aux prevues historiques; le second, aux preuves généalogiques; paraphé à chaque page, attesté et signé par ces deux roi d'armes, et scellé du sceau de leur office à Londres, le 8 juin, 1776.

METCALF, Sir Aubrey. "History of the Descendants of Richard, the MacGillycuddy of the Reeks (1826–1866) by his grandson. 1957." Duplicated and distributed by the MacGillycuddy Clan Society.

O'DOGHERTY, Rear Admiral Pascual. "The Genealogy of the O'Doghertys; Chiefs of Inish-Owen." Unpublished mss, together with cuttings and other material.

O'DONOVAN, The. "Letters of Dr. John O'Donovan to Morgan William O'Donovan," vol. 1 (1841–43); vol. 2 (1843–1854) and vol. 3 (1855–1861). Privately held by the O'Donovan.

O'DONEL (Duke of Tetuan). "The O'Donel Pedigree" Commissioned by the Duques of Tetuan, Spain, in possession of the Duque de Tetuan y Lara.

BOOKS BY THE SOI-DISANT MACCARTHY MÓR (TERENCE MACCARTHY):

MacCARTHY MÓR, Samuel Trant McCarthy. *The MacCarthys of Munster: The Story of a Great Irish Sept*, (first published by the Dundalgen Press, 1922); a facsimile edition with an introduction and commentary by the MacCarthy Mór, Prince of Desmond. Little Rock, Arkansas: Gryfons Publishers. 1997.

———. The Prince of Desmond. *Historical Essays on the Kingdom of Munster.* Kansas City, Missouri: The Irish Genealogical Foundation. 1994.

———. *Ulster's Office 1552–1800: A History of the Irish Office of Arms from the Tudor Plantations to the Act of Union;* with a foreword by John P. B. Brook-Little, Clarenceux King of Arms. Little Rock, Arkansas: Gryfons Publishers. 1996.

———, with CLANDERMOND, The Count of. *An Irish Miscellany: Essays Heraldic, Historical and Genealogical.* Little Rock, Arkansas: Gryfons Publishers. 1998.

O'DUGAN, John. *The Kings of the Race of Eibhear, A Chronological Poem*, foreword by Peter Berresford Ellis, with commentary and appendices by the MacCarthy Mór, Prince of Desmond. Clonmel: A Royal Eóghanacht Publication. 1999.

BOOKS AND ARTICLES BY THE SOI-DISANT COUNT OF CLANDERMOND (ANDREW DAVISON):

CLANDERMOND, The Count of. "Gaelic Feudalism and the Kingdom of Desmond." *The Augustan Omnibus* 14, vol. 30 (1993).

———. *Three Centuries of Niadh Nask Bookplates.* Foreword by the MacCarthy Mór, Prince of Desmond. Country Antrim, Ireland: The Black Eagle Press for the Niadh Nask. 1997.

———, ed. *Links in a Golden Chain: A Collection of Essays on the History of the Niadh Nask or The Military Order of the Golden Chain.* Foreword by Peter Berresford Ellis. Little Rock, Arkansas: Gryfons Publishers for the Royal Eóghanacht Society. 1998.

———, ed. *A New Book of Rights: A Complete Transcript of the Legal Verdicts Handed Down by the Courts of the Republic of Italy Concerning the Heraldic Rights, Status and Prerogative of the MacCarthy Mór, Prince of Desmond, Chief of the Name and Arms and Head of the Eóghanacht Royal House of Munster & etc.* Little Rock, Arkansas: Gryfons Publishers for the Royal Eóghanacht Society. 1998.

MEDIEVAL MANUSCRIPT BOOKS

Within the text are references from the many medieval manuscript annuals, chronicles and books. These are self-explanatory. But readers may like to know that these works are available in facsimile and/or translated editions. As examples: *Annals of Connacht (Annála Connacht)* chronicling the years 1224–1554 were edited and translated by A. Martin Freeman, Dublin Institute for Advanced Studies, 1944; the *Annals of Innisfallen*, written between the eleventh and the fourteenth centuries, has been translated and edited several times. Particularly recommended is R. I. Best and Eoin Mac Néill, Dublin: Royal Irish Academy, 1933; the *Annals of Clonmacnoise*, covering early times to A.D. 1408, was actually translated into English as early as 1627 and published by Dublin University Press in 1896; the *Annals of the Four Masters (Annales Rioghachta Éireann)* was edited by John O'Donovan in several volumes in Dublin, 1849–51; the *Annals of Tighernach*, composed in the late eleventh century, was published in the *Revue Celtique*, Paris, 1896–97. The *Annals of Ulster*, compiled in 1498 by Cathal Mac Magnus Mheg Uidir, Archdeacon of Clogher, has also been edited seven times, most recently by Gearóid MacNiocaill in Dublin, 1984.

In addition to the annals, such as the above, there are countless manuscript books which are referred to, and some of these are also available in modern forms. Examples of these include the *Book of Armagh*, compiled by Feardomhnach about A.D. 807: A facsimile edition was published by the Irish Mss Commission in Dublin in 1937; the *Book of Ballymote*, compiled in 1390 by Maghnus Ó Duibhgeánnáin, contained the *Lebor na gCert* or "Book of Rights," which was published by the Royal Irish Academy, Dublin, 1887; the *Book of Duniry*, or the *Leabhar Breac*, written by the Mac Egan family ca. 1400, was published by the Royal Irish Academy, 2 volumes, Dublin 1872 and 1876. *The Great Book of Lecan* and the *Yellow Book of Lecan*, complied by Giolla Íosa Mór Mac Firbisigh (ca. 1360–1430) were edited by Kathleen Mulchrone for the Irish Mss Commission in 1937 and Robert Atkinson, Dublin, 1896, respectively. *The Book of Leinster (Lebar na Nuachonghbala)* compiled by Fionn MacGormain, ca. 1150, was edited for the Dublin Institute of Advanced Studies by R. I. Best, Osborn Bergin and M. A. O'Brien, and published in five volumes, 1954, 1956, 1957, 1965 and 1967. Finally the *Book of the Dun Cow*, or *Leabhar na hUidri*, written in Clonmacnoise about 1100 by Mael Muire Mac Ceilachair (d. 1106) has also been translated several times. The recommended version is by R. I. Best and Osborn Bergin (Dublin: Royal Irish Academy, 1929).

Dubhaltach Mac Firbisigh (1585–1670) wrote, among many other works, *Genealogies of the Families in Ireland*. This was edited by J. O. Raithbheartaigh for the Irish Manuscript Commission, Dublin, 1932.

For readers interested in further details the many poets and writers writing in the Irish language mentioned in the text, a handy quick reference is *A Biographical Dictionary of Irish Writers*, compiled by Anne M. Brady and Brian Cleeve (part two—Writers in Irish and Latin), the Lilliput Press, Mullingar, Ireland, 1985.

INDEX